ID0629782

Scanner Data and Price Indexes

Studies in Income and Wealth
Volume 64

National Bureau of Economic Research
Conference on Research in Income and Wealth

Scanner Data and Price Indexes

Edited by **Robert C. Feenstra and Matthew D. Shapiro**

The University of Chicago Press

Chicago and London

ROBERT C. FEENSTRA is professor of economics at the University of California, Davis, and a research associate of the National Bureau of Economic Research. MATTHEW D. SHAPIRO is professor of economics at the University of Michigan and a research associate of the National Bureau of Economic Research.

The University of Chicago Press, Chicago 60637
The University of Chicago Press, Ltd., London
© 2003 by the National Bureau of Economic Research
All rights reserved. Published 2003
Printed in the United States of America
12 11 10 09 08 07 06 05 04 03   1 2 3 4 5
ISBN: 0-226-23965-9 (cloth)

Copyright is not claimed for chapter 2 by David H. Richardson; "Comment" by Dennis Fixler in the Roundtable Discussion; "Comment" by John S. Greenlees in the Roundtable Discussion; "Comment" on chapter 5 by Marshall B. Reinsdorf.

Library of Congress Cataloging-in-Publication Data

Scanner data and price indexes / edited by Robert C. Feenstra and
   Matthew D. Shapiro.
      p. cm. — (Studies in income and wealth ; v. 64)
   Includes bibliographical references and index.
   ISBN 0-226-23965-9 (cloth) — ISBN 0-226-23966-7 (electronic)
   1. Consumer price indexes—Data processing. 2. Consumer price
indexes—Methodology. 3. Price indexes—Data processing. 4. Price
indexes—Methodology. 5. Prices—Data processing. 6. Prices—
Statistical methods. 7. Point-of-sale systems. 8. Scanning systems.
I. Feenstra, Robert C. II. Shapiro, Matthew D. (Matthew David)
III. Series.

HC106.3 .C714 vol. 64
[HB225]
330 s—dc21
[338.5'28'0285574]
                                                         2002075288

♾ The paper used in this publication meets the minimum requirements of the American National Standard for Information Sciences—Permanence of Paper for Printed Library Materials, ANSI Z39.48-1992.

National Bureau of Economic Research

Officers

Carl F. Christ, *chairman*
Michael H. Moskow, *vice-chairman*
Martin Feldstein, *president and chief executive officer*
Susan Colligan, *vice president for administration and budget and corporate secretary*

Robert Mednick, *treasurer*
Kelly Horak, *controller and assistant corporate secretary*
Gerardine Johnson, *assistant corporate secretary*

Directors at Large

Peter C. Aldrich
Elizabeth E. Bailey
John H. Biggs
Andrew Brimmer
Carl F. Christ
John S. Clarkeson
Don R. Conlan
George C. Eads

Martin Feldstein
Stephen Friedman
Judith M. Gueron
George Hatsopoulos
Karen N. Horn
Judy C. Lewent
John Lipsky
Michael H. Moskow

Alicia H. Munnell
Rudolph A. Oswald
Robert T. Parry
Peter G. Peterson
Richard N. Rosett
Kathleen P. Utgoff
Marina v. N. Whitman
Martin B. Zimmerman

Directors by University Appointment

George Akerlof, *California, Berkeley*
Jagdish Bhagwati, *Columbia*
William C. Brainard, *Yale*
Glen G. Cain, *Wisconsin*
Franklin Fisher, *Massachusetts Institute of Technology*
Saul H. Hymans, *Michigan*
Marjorie B. McElroy, *Duke*

Joel Mokyr, *Northwestern*
Michael J. Brennan, *California, Los Angeles*
Andrew Postlewaite, *Pennsylvania*
Nathan Rosenberg, *Stanford*
Michael Rothschild, *Princeton*
Craig Swan, *Minnesota*
David B. Yoffie, *Harvard*
Arnold Zellner, *Chicago*

Directors by Appointment of Other Organizations

Mark Drabenstott, *American Agricultural Economics Association*
Gail D. Fosler, *The Conference Board*
A. Ronald Gallant, *American Statistical Association*
Robert S. Hamada, *American Finance Association*
Robert Mednick, *American Institute of Certified Public Accountants*
Angelo Melino, *Canadian Economics Association*

Richard D. Rippe, *National Association for Business Economics*
John J. Siegfried, *American Economic Association*
David A. Smith, *American Federation of Labor and Congress of Industrial Organizations*
Josh S. Weston, *Committee for Economic Development*
Gavin Wright, *Economic History Association*

Directors Emeriti

Thomas D. Flynn
Lawrence R. Klein

Franklin A. Lindsay
Paul W. McCracken

Bert Seidman
Eli Shapiro

Since this volume is a record of conference proceedings, it has been exempted from the rules governing critical review of manuscripts by the Board of Directors of the National Bureau (resolution adopted 8 June 1948, as revised 21 November 1949 and 20 April 1968).

Contents

Prefatory Note

This volume contains revised versions of most of the papers and discussion presented at the Conference on Research in Income and Wealth entitled "Scanner Data and Price Indexes," held in Arlington, Virginia, on 15–16 September 2000.

Funds for the Conference on Research in Income and Wealth are supplied by the Bureau of Labor Statistics, the Bureau of Economic Analysis, the Federal Reserve Board, and the Bureau of the Census; we are indebted to them for their support.

We thank Robert C. Feenstra and Matthew D. Shapiro, who served as conference organizers and editors of the volume, and the NBER staff and NBER and UCP editors for their assistance in organizing the conference and editing the volume.

CRIW Executive Committee Membership
Spring 2002

John M. Abowd, Cornell University
Susanto Basu, University of Michigan
Ernst R. Berndt,* Sloan School of Management
Carol A. Corrado, Board of Governors of the Federal Reserve
Robert C. Feenstra,* UC Davis
John Greenlees, Bureau of Labor Statistics
John C. Haltiwanger, University of Maryland
Michael J. Harper, Bureau of Labor Statistics
Charles R. Hulten (chair), University of Maryland
John Bradford Jensen, Bureau of the Census

Lawrence Katz,* Harvard University
J. Steven Landefeld, Bureau of Economic Analysis
Brent Moulton, Bureau of Economic Analysis
Mark J. Roberts, Pennsylvania State University
Matthew D. Shapiro,* University of Michigan
David W. Wilcox, Board of Governors of the Federal Reserve

* NBER Appointees

Volume Editors' Acknowledgments

We are grateful to ACNielsen for providing data for some of the papers. We also thank Bill Hawkes for his longstanding support for the use of scanner data in research.

Introduction

Robert C. Feenstra and Matthew D. Shapiro

New technologies for processing transactions, together with increases in the ability to store and process information, provide tremendous opportunities for measurement. When data are based on actual transactions, as opposed survey samples of price quotations, revenues, and expenditures, there is the potential for measurement to closely reflect the underlying variable being measured. Basing data on actual transactions also creates opportunities for modeling the behavior underlying the transactions. Such analysis can both improve measurement and be used to study a wide range of economic phenomena.

This volume examines how scanner data can improve price measurement. What are scanner data? Scanner data are electronic records of transactions that establishments collect as part of the operation of their businesses. The most familiar and now ubiquitous form of scanner data is the scanning of bar codes at checkout lines of retail stores. The scanning of goods has a number of purposes for the stores. At a minimum, it provides a relatively automated way for totaling customers' bills. The information collected at the cash registers can also feed information to inform a wide vari-

Robert C. Feenstra is professor of economics at the University of California, Davis, and a research associate of the National Bureau of Economic Research. Matthew D. Shapiro is professor of economics at the University of Michigan and a research associate of the National Bureau of Economic Research.

Although many persons provided invaluable suggestions for the organization of the conference, the editors would like to take this opportunity to thank William Hawkes for helping to promote the use of scanner data for research and to secure the scanner data used in some of the papers. In particular, the paper by the editors makes use of the ACNielsen academic database (for tuna). The editors hope that continued cooperation among the private and public agencies using scanner data and researchers in academia will ensure that these data are used to address some of the difficult and important issues in the construction of price indexes.

1

ety of decisions faced by firms regarding operations that include restocking shelves and stores, reordering goods, and scheduling production. It can also be used to monitor the effectiveness of promotions and to evaluate changes in purchase patterns. Stores are increasingly linking the data on individual transactions to other information, for example, through the use of affinity cards that tracks individuals' purchases and offer targeted promotions.

Although most of the papers in this volume focus on retailing, scanner data or their equivalents are collected by many enterprises. One paper in this volume uses extensive databases on prescription drugs transactions. Similar data are collected by all components of the health care system to track patient care and provide the accounting needed for billing and third-party payment. Catalog companies and on-line businesses integrate ordering, delivery, and billing in their information systems. Many nonretail consumer purchases (e.g., utility bills and airline tickets) are accounted for electronically. Increased computerization and networking provide enormous scope for measuring consumer activity transaction by transaction. Finally, electronic data are not limited to the purchases of goods and services. Increased computerization and improvements in information technology also provide opportunities for data collection on production, employment, and payrolls.

Opportunities

Scanner data and other electronic records of transactions create tremendous opportunities for improving economic measurement. Scanner data provide a census of all transactions rather than a statistical sample. Scanner data are collected continuously, rather than at discrete and perhaps infrequent intervals. Scanner data provide simultaneous and consistent observations on both price and quantity. Electronic transmission of scanner data from point of collection to point of analysis can provide for substantial increases in the timeliness and accuracy of observations. Scanner data can allow the process of collecting and summarizing data to be reengineered, with the promise of improvements in the quality and timeliness of official statistics and the potential for providing these improvements at low incremental cost. They allow conceptual as well as functional changes in price measurement.

Census of Transactions

Scanner data provide a record of virtually all transactions. Having a census rather than a sample of transactions has a number of obvious benefits. The most obvious of these is the elimination of sampling error inherent in estimating the average price paid based on a relatively small sample of prices for an item. The limitation on observations per item is only one of the serious constraints imposed by measurement systems that must rely on a sample of prices. Statistical agencies can only sample a limited number of items, and they must sample these items in only a limited number of establishments. The Bureau of Labor Statistics (BLS) uses sophisticated surveys to measure what consumers buy and where they purchase it. It then uses a probability sampling to assure that the items to be priced are a representative sample of consumer purchases. It also collaborates with store managers to use information on sales of items within stores as an input into the probability sampling of items to be priced. Nonetheless, the use of a probability sample inherently involves sampling error. Moreover, the surveys of spending patterns can only be conducted infrequently, and it takes time to introduce the finding of these surveys into the data collection process. In contrast, scanner data can reduce the need to measure prices for a limited number of items at a limited number of outlets.

Surveillance for New Goods

Scanner data provide enormous opportunities for increasing the surveillance of new goods and new outlets by providing timely information on their appearance.[1] The slow incorporation of changes in goods and shopping patterns is an important source of overstatement of inflation by the Consumer Price Index (see Boskin et al. 1996; Shapiro and Wilcox 1996). Eliminating new goods or new outlet bias does not only depend, however, on incorporating new goods rapidly into the sample. Current BLS techniques, for example, link out differences in levels of prices when bringing new establishments into the sample. Scanner data could provide new opportunities to make comparisons of levels of prices or unit values across establishments.

Continuous-Time Data

Scanner data also liberate the data collection process in the time dimension. Prices must be sampled at a particular point in time. These points in time might not be representative of the times when consumers purchased goods (e.g., time of month, day of week, holiday versus nonholiday, time of day, during a sale or promotion). Prices might vary according to time of purchases as firms adjust prices in response to the timing of demand and as consumers simultaneously respond to changes in prices. Prices sampled at fixed points within the calendar or clock might overstate or understate the prices that consumers pay on average.[2] The BLS collects data throughout the month, but not in a way that reflects variation in sales. If there are changes in consumers' spending patterns or in firms' pricing strategies,

1. Hausman (1999) notes how scanner data can be used to alert statistical agencies to the appearance of new goods.
2. Warner and Barsky (1995) find a significant "seasonal" over the week—specifically, that prices are lower on the weekend. Chevalier, Kashyap, and Rossi (2002) find similar price patterns related to weather and holidays.

sampling at fixed points in time could lead to a mismeasurement of the changes in average price paid. By synchronizing the price measurement with the purchase, scanner data eliminate these problems.

Price and Quantity Observed Simultaneously

The simultaneous collection of price and quantity data is another substantial advantage of scanner data over conventional techniques that measure price and revenues separately. At the retail level, prices and sales are collected by entirely different statistical programs. Integrating the data collection of prices and revenues could deliver substantial benefits in terms of cost reduction for both the statistical agencies and the respondents. It would also yield consistent measurement of price and revenues, which would provide opportunities for improving data quality and for increasing their utility for research.

The simultaneous collection of price and quantity data has the potential for greatly improving the ability to construct price indexes that accurately track the cost of living. In the current statistical system in the United States, prices are collected at monthly frequency. These data on price change are available at a very short lag. The Consumer Price Index (CPI) is typically released within a week or two of the end of the month to which it refers. The Consumer Expenditure Survey (CEX) provides the expenditure data necessary for construction of the CPI. These include weights that are used for sampling prices and for aggregating elementary price indexes into the CPI and its components. The CEX has evolved considerably over the years. It now provides a continuous rather than periodic sample of households. The sample size and timeliness of the data have improved over time. Nonetheless, expenditure data are collected at lower than monthly frequency and are only available with a substantial lag.

The lag in the availability of expenditure data creates substantial challenges for price measurement. A fundamental principle of economics is that consumers economize by buying more of goods that become less expensive and fewer of goods that become more expensive. This substitution effect operates at various levels of aggregation: at high levels of aggregation (e.g., chicken vs. beef, medical care vs. entertainment), at low levels of aggregation (e.g., brand X vs. brand Y of canned tuna, branded vs. generic goods), and across outlets (e.g., department stores vs. discount stores, stores having promotions vs. those without them). Price indexes have traditionally been calculated using the Laspeyres formula, which assumes no substitution away from items owing to price changes. In recent years, statistical agencies have made substantial improvements in their methodologies to address substitution effects. For example, the Bureau of Economic Analysis (BEA) now uses chain-weighted indexes that, to a second-order approximation, completely account for substitution effects at a high level of aggregation in the National Income and Product Accounts (NIPA). The

BLS changed its construction of a fraction of its elementary price indexes (from Laspeyres to geometric index formulas) in the CPI to account for low-level substitution of purchases within narrowly defined items. These improvements in the CPI are also reflected in the NIPA because the BEA uses CPI components to deflate personal consumption expenditures. In August 2002, the BLS began publishing the Chained Consumer Price Index that accounts for high-level substitution.

The scope for further improvement in price indexes in how they reflect substitution effects is limited by data availability. To account for substitution, price and quantity (or expenditure) must be measured simultaneously. The existing system of collecting data provides high-frequency information on price but provides information on quantity at low frequency and with greater lags. In the case of the low-level indexes, BLS use of (unweighted) geometric means obviates the need for quantity data by implicitly assuming a unit elasticity of substitution.[3] In the case of high-level substitution, it is possible to project expenditures using an estimate of demand elasticities (see Shapiro and Wilcox 1997) or to report or revise the price index with a lag once expenditure data become available.

Scanner data provide simultaneous data on quantity and expenditure. These data are available with a very short lag and are consistently measured. Having simultaneous quantity and expenditure data creates the possibility of creating price indexes that account for the substitution of consumers away from goods that have price increases. Hence, it is possible to implement superlative index formulas, which account for substitution effects to a second-order approximation, at all levels of aggregation with virtually no time lag. This possibility creates great promise for scanner data, but, as the papers in this volume make clear, the mechanical application of superlative index formulas to scanner data introduces new problems for measurement.

Product Attributes and the Measurement of Quality

Scanner data can be linked with a large range of information in addition to quantities sold. Databases contain detailed information about product attributes, information that has several uses. First, scanner data can be monitored to alert statistical agencies to the appearance of new goods or changes in the attributes of existing goods. Second, as several of the papers in this volume emphasize, information about the attributes of goods can be used to make quality adjustments that are necessary to assure accurate measurement of changes in the cost of living. Information from scanner data can be used to make hedonic adjustments that use many more attributes, larger datasets, and more frequent observations than are available

3. The Bureau of Labor Statistics has found this to be a good assumption on average, but it is likely not to be very accurate when looking across goods.

with conventional hedonic adjustment procedures. Information on product attributes from scanner data can also be used to link observations more accurately when models change and to increase the level of assurance that changes in quality are not linked out of price indexes.

Challenges

The papers in this volume demonstrate that, although scanner data provide significant opportunities for improving on price measurement, incorporating scanner data into the statistical system creates substantial challenges.

First, scanner data pose significant challenges for economic and index number theory. Because scanner data capture individual transactions rather than consumption, they do not map as cleanly into economic aggregates as one might hope. In particular, because of the distinction between purchase and consumption, standard index number formulas cannot be mechanically applied, at least not at high frequency.

Second, the use of scanner data probably would not automatically reduce the cost of collecting price data. Although a price quotation from a scanner record is available at essentially zero marginal cost, the costs of processing scanner data may be high. An agency would have to deal with a tidal wave of information. It would need to address problems of missing data or new goods. Moreover, since much of the cost of pricing an item by hand involves the fixed cost of visiting the outlet, the system of collecting prices by hand would still be quite costly unless all price quotations were made by scanner data.

Third, the use of scanner data requires the participation and cooperation of private firms—both those that are the source of the scanned prices and firms such as ACNielsen, which collects and processes these data. To assure the continuity of the statistical system, the statistical agencies must be assured of long-term, consistent, and timely access to the information need to construct price indexes.

Fourth, the availability of more data does not always lead to better analysis. The electronic economy creates a flood of information. Statistical agencies must develop new modes of operating to convert the huge flow of information into useful statistics.

Summary of the Conference

This volume contains papers originally presented at the Conference on Research in Income and Wealth (CRIW) meeting "Scanner Data and Price Indexes" on 15–16 September 2000 in Arlington, Virginia. The CRIW brings together experts from the statistical agencies and academics with an interest in measurement. The papers in this volume give a good picture of both the promise and the challenge of using scanner data to produce economic statistics.

Scanner Data in Official Statistics: Advancing the State of the Art

William J. Hawkes and Frank Piotrowski present an invaluable case study of using scanner data for price measurement of ice cream. Their paper begins with a discussion of how scanner data can be used to improve price measurement. It also traces important conceptual and practical differences between the ways the CPI program and the Scantrack data system view the markets and goods—ice cream in particular. The paper's analysis is based on a virtual census of retail purchases of ice cream in the United States in 1999. They find that the CPI quite closely tracks the change in the price of bulk ice cream, although this price change is not representative of the entire ice cream category in Scantrack. As noted above, scanner data provide substantial scope for measuring quantities as well as price. This paper is the only one in the volume to have comprehensive coverage for a good. It finds that CEX understates sales by almost 20 percent. Hawkes and Piotrowski also provide an indication of the range of data available for hedonic adjustment. For ice cream, the ACNielsen Product Reference codes over fifty attributes. The impression the authors leave is that a substantial amount of product-specific expertise would be required to make use of such data.

The statistical agencies have substantial research in progress on the use of scanner data for price measurement. This volume includes three reports on this research, from the U.S. Bureau of Labor Statistics, from the U.K. Office for National Statistics, and from Statistics Canada.

The BLS has a pilot project to investigate the feasibility of incorporating pricing information from scanner data into the monthly production of the CPI. This pilot is based on the market for breakfast cereal in New York. The paper by David H. Richardson makes two broad contributions. First, it provides an overview of the use of scanner data in the statistical system based on the actual experience of using them to construct a price index designed to be a practical alternative to a price index based on conventionally collected data: Scanner data are continuous, whereas CPI price observations are collected at particular times of the month, days of the week, and times of the day. Scanner data represent transactions, whereas CPI price observations are based on quoted prices (e.g., the price of a box of cereal on the shelf) whether or not there is a transaction at that price. The BLS knows the exact location of a price quotation, whereas the scanner data are currently anonymous. This anonymity complicates the addition of the appropriate sales tax to the transaction. New procedures are needed for imputing missing prices (see also the paper by Ralph Bradley in this volume) and for cleaning data.

Second, the paper compares the New York price index for breakfast cereal from the CPI program to various indexes computed from the scanner data. The indexes based on scanner data have a similar trend to the CPI index over 1999 to 2000. The CPI is substantially more variable. During the first part of the sample, it runs ahead of the indexes for scanners, whereas it runs behind during the second half. Of the scanner indexes, the superlative indexes increase faster than the geometric index. Given that the elasticity of substitution between different types of cereal is likely to be higher than 1, one would have expected the superlative indexes to grow more slowly. This difficulty of mechanically implementing formulas for price indexes is one of the main themes of this volume.

David Fenwick, Adrian Ball, Peter Morgan, and Mick Silver discuss the U.K. Office for National Statistics's experience in comparing scanner data with conventionally collected data from its Retail Price Index (RPI). This experience highlights another theme of this conference—that the promise of scanner data is perhaps more an increase in quality of price measurement than simply an alternative means to collect data that would otherwise be collected by hand. In contrast with the BLS's pilot, which used breakfast cereals, the U.K. study examines high-unit-value consumer durables. An aim of the study is to evaluate whether scanner data can help improve the representativeness of items priced. In consumer durables, there is substantial heterogeneity in attributes of items, models and items change frequently, and model changes and price changes interact through sale pricing of old models and price changes that occur when new models are introduced. Fenwick and his colleagues find that the universe of scanner data provides different measures of price change than the subset matched with the items in the RPI over the several months compared. However, there is no general lesson. For some of the goods, the RPI-based sample has greater price increase than the scanner universe, whereas the opposite is true for other goods. The authors' recommendation is that scanner data be used for weighting price quotations, either through quotas based on scanner data or the weighting of price quotations based on sales measured by scanners. They do not go so far as to recommend using unit values from scanners to replace price measurements for these goods.

Robin Lowe and Candace Ruscher's paper reports on Statistics Canada's research on the price of televisions. Technical change has led to both price declines and quality improvements in televisions. As has just been noted, the interactions of these quality changes, changes in models, and changes in prices pose very difficult challenges for the statistical agencies in obtaining accurate measures of prices for consumer durables. The paper first discusses the current practice of Statistics Canada for dealing this these problems and uses a relatively long span of data, from 1990 to 1997, to document how different procedures have noticeable implications for measures of price change. The paper then examines an experimental data set using scanner data for televisions over a two-year period. It discusses how scanner data can alert the statistical agency to the existence of new models, but it also highlights the practical difficulties of using these data to compute price indexes. As with prices for the official CPI, these new models must be linked in to the existing database. Doing so requires assumptions about whether or not their attributes are comparable to the ones they replace. The authors investigate using regression analysis as an alternative to making judgments about this issue. For this approach to be practical, substantial data on attributes of the models would need to be collected, and the regression analysis would need to be carried out quickly. It would not be practical to perform such analysis for all goods in the scanner database, so the agency would need to resort to sampling of these data.

In addition to reports on these specific projects, the volume also includes a roundtable discussion of ongoing projects at the statistical agencies. Participants in the roundtable are Dennis Fixler (BLS), John S. Greenlees (BLS), David Fenwick (U.K. Office of National Statistics), Robin Lowe (Statistics Canada), and Mick Silver (Cardiff University). This discussion highlights a number of the key findings of the pilot projects relating to variance, replication of official practice, and quality adjustment. It also raises the issues of the pecuniary and practical issues raised by the use of scanner data. The pecuniary cost of collecting prices by visiting stores is quite low, especially for the marginal price quotation. Scanner data are produced commercially and typically are quite expensive to purchase. Hence, using scanner data, especially when workers from statistical agencies must visit stores for other purposes (e.g., to get other price quotations, to get information about products, etc.) might add to the cost of the statistical system, particularly during a period of transition to increased use of electronic data. Also, the statistical agencies would need to develop long-term contracts with the commercial sources of scanner data to assure the timeliness and continuity of its data sources.

Aggregation Across Time

Conventional price measurement typically involves some averaging over time. Equilibrium prices and quantities, however, vary continuously as sellers strategically set prices and as consumers respond to price variation. By making actual rather than average transactions observable, scanner data both create the opportunity for studying these market outcomes and provide challenges for mapping transactions data into price index numbers.

Robert C. Feenstra and Matthew D. Shapiro study the behavior of price indexes constructed from high-frequency scanner data. Jack E. Triplett reflects on a number of issues of price index construction and uses a small data set to show how consumer shopping behavior can dramatically alter the true price paid relative to what a price index based on survey sampling might measure. Feenstra and Shapiro find that mechanical application of standard index number formulas to these weekly data lead to surprising results. Superlative price indexes should grow more slowly than fixed-weighted indexes because they are designed to account for substitution by consumers away from goods whose price is increasing. Yet, in their sample of weekly data, the superlative indexes show increases relative to the fixed-weight indexes. The studies by the statistical agencies in this volume provide similar examples of unexpected behavior of superlative indexes.

The papers by both Feenstra and Shapiro and by Triplett note that movements in high-frequency data on purchases by consumer can be dominated by shopping behavior rather than consumption behavior. Even goods that are nondurable may be storable, so the high-frequency purchases might be dominated by consumers' economizing by buying (rather than consuming) when the price is low. This consumer behavior is also affected by strategic behavior of the stores, especially nonprice promotion (e.g., advertising). These promotions cause bursts of purchases at times when the price may not be the lowest, leading to apparent failures of the law of demand and the surprising behavior of superlative indexes. Feenstra and Shapiro present a model due to Betancourt and Gautschi (1992) that distinguishes shopping and consumption. It implies an index number formula that compares prices over entire planning horizons (e.g., from one year to the next). This formula appears to work well in practice. They also provide econometric evidence that consumers respond to sales and promotions as the theory predicts.

Using Price Data to Study Market Structure

Robert Barsky, Mark Bergen, Shantanu Dutta, and Daniel Levy use an original data set that combines retail and wholesale data for a grocery store chain. The differences in prices between branded goods and store labels can provide an estimate of the markup. Since store labels will not be sold at less than marginal cost, the ratio of the retail prices of branded to store labeled goods is a lower bound on the markup of the branded goods. Moreover, since they have data on the wholesale prices of both goods, they can provide additional estimates of the markups that include the cost of retailing. They find that markup ratios can be substantial—over 3 for toothbrushes and over 2 for soft drinks. There is also substantial heterogeneity in markup ratios, with some being quite low and most ranging from 1.5 to 2.

The existence of substantial markups has very important implications for industrial organization and macroeconomics. It also has important implications for price measurement and the use of scanner data. That markups can be large also means there is substantial scope for them to vary over time. (If perfect competition reigned supreme, not only would markups be low, but they would always be the same.) There are good reasons to expect that markups should vary with the level of demand (see Rotemberg and Saloner 1986). Demand can vary over the business cycle, but also at much higher frequency. Warner and Barsky (1995) emphasize how markups can change over the days of the week depending on the shopping behavior of consumers, and Chevalier, Kashyap, and Rossi (2002) make the same point for the time of year. Since scanner data record prices continuously, they will capture the changes in prices resulting from changes in the markup that may occur at high frequency. Statistical agencies could miss some of these price changes to the extent that price data are collected during normal business hours and days.

One of the most difficult practical and conceptual problems for statistical agencies is the incorporation of new goods into the price index. A key practical difficulty is monitoring the arrival of new goods and the selectivity and bias created by lagged incorporation of successful new goods. Scanner data can be helpful in this regard because they can provide more timely information about the arrival of new goods than can surveys of consumers. John S. Greenlees emphasizes this point in his roundtable discussion. Nonetheless, the conceptual issues of how to incorporate them into a price index remain. Ernst R. Berndt, Davina C. Ling, and Margaret K. Kyle study the interactions of prescription versus over-the-counter versions of the same pharmaceutical compound during the period around the expiration of the patent for the compound. They contrast different techniques for accounting for the value of new goods—one by Feenstra (1994, 1997), which estimates the elasticity of substitution across the goods, and one by Griliches and Cockburn (1994), which relies on a distribution of tastes across consumers for branded versus generic versions of the pharmaceuticals. Their analysis makes use of monthly data on shipments of the compounds by their manufacturers (quantity, revenue, and promotional information) collected by IMS Health. Like scanner data for a grocery store, these data provide a census of transactions for the goods in question. The authors find that marketing is very important in explaining the relative success of pharmaceuticals and the demand for them following patent expiration. They also provide a comparative analysis of the Feenstra and Griliches-Cockburn procedures for incorporating new goods into price indexes. They find that functional form assumptions, although not inherent to Feenstra's procedure, have significant impact on the calculations. They speculate that the simple functional forms used by Feenstra might operate better at higher levels of aggregation (e.g., new classes of pharmaceuticals instead of close substitutes within a class).

Measuring Change in Quality and Imputing Missing Observations

The paper by Mick Silver and Saeed Heravi examines alternative approaches to using scanner data for adjusting prices for quality change. It contrasts three approaches: matching of similar models; hedonic regression using a limited set of dummy variables for characteristics; and hedonic regression using the larger set of characteristics readily observed in scanner data. The paper examines data for 1998 on washing machine sales. The scanner data provide model numbers for each transaction, which are keyed to information about the characteristics of the models from the manufacturers. For the authors' data, the three approaches to quality adjustment perform not dissimilarly. The authors extend their framework to discuss the problem of missing data as confronted by statistical agencies in practice. In contrast with the case of cereal examined by Bradley, missing data for consumer durables are likely to occur with model changes that require hedonic adjustments.

Erwin Diewert's discussion of Silver and Heravi's paper developed into an examination of the foundations of hedonic price adjustment, which is included as a chapter in this volume. It shows how simple linear models are hard to justify with economic theory. It also shows that the traditional practice of statistical agencies replicates exact hedonics under some circumstances. Additionally, it uses the economic analysis to inform econometric practice for estimating hedonic relationships.

Scanners record transactions. If a good is not sold during a specific week at a specific outlet, there will be no information about its price. Since goods are very narrowly defined (there are different Universal Product Codes for slight variants of products—e.g., the 16-oz. vs. the 20-oz. box of Cheerios), there is a substantial probability that observations will be missing. In contrast, the CPI will price an item if it is on the shelf, regardless of whether it is sold. It will generate a missing observation if it is stocked out. A stock out could mean either that the item is not available (and therefore not sold) or that it is sold out (and therefore had possibly substantial sales). Ralph Bradley investigates alternative methods for dealing with these missing observations. In particular, he proposes an econometric procedure that assigns a virtual price and contrasts it to other procedures (carrying forward the last observation, using unit values at a higher level of aggregation that does not have missing values, the BLS method of imputation). For his sample, the procedures lead to similar indexes over time, although the variability of the indexes differs.

References

Betancourt, Roger R., and David Gautschi. 1992. The demand for retail products and the household production model: New views on complementarity and substitution. *Journal of Economics Behavior and Organization* 17:257–75.

Boskin, Michael J., Ellen R. Dulberger, Robert J. Gordon, Zvi Griliches, and Dale W. Jorgensen. 1996. Toward a more accurate measure of the cost of living: Final report to the Senate Finance Committee from the Advisory Commission to Study the Consumer Price Index. Washington, D.C.: Senate Finance Committee, December.

Chevalier, Judith, Anil Kashyap, and Peter Rossi. 2002. Why don't prices rise during peak demand periods? Evidence from scanner data. *American Economic Review,* forthcoming.

Feenstra, Robert C. 1994. New product varieties and the measurement of international prices. *American Economic Review* 84:157–77.

———. 1997. Generics and new goods in pharmaceutical price indexes: Comment. *American Economic Review* 87:760–67.

Griliches, Zvi, and Ian M. Cockburn. 1994. Generics and new goods in pharmaceutical price indexes. *American Economic Review* 84:1213–32.

Hausman, Jerry. 1999. Cellular telephone, new products, and the CPI. *Journal of Business and Economics Statistics* 17:188–94.

Rotemberg, Julio, and Garth Saloner. 1986. A supergame-theoretic model of price wars during booms. *American Economic Review* 76:390–407.

Shapiro, Matthew D., and David W. Wilcox. 1996. Mismeasurement in the Consumer Price Index: An evaluation. *NBER macroeconomics annual 1996,* ed. Ben S. Bernanke and Julio J. Rotemberg, 93–142. Cambridge: MIT Press.

———. 1997. Alternative strategies for aggregating prices in the CPI. *Federal Reserve Bank of St. Louis Review* 79 (May/June): 113–25.

Warner, Elizabeth J., and Robert B. Barsky. 1995. The timing and magnitude of retail store markdowns: Evidence from weekends and holidays. *Quarterly Journal of Economics* 110:321–52.

Scanner Data in Official Statistics
Advancing the State of the Art

Using Scanner Data to Improve the Quality of Measurement in the Consumer Price Index

William J. Hawkes and Frank W. Piotrowski

"The only emperor is the emperor of ice cream."
—Wallace Stevens, 1922

1.1 Introduction

Twenty-five years ago, a major technological change swept through U.S. retailing and left the field of marketing research profoundly altered in its wake. Since then, the same tidal wave has moved across most of Europe and the developed countries of Asia and Latin America as well. This technological change involved the source-coding of most fast-moving packaged consumer goods by their manufacturers, using the newly developed Universal Product Code. It also involved the installation, by retailers, of electronic scanning equipment at the checkout counter to "read" and record each item purchased in the store. Subsequently, other kinds of electronic point-of-sale (EPOS) systems were introduced to record transactions of durable goods (e.g., toasters and refrigerators) that had not been source-coded at the manufacturer level.

As a result of this new method of data collection, market research firms were able to obtain and summarize information on consumer sales and retail prices in a much faster, more detailed, and more cost-efficient manner than before. Scanner-based data quickly became the "common language" used by manufacturers, retailers, and marketing research companies to describe and interpret developments in the retail marketplace.

As shown in table 1.1 below, currently in the United States around 10 percent of total consumer expenditures, and around one-quarter of consumer

William J. Hawkes is the former chief statistical officer of ACNielsen and is presently a marketing research consultant. Frank W. Piotrowski is vice-president and chief of the measurement science department of ACNielsen.

The authors thank Bill Cook and Dave Richardson for their comments on an earlier draft of this paper.

Table 1.1   **Consumer Expenditures Scannable through Supermarkets, Drugstores, and Mass Merchandisers in CIP (as of December 1999)**

CPI Expenditure Categories	Number of CPI Categories	% of Consumer Expenditures Included in These Categories	
		All Expenditures	Expenditures for Goods
Food at home	53	9.6	22.8
Perishables	19	3.2	7.5
Scannable edibles (row 1 less row 2)	34	6.4	15.2
Other supermarket item strata	9	3.8	9.0
Total supermarket scannables (row 3 plus row 4)	43	10.2	24.2

Table 1.2   **A Brief Lexical Concordance between Market Research and Consumer Price Index Terminology**

Marketing Research	Price Index
Retail selling price	Price (p)
Consumer sales equivalent units	Quantity (q)
Consumer sales dollars	Expenditures (pq)

expenditures on goods (as opposed to services, such as housing services and haircuts), are made in categories that can, in large measure, be represented through scanning data obtained from supermarkets, mass merchandisers, and drugstores.

Price index theorists and practitioners have long been observing and measuring the same consumer behavior as have marketing researchers, even though they sometimes use a slightly different vocabulary to describe the transactions that they are studying, as shown in table 1.2 below. Both price index and marketing research theorists are concerned with the response, or elasticity, of consumer purchases to changes in retail price. Despite this commonality of interest, the public sector involved in producing consumer price indexes has been slower than the private sector of marketing research to utilize and benefit from this new technology. Recently, however, government statistical agencies in many countries have to begun to investigate and utilize this new source of data in their consumer price indexes.

This paper, written from the perspective of market researchers who have spent the past twenty-five years working with scanner data, discusses specific ways in which the quality of consumer price information can be improved using this new data source. It also shows how the measurement of product quality can be enhanced through the use of these data. The paper will make use of actual scanner data for a particular product category and will, we believe for the first time, present and discuss a "total U.S." simulated price index for a specific Consumer Price Index (CPI) "food-at-home" commodity (item stratum), comparing the results with the corresponding "urban U.S." figures produced by the U.S. Bureau of Labor Statistics. The paper concludes with a discussion of data aggregation issues in CPI construction.

1.2   How Scanner Data Can Improve the Quality of Consumer Price Indexes' Measurements

The potential benefits from using scanner or other EPOS data in CPIs can be grouped into three categories: (a) more data and, consequently, less variance; (b) better data and, consequently, less bias; and (c) better methods. We shall consider each in turn.

1.2.1   More Data

In most developed countries, scanner data for supermarket items are based on a number of data points (outlets, items, and weeks) that exceed those currently used in these countries' CPIs by several orders of magnitude—generally in the range of 1,000 to 1. To cite one example, CPI data for the U.S. breakfast cereals "item stratum" are based on around 675 individual price observations, one observation per month for two or three items per store in a sample of around 300 individual outlets. In contrast, ACNielsen scanner data for supermarkets are based on four or five price observations per month for over 200 cereal items per store in a sample of around 3,000 supermarkets. If the scanner data reporting period, for CPI purposes, is constrained to the first three weeks of each month, then scanner data consist of 1,800,000 price observations per month ($3 \times 200 \times 3000$). This is 2,700 times as many price observations as are currently being obtained for breakfast cereals (1,800,000 divided by 675) in the CPI program. These price records are, in every case, accompanied by actual quantities sold, each week, in each supermarket for each item, in contrast to the implicit quantity weights for each price observation in the CPI, which usually remain unchanged for four or five years.

1.2.2   Better Data

Even within the framework of current CPI designs in most countries, scanner data provide the opportunity for significant quality improvement in terms of bias reduction along several dimensions:

1. *Sample outlet selection.* Scanner retail outlet samples are generally selected from a well-defined frame that lists all universe supermarkets, mass merchandisers, and large drugstores. For the U.S. CPI, sample retail outlets are drawn from a list of "point-of-purchase" outlets obtained from a

sample of around 3,500 households nationally. In many other countries, individual CPI retail outlets are selected from incomplete or geographically restricted frames.

2. *Outlet sample updating.* Scanner samples are usually designed to incorporate new outlets with minimum delay. Consumer price index outlet samples, in most countries, are refreshed or replaced only at periodic intervals, generally once every several years.

3. *Item selection.* Designation of individual items to be priced is carried out, in most countries, in one of two ways:

- Selection of items within a store with probability proportionate to measures of size, in theory based on actual expenditures but often based on shop owners' memory or estimates, or shelf space, or some other "proxy" means. This is the procedure currently used in the United States.
- Purposive or judgmental selection of items by product characteristics, with specific products, or varieties then chosen in the field or, in certain instances, centrally designated. This is the procedure currently used in the United Kingdom and in Canada.

In contrast, scanner data are provided for every item in every category handled and scanned by the store. At the very least, scanner data could be used to check out the validity of the "purposive" item selection methods used in areas such as the United Kingdom and Canada.

4. *Item updating.* Scanner data automatically include all new items appearing in each sampled retail outlet, generally in "real time," or with a delay of a few weeks at most to allow for a full product description to be defined for each new item code. In contrast, CPI new items are brought in only when existing items are discontinued at the individual outlet level or when a complete item reselection is carried out, generally once every several years.[1] Both new items and new outlets are generally linked to the previous price index generated by the old items and old outlets, with no allowance for differences in price levels between new and old, except for item strata where explicit hedonic adjustments can be made. In an important paper, Reinsdorf (1993) showed that the combined effect of new items and new outlets in the U.S. CPI for food-at-home items was to reduce average price levels for food-at-home commodities by 0.25 percent per year.

5. *Better lower-level (within item stratum) expenditure weights.* Lower-level item expenditure or quantity weights used in CPI construction are generally based on estimates made at infrequent intervals from a variety of sources: consumers' recall, consumer purchase diaries, and shopkeepers' estimates. Use of out-of-date expenditure weights is likely to result in an

---

1. When the CPI's telephone point-of-purchase surveys (POPS) rotation scheme is fully operational, POPS categories will be reselected on an ongoing basis, with a complete outlet or item recycling at four- or five-year intervals.

overstatement of inflation. In contrast, scanner data provide current, up-to-date expenditure weights each week.

1.2.3 Improved CPI Scope, Definitions, or Methods

For many years, price theorists have written of "superlative" or "ideal" price indexes more as a concept than as a reality, since current period quantities have generally not been available. In a scanning environment, this restriction no longer exists. Accordingly, a number of methodological questions come immediately to mind. Scanning data can help provide answers to these important questions:

1. Should expenditure weights be computed for each specific month, or is it better to use more stable weights (e.g., for the most recent year), on the assumption that trading off some temporal "characteristicity" in weights will be more than offset by reducing the greater intransitivity associated with chaining true Fisher or Törnqvist indexes? Triplett (1998) has pointed out the instability and intransitivity that can result from the chaining together of even superlative indexes when quantities and prices change abruptly from month to month. Recent studies at the Bureau of Labor Statistics (BLS) seem to support the desirability of using the most recent annual quantity weights with scanning data, updated each year, rather than using the monthly quantity weights that accompany the monthly prices. Silver (1995) and Diewert (2000b) advocate constructing an annual moving weight to avoid seasonal bounce.

2. To what extent should weekly sales and quantities for individual items in individual outlets be aggregated to construct "unit values" across items, outlets, and time? Although a unit value index fails the identity and proportionality tests and thus, according to Balk (1998), "cannot be called a price index," it is also true that the unit value index passes the circularity or transitivity test (cited by Balk as a further axiomatic test for a price index), which the Fisher and the Törnqvist, both considered superlative, are guaranteed to fail![2] The same is true of the "consistency in aggregation" test: the unit value passes this test, whereas the above superlative indexes fail it. Moreover, the unit value is (or can be) automatically adjusted for new items and new outlets. The question of aggregation is discussed at greater length in section 1.5 of this paper.

3. How can scanner data be used to improve the stratum weights used to aggregate the city-by-category lower-level indexes into higher-level indexes? In a recent paper, Diewert (2000b, 26) has cited the "large measurement errors" in these weights as a serious problem in producing an accurate national price index. Certainly the current need to produce expenditure

---

2. See discussions in Frisch (1930) and Olt (1996). "Transitivity" simply means that the product of comparative price levels between countries A and B, and between countries B and C, will equal the comparative price level between countries A and C.

weights for the 1,292 "scannable food-at-home" strata (thirty-eight geographic areas times thirty-four item strata) places a high degree of stress on the sample of roughly 10,000 households each providing two weeks of expenditure data in the U.S. Consumer Expenditure Survey.

An obvious alternative is to make use of aggregate outlet-based scanner data for this purpose. As shown in table 1.3 below, Consumer Expenditure Survey data for 1998 and 1997 agree fairly closely at the national level with ACNielsen ScanTrack data for one product category that will be examined extensively in this paper, but this apparent agreement obscures the fact that the Consumer Expenditure data are probably around 16 percent too low when nonscanning outlet types, sales taxes, and Alaska and Hawaii are taken into account. It would seem an easier matter to estimate this missing 16 percent from the BLS point-of-purchase survey or from household-based scanner data than to estimate the entire 100 percent from the Consumer Expenditure Survey.

In addition to using scanner-based data, ACNielsen also measures consumer sales directly through a 55,000 household sample. The sampled households are supplied a hand-held scanner with a downloaded list of retail establishments in their neighborhood. Households are instructed to scan all UPC coded items they purchase and identify the retail establishment where the purchase occurred. The ACNielsen HomeScan service indicates that 89 percent of ice cream–type products are purchased in traditional supermarkets. This would support the claim that the Consumer Expenditure data may underestimate true sales.

In any event, it would be a useful exercise to carry out this comparison for the thirty-three other scannable edible item strata as well, first at the national level and eventually at the geographic area level as well.

4. How should product categories be defined and subdivided in such a

Table 1.3   Total U.S. Sales of Ice Cream and Related Products, 1997 and 1998 (based on Consumer Expenditure Survey and ScanTrack; sales in $millions)

Year	CES	ScanTrack	ScanTrack vs. CES
1997	5586	5580	−0.1%
1998	5682	5810	+2.3%
1997–98 % change	+1.7	+4.1	+2.4
Adjustments to make 1998 ScanTrack comparable to CES			
Outlets other than supermarkets	14%		
Alaska and Hawaii	1%		
Sales taxes	2%		
Subtotal	17%		
Reported difference	2%		
Adjusted difference, ScanTrack vs. CES	19%		

way as to maximize the temporal and geographic transitivity of the resulting indexes and to avoid item "churn" (i.e., excessive item turnover) while enhancing the comparability of items across time and across geography?

5. The foregoing leads to the next question: how many item strata should there be in the CPI, and how should they be defined? The current fifty-three food-at-home item strata have changed very little in the past twenty years. Essentially, the number of item strata has been determined by the limitations of the 10,000-household Consumer Expenditure Survey sample, the need for continuity and for seasonal adjustment, and the data collection budget. If we were freed from these constraints, how might we want to proceed?

An orthogonal view, or at least an alternative view, of the food-at-home universe is shown in table 1.4. Note that the ACNielsen item structure tends to reflect the "department" or physical layout of the typical supermarket, whereas the BLS structure is driven by classification of item complements and substitutes. Thus, ACNielsen classifies Ice Cream as a frozen food, rather than as a dairy product; ACNielsen classifies vegetables in three different places: frozen, canned, and perishable, just as they are found in the supermarket, whereas BLS groups them together under the fruits and vegetables heading and then divides them into subgroups by form.

Obviously, there is no right or wrong in these taxonomies, but there are differences. Of greater interest is that ACNielsen has further subdivided its 64 categories into 603 separate modules. To some extent BLS also carries out further subdivisions of its 34 item strata, both explicitly into its 44 "entry-level items" (ELIs), and implicitly (for sampling purposes of individual items to be priced in specified outlets) through a "disaggregation" procedure that partitions "entry-level items" down into successively smaller subgroupings based on criteria such as form and package size. Through this

Table 1.4   **How ACNielsen and BLS View the World of Food-at-Home**

	ACNielsen	BLS
Division of food-at-home items	6 departments (dry grocery, frozen foods, dairy, deli, packaged meats, perishables); 64 categories (excludes fresh meat and produce); 603 modules (excludes fresh meat and produce)	6 commodity groups (cereals & bakery products, meat, poultry, eggs & fish, dairy, fruits & vegetables, nonalcoholic beverages, other); 18 expenditure classes; 53 item strata (of which 34 exclude fresh meat and produce); 65 entry-level items (of which 44 exclude fresh meat and produce)
Division of "ice cream and related products"	4 modules in 2 categories under "frozen foods"	1 entry-level item in 1 item stratum under "dairy"
Classification of ice cream	frozen food	dairy product

process, the 34 "scannable edible" item strata are thus further subdivided into 79 "clusters" or mutually exclusive and exhaustive building blocks. These 79 clusters might be a natural next level for category detail to be used as input to higher-level index aggregates in the CPI if resources allowed.

However, the conceptual distinction between what should be a cluster and what should merely be a disaggregation criterion is not always clear. In the CPI example above, fresh fruits and vegetables are divided into eight separate item strata, whereas canned vegetables share an item stratum with canned fruits, although the item stratum is subdivided two separate clusters, one for fruits and one for vegetables. ACNielsen has sixty-nine separate modules for canned fruits and vegetables. Is sixty-nine too many? Is one too few? Is two?

With scanner data, alternative partitionings of the entire product space can be carried out on an experimental basis to determine what the optimal clustering rules should be, in order to produce the most reliable and efficient overall index at various geographical levels.

6. There has been a blizzard of papers written over the past decade, both within BLS and from interested observers, on the subject of within-stratum price elasticity. These papers have been written in the context of two very real and important issues:

- Did the Laspeyres assumption of a Leontief preference function lead to a serious upward bias in the CPI prior to 1999?
- Has the geometric mean formula used in lower-level index construction starting in 1999, which assumes Cobb-Douglas preferences and unit elasticities, fully corrected the problem?

With few exceptions, such as a reference by Moulton (1993) to one earlier article by Tellis (1988), most of the literature on this subject has been informed more by opinions or "a prioristic" arguments than by factual evidence. Until recent years, in the absence of good information on quantities to accompany price information, economists had little choice but to speculate about these elasticities. However, scanner data provide a veritable library of information pertaining to individual item elasticities and cross-elasticities. In the United States and many other countries, manufacturers and retailers conduct and commission literally hundreds of studies each year in which outlet-level scanner data are used to measure these elasticities for the purpose of planning their pricing and promotional strategies. Certainly the public sector (e.g., the BLS and its counterpart agencies in other countries) could and should make use of the same data source in order to answer these critical questions on price elasticities, functional forms, and biases.

7. A final opportunity for improving the quality of measurement is one that also improves the measurement of quality. By "measurement of quality" we are referring to the measurement of product quality for use in price index construction. This can be done by relating bundles of product char-

acteristics to the price of each product in such a way as to generate hedonic quality coefficients on each characteristic and thereby enable new items to be linked together with old or existing items in a price index without loss of continuity. This will be the topic of the next section.

1.3   How Scanner Data Can Improve the Measurement of (Product) Quality in the Consumer Price Index

There are (at least) four different methods[3] that have been proposed or used to adjust for quality changes in the CPI framework, or for quality differences in an interarea price comparison framework.

1.3.1   Direct Adjustment

This procedure is normally used when the new product differs from the old only by a factor of size—generally package size. For example, if a manufacturer downsizes from a 220-gram size to a 200 gram size but leaves the price unchanged, this would be treated as a 10 percent price increase under a "direct adjustment" procedure. This method assumes a linear, nonzero intercept pricing model. This assumption is generally a good one when the size change is small, but it tends to break down when substantially different package sizes are being compared (see table 1.5 for some real examples).

1.3.2   Manufacturer's Cost Adjustment

When a new product attribute, or a change in product attributes, has been introduced, a value on this new or changed attribute can sometimes be obtained from manufacturer's cost information. The accompanying change in retail price can then be partitioned into a pure price increase component and a quality change component, based on the manufacturer's cost information. This method has been used, for example, in making some quality change adjustments for new automobiles.

1.3.3   Hedonic Adjustment

In this method, which dates back at least to Court (1939), implicit price components for each of a bundle of product characteristics are determined by a regression procedure that expresses the price of a product as a function of the coefficients associated with each characteristic. The price of a new product (or different product) can then be compared with that of the previously existing product when one utilizes these coefficients.

There are three potential difficulties with this method. One is that the he-

---

3. Jack Triplett tells me (WJH) that there are actually a lot more than four, and he is probably right. Most of the other candidates strike me as variants of the four that we have listed. (see, for example, Wynne and Sigalla 1994). Methods have also been developed to partition an observed difference into a pure price change component and a quality change component. Greenlees (2000) discusses these issues in detail, as does Triplett (1997).

Table 1.5   **Examples of Nonlinear Pricing: Organization "Y"**

Product and Size	Price ($)	Price per Unit ($)
Brand "A" Corn Oil		
16 oz.	1.53	3.06 (per quart)
24 oz.	1.95	2.60
32 oz.	2.45	2.45
48 oz.	3.15	2.10
64 oz.	4.13	2.07
128 oz.	7.87	1.97
Brand "B" Coffee		
13 oz.	2.71	3.34 (per pound)
26 oz.	5.23	3.22
39 oz.	7.59	3.11
Brand "C" Rice		
1 lb.	0.63	0.63 (per pound)
2 lb.	1.19	0.59
5 lb.	2.75	0.55
10 lb.	4.79	0.48
Brand "D" Peanut Butter		
12 oz.	1.65	2.20 (per pound)
18 oz.	1.89	1.68
28 oz.	3.09	1.77
40 oz.	4.35	1.74
64 oz.	6.85	1.71
Brand "E" Sugar		
1 lb.	0.63	0.63 (per pound)
2 lb.	1.01	0.51
5 lb.	1.99	0.40
10 lb.	3.95	0.39
Brand "F" Large Eggs		
6	0.79	0.131 (per egg)
12	1.29	0.107
18	1.95	0.108
Brand "G" 2% Milk		
1 qt.	0.95	0.95 (per quart)
1/2 gal.	1.69	0.84
1 gal.	2.69	0.67
Brand "H" Catsup		
14 oz.	0.91	2.08 (per quart)
20 oz.	1.12	1.79
28 oz.	1.95	2.23
40 oz.	2.59	2.07
60 oz.	3.59	1.80

donic coefficients can be unstable across time and across geography. Another is that the hedonic variables can be intercorrelated, leading to all the usual problems of out-of-sample forecasts based on least squares. Finally, reliable calculation of the hedonic factors requires a large number of observations— often larger than the number of CPI quotes available to estimate them.

Scanning or EPOS data offer a way around many of these obstacles, especially for certain Durable goods items where product turnover is rapid, the number of relevant characteristics is large, and the CPI sample size is small. For this reason, hedonic adjustment research using EPOS data in theUnited States, Canada, and theUnited Kingdom has tended to focus on durable goods, as evidenced by a number of papers on this topic presented at this and other recent conferences (see, e.g., Lowe 1998; Ioannides and Silver 1997).

Hedonic adjustment procedures, however, can also be used for fast-moving consumer goods, such as packaged foods and household products. For example, a few years ago the packaged laundry detergent industry switched to a new "high-density" formulation that made direct comparison of new and old product prices impossible without taking this product reformulation into account. A similar discontinuity arose with the introduction of "high yield" extraction coffee roasting techniques fifteen or twenty years ago. Other examples could easily be cited.

The richness of the scanner-based data sets, not only in number of observations but also in the systematic collection of detailed product characteristics, makes hedonic adjustment for new items in these fast-moving consumer goods much easier to carry out. Beyond that, however, it can also greatly facilitate the process of disaggregation in the current CPI system, in which individual items are selected for pricing in the store based on a hierarchical list of price-determining characteristics. This process of identifying and ranking the relevant price-determining characteristics for each cluster, ELI, or item stratum can be greatly refined with the use of scanning data.

1.3.4 Characteristic-Based Subgroups

Finally, a robust alternative to making explicit hedonic adjustments in certain cases involves using the hedonic coefficients to identify price-determining characteristics and then combining items into subgroups based on these characteristics, with a unit value price computed across the items in each subgroup. Such a procedure would make it possible to compare prices across cities, regions, and even countries where the set of brands handled differs from place to place. It would also provide a mechanism for handling new items (e.g., flavors) within existing brands or even the introduction of an existing brand into a new region of the United States.

The number of detailed product characteristics available for such analyses in the ACNielsen ScanTrack product reference file is substantial. Currently, ACNielsen has over 3 million unique UPCs coded in its item dictionary, with over 3,000 new entries added on a weekly basis. The product reference file contains nearly 600 unique characteristics. Each specific product category has a set of mandatory characteristics that are coded with product in hand by ACNielsen associates. Many of these characteristics could be considered price-determining for their category. Appendix C provides a listing of characteristics associated with the ice cream category. Values for these characteristics are only populated if present on product packaging.

1.4   An Extended Example Using One Item Stratum

One of the thirty-four "scannable edible" item strata for which separate price indexes are computed in the CPI is "ice cream and related products." This item stratum corresponds to a total of four ACNielsen ScanTrack "product modules": bulk ice cream, ice milk and sherbet, frozen yogurt, and frozen novelties. Each module can be approximated by a combination of characteristics used in the CPI disaggregation procedure for the "ice cream and related products" item stratum. One of the modules—bulk ice cream—is identical to a commodity that is included in the CPI "average price" series.

A profile of this product category is shown on tables 1.6 and 1.7. Note

Table 1.6   How Many Different Kinds of Ice Cream and Related Products Are There, and How Many of Them Are New?

| | Number of Different Items in 1999 | | | % of 1999 $ Sales |
ScanTrack Module	Total	Old	New	from New Items
Bulk ice cream	8,056	7,422	634	4.2
Ice milk and sherbet	788	756	32	4.1
Frozen yogurt	900	865	35	3.0
Frozen novelties	3,106	2,785	321	4.9
Total	12,850	11,828	1,022	4.4

Note: An item is defined as a particular flavor of a particular size of a particular type of a particular brand. This generally, but not always, corresponds to one UPC. New items are items sold in 1999 but not in 1998.

Table 1.7   Profile of "Ice Cream and Related Products" Item Stratum Based on ScanTrack Data for 1999

| | 1999 Sales | % of Item Stratum | % of Sales on Promotion | |
Type	($millions)	1999 $ Sales	Dollars	Quantities
Bulk ice cream	3,895	64.0	11.8	15.0
Ice milk and sherbet	133	2.2	9.1	12.6
Frozen yogurt	264	4.4	12.6	19.2
Frozen novelties	1,788	29.4	22.7	30.3
Total	6,082	100.0	15.0	n.a.

Note: n.a. = not available.

that there were nearly 13,000 separate items of "ice cream and related products" sold somewhere in the United States at some time during 1999. More than 1,000 of these items were new (i.e., not found in 1998), and these new items accounted for more than 4 percent of U.S. ice cream expenditures in 1999 (this could imply an annual rate of 8 percent at year end). Fifteen percent of total expenditures on ice cream and related products were for items that were on promotion during the week in which they were purchased ("on promotion" means that they were on display, were advertised by the retailer, or had a temporary price reduction). The typical U.S. supermarket, incidentally, stocks more than 500 of these items.

Because of the close correspondence between the ACNielsen and CPI category definitions, it is possible to compare CPI with ScanTrack "price index" data for the item stratum as a whole, and CPI with ScanTrack "average price" data for the "bulk ice cream" module. The results of these comparisons are set forth on tables 1.8 and 1.9.

In table 1.8, note that the two "average price" series are in very close agreement. Note also, however, that the ScanTrack "average price" in 1999

Table 1.8   **Average U.S. Price of Bulk Ice Cream per 64 oz. Equivalent Unit**

Source	1998	1999	Average Price Ratio × 100
CPI[a]	$3.127	$3.296	105.42
ScanTrack[b]	$3.171	$3.360	105.96
ScanTrack vs. CPI	+1.4%	+1.9%	
ScanTrack[b] less 2 new brands	$3.171	$3.330	105.01
ScanTrack less 2 new brands vs. CPI	+1.4%	+1.0%	

[a]Based on linear average of monthly average price series.
[b]Annual dollar sales divided by annual equivalent unit sales.

Table 1.9   **1998–99 U.S. Ice Cream Price Trends Reported by ScanTrack and CPI**

		1999 Index (1998 = 100) by Module				
Source	Index Type	Bulk Ice Cream	Ice Milk and Sherbet	Frozen Yogurt	Frozen Novelties	Total
CPI	Geomean	n.a.	n.a.	n.a.	n.a.	*1.0400*
ScanTrack	Geomean	1.050	1.043	1.036	1.028	*1.0422*
ScanTrack	Törnqvist	1.049	1.046	1.035	1.027	1.0420
ScanTrack	Laspeyres	1.051	1.044	1.037	1.029	1.0433
ScanTrack	Fisher	1.049	1.046	1.036	1.028	1.0420
ScanTrack	Unit value[a]	*1.060*	1.027	1.023	1.029	n.a.
CPI	Unit value[b]	*1.054*				

Notes: n.a. = not available. Figures in italics indicate agreement between CPI and ScanTrack values.
[a]Price based on annual dollar sales divided by annual equivalent sales.
[b]Prices based on linear average of monthly "average price" series.

was increased, by 1 full percent, by the appearance in the market of two new "luxury" brands that could not have been included in the CPI "average price" series in 1999 because of the delay from the time that a new item comes into the marketplace to the time that it has a chance of selection in the CPI. To some extent, this calls into question the belief that the "average price" series correctly reflects only the downward price pressures that Reinsdorf (1993) characterized as resulting from "Schumpeterian creative destruction." We now see that new items can raise average price levels as well as lower them. Other recent examples of this phenomenon are "boutique brewery" brands of beer and "gourmet" brands of coffee. In theory, the right hedonics should be able to identify and correct for these instances, but it would not be an easy job.

In table 1.9, the relationship between CPI and ScanTrack year-to-year price index trends is surprisingly close, although the high degree of correspondence among Laspeyres, Fisher, Geomean, and Törnqvist indexes suggests that inter-item price elasticities in this category may indeed be close to unity. For ScanTrack Geomean and Laspeyres indexes, 1998 was used as the base year, in contrast to the implicit weights generated by the CPI outlet and item selection process, which probably reflect an average product mix dating back to around 1996.

It is obvious that dividing "ice cream and related items" into four separate modules would result in a moderate reduction in variance in measuring year-to-year change at the item stratum level, since the subgroups differ among themselves in their year-to-year change.

Finally, it is interesting to note that ice cream is a category with moderately strong seasonal variation. The weekly seasonal expenditure peak (4 July) is roughly twice as high as the seasonal trough (New Year's week).

1.5   A Coda (or Cadenza) on Aggregation

Henri Theil gives a useful characterization of data aggregation issues in his *Linear Aggregation of Economic Relations* (Theil 1955) and elaborates on it in his *Economics and Information Theory* (Theil 1967). In the earlier book, Theil identifies three dimensions of aggregation: aggregation over individuals, aggregation over commodities, and aggregation over time. In the later book Theil goes on to discuss application of his ideas to price index theory.

For convenience, I have shown in table 1.10 five potential levels of aggregation for each dimension with scanner data. Current CPI practice is generally to choose level 1 for time, level 2 for space, and level 3 for entity. For our simulated CPI using scanning data, we have aggregated time and space to level 5 but used level 2 for entity.

Using somewhat different terminology, Parsons and Schultz (1976) apply these notions of aggregation to the field of Marketing Research in their

Table 1.10   **Potential Aggregation Levels for Price Index Construction Using Scanner Data**

Aggregation Level	Dimension		
	Time	Space	Entity
5 (highest)	Annual	U.S.	Category
4	Monthly	"City"	Segment
3	Weekly	Organization within city	Type by size within brand
2	Price point within week	Outlet	Item
1 (lowest)	Daily[a]	Household	UPC

[a]In Japan, for example, where many price promotions are in effect for one, two, or three days, scanning data are supplied by retailers on a daily basis.

book *Marketing Models and Economic Research.* The relevant chapter in their book was actually written by Dick Wittink, who has subsequently written several papers on the subject using scanning data. In these articles Wittink (see, e.g., Foekens, Leeflang, and Wittnik 1997) finds that it is difficult (and in certain circumstances impossible) to estimate price elasticities reliably using data that have been aggregated across outlets, especially when different prices have been collapsed in the aggregation.

Is this also true for price indexes? Consider the following two questions: (a) Do eggs cost more in stores east of the Mississippi this year than they did last year? (b) Do eggs cost more in stores east of the Mississippi this year than they do in stores west of the Mississippi?

Are these equivalent questions? More precisely, should we use equivalent methods in comparing prices across time as we do in comparing prices across geography?

According to Peter Hill, the answer might well be "yes." In chapter 16 of *Systems of National Accounts,* Hill (1993) writes that "A price index is an average of the proportionate changes in the prices of a specified set of goods and services between two periods in time."

Hill goes on to state that "It is possible to compare prices and volumes between countries using the same general methodology as for intertemporal comparisons within a single country."

Thus, Hill's two statements might be combined as follows: "A price index is the average of the proportional differences in the prices of a specified set of goods and services between two price regimes," where "regime" is used to denote a particular time and place.

In trying to apply this principle to our egg price question, however, we run into an immediate problem: in comparing prices across time, we normally make use of outlet-level data, lining up or "lacing together" the individual outlet prices across time and then combining the resulting price ratios using a Laspeyres, Geomean, Törnqvist, or some other aggregation formula.

When we try to compare egg prices across geography, however, we find that lacing across outlets won't work, because the eyelets on one side of the shoe (or outlets on one side of the river) don't match up with those on the other side. Thus, in making interspatial comparisons, we have no choice but to aggregate outlets all the way up to the regional (or, in the case of purchasing power parities, national) level. We have no hesitation about doing this for interspatial comparisons, but we are reluctant to do so for intertemporal ones. Why is this?

One of the attractive properties of the Geomean is that, with it, the operational problem goes away, since the product of ratios is the same as the ratio of products so long as the weights stay constant. However, the conceptual problem stays. At the very least, obtaining the price ratios from an identical set of outlets has substantial variance implications because of the correlation between item prices across time at the individual outlet level. Aggregated data can also take into account new outlets and items. The question is whether they should do so.

There has been surprisingly little discussion of this issue in the literature, although a few authors have come close. Dalen (1992) has pointed out the difference in concept between the two methods as they apply in a time-series context, but he avoids taking sides. Empirically, Reinsdorf (1998), examining a scanner data set for coffee in two geographic markets, finds little difference between time-series indexes resulting from the use of data aggregated or disaggregated across outlets, but he expresses no preference between them. Kokoski, Moulton, and Zieschang (1996) have written a lengthly article describing a method for comparing prices across cities using hedonic procedures, in which they mention that the procedure can be adapted to time-series comparisons and for achieving transitivity between temporal and spatial measures, but they do not consider the effect of different across-outlet aggregation methods in achieving this transitivity.

Diewert (1995a) suggests that "if individual outlet data or transactions were not available or were considered to be too detailed, then unit values for a homogenous commodity over all outlets might form the lowest level of aggregation." Saglio (1994) starts with data aggregated across all outlets in France by six different shop types and never even considers whether the data should be kept disaggregated by outlet. Magnien and Pougnard (1999) use a similar procedure on French scanner data. Dalen (1997), presenting the results of Swedish scanner data both ways (aggregated vs. disaggregated across outlets), merely argues "for the use of unit values at least over time and *perhaps* also over outlets in a market area"(emphasis added). De Haan and Opperdoes (1997), presenting scanner data for the Netherlands, look at the data both ways but do not reach a conclusion, either. Pollock (1995) briefly considers the issue but simply concludes that "there are opportunities here for empirical work." No one seems to have devised a general rule or even considered the difference between time-series and geographic approaches to aggregation across outlets.

In the price indexes that we have constructed for the ice cream and related products item stratum, we have aggregated the outlet data into a single unit value all the way up to the national level but have kept the item detail fully disaggregated for all 12,000 items common to both years. We have done this largely as a matter of computational ease rather than methodological preference. It seems to us unlikely that we would get a substantially different answer if we had kept the item detail disaggregated by outlet, but we cannot guarantee it.

This is, in our opinion, a methodological issue worthy of further theoretical and empirical consideration. Obviously the concept of interspatial price comparisons has little meaning when viewed from the perspective of the consumer, except for the rare consumer who may be trying to decide on which side of the Mississippi he should buy his eggs.

There are related issues in regard to aggregation across time, especially for products with strong seasonal variations in sales. These have been discussed by Diewert (1996, 2000b) and by Turvey (1998). Scanner data provide an opportunity to examine these issues as well. The effect of various temporal aggregation procedures is shown in table 1.11. Echoing Turvey's

Table 1.11   **1988–99 Annual Comparison of Price Index Trends for "Ice Cream and Related Products" Using Various Methods for Aggregating Monthly Price Indexes**

| | CPI (1982-84 = 100) | | | ACNielsen ScanTrack Share of Annual | | | |
| | Year | | | Expenditures | | Quantities | |
Month	1998	1999	1999 ÷ 1998	1998	1999	1998	1999
January	153.5	165.2	1.0762	0.0617	0.0623	0.0632	0.0606
February	150.8	163.5	1.0842	0.0681	0.0704	0.0708	0.0704
March	150.0	160.2	1.0680	0.0712	0.0728	0.0747	0.0741
April	152.4	162.4	1.0656	0.0773	0.0782	0.0787	0.0787
May	150.9	160.0	1.0603	0.0959	0.0939	0.0997	0.0966
June	153.2	161.7	1.0555	0.1078	0.1133	0.1108	0.1127
July	153.1	158.8	1.0372	0.1186	0.1180	0.1179	0.1198
August	155.2	159.2	1.0258	0.1041	0.1011	0.1031	0.1022
September	157.9	159.8	1.0120	0.0896	0.0863	0.0876	0.0865
October	162.3	163.8	1.0092	0.0762	0.0767	0.0726	0.0745
November	163.9	162.0	0.9984	0.0682	0.0671	0.0630	0.0661
December	162.8	164.1	1.0080	0.0614	0.0600	0.0579	0.0579
Annual	155.5	161.725	n.a.	1.0000	1.0000	1.0000	1.0000

1999 ÷ 1998

"Official" CPI (Dutot aggregation)	1.0400
Unweighted CPI (Jevons aggregation)	1.0413
Unweighted CPI (Carli aggregation)	1.0417
Weighted CPI (Törnqvist-Theil aggregation)	1.0412
Weighted CPI (unit value aggregation)	1.0410

Note: n.a. = not applicable.

conclusion on a different set of data, we find that the differences "are very small, but they do exist."

Appendix A
Formulas Used for Table 1.9

CPI Geomean. See description in "The Experimental CPI using Geometric Means" (U.S. Bureau of Labor Statistics Research Paper, 1997).

$$\text{ScanTrack Geomean} = \prod_i \left(\frac{p_i^{99}}{p_i^{98}} \right)^{S_{98}^i}$$

Where p_i is an annual total U.S. unit value price for the ith item with sales in both 1998 and 1999.

$$S_i^{98} = \frac{E_i^{98}}{\sum E_i^{98}}, \text{ and } E = p_i q_i = \text{price} \times \text{quantity for the item}$$

$$\text{ScanTrack Törnqvist} = \prod_i \left(\frac{p_i^{99}}{p_i^{98}} \right)^{(S_i^{98}+S_i^{99})/2}$$

Where S_i^{99} is defined as for S_i^{98}, above.

$$\text{ScanTrack Laspeyres} = \frac{\sum_i p_i^{99} q_i^{98}}{\sum_i p_i^{98} q_i^{98}}$$

$$\text{ScanTrack Fisher} = \left(\frac{\sum_i p_i^{99} q_i^{98}}{\sum_i p_i^{98} q_i^{98}} \times \frac{\sum_i p_i^{99} q_i^{99}}{\sum_i p_i^{98} q_i^{99}} \right)^{1/2}$$

Appendix B
Formulas Used for Table 1.11

Here I have borrowed the notation of Diewert (2000b).

$$\text{Carli: } P_C(p_n^0, p_n') \equiv \sum_{m=1}^{12} \left(\frac{1}{12} \right) \left(\frac{p_n^{t,m}}{p_n^{0,m}} \right); \quad n = 1, \dots, N; \quad t = 1, \dots T$$

where $p_n^{t,m}$ denotes the price for commodity n in month m in year t.

Jevons: $P_J(p_n^0, p_n^t) \equiv \sum_{m=1}^{12} \left(\frac{p_n^{t,m}}{p_n^{0,m}}\right)^{1/12}$; $n = 1, \ldots, N$; $t = 1, \ldots, T$

Dutot: $P_D(p_n^0, p_n^t) \equiv \left[\sum_{m=1}^{12} \left(\frac{1}{12}\right) p_n^{t,m}\right] \Big/ \left[\sum_{m=1}^{12} \left(\frac{1}{12}\right) p_n^{0,m}\right]$;

$$n = 1, \ldots, N;   t = 1, \ldots, T,$$

where the year-to-price vector for commodity n is

$$\mathbf{p}_n^t \equiv (\mathbf{p}_n^{t,1}, \mathbf{p}_n^{t,2}, \ldots, \mathbf{p}_n^{t,12});   n = 1, \ldots, N;   t = 0, 1, \ldots, T.$$

Törnqvist-Theil: $P_T(p_n^0, p_n^t, s_n^0, s_n^t) \equiv \sum_{m=1}^{12} \left(\frac{1}{2}\right) [s_n^{0,m} + s_n^{t,m}] \ln\left(\frac{p_n^{t,m}}{p_n^{0,m}}\right)$;

$$n = 1, \ldots, N;   t = 1, \ldots, T,$$

where the year t vector of monthly expenditure shares for commodity n is

$$\mathbf{s}_n^t \equiv (\mathbf{s}_n^{t,1}, \mathbf{s}_n^{t,2}, \ldots, \mathbf{s}_n^{t,12});   n = 1, \ldots, N;   t = 0, 1, \ldots, T.$$

Unit value: $\dfrac{P_n^t}{P_n^0} \equiv \dfrac{\sum_{m=1}^{12} \sigma_n^{t,m} p_n^{t,m}}{\sum_{m=1}^{12} \sigma_n^{0,m} p_n^{0,m}}$; $n = 1, \ldots, N$; $t = 0, 1, \ldots, T.$

where $\sigma_n^{t,m}$ is defined as

$$\sigma_n^{t,m} \equiv \frac{q_n^{t,m}}{Q_n^t};   n = 1, \ldots, N;   t = 0, 1, \ldots, T.$$

Appendix C

Ice Cream Category Item Characteristics (from ACNielsen product reference)

Characteristic Typename
Artificial color flavor presence claim
Bonus pack
Branded component or flavor
Calcium presence claim
Calorie Claim
Calories per serving size
Cholesterol
Cholesterol presence claim
Claim

Commodity group
Common consumer name
Dietary fiber
Endorsement
Enrobing flavor
Fat calorie per serving size
Fat presence claim
Fat substitute type
Flavor
Form
Imported or domestic
Lactose presence claim
Licensed trademark
Manufacturer suggested price claim
Manufacturing process
Milk fat
Monounsaturated fat gram
Naked product source
Natural or artificial ingredient claim
Origin
Product storage as stated
Product weight
Protein gram
Saturated fat gram
Season
Serving per container
Serving size household
Serving size metric
Sodium
Sodium presence claim
Sorbitol
Strategic ingredient presence claim
Sugar alcohol
Sugar gram
Sweetener presence claim
Sweetener type
Target group condition
Total fat gram
Vitamin presence claim
Package general shape
Polyunsaturated fat gram
Potassium
Preparation method
Prepriced

Preservative presence claim
Product claim
Product count
Product size

References

Balk, B. 1998. On the use of unit value indices as consumer price subindices. *Proceedings of the fourth meeting of the International Working Group on Price Indices,* 112–120. Washington, D.C.: U.S. Department of Labor, Bureau of Labor Statistics.

Court, A. J. 1939. Hedonic price indexes with automotive examples. In *The Dynamics of Automobile Demand,* 95–119. New York: General Motors.

Dalen, J. 1992. Computing elementary aggregates in the Swedish consumer price index. *Journal of Official Statistics* 8:129–47.

———. 1997. Experiments with Swedish scanner data. In *Proceedings of the third meeting of the International Working Group on Price Indices,* ed. Bert Balk, 163–68. Research Paper no. 9806. Voorburg, the Netherlands: Statistics Netherlands, Division of Research and Development, Department of Statistical Methods.

Diewert, W. E. 1995a. Axiomatic and Economic approaches to international comparisons. Discussion Paper no. 95-01. Vancouver, Canada: University of British Columbia, Department of Economics.

———. 1995b. Price and volume measures in the system of national accounts. Discussion Paper no. 95-02. Vancouver, Canada: University of British Columbia, Department of Economics.

———. 1996. Seasonal commodities, high inflation, and index number theory. Discussion Paper no. 96-06. Vancouver, Canada: University of British Columbia, Department of Economics.

———. 2000a. The Consumer Price Index and index number purpose. Discussion Paper no. 00-02. Vancouver, Canada: University of British Columbia, Department of Economics.

———. 2000b. Notes on producing an annual superlative index using monthly price data. Discussion Paper no. 00-08. Vancouver, Canada: University of British Columbia, Department of Economics.

Foekens, E. W., P. Leeflang, and D. Wittnik. 1997. Hierarchical versus other market share models for markets with many items. *International Journal of Research in Marketing* 14:359–78.

Frisch, R. 1930. The problem of index numbers. *Journal of the American Statistical Association* 25 (December): 397–406.

Greenlees, J. S. 2000. Consumer price indexes: Methods for quality and variety change. *Statistical Journal of the United Nations* 17:59–74.

Haan, J. de, and E. Opperdoes. 1997. Estimation of the coffee price index using scanner data: The choice of the micro index. In *Proceedings of the third meeting of the International Working Group on Price Indices,* ed. Bert Balk, 191–202. Research Paper no. 9806. Voorburg, the Netherlands: Statistics Netherlands, Division of Research and Development, Department of Statistical Methods.

Hill, P. 1993. Price and volume measures. In *System of National Accounts 1993,* Organization for Economic Cooperation and Development staff, 379–406. N.p.: United Nations Publications.

Ioannides, C. and M. Silver. 1997. Chained, exact, and superlative hedonic price changes: Estimates from micro data. In *Proceedings of the third meeting of the International Working Group on Price Indices*, ed. Balk, 215–224. Research Paper no. 9806. Voorburg, the Netherlands: Statistics Netherlands, Division of Research and Development, Department of Statistical Methods.

Kokoski, M. F., B. Moulton, and K. Zieschang. 1996. Interarea price comparisons for heterogeneous goods and several levels of commodity aggregation. Working Paper no. 291. Washington, D.C.: U.S. Department of Labor, Bureau of Labor Statistics.

Lowe, R. 1998. Televisions: Quality changes and scanner data. In *Proceedings of the fourth meeting of the International Working Group on Price Indices*, 5–20. Washington, D.C.: U.S. Department of Labor, Bureau of Labor Statistics.

Magnien, F., and J. Pougnard. 1999. Non-parametric approach to the cost-of-living index. In *Proceedings of the Measurement of Inflation Conference*, ed. Mick Silver and David Fenwick, 345–76. Cardiff, Wales: Cardiff University.

Moulton, B. 1993. Basic components of the CPI: Estimation of price changes. *Monthly Labor Review* (December): 13–24. Washington, D.C.: Bureau of Labor Statistics.

Olt, B. 1996. *Axiom und Struktur in der Statistischen Preisindextheorie* (Axiom and structure in statistical price index theory). Frankfurt, Germany: Peter Lang.

Parsons, L., and R. Schultz. 1976. *Marketing models and econometric research*. Amsterdam: North-Holland Publishing Company

Pollock, R. A. 1995. Elementary aggregates in the CPI. Paper prepared for U.S. Bureau of Labor Statistics. University of Washington, Department of Economics.

Reinsdorf, M. 1993. The effect of outlet price differentials on the U.S. Consumer Price Index. In *Price Measurements and their Uses*, ed. M. F. Foss, M. E. Manser, and A. H. Young, 227–54. Chicago: University of Chicago Press.

———. 1998. Constructing basic components for the U.S. CPI from scanner data: A test using data on coffee. Working Paper no. 277. Washington, D.C.: U.S. Bureau of Labor Statistics.

Saglio, A. 1994. Comparative changes in average price and a price index: Two case studies. Paper presented at the International Conference on Price Indices. October 31–November 2, Ottawa, Canada.

Silver, M. 1995. Elementary aggregates, micro-indices, and scanner data: Some issues in the compilation of consumer price indices. *Review of Income and Wealth* 41 (4): 427–35. Cardiff, Wales: Cardiff University, Cardiff Business School.

Tellis, G. 1988. The price elasticity of selective demand: A meta-analysis of econometric models to sales. *Journal of Marketing Research* 25:331–41.

Theil, H. 1955. *Economics and information theory.* Amsterdam: North-Holland Publishing Company.

———. 1967. *Linear aggregation of economic relations.* Amsterdam: North-Holland Publishing Company.

Triplett, J. 1997. Measuring consumption: The post-1973 slowdown and the research issues. *St. Louis Federal Reserve Bank Review* 79 (3): 9–46.

———. 1998. Elementary indexes for a consumer price index. In *Proceedings of the fourth meeting of the International Working Group on Price Indices*, 176–97. Washington, D.C.: U.S. Department of Labor, Bureau of Labor Statistics.

Turvey, R. 1998. Months versus years. In *Proceedings of the fourth meeting of the International Working Group on Price Indices*, 198–202. Washington, D.C.: U.S. Department of Labor, Bureau of Labor Statistics.

Wynne, M., and F. Sigalla. 1994. The Consumer Price Index. *Economic Review* (second quarter): 1–22.

2

Scanner Indexes for the Consumer Price Index

David H. Richardson

2.1 Introduction

The Consumer Price Index (CPI) is the nation's primary measure of the price change of consumer goods and services. To produce the CPI, the Bureau of Labor Statistics (BLS) staff tracks the prices of a sample of consumer items in the various categories of consumer spending in stores and other retail outlets. In some of those categories, virtually all of the items have a manufacturer-supplied Universal Product Code (UPC) printed on the products to be read by scanners (McKaig 1999). Retailers set prices by UPC for efficiency at the checkout and for inventory management. Consequently, the retailers create computerized records by UPC of the prices and number of units they have sold, records that are commonly called *scanner data*. Scanner data are also used in marketing research to track promotions and variations in packaging, product size, and pricing. In a report to the Senate Finance Committee, Boskin et al. (1996) suggested that scanner data could be used in the CPI for additional commodity detail, as have the Conference Board (1999) and de Haan and Opperdoes (1997a,b). Previous BLS work on scanner data includes Bradley et al. (1997) and Reinsdorf (1997).

The data used in the basic indexes of most item strata are collected by BLS field economists, typically by personal visits to the store or other retail outlet. In retail outlets such as supermarkets, the collection is by observa-

David H. Richardson is an economist at the U.S. Bureau of Labor Statistics working in the CPI program.

Many thanks to all of the members of the ScanData team; this paper is really a group effort. Special thanks to Ralph Bradley, Bill Cook, Dennis Fixler, John Greenlees, Bill Hawkes, and Walter Lane for helpful comments, to Lyubov Rozental for the programming assistance that made it all possi ble, and to Scott Pinkerton for cereal analysis. All remaining errors are of course the author's own.

tion of the prices on the shelves. Each of these prices is called a quote, whether a price was actually collected or whether an unsuccessful attempt was made. The outlets and items are chosen using a probability of selection proportional to sales (PPS) approach. The outlet sample for most strata is based on the point-of-purchase survey (POPS), a telephone inquiry of where items are purchased by consumers in the urban United States. The result is that the CPI tracks prices in the outlets where people actually shop. Within the sample outlets, the item samples are selected in proportion to the outlets' sales within the item category. The same items are priced each month to the extent possible, and new items are substituted as the current items disappear from the market.[1] The outlet sample is rotated approximately every four years, and new item samples are initiated at that time.

It has long been thought that scanner data can be of benefit to the CPI for some or all of the following reasons:

1. Scanner indexes promise greater precision or lower variance than traditionally collected price data.

2. Scanner data record transactions that have actually taken place, whereas the CPI collects the prices of items on the shelf whether transactions actually took place at these prices in the given month or not.

3. Scanner data result in indexes with finer "granularity"—greater commodity detail.

4. The scanner sample is more representative of the universe because the weights are estimated more accurately and updated more frequently.

5. The scanner data are cleaned according to rules that can be applied consistently and studied academically.

6. Scanner data present the opportunity to implement superlative indexes.

This paper explores one way that the CPI could use scanner data in place of traditionally collected price data.

ACNielsen and Information Resources are the only major U.S. vendors of supermarket scanner data, routinely collecting scanner data from the retailers (e.g., Kroger, Safeway, and Giant) and marketing them to the manufacturers (e.g., General Mills, Nabisco, and Pepsi). Although the manufacturers could collect these data themselves, there are clear economies of scale enjoyed by the vendors, and in fact no manufacturer collects these data directly. The vendors add value by sorting the data into useful categories (e.g., cereal), subjecting them to range and consistency checks, and making them available in a standard format. The data contain three principal dimensions—product, time, and geography—and any desired subset is available. Thus, BLS can theoretically request data for the items that are currently

---

1. Occasionally new outlets are chosen to augment the sample in cases in which serious attrition has occurred due to the closing of outlets.

priced (i.e., according to BLS item definitions) and also for the CPI index areas. This paper is a progress report on a CPI program initiative to construct scanner-based test indexes for breakfast cereal in the New York metropolitan area.

The CPI is calculated in two stages based on the BLS partition of the consumption universe into 211 item strata and 38 geographical index areas. In the first stage a basic index is calculated for each of the $211 \times 38 = 8,018$ index area–stratum combinations. The basic indexes for most item strata are constructed using a weighted geometric mean (Geomean) formula; the few remaining item strata use a modified Laspeyres formula. The second stage of the calculation uses the Laspeyres formula to combine appropriate sets of basic indexes to yield various higher level aggregates. These aggregates include the national all-items CPI along with intermediate-level aggregations, for example, national food and beverages, or geographical areas such as New York all-items. The CPI for the New York consolidated metropolitan statistical area (referred to in the CPI as A101) is the aggregation of three basic index areas, A109 (New York city), A110 (New York-Connecticut suburbs), and A111 (New Jersey-Pennsylvania suburbs).

To evaluate the possibility of improving the accuracy of the CPI by using scanner data, BLS created the ScanData team. ScanData's objective was to determine the feasibility of incorporating scanner data into the monthly CPI production process. The method has been to produce demonstration or test indexes for breakfast cereal in A101 New York using scanner data. A success in producing such indexes would confirm that it is indeed possible to improve the CPI using scanner data, whereas a failure would be evidence to the contrary. The goal is indexes that

1. Are produced on the CPI production schedule;
2. Cover the entire domain of a basic item or area stratum by combining or "amalgamating" scanner and CPI data to eliminate outlet and geographic gaps;
3. Are consistent with CPI sampling principles;
4. Are based on a sample that is rotated and refreshed at least as often as under the current CPI procedure;
5. Use both the standard CPI geometric mean formula and a superlative index formula;
6. Use data cleaned at least to current BLS standards; and
7. Use prices with tax.

ScanData has constructed test indexes based on Nielsen breakfast cereal data for New York monthly in real time since March 1998, and it has similar indexes based on back data in a somewhat different format from September 1994 to January 1998. These data have been used to construct Geomeans, Laspeyres, Törnqvist, and Sato-Vartia indexes. The fixed-weight indexes (i.e., Geomeans and Laspeyres) use weights based on the previous calendar year, whereas the weights for the Törnqvist and the Sato-Vartia are updated monthly.

The results show that, over the whole sample period, March 1998 through December 2000, the A101 scanner Geomean index was 105.2 and the CPI was 99.5 on a February 1998 = 100 base. On average, the scanner indexes have less variability than the current CPI. There are about 80,000 scanner quotes collected each month in New York and about 55 traditional CPI quotes, and hence there is a potential reduction in the standard error by a factor of about $\sqrt{80,000/55} = 38.1$. In fact, this is quite a bit too optimistic, mainly because the scanner data allocate the sample very inefficiently from the CPI point of view. Another indication of the reduction in the standard error is the mean absolute percent error (MAPE) about the mean. If the level were constant from month to month, the MAPE would be a measure of the spread of the distribution. As it is, the MAPE includes both the percentage error and the change in the level. Through December 2000, the CPI Geomean relatives have a MAPE of 2.63 percent compared with 1.23 percent for the scanner Geomean relatives, an indication that the scanner relatives are more precise but not nearly by a factor of 38.1.

Section 2.2 discusses the majority of the known technical issues in the implementation of the scanner indexes. The unit values issues are deferred to section 2.3. The scanner data are used to compute a variety of indexes, the formulas for which are presented in section 2.4. Section 2.5 presents a sample of the results of the real time experiment from March 1998 to December 2000 and also the earlier data referring to October 1994 through January 1998. Some conclusions are presented in section 2.6.

2.2 Technical Issues

The production of scanner indexes has involved dealing with a host of technical issues, some of which have been considered in the academic literature, others of which have not. The technical issues other than unit values and the index calculation are considered here. A summary of the status of these technical issues is found in table 2.1, followed by a definition and a more detailed discussion. A "Y" in the "Envisioned" column indicates that ScanData has a solution to the issue in mind, whereas an "N" is an indication simply that there is work to do. The solution to a given issue is said to be "Designed" if there is a mathematical solution on paper and agreement on the appropriate procedure. A solution is said to be "Implemented" if it exists at present in the ScanData computer program. There are "Results" if data have been produced using the implemented solution.

2.2.1 Quote Timing

The CPI collects data for the first eighteen business days (i.e., Mondays through Fridays, excluding holidays) in the month, except for November

Table 2.1   **Status of Scanner Issues**

Issue	Envisioned	Designed	Implemented	Results
Quote timing	Y	Y	Y	Y
Refreshing sample	Y	Y	Y	Y
Quote eligibility	Y	Y	Y	Y
Sales taxes	Y	N	N	N
Amalgamation	Y	Y	Y	Y
Migrating quotes	Y	N	N	N
Data cleaning	Y	Y	Y	Y
Imputation	Y	Y[a]	Y[a]	Y[a]
Variances	Y	Y	Y	Y
Geography	Y	Y	Y	Y
Average prices	Y	N	N	N
Supply disruptions	Y	Y	Y	Y
Aggregation	Y	Y	Y	Y

[a]Decision being reconsidered.

and December, in which months it collects data for the first fifteen days. Each CPI quote is assigned to one of three pricing periods of five or six business days each, and the data from all three pricing periods are used to produce a monthly index. Nielsen scanner data, by contrast, are collected weekly (a week is Sunday to Saturday) and ScanData receives monthly shipments with either four or five weeks of data. The last week in each shipment is the third week of the calendar month, and the data are due ten business days after the end of the third week. The data have almost always arrived two or three days early. The first week of the month is defined as the first week with at least five days in the given month, irrespective of any holidays. Thus, the designated "first" week of the month occasionally includes the last day or two of the previous month, but never more than this. Since the prices generally refer to a whole week, they are also the prices for the actual first week of the month. ScanData is able to use data for the first three weeks of the month in the test indexes and can produce the test indexes a few days earlier than they would have been needed for the regular CPI computation. The indexes compare prices in the first three weeks of the current month to the first three weeks of the previous month.

The result of these collection rules for calendar year 2000 has been that the median CPI collection period covers the first through the twenty-fifth of each month, and the median scanner collection period covers the second through the twenty-second. Therefore:

1. The CPI and the scanner indexes cover very similar time periods within the month.

2. The CPI data are collected a little later in the month.

3. The scanner data explicitly cover Saturday, Sunday, and holidays.

2.2.2 Refreshing the Sample

As noted above, the CPI outlet and item samples are rotated (the old sample is dropped and a new one takes its place) every four years in current practice. Nielsen refreshes (i.e., adds units to) the outlet sample periodically to maintain sample size and to ensure that it continues to reflect the market in terms of the distribution of outlets by geography, organization,[2] format type, size, and age. Since the scanner data consist of a census of the items in the category in the sampled stores, the scanner item samples are refreshed continuously. For the test indexes that use the Geomeans or the Laspeyres formulas, ScanData refreshes both the weights and the item sample each year using the expenditure patterns of the previous year. Thus the 1999 scanner weights for New York cereal are based on 1998 expenditures, the weights for 2000 are based on 1999, and so on.[3]

2.2.3 Quote Eligibility

Quotes in the CPI are eligible for pricing if they were selected in the most recent PPS sample. Scanner quotes are eligible simply if the items have been sold in the previous year. Once a quote is selected, the CPI collects its price if it is present on the shelf regardless of whether it has been sold at that price recently or at all. Scanner prices, on the other hand, are "transaction" prices: that is, there is a price if and only if the item was sold during the given week, regardless of whether it is on the shelf at any particular time. Consumer Price Index quotes are imputed if the item is not available for purchase when the CPI data collector appears. Scanner quotes are imputed if they are eligible and if there were no sales in the first three weeks of the month.

2.2.4 Sales Taxes

For cereal as for most other items, the CPI collects prices net of any applicable tax. The sales tax is applied subsequently, using a secondary source with the sales tax rates for all of the jurisdictions in which there are CPI outlets. Scanner prices are also collected untaxed. For confidentiality, however, the vendors will not disclose the exact location of the outlets, so ScanData cannot add the sales taxes in the same manner as for CPI data. This is not a problem here, because breakfast cereal is not taxed in the New York

2. The term "organization" is used rather than "chain" to denote what is normally referred to as a supermarket chain in order to avoid confusion with the technical term "index chaining." In addition, some organizations that appear to be supermarket chains to the consumer actually consist of independently owned stores with a common logo.

3. One exception should be noted: the Nielsen data for the three New York index areas became available in the current format only in February 1998, and hence both the 1998 and 1999 weights for New York were based on eleven months of data rather than the desired entire year. In addition, the 1998 indexes were based on the 1998 weights rather than, as would have been preferred, the 1997 weights.

CMSA. ScanData has not designed a solution to this problem as yet. It is hoped that Nielsen can help with the taxes, with the caveat that Nielsen may not realize what a complex problem it is. A second best solution, which BLS can implement independently, is to calculate a population-weighted average sales tax each month for each item stratum in each index area and apply the average sales tax to all of the outlets in the index area.

2.2.5   Amalgamation

The current CPI is designed so that every item in every outlet in all of the urban areas of the United States has a chance of selection in accordance with the PPS methodology. The scanner database is a proper subset of the universe covered by the current CPI. Therefore the scanner index will not cover the appropriate universe unless the outlets not covered by scanner data (for example, because of their type—as in the case of independent grocers—or location) are covered by retaining existing CPI quotes.[4]

The indexes reported in this paper combine preliminary scanner indexes (using scanner data only) with indexes constructed from CPI data for the nonscanner universe, a procedure called amalgamation. In particular, from 1998 through 2000 in New York there were four CPI quotes not in the scanner universe, all of which were from mass merchandisers or wholesale clubs. The mass merchandisers will be covered in future Nielsen data deliveries. The results show that the amalgamation in the New York cereal indexes did make a difference, and given that the CPI must be unbiased, it is necessary.

The amalgamation uses CPI weights, which come from the POPS. For example, if the current CPI had ten quotes and nine of them were from outlets covered by scanner data, the price relative computed from the scanner data would receive the sum of the weights of the nine quotes, and the nonscanner quote would retain its original weight. To date the Geomean formula has been used for amalgamation. Since the Törnqvist and the Sato-Vartia indexes rely on current period quantities, these formulas cannot be used for amalgamation. In a hypothetical production mode, Laspeyres amalgamation would be used in the Laspeyres strata.

2.2.6   Migrating Quotes

The CPI objective is to track changes in the prices paid by the residents of a particular index area for items in a particular item stratum. The CPI outlet surveys reveal that consumers make some purchases in outlets located outside the consumers' home areas. Hence, some of the CPI quotes are not collected in the area to which the index refers but represent purchases of consumers from the given area in other places because of travel,

---

4. Since the scanner markets are based on television markets, they do not always contain the corresponding census index areas as proper subsets. On the other hand, Nielsen has done a good job of reconfiguring its data to the CPI areas.

mail order, or other factors. Scanner data refer to the prices charged by the outlets in an index area, which is not quite the same as the prices paid by the residents of the index area. Thus, a scanner index based on outlets in a given area will not represent the CPI objective. None of the current New York CPI cereal quotes has "migrated" out of the New York metropolitan area, although some of the current CPI quotes for index area A109 are collected in A110 and A111. For this reason, a more adequate treatment would involve making the index for A109 a weighted average of the indexes for all three index areas.

2.2.7 Data Cleaning

Before indexes can be computed, the data quality must be assessed and questionable observations deleted. This is an automatic process that corresponds to the current CPI procedure wherein a BLS economist (called a commodity analyst) investigates quotes with large price changes and makes decisions whether or not to use them in the index. Although Nielsen does implement quality checks, for purposes of the CPI they must be supplemented by BLS efforts. Therefore ScanData has developed a procedure for automatically cleaning the cereal data based on the following five rules:

1. Accept all quotes that do not decline more than 37.5 percent or increase more than 60 percent in a given month.

2. On quotes with a promotion on the lower price, accept all quotes that do not decline more than 60 percent or increase more than 150 percent.

3. Accept all quotes for which the elasticity implied by the two months is at least as large as the 1.0 implied by the Geomeans calculation. In other words, if the price goes down, the volume must increase more than proportionately (so that revenue does not decline), and conversely.

4. Accept all quotes if, in the last twelve months, the price has been as high as or higher than the current price, and if the price has been as low as or lower than the current price.

5. Do not use any quote that does not satisfy at least one of the preceding rules.

If the item is sold in multiple units, for example, as a "two-fer" or a "three-fer," in one but not both of the relevant time periods, rules 1 and 2 are modified as follows:

1'. Accept all quotes that do not decline more than 50 percent or increase more than 100 percent in a given month.

2'. On quotes with a promotion on the lower price, accept all quotes that do not decline more than 68 percent or increase more than 212.5 percent.

Rule 5 applies in both cases: that is, a quote must pass only one of rules (1 or 1'), (2 or 2'), 3, or 4. It has been found that the application of these rules deletes a few questionable quotes but accepts most of the data.

2.2.8   Imputation of Missing and Suspect Prices

In both the current CPI and the scanner index, the cleaned database contains a record for each quote. The record includes (if available) the quote's collected price, its effective (per ounce) price, and its derived price. The derived price (also per ounce) is either the effective price, where acceptable, or the imputed price otherwise. As in the CPI, only quotes with both an acceptable price in the current month and a derived price in the previous month are used in scanner index calculation.

Missing data for the scanner indexes (as for CPI data) are imputed for use in future months, and unacceptable prices are treated as missing data. In this process, missing prices are imputed by moving the last acceptable price forward by the (chain of) stratum relative(s). This is equivalent to current CPI practice, according to which the last acceptable price is moved forward each month by the index area–stratum relative. Once the indexes have been calculated, the imputed prices are calculated explicitly and entered as derived prices in the database for use in future months.

In the CPI, if an item is not on the shelf, is not expected to be restocked shortly, and has not been sold in the last few days, it is reported as missing. In cases in which the item is not expected to return, the CPI field representative will select a replacement. In the scanner procedure, if an item were not sold in any of the first three weeks of the month, it would be treated as missing. In scanner data indexes, however, replacements for missing items are not sought, since the data already include all possible items.

There is a new issue that arises in full force with scanner data. Because of the 100 percent sampling rate for items within an outlet, new items appear in scanner data much more often than in the CPI; moreover, there is virtually no lag between the time a new item appears in the outlet and the time it is available for our use. Often, at least for cereal, the prices of goods newly introduced into the market are not equilibrium prices but rather test prices set by the cereal manufacturer's product manager in the hope of obtaining a relatively stable volume at an acceptable price. They are erratic, sometimes beginning quite low and then increasing to a level comparable to similar products, and at other times beginning at a comparable level, declining in a deep sale, and then returning to a comparable level. This process can be repeated for a single item over its first few months. It can be fascinating to observe the resulting price trajectories, but any information on inflation is swamped by the wide variations in the prices resulting from the marketing process. The CPI has long faced the similar problem of products that disappear after a dramatic price reduction or a "closeout special." Since in formulas with constant weights (such as the Geomeans) the long-run effect on an index of a product that appears and then, after some time, disappears is just the ratio of the first and last prices, the introduction and withdrawal of items from the market can have a nontrivial effect on the index. The solution to this problem is in an imputation system that is based on something other than the last acceptable collected price. Thus, in table 2.1 the imputation design is labeled as a decision being reconsidered.

2.2.9   Variances and Replicates

The CPI variances are computed on the basis of replicates.[5] In the current CPI, the small sample sizes mean that there are just two replicates for most index areas to serve as the basis of an estimate of the sampling variance. Leaver and Larson (2001) used a stratified jackknife calculation based on a segmentation of the scanner sample into separate index area–organization-identified strata: one for each of three to eight major organizations and one for the remaining scanner outlets within each index area. Within each stratum they created clusters of from one to three outlets each, and a replicate consisted of the whole sample with one of these clusters deleted. In this way the much larger scanner sample could support 126 clusters with one replicate for each of them.

The result was a much more precise estimate of the variance. It turns out that the actual reduction in the standard error is by a factor of 7.0 for the one-month comparison and 5.7 over twelve months. This is quite a bit less than the 38.1 factor calculated above on the basis simply of the relative number of quotes. The reason for this divergence is that the CPI sample is optimized for the calculation of the CPI, whereas the scanner sample is optimized for quite different purposes. In particular, the scanner data samples in the larger organizations are relatively much larger than in the small chains and independents, and this small sample makes a great deal of difference in the variance estimates. Leaver and Larson discovered the importance of this factor. It is as if we reduced the variance of a part of the sample with half the weight to zero while leaving the rest alone. The variance of the whole sample would simply be reduced by half, whereas the standard error would be reduced by only $\sqrt{1/2}$, regardless of how much we oversampled.

2.2.10   Northeast and National Geography

The population target of the CPI is the noninstitutional population living in metropolitan or urban nonmetropolitan areas. As noted above, the CPI has partitioned the urban United States into thirty-eight index areas.[6] Scanner data are available for "markets," which are generally smaller than the U.S. Census–defined metropolitan areas. To reconcile the geography, Nielsen has mapped its entire U.S. sample into the CPI index areas. The result is coverage of all of the thirty-one self-representing metropolitan areas

---

5. See Swanson (1999). A replicate is a sample consisting of only part of the universe of available quotes. An estimate of the sampling variance can be obtained by comparing the indexes estimated from the replicates.

6. The index areas are thirty-one self-representing metropolitan areas and seven "region-size classes" for the remainder of the covered population; for details, see Williams (1996).

except Anchorage, where Nielsen does not collect data. All seven non–self-representing areas were covered, and all of the data for the smaller places were used. Thus, the coverage of the smaller places was more complete than in the CPI, since these places are currently sampled.

2.2.11   Average Prices

The CPI computes average prices for a number of items for the convenience of users. It is clear that extremely accurate average prices could be computed using scanner data. To date there has been no decision as to which average prices to compute—that is, whether to simply continue the current set or expand it.

2.2.12   Protection against Data Supply Disruptions

The CPI program collects most of the prices it uses; consequently, the data supply is controlled within the program, and the program is responsible for any data supply disruptions. Delegating the basic data collection to a scanner data vendor, however, creates the possibility of data supply disruptions that are not under the direct control of the CPI. Therefore, in order for the CPI to fulfill its responsibility for a continuous flow of data, there must be a backup. One backup could be to continue to process the POPS as it is currently done to obtain (a) the weights required for the scanner amalgamation procedure and (b) a sample of quotes that could be initiated as a fallback in case of need, including a vendor supply disruption. No supply disruptions have occurred while we have been purchasing scanner data on a flow basis, and none is expected. The effect of a backup would be to preserve the ability of BLS to begin collecting prices for the scanner items in case of need.

2.2.13   Aggregation

The three New York areas are being combined to the A101, New York Metro, level, using the current CPI weights and the current Laspeyres calculation.

2.3   Unit Value Issues

This section considers three technical issues: weekly unit values, item definition, and organization-level, as opposed to outlet-level, indexes. The reason for considering these issues together in a separate section is that they all touch on the unit value issue in one way or another. A unit value is a quantity-weighted average price of an item. One way to compute a unit value is to divide the revenue for the item by the number of units sold. Unit values are currently used for the basic area-item indexes in most countries; they are not used in the United States because a weight is assigned to each individual quote.

Unit values are frequently encountered in scanner data since, for example, if an outlet has two different prices on an item in a week, the reported price is often the revenue for the item divided by the number of units sold. On the other hand, it may be appropriate to use unit values to combine observations over several weeks in the same month, or over outlets, or over similar items. Since a unit value is not a price in that often no one pays the unit value exactly, there is some controversy over whether our calculations should use them as if they were prices. ScanData is using unit values to combine the weeks of the month, UPC codes with minor differences, and the outlets within an organization in a given CPI area.

2.3.1 Weekly Unit Values

ScanData combines data for the three weeks of the month using unit values: the quantity-weighted average of prices for a given item.[7] The price relative of an item is its unit value (averaged over the three weeks) for the current month divided by its unit value for the previous month. ScanData then computes the Laspeyres, Geomean, and other price indexes using these price relatives of item unit values with the appropriate PPS weights. One condition that must be satisfied for this to make sense is that the quantities must all be measured in the same units, a condition that is clearly satisfied here.

Instead of combining these prices and quantities in a unit value, one could combine them using the chosen index formula, in the same way that prices and quantities of different items are combined. However, the unit value approach more accurately reflects the preferences of the shopper who searches out the lowest prices each week, and also the consumer who stockpiles during a particularly good special, but then purchases nothing until the next special (see Triplett 1999). Consider the problems that arise by *not* using unit values and considering purchases in different weeks as different goods:

1. The weeks are arbitrarily defined, starting as early as the penultimate day of the preceding month, and as late as the fifth day of the current month. Thus, a purchase made every month on a particular date (e.g., any day between the sixth and the eleventh) will sometimes be allocated to the first week of the month and sometimes to the second.

2. The commodities purchased in the different weeks seem to satisfy the same needs and desires on the part of the consumer.

3. Unit values are required at some level in order to construct an index at all.

4. Consumers who stockpile are not indexed correctly without unit values over the weeks.

---

7. An item is commonly but not always a given UPC in a given store; see the subsection on Item Definition below.

5. *Not* using unit values implies an inherent rigidity in consumer behavior since it is assumed that the items in each of the three weeks are unrelated and that the elasticity of substitution among them is zero.

6. Defining items with a finer granularity, as is the case if quotes in different weeks are treated as separate items, results in more missing data and more imputations.

Thus, real inaccuracies can be introduced by *not* grouping identical commodities using unit values, and there is a powerful argument for considering purchases in the different weeks of the month as the same good.

2.3.2   Item Definition

Occasionally a manufacturer will keep the product constant but will create a new package with a new UPC code, a process called "churning." Alternatively, and more interestingly, new UPCs sometimes appear that involve only small changes in the package size or flavor (e.g., blueberry vs. raspberry) that almost always sell at the same price. Changes in the package size can be used to indirectly raise or lower the effective (per ounce) price while keeping the shelf price constant. Both to reduce attrition and to capture these indirect price changes, it is important that these small to nonexistent variations in the product be grouped together into a single item for index calculation.

Each month Nielsen supplies a list of new UPC codes together with the respective sizes and product descriptions. These are compared to the UPC codes already in use, and, if in the analyst's judgment the differences are sufficiently small that the products are interchangeable, they are combined into a single item. The quantity (in ounces) of these combined items is the sum of the quantities sold of the constituent UPCs, the expenditure is the sum of the expenditures, and the price is the average price or unit value per ounce.

2.3.3   Organization-Level Indexes

The CPI is based on the price of a given item at a given outlet at a given time. Scanner data are available at the outlet level, and outlet data can easily be aggregated up to the organization level, in which case the quote is the unit value of a given item in a given organization at a given time. The organization-level index is based on the unit value or average price of an item at the outlets in an organization.[8] It may be that unit values across outlets are appropriate: "if individual outlet data on transactions were not avail-

---

8. Each month the scanner data come with codes for each organization, without identifying the particular organization. There is always an "Other" organization representing smaller stores and independents. Heretofore the organization level index has been computed treating the other stores as if they constituted an actual organization. It has been proposed to modify this by treating each of the other stores as if it was a separate organization.

able or were considered to be too detailed, then unit values for a homogenous commodity over all outlets in a market area might form the lowest level of aggregation" (Diewert 1995, 22). In fact, "everyday life suggests—and the suggestion is confirmed by our coffee data set—that consumers easily switch between outlets in response to relative price changes" (de Haan 1999, 64). Thus it has been thought that aggregation across outlets in general is not particularly controversial, and aggregation across different outlets in the same organization would seem to be even less so. The extra detail provided by outlet-level data is not much trouble to process, but it turns out that organization-level data are less expensive than outlet-level data because there are only a fraction as many data points. Perhaps of more significance is the need to reflect adequately the shoppers who search out the best sale, on the one hand, as opposed to the ones who always shop at the same outlet.

So far, the organization-level and outlet-level indexes for cereal have been quite close. In a hypothetical production mode, budget constraints may make organization-level indexes appealing. Nevertheless, there are three compelling reasons to continue to receive outlet-level data in a research project:

1. Outlet-level data allow the study of the differences between organization-level and outlet-level indexes.
2. Outlet-level data allow ScanData more control of the data quality.
3. Outlet-level data facilitate variance estimation.

2.4   Index Formulas

The scanner project originally was intended to produce Geomean indexes comparable to the current CPI. However, the scanner sample leads naturally to superlative indexes since the quantity of each item is collected each month along with the price. Therefore, Törnqvist and Sato-Vartia formulas have also been computed, along with the Laspeyres. The status of the various alternative index calculations is summarized in table 2.2.

As noted above, the second stage of CPI calculation is aggregation of basic indexes. The CPI for A101 New York cereal is the aggregate of the three

Table 2.2   Status of Index Formulas

Index	Envisioned	Designed	Implemented	Results
Geomean	Y	Y	Y	Y
Monthly Törnqvist	Y	Y	Y	Y
Annual Törnqvist	Y	Y	N	N
Laspeyres	Y	Y	Y	Y
Sato-Vartia	Y	Y	Y	Y

basic indexes for A019, A110, and A111. With respect to any index formula X, the A101 index at t compared with base month b is calculated from what are referred to in CPI terminology as "cost weights." The month t cost weight for A101 is aggregated from the three constituent index area cost weights,

$$(1) \qquad C_X^t = \sum_{m=1}^{3} C_{Xm}^t.$$

The cost weight for index area m at time t is the product of A_m, the population-expenditure weight for cereal in index area m, and all of the period-to-period index relatives since the base time b,

$$(2) \qquad C_{Xm}^t = A_m \prod_{p=b+1}^{t} R_{Xm}^{p,p-1}.$$

The index of the price change from $t - k$ to t with respect to index formula X is just the ratio of the relevant cost weights from equation (1),

$$(3) \qquad X^{t,t-k} = \frac{C_X^t}{C_X^{t-k}}.$$

The calculation equation (1) minus equation (3) corresponds exactly to the current CPI.

2.4.1   Geomean

The calculation of the Geomean relative used in the current CPI is

$$R_{Gm}^{t,t-1} = \prod_{j} I_j^t \left(\frac{p_j^t}{p_j^{t-1}} \right)^{S_j^0}.$$

Here j indexes the quotes in index area m, I_j^t is the indicator function for the presence of quote j in month t, and the quotes are weighted by S_j^0, the expenditure share of quote j at time 0, $S_j^0 = E_j^0 / \sum_i E_i^0$. If there is no price in month $t - 1$, an imputed price is used if it is available.

The scanner Geomean relative in index area m from month $t - 1$ to t is

$$R_{Gm}^{t,t-1} = \prod_{c=1}^{n_m} \prod_{j} I_j^t \left(\frac{p_j^t}{p_j^{t-1}} \right)^{S_{cj}^0}.$$

In equation (4) each index area m is composed of n_m organizations c, j refers to the different quotes within an organization, and the quotes are weighted by the expenditure share of quote j in organization c at time 0, except for 1998 the previous calendar year,

$$(5) \qquad S_{cj}^0 = \frac{E_{cj}^0}{\sum_i E_{ci}^0}.$$

The price p_j^t is the unit value of commodity j in organization c at time t,

(6)
$$p_j^t = \frac{\sum_{t=1}^{n_{mc}} P_{ij}^t Q_{ij}^t}{q_j^t},$$

where P_{ij}^t and Q_{ij}^t are the prices and quantities, respectively, of j at the different outlets at time t, $q_j^t = \sum_{i=1}^{n_{mc}} Q_{ij}^t$ and there are n_{mc} quotes in each organization c. The A101 cost weight, using equation (4) in equation (2) with $X = G$, and then substituting into equations (1) and (3), results in the Geomean index $G^{i,t-k} = 100 C_G^t / C_G^{t-k}$.

2.4.2   Monthly Törnqvist

This is the chained Törnqvist calculation, the geometric mean of the item relatives with weights equal to the average expenditure shares of the current and preceding months. Thus, with $W_{cj} = (S_{cj}^{t-1} + S_{cj}^t)/2$,

(7)
$$R_{Tm}^{t,t-1} = \prod_{c=1}^{n_m} \prod_j I_j^t \left(\frac{p_j^t}{p_j^{t-1}}\right)^{W_{cj}}.$$

The A101 cost weight, using equation (7) in (1)–(3) with $X=T$ results in the Törnqvist index $T^{t,t-k} = 100 C_T^t / C_T^{t-k}$. The monthly Törnqvist relative has been calculated and amalgamated with CPI data from March 1998 forward. This amalgamation perforce uses the Geomean formula since there are no monthly expenditure weights for the CPI quotes.

2.4.3   Annual Törnqvist

In this form of the calculation, the base for the Törnqvist would be one fixed month that is used for a whole year. The current and base periods are single months. Assume, for example, that January were chosen as the base month. In this case, the February relative would be calculated as in the monthly Törnqvist above. The March relative, however, would be the Törnqvist of the March to January prices as if the February data did not exist: that is, the time zero prices and expenditure shares would refer to January. This would give up the pretense of the discrete time approximation to the Divisia but would eliminate any monthly chaining bias.

2.4.4   Laspeyres Index

This is the textbook Laspeyres, without any correction for formula bias, using weights updated once per year just as the Geomean. Thus the Laspeyres relative is

(8)
$$R_m^{t,t-1} = \frac{\sum_{c=1}^{n_m} \sum_j I_j^t p_j^t q_j^0}{\sum_{c=1}^{n_m} \sum_j p_j^{t-1} q_j^0} = \sum_{c=1}^{n_m} \sum_j I_j^t S_{cj} \frac{p_j^t}{p_j^{t-1}},$$

where the shares S_{cj} are defined in equation (5). The A101 cost weight, using equation (8) in (1)–(3) with $X = L$, results in the Laspeyres index $L^{t,t-k} =$

$100C_L^t/C_L^{t-k}$. The Laspeyres provides an upper bound with which to test the other indexes.

2.4.5   Sato-Vartia Index

The Sato-Vartia relative is a logarithmically weighted geometric average of the price relatives in which the weights W_{cj} are proportional to $m_{cj} = S_{cj}^t - S_{cj}^{t-1}/\ln S_{cj}^t - \ln S_{cj}^{t-1}$, so that

$$(9) \qquad\qquad R_{Sm}^{t,t-1} = \prod_{c=1}^{n_m} \prod_j I_j^t \left(\frac{p_j^t}{p_j^{t-1}} \right)^{W_{cj}}.$$

The A101 cost weight, using equation (9) in (1) – (3) with $X=S$, results in the Sato-Vartia index $S^{t,t-k} = 100C_S^t/C_S^{t-k}$. The Sato-Vartia amalgamation uses the Geomean formula since there are no expenditure weights for the CPI quotes. Along with the Fisher, the Sato-Vartia satisfies more of the statistical axioms describing a desirable index than any other does. However, like the Törnqvist, it does not satisfy the monotonicity axiom (Reinsdorf and Dorfman 1999).

2.5   Results

Scanner indexes were calculated for the three New York index areas on the basis of February 1998=100 through December 2000. These were aggregated—using the appropriate weights—across the three areas. Table 2.3 below gives the various scanner indexes' results along with the CPI for cereal for A101.[9] As we see from table 2.3, by the end of this period, the A101 CPI had fallen to 99.5, a decrease of 0.5 percent over thirty-four months. Over the same period all of the scanner indexes, whether amalgamated or not, increased, and ended in the 104.9–107.8 range. In addition, there were several large month-to-month changes in the A101 CPI, especially in October 1999, for which there was no corresponding change in the scanner indexes; there is no obvious explanation save the CPI's small sample size. Looking ahead, we see that this pattern was much attenuated in the national cereal CPI.

Unless there is some systematic divergence in price change between the scanner universe and the CPI universe, the scanner indexes will give a more accurate measure of inflation. By the end of the thirty-four-month sample period, the A101 CPI was 5.5 percent lower than the scanner Geomean index and 5.7 percent lower than the amalgamated Geomean. The Törnqvist, whether amalgamated or not, showed a bit less inflation than the Geomean,

9. The BLS does not publish an index for breakfast cereal below the national level. The New York cereal indexes reported here are unpublished, primarily because of the small sample sizes on which they are based and the resulting high variances. The comparison is somewhat muddied because the CPI switched from the Laspeyres to the Geomean for the lower level cereal indexes in January 1999.

Table 2.3 Organization-Level Scanner Indexes, 1998–2000

Month	A101 CPI	Geomean		Törnqvist		Sato-Vartia	
		Scanner	Amalgamated	Scanner	Amalgamated	Scanner	Amalgamated
March 1998	98.8	100.7	100.7	100.7	100.7	100.8	100.8
April 1998	99.6	100.2	100.2	100.2	100.2	100.4	100.4
May 1998	99.9	100.5	100.5	101.2	101.1	101.0	101.0
June 1998	101.6	100.2	100.1	98.4	98.5	99.2	99.2
July 1998	102.1	99.8	99.8	99.1	99.1	99.5	99.5
August 1998	101.4	100.2	100.2	100.1	100.1	100.4	100.4
September 1998	99.6	97.6	97.7	97.0	97.1	97.5	97.6
October 1998	101.1	98.3	98.4	97.0	97.1	97.8	97.8
November 1998	101.4	100.4	100.4	100.8	100.7	101.3	101.2
December 1998	102.1	100.8	100.8	101.1	101.0	101.8	101.7
January 1999	103.3	100.6	100.7	100.1	100.3	100.5	100.7
February 1999	102.5	100.0	100.1	97.0	97.2	98.4	98.5
March 1999	104.9	100.2	100.4	97.0	97.2	98.6	98.8
April 1999	102.1	100.7	100.8	98.5	98.7	100.1	100.3
May 1999	101.7	102.1	102.2	100.5	100.7	101.8	101.9
June 1999	104.7	101.8	102.2	98.3	98.8	100.4	100.9
July 1999	103.8	103.0	103.5	100.3	100.8	102.2	102.7

August 1999	103.2	102.8	103.2	100.6	101.1	102.3	102.8
September 1999	104.6	100.3	100.9	98.4	99.1	100.0	100.6
October 1999	99.1	102.9	103.3	100.5	100.9	102.8	103.2
November 1999	98.7	105.3	105.6	105.7	105.9	107.3	107.5
December 1999	100.9	104.6	105.0	102.3	102.7	104.9	105.2
January 2000	97.5	103.0	103.5	101.3	101.9	103.0	103.6
February 2000	102.8	101.9	102.5	98.4	99.1	100.9	101.5
March 2000	100.7	102.9	103.3	100.4	100.9	102.7	103.1
April 2000	104.0	104.9	105.2	102.5	103.0	105.2	105.6
May 2000	104.7	105.2	105.5	102.9	103.3	105.4	105.7
June 2000	101.1	103.9	104.3	99.0	99.5	102.4	102.8
July 2000	100.0	104.1	104.4	100.8	101.2	103.6	103.9
August 2000	101.6	104.1	103.9	101.3	101.3	104.1	103.9
September 2000	98.6	100.6	101.2	98.2	98.9	100.7	101.3
October 2000	102.7	103.1	103.6	100.3	100.9	103.3	103.8
November 2000	99.7	106.7	107.0	106.4	106.9	109.2	109.4
December 2000	99.5	105.0	105.2	104.9	105.1	107.7	107.8

whereas the Sato-Vartia showed quite a bit more. The very slightly less Törnqvist inflation, compared with the corresponding Geomean, cannot plausibly be taken as evidence that the elasticity of substitution is less than the 1.0 assumed by the Geomean. On the other hand, the divergence between the Törnqvist and the Sato-Vartia may lead us to question the degree to which the latter is "nearly superlative."

The amalgamated indexes from table 2.3 are plotted against the CPI in figure 2.1. The CPI used the Laspeyres formula, an upper bound to the true cost-of-living index, through December 1998, and the A101 CPI shows more inflation than any of the scanner indexes through September 1999 before dropping convincingly below.

The corresponding scanner indexes (i.e., those that are not amalgamated) are plotted in figure 2.2 below. There is no particular reason to expect that the Geomean, Törnqvist, and Sato-Vartia should bear any particular relationship to each other. It is interesting that once again the superlative Törnqvist and the nearly superlative Sato-Vartia do not track each other particularly closely. In fact, the Törnqvist was below the other two for seventeen of the twenty-two comparison months, including all of the last thirteen, before almost catching up at the end to finish slightly below the Geomean.

Figure 2.3 below considers the scanner indexes without amalgamation

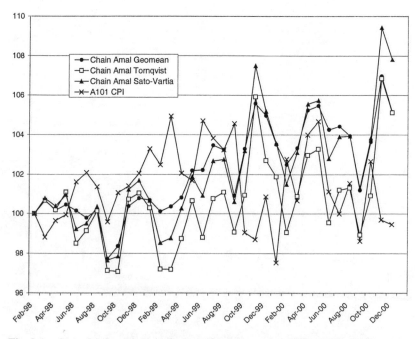

Fig. 2.1   Organization-level amalgamated indexes and the CPI, 1998–2000

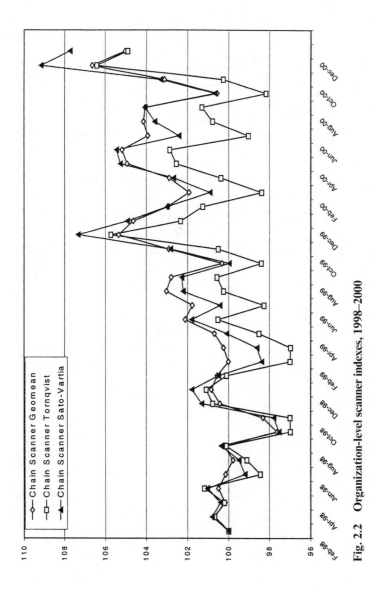

Fig. 2.2 Organization-level scanner indexes, 1998–2000

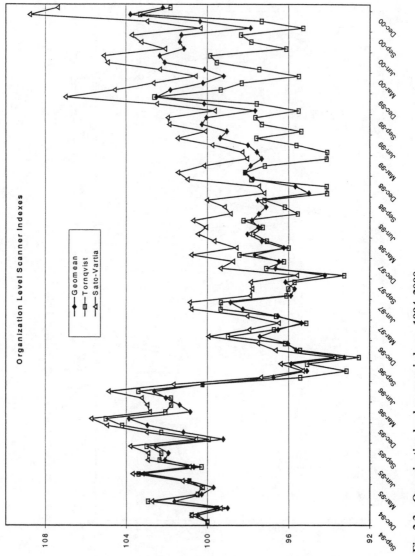

Fig. 2.3 Organization-level scanner indexes, 1994–2000

Table 2.4   **Relatives by Month**

Month	Product of Relatives		Ratio	Ratio per Month
	Geomean	Törnqvist		
January	0.918	0.886	1.036	1.006
February	0.983	0.932	1.055	1.009
March	1.051	1.049	1.002	1.000
April	1.065	1.106	0.964	0.994
May	0.978	0.972	1.006	1.001
June	0.932	0.861	1.083	1.013
July	0.990	1.019	0.972	0.995
August	1.020	1.044	0.977	0.996
September	0.848	0.845	1.003	1.001
October	1.141	1.155	0.988	0.998
November	1.087	1.166	0.932	0.990
December	1.044	1.049	0.995	0.999
Total	1.0219	1.0181	1.0037	1.0027

back to September 1994, the beginning of the cereal data available to Scan-Data.[10] Here the final ranking of the formulas is the same as in the more recent period, and once again the Törnqvist is below the others during most of the later period, despite almost catching up at the end. In fact, although the Törnqvist was ahead of the Geomean for seventeen of the first twenty months, through May 1996, it is ahead for only two of the last thirty-one months, beginning in June 1998.

Some understanding of this unexpected temporal relationship between the Geomean and the Törnqvist can be found in an unanticipated seasonal pattern. The ratio of the Geomean to the Törnqvist in December 2000 from table 2.3 is 1.00372: the Geomean has outpaced the Törnqvist by about 0.37 percent over seventy-five months. However, the relationship between the indexes varies substantially over the months of the year. Table 2.4 presents the product of the Geomean and Törnqvist relatives by month over the whole sample period. The cell in the January row and the Geomean column is the product of the relatives for the six Januaries in the sample, and so forth through September. The entries for October through December are the product of the seven relatives for these months. The column labeled "Ratio" is just the Geomean entry divided by the corresponding Törnqvist entry.

10. Figure 2.3 is subject to the caveat that the format of the scanner data changed between January and February 1998 in a way that caused a break in the series. This problem was resolved here by arbitrarily making all of the scanner relatives for February compared with January 1998 equal to the corresponding national CPI relative. Note also that (except for the A101 CPI) the data in figure 2.3 are the scanner indexes *not* amalgamated with any CPI data. The reason for this is that the data from September 1994 through January 1998 were not received in real time, and hence it was not possible to amalgamate the CPI quotes not covered in the scanner universe.

"Ratio per Month" is either sixth or seventh root of the ratio—that is, the geometric mean of the corresponding ratio. The totals at the bottom are just the products of all of the entries in the given column.

It is clear from table 2.4 that there is a distinct seasonal pattern in the relatives, with the Geomean gaining during the first half of the year, January through June, and the Törnqvist catching up during the second half, especially during November. The reason that the Törnqvist tended to lead for the first part of the sample period is that the first comparison month was October, and hence the Törnqvist was ahead at the start due to this seasonal effect. Nevertheless, the Törnqvist tended to fall behind over time and ended, as mentioned, 0.37 percent behind the Geomean. The total in the "Ratio per Month" column shows that over an average year the Geomean gained 0.27 percent, and hence, had we corrected for the seasonal effects the Geomean would have ended $1.00272^{6.25} - 1 = 1.71$ percent ahead of the Törnqvist. A more direct calculation confirms this general idea and gives an even larger difference between the indexes. The annual relatives of both the Geomean and the Törnqvist indexes were calculated, and also the ratios between them. This eliminated eleven observations and reduced the sample to sixty-four annual comparisons. The geometric mean of the sixty-four annual relatives was 1.00554, a gain of 0.55 percent per year for the Geomean and of 2.99 percent over the whole sample.

These differences are quite striking since both the prices and the form of the index formula were the same, the only difference being in the weights. It would appear that this is a manifestation of the "high-frequency" phenomenon discussed by Feenstra and Shapiro (F&S) in this volume. In the F&S data the Törnqvist (their "chained Törnqvist") resulted in much higher estimates of inflation than the Geomean, the opposite of the findings here. Feenstra and Shapiro found that often an item went on sale a week or two before ads appeared and that the ad appeared the last week of the sale. The result was that the increase in price at the end of the sale was weighted more heavily than the previous decline, and hence the Törnqvist increased too rapidly.

Feenstra and Shapiro present a sample data set of two items over six months in which the beginning and ending prices are the same for both items, and hence the ending index should be equal to 100. The Törnqvist index, however, stood at 154.1 at the end, whereas summing the data into months as in the ScanData methodology resulted in an ending Törnqvist of 95.2.[11] Thus, the monthly Törnqvist gave a low measure, whereas the weekly Törnqvist gave a high measure based on the same data. It would appear that item volume the month before a sale tends to be normal, but vol-

---

11. This is slightly different from the 145.2 figure given by F&S in their table 3, even after taking account of their initial index value of 92.7, due to rounding. The basic data are in their table 1.

ume after the sale tends to be suppressed due to stockpiling. Feenstra and Shapiro also present a "fixed-base Törnqvist" index, which ends at 103.0. However, since the beginning and ending prices were equal, none of these is correct. The evident inventory effect invalidates the assumption of static utility maximization underlying the Törnqvist formula. The F&S "fixed-base Törnqvist" formula is one attempt to deal with this, but clearly more work is required before such a formula can be used in the National Income Accounts.

In figure 2.4 below we plot the national CPI for breakfast cereal against the A101 CPI and the scanner Geomean indexes at the outlet and organization levels. The organization-level and outlet-level Geomean indexes track quite well, the organization level index trailing by only 0.38 percent after sixty-eight months, an indication that the unit value at the organization level results in only a small correction. The national CPI and the A101 CPI do not track each other very well at all, however, and hence, despite possible differences between the national and New York markets, we must suspect considerable small sample variability in the A101 CPI. In particu-

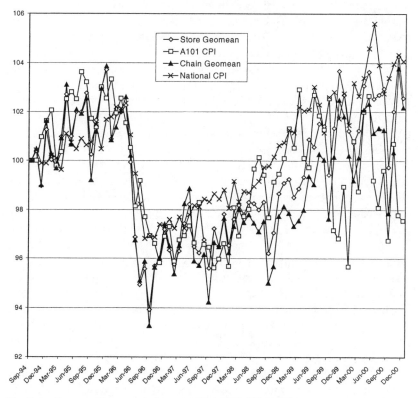

Fig. 2.4   Scanner Geomean indexes and the CPI, 1994–2000

lar the pronounced October 1999 dip in the A101 CPI is not reflected at all in the national CPI. By December 2000 the national CPI is above the New York scanner indexes, whereas the A101 CPI is far below them.

2.6 Conclusions

There have been numerous suggestions that scanner data could be used in the CPI for additional commodity detail. It has also been hoped that scanner data could result in more accurate low-level indexes and also provide the opportunity to implement superlative indexes at the lowest level. Another possible advantage is that the scanner sample may be more representative of the relevant universe because the weights are estimated more accurately and updated more frequently. Yet another advantage is that scanner data can be cleaned according to rules that can be applied consistently and studied academically. The purpose of the ScanData project was to study these propositions.

ACNielsen has been an excellent vendor, supplying the scanner data on time and dealing with issues as they arose. A computer program has been developed and extensively acceptance-tested to construct scanner-based test indexes for breakfast cereal in the New York metropolitan area. The technical issues have been largely dealt with, as we saw in sections 2.2–2.4. The data have been received on a schedule such that they could have been used in the CPI, the scanner sample has been refreshed appropriately, and the standards for quote eligibility are more closely related to the relevant theory than are those of the current CPI. The scanner data have been amalgamated with the few CPI quotes from nonscanner outlets to produce indexes that cover the CPI target universe. The automated computer data-cleaning system has been found to work adequately. Missing prices have been imputed using rules similar to those of the current CPI, and in the process defects have been discovered in those rules. The more accurate variance calculations that are possible with scanner data have been carried out. The scanner indexes have been aggregated to the appropriate higher levels and some protection has been found against supply disruptions in a hypothetical production environment. Issues with respect to average prices and taxes remain, but it would appear that these can be solved with a bit more effort. Issues revolving around unit values have been dealt with, and the index formulas have been implemented.

The results of Leaver and Larson (2001) show that the standard errors of the scanner indexes are about one-sixth of those of the current CPI, a significant reduction but not nearly what would have been expected simply on the basis of the increase in sample size. The calculation of the superlative Törnqvist index has revealed unforeseen problems with the superlative methodology. Although it has long been known that stockpiling and search behavior cause problems for price indexes, they are of such magnitude as to preclude the traditional superlative indexes' being used with this fine a granularity in the product, time, and geographical dimensions. Although the use of more aggregated data would mitigate the problems of the superlatives, they are so fundamental that it is not clear that they would disappear at any level of aggregation.

References

Boskin, Michael J., Ellen R. Dulberger, Robert J. Gordon, Zvi Griliches, and Dale Jorgenson. 1996. *Final report of the Commission to Study the Consumer Price Index.* U.S. Senate, Committee on Finance. Washington, D.C.: U.S. Government Printing Office.

Bradley, Ralph, Bill Cook, Sylvia G. Leaver, and Brent R. Moulton. 1997. An overview of research on potential uses of scanner data in the U.S. CPI. In *Proceedings of the third meeting of the International Working Group on Price Indices,* ed. Bert M. Balk, 169–82. Voorburg, the Netherlands: Statistics Netherlands.

Conference Board, The. 1999. *Measuring prices in a dynamic economy.*

Diewert, W. Erwin. 1995. Axiomatic and economic approaches to elementary price indexes. Discussion Paper no. 95-01. Vancouver, Canada: University of British Columbia, Department of Economics.

Haan, Jan de. 1999. *Empirical studies on Consumer Price Index construction.* Voorburg, the Netherlands: Statistics Netherlands.

Haan, Jan de, and Eddy Opperdoes. 1997a. Estimation of the coffee price index using scanner data: The choice of the micro index. In *Proceedings of the third meeting of the International Working Group on Price Indices,* ed. Bert M. Balk, 191–202. Voorburg, the Netherlands: Statistics Netherlands.

———. 1997b. Estimation of the coffee price index using scanner data: The sampling of commodities. In *Proceedings of the third meeting of the International Working Group on Price Indices,* ed. Bert M. Balk. Voorburg, the Netherlands: Statistics Netherlands.

Leaver, Sylvia G., and William E. Larson. 2001. Estimating variances for a scanner-based consumer price index. *Proceedings of the American Statistical Association, Government Statistics Section.*

McKaig, S. Kate. 1999. Universal Product Codes. Washington, D.C.: CPI Tech. Memo, April.

Reinsdorf, Marshall B. 1997. Constructing basic component indexes for the U.S. CPI from scanner data: A test using data on coffee. BLS Working Paper no. 277. Washington, D.C.: Bureau of Labor Statistics.

Reinsdorf, Marshall B., and Alan H. Dorfman. 1999. The Sato-Vartia index and the monotonicity axiom. *Journal of Econometrics* 90:45–61.

Swanson, David. 1999. Variance estimates for changes in the Consumer Price Index, January 1998–December 1998. CPI detailed report. Washington, D.C.: Bureau of Labor Statistics, December.

Triplett, Jack E. 1999. Should the Cost-of-Living Index provide the conceptual framework for a consumer price index? *Economic Journal* 111 (472): F311–34.

Williams, Janet. 1996. The redesign of the CPI geographic sample. *Monthly Labor Review* 119 (12): 10–17.

3

Price Collection and Quality Assurance of Item Sampling in the Retail Prices Index
How Can Scanner Data Help?

David Fenwick, Adrian Ball, Peter Morgan, and Mick Silver

Introduction

The U.K. Retail Prices Index (RPI) is an important and widely used macro-economic indicator both in the formation and monitoring of economic policy and for the indexation of welfare and other state benefits. Its accuracy is of paramount importance. A 0.1 percentage point overstatement or understatement of the inflation rate would affect government expenditure and receipts by about £100 million a year and could mislead managers of the economy. The Office for National Statistics continually seeks improvements in the methodology used to compile the RPI and so has a continuous research program, with the primary aim of ensuring that the best possible statistical methods are used.

A number of studies[1] in the past have pointed to the possibility of scanner data's being used in the compilation of consumer price indexes either as a direct source of price data in its own right or for the estimation of appropriate quality adjustments when collectors are forced to select new items with different characteristics from the original. In addition, it has been suggested that scanner data have the potential to contribute to the effectiveness of probability sampling procedures.

The results of the study highlight the difficulties faced when trying to pro-

The views expressed in this paper are those of the authors and not the Office for National Statistics.

David Fenwick is director of the Consumer Prices and General Inflation Division of the U.K. Office for National Statistics. Adrian Ball is head of research and methodology for the Retail Prices Index at the U.K. Office for National Statistics. Peter Morgan is senior lecturer in quantitative analysis at Cardiff Business School, Cardiff University. Mick Silver is professor of business statistics at Cardiff Business School, Cardiff University.

1. These include Silver (1995), Bradley et al. (1998), and Richardson (chap. 2 in this volume).

duce a representative sample for use in consumer price indexes. The comparison of prices for six products obtained from sampling procedures of the U.K. RPI, when compared to unit values from scanner data, highlight difficulties in using each data set. In particular, existing sampling techniques run the risk of not having a representative sample, whereas scanner data have the opposite problem of including price quotes for items not wanted in the RPI, such as damaged goods or closeout sales.

We try to identify an approach that takes the advantages of each type of data and combines them to produce a more accurate sample from which pricing information can be taken. In this case, we recommend either using the scanner data to inform selection of items for the RPI data collection or, alternatively, using the expenditure weights implicit in scanner data to post-weight the RPI collection data into a representative formula.

3.1   The Retail Prices Index Data Collection System[2]

This section gives details of the RPI data collection system. It highlights the main characteristics of the collection system. Some of these characteristics will be the subject of further comment in the context of the results of the comparative analysis of the RPI and scanner data samples mentioned above and the subject of this paper.

3.1.1   Background

Data are collected for the RPI in two ways: local collection by price collectors who visit shops to determine prices available in each location and a central collection for those stores with a national pricing policy or for items for which a local collection would not be cost effective. Since 1995 the local collection of price data has been contracted out to a private-sector company. The tendering process leading up to the award of the contract acted as a catalyst for a number of initiatives. These included the move from a purposive sample to a random sample of outlets and the introduction of hand-held computers for the collection of price data in the field.

3.1.2   Sampling Procedures for Local Price Collection

Current methodology for the selection of locations from which we collect local prices, introduced in 2000, aims to give each shopping center in the United Kingdom a probability of being selected for the price collection equal to its proportion of total consumer expenditure. This is achieved using a two-stage hierarchical sampling frame based on geographical regions. A total of 141 locations is required for local price collection, and the number to be selected within each of the regions is determined by taking a pro-

2. Details of the RPI methodology are given in Baxter (1998).

portion equal to the proportion of total U.K. expenditure that each region attracts. This is the first stage of the sample and is based on information obtained from household expenditure surveys. Within each region, locations are selected on a probability proportional to size basis, using the number of employees in the retail sector as a proxy for expenditure. Practical considerations mean that this basic principle is modified in two ways. Firstly, it is not cost effective to collect from areas too small to provide a reasonable proportion of the full list of items, therefore, locations that had fewer than 250 outlets were excluded. Second, and for similar reasons, out-of-town shopping areas, in which a high level of expenditure takes place, but from which it is not possible to obtain all items, are paired with smaller locations nearby from which the rest of the items can be obtained. This joint location is then used as a single location in the probability sampling, producing a final sample of locations.

Each selected location is then enumerated by price collectors to produce a sampling frame from which outlets are randomly selected. Multiple and independent retailers are separately identified.

The selection of representative items to be used to calculate the RPI is, in contrast to outlet sampling, purposive (i.e., judgmental, not random). All categories of expenditure on which, according to the household expenditure survey, significant amounts of money are spent are arranged into about eighty sections, and items are chosen to be representative of each section. The number of representative items for each section depends on both the weight given to that section and the variability of the prices of the items covered by that section. Around 650 representative items are chosen centrally by commodity specialists and reviewed each January to ensure that they continue to be representative of the section. New items are chosen to represent new or increasing areas of expenditure or to reduce the volatility of higher level aggregates. Other items are removed if expenditure on them falls to insignificant levels. Decisions are informed by market research reports, newspapers, trade journals, and price collectors in the field. This enables the basket to be kept up-to-date, but it does not guarantee sample representativity. The descriptions are generic rather than prescriptive, leaving the price collector with the task of choosing the precise product or variety to be priced.

The selection by the price collector of the products and varieties to represent the selected items is also purposive and carried out in the field. Price collectors are instructed to choose the product or variety in the selected shop that most represents sales in the area of that particular item. In practice, the price collector will normally get the assistance of the shopkeeper to help in this process by asking which is the best-selling product or variety. This is, in most cases, the one that is chosen as the representative item for price monitoring. This sampling procedure has the advantage of increasing the achieved sample size by overcoming the problem of particular shops not stocking a particular product or variety. In addition, it spreads the sample to include a wider range of products and varieties than would be covered if a very tight description were employed.

3.1.3 Sampling for Centrally Collected Prices and Prices Obtained over the Telephone

In some instances prices are collected centrally without resorting to the expensive activity of sending price collectors into the field. Central price collection is done for two distinct groups:

1. Central shops, where, for cost effectiveness, prices are collected direct from the headquarters of multiples with national pricing policies. These prices are then combined with prices collected locally from other outlets in proportion to the number of outlets originally chosen in the selected locations.
2. Central items, for which there are a limited number of suppliers and purchases of which do not normally take place at local outlets. Examples of these include gas, electricity, and water, whose prices are extracted from tariffs supplied direct by the head offices of the companies involved. These data will be used to create subindexes that are combined with other subindexes to produce the all-items RPI.

In addition, the prices of some locally collected items are collected over the telephone, with the retailer being visited in person only occasionally to ensure that the quality of response is being maintained. Such prices include electrician's charges, for which there is no outlet as such, and entrance fees to leisure centers, for which there are unlikely to be any ambiguities over pricing and in cases in which a trip to the center may be relatively time-consuming for the collection of just one price. These prices are combined with data obtained by price collectors as necessary.

3.1.4 Price Reference Day

The price reference day is the second or third Tuesday in the month.

3.1.5 Coverage of the RPI

The RPI is an average measure of the change in the prices of goods and services bought for the purpose of consumption by the vast majority of households in the United Kingdom. The reference population is all private households with the exception of (a) pensioner households that derive at least three-quarters of their total income from state pensions and benefits, and (b) high-income households whose total household income lies within the top 4 percent of all households. The reference expenditure items are the goods and services bought by the reference population for consumption. Prices used in the calculation of the index should reflect the cash prices typically paid by the reference population for these goods and services. The index is compiled mainly on an acquisition basis—in other words, on the total value of goods and services acquired during a given period regardless of whether they are wholly paid for in that period. The main exception is owner-occupied housing, for which a user cost approach is adopted.

3.2   Characteristics of Scanner Data

Scanner data are based on electronic point-of-sale (EPOS) data recorded by bar code readers at the time and point of purchase. As more shops move over to bar code readers, the potential benefits to compilers of consumer price indexes increase. Scanner data provide the potential to deliver up-to-date and accurate information on

1. The number of sales over a chosen period of individual products uniquely identified by the bar code number,
2. The total value of those sales and by implication the average transaction "price" or unit cost, and
3. An analysis by the characteristics, outlet type, and geographical location of the individual products concerned.

In reality, the market coverage of scanner data varies between different shop types and products, and the amount and detail of data actually available can vary depending on the commercial source and which product is being examined. In addition, definitions may not be compatible with index compilation. For example, the average transaction "price" (unit cost) recorded by scanner data does not take into account the specific needs of index compilers to measure according to a strict set of predetermined rules that disallow certain discounts, such as those relating to damaged stock. The latter should be excluded from the RPI but will be included implicitly in scanner data (see next section).

In addition, experience indicates that a great deal of expertise and effort is needed to clean scanner data, adjusting for such things as reused bar codes, in order to make them usable for statistical purposes.

3.2.1   Main Definitional Differences between Scanner Data and Data Collected Locally for the Retail Prices Index

The main differences between the two data sets are the following:

1. The RPI is a sample that covers all transactions conducted in retail outlets by private households for private domestic consumption. Scanner data cover EPOS sales (coverage of prices for outlets not using bar code

scanning is dependent on a survey and is not of equal quality) and may exclude "own" brands. It does not distinguish between commercial customers and others in the sales figures it provides.

2. RPI data measure individual transaction prices according to RPI conventions, mainly by taking display price. They therefore exclude conditional discounts (for example, where a "club" card is required), two-for-one offers, personal discounts offered on a one-time basis by shop managers, and discounts on discontinued or damaged stock. Scanner data measure average revenue generated after discounts given by whatever method; they will include discontinued or shop-soiled stock and may attribute discounts to the scanner code rather than to the transaction (for example, free video tapes given away with a recorder will be shown as a reduction in average revenue for video tapes).

3. RPI data relate to prices charged in a set sample of outlets and therefore do not include the effects of outlet substitution. Scanner data, on the other hand, relate to current transactions in all outlets and therefore include outlet substitution.

The numerical impact of these differences is not known. However, it is clear that the impact will not necessarily be constant over time but, rather, will vary with market circumstances, and that differences are likely to be greater for some goods than others.

In addition to the main differences, other characteristics of the two data sources need to be borne in mind when one compares display prices in shops and corresponding scanner data. In particular,

1. In the case of prices collected from shops there is the potential for a relatively large sampling error due to the small number of prices that may be gathered for a particular product variety (the RPI sample is not designed to provide reliable information at this level of detail, particularly for goods and services for which there has traditionally been a wide variation in price). Scanner data can provide almost total coverage.

2. The RPI records prices for a particular day in the month, whereas the scanner data used for this exercise cover a whole month.

3. The sample for local price collection is designed to be self-weighting, and therefore the data set of prices does not distinguish between different types of retailers such as multiple and independent. This is unlike the unit values available from scanner data, which can identify different outlet types separately (although the detail of the categorization varies between market sectors). This means that there is a potential problem with differences in the mix of outlet types between the two data sources, both in a single month and varying over time. This can lead to inconsistencies in the comparisons that cannot be easily corrected for. (This is countered by the fact that scanner data provide full weighting information so that actual, rather than implicit, weights can be applied.)

3.3   Research Design

The research consisted of two separate but related exercises: (a) the benchmarking of RPI product and variety selection against corresponding scanner data, and (b) a comparison of RPI average unit prices and price changes with the corresponding unit values (i.e., average revenue generation) and unit value movements obtained from scanner data.

The benchmarking exercise involved a comparison of the relative distributions by product and variety for each of five preselected items: televisions, washing machines, vacuum cleaners, dishwashers, and cameras.

3.4   Representativity of Product and Variety Selection

The purpose of this stage of the research was to determine the extent to which current selection practices may lead to the choice of an unrepresentative sample of products and varieties for pricing. It looked at overall distributions obtained from the selection procedures used in the RPI and compared these with the overall distributions of sales given by scanner data. Monthly data were compared for the period from January 1998 to December 1998. This was done at an aggregate level; RPI and scanner data were not linked in any way to facilitate this exercise.

3.4.1   Summary of Results

Table 3.1 shows a comparison between the proportionate coverage of scanner data and data collected for the RPI. The figures are ordered to show the top ten sellers for each product group in September 1999 according to sales volume from scanner data, alongside which is the proportion of quotes that are taken for the RPI collection for that item.

The results show some very interesting patterns. In general collectors tended to choose items that were good sellers, although frequently they overcollected from models that were only mildly popular. Some of the most obvious examples of discrepancies were within dishwashers. Here the top-selling model, which accounted for around one-fifth of sales, was represented by just 2 percent of quotes, and the seventh most popular, which only accounted for 4 percent of sales, was represented by over 20 percent of quotes. This pattern was repeated in other items.

Even if we investigate a cumulative distribution, problems are evident. In all cases the proportion of RPI quotes that represent the top ten selling models are significantly lower than their sales figures. The reasons for this are not obvious but may be illustrated by an example. In September there is a particular model of washing machine that attracts almost 10 percent of RPI quotes, whereas scanner data indicate that no sales of this particular model took place. This is clearly an anomaly and represents a real difficulty in maintaining the representativity of the sample. It should be noted that

Table 3.1   Top-Ten Selling Items According to Scanner Data, and Associated Percentage of RPI Quotes

Model	14" Televisions		21" Televisions		Vacuum Cleaners	
	Percentage of Scanner Data	Percentage of RPI Quotes	Percentage of Scanner Data	Percentage of RPI Quotes	Percentage of Scanner Data	Percentage of RPI Quotes
Model 1	17.7	1.0	16.2	10.5	30.1	18.7
Model 2	13.9	25.0	12.8	4.4	13.2	3.0
Model 3	11.0	1.9	11.7	1.8	8.7	1.2
Model 4	8.5	28.6	10.2	8.8	5.7	1.2
Model 5	8.2	3.8	10.1	31.6	4.4	0.6
Model 6	6.9	4.8	10.1	3.5	4.1	20.5
Model 7	6.6	1.9	6.1	8.8	4.1	0.6
Model 8	4.9	4.8	5.6	0.8	3.8	1.2
Model 9	4.4	1.0	4.1	1.7	3.5	0.6
Model 10	3.9	3.8	1.8	1.7	3.4	6.6

Model	Cameras		Dishwashers		Washing Machines	
	Percentage of Scanner Data	Percentage of RPI Quotes	Percentage of Scanner Data	Percentage of RPI Quotes	Percentage of Scanner Data	Percentage of RPI Quotes
Model 1	28.4	38.4	17.2	2.2	12.0	6.5
Model 2	13.6	1.2	17.1	16.3	11.2	20.3
Model 3	11.9	12.8	9.4	11.9	11.2	2.3
Model 4	7.6	3.5	7.8	5.9	9.8	5.8
Model 5	6.7	1.2	7.3	6.7	6.9	1.4
Model 6	5.6	2.3	5.8	0.7	5.1	4.3
Model 7	4.4	15.1	5.1	23.0	5.1	2.9
Model 8	4.3	3.5	5.1	0.7	4.4	1.4
Model 9	4.0	1.2	4.8	3.0	4.2	1.4
Model 10	3.4	1.2	4.1	0.7	4.1	4.3

the data relate to September, and it is quite possible that a model chosen by a price collector at the start of the year is still on the shop floor being priced but may have limited, if any, sales.

3.4.2   Interpretation

Any interpretation of the results clearly depends as much on the quality and coverage of the scanner data as on the representativity of the RPI sample. However, it does seem to indicate two things:

1. Despite the instruction to the price collector to chose a product variety that is representative of the sales of that item in each area, often through asking the shopkeeper which is the best-selling item, the pricing of items can apparently be skewed toward products and varieties that scanner data indicate have relatively small sales. Conversely, there is the nonselection of some big-selling items. This at first sight seems odd, given that the instructions to price collectors would encourage the selection of the big sellers and, therefore, may be more to do with outlet selection. Initial indications suggest that another cause may be brand loyalty on the part of collectors. Collectors identify a popular brand early on in their careers as collectors and tend to stay with it, even when their sales fall.

2. The fixed basket approach, in which products and varieties as well as items are only reviewed on an annual basis (except where a replacement is forced on the price collector because an item becomes obsolete and is no longer found in shops), leads to the sample's becoming increasingly unrepresentative as the "fixed" selection of goods in the basket ages over the year. This is not surprising but does raise the issue of whether, for certain items for which models change very quickly, updating of the basket should occur more frequently than once a year. Certainly it suggests that replacements should be introduced before models disappear and the volume of sales contracts to the point that very few purchases are made.

But do these things matter? Clearly this depends on the extent to which there is a noticeable impact on the published index and the measured rate of inflation. The following section reports on the second stage of the research designed to test whether this is so.

3.5   Average Unit Prices and Price Changes

The purpose of this stage of the research was to observe for specific product varieties the extent to which the price levels and changes observed by price collectors in the field differed from the price levels and changes shown by scanner data. Resource constraints limited the exercise to the three months from August to October 1999. The process of matching price data from the RPI with scanner data on unit values was not always successful despite a series of reconciliation and validity checks. In part this was due to the fact that descriptions provided by price collectors in the field were inadequate for the process of matching (although generally adequate for the identification of product varieties in shops). For instance, a maker's name and a select number of attributes may be all that is required to identify a product variety in a shop, but the model number, which in many cases will not be listed, will be required to unambiguously match the product variety with one shown on the scanner list.

3.5.1   Practical Limitations of the Matching Process

The degree of successful matching varied between the five items selected. It was most successful for dishwashers, washing machines, and vacuum cleaners, for which over 70 percent of RPI observations (representing about 50 percent of RPI product varieties) were successfully linked to scanner data. Matching was most problematic for cameras, for which only about one-half of RPI quotes (representing about one-third of RPI product varieties) were matched to scanner data (see table 3.2). Further analysis indicated that in some instances there were significant differences between the mean *average price level* for the full set of RPI quotes and the subset in which there was a successful match with scanner data for a product variety. This was most marked for television sets and washing machines. The figures suggest that, in general, there is no pattern across the items as to whether the matched sample had a higher or lower mean price than that for all RPI quotes. However, within an item the direction of the difference remained the same over time, with the sole exception of cameras, for which the differences are small. This may suggest that an effect is present within items, although this is difficult to test with a weighted mean, and a serially correlated sample. Differences were also detected between average price *changes* shown by the full scanner data set and those shown by the matched set. This was explored by calculating Laspeyres, Paasche, and Fisher indexes,[3] both for the full RPI set of price data and for the subsample representing matched observations. The results for a Fisher index are shown in figure 3.1 and indicate that the price changes from the subsample followed similar, but not necessarily identical, patterns to those in the full scanner data.

3.5.2   The Results

Despite the limitations to the exercise arising from problems of matching, the results are nevertheless instructive. Table 3.3 gives an overview of matched comparative prices and unit values expressed in terms of both monetary amounts and the percentage of product varieties for which the mean collected for the RPI is higher than that produced by scanner data unit values. We found that for a particular product variety the average price

3. See appendix.

Table 3.2   Percentage Coverage of Matched Data and Comparison Between Means of Prices for the Whole RPI and the Matched Sample (means in £s): August to October 1999

	August			September			October		
	% Matched	Mean of All RPI Quotes	Mean of Matched Sample	% Matched	Mean of All RPI Quotes	Mean of Matched Sample	% Matched	Mean of All RPI Quotes	Mean of Matched Sample
14" televisions	39	135.5	146.7	46	130.8	148.9	46	129.2	150.7
21" televisions	48	249.7	291.3	56	246.5	283.8	58	240.1	268.4
Vacuum cleaners	76	129.5	129.1	77	130.0	130.9	78	128.9	130.2
Cameras	55	55.4	56.9	50	56.5	59.9	53	57.3	56.4
Dishwashers	71	339.5	332.3	73	337.9	330.8	69	333.3	328.5
Washing machines	81	345.3	349.7	75	354.0	323.2	76	348.9	317.8

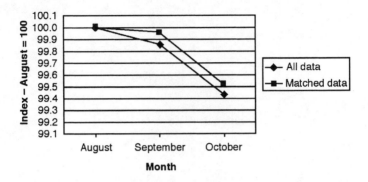

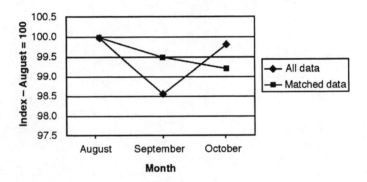

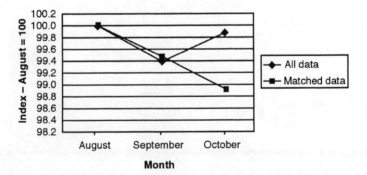

Fig. 3.1   Price indexes for each item calculated using all scanner data and the
matched subset, using a Fisher index: August to October 1999

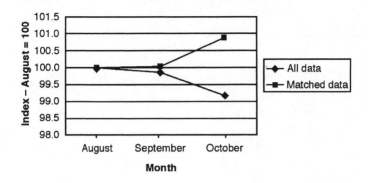

Washing Machines

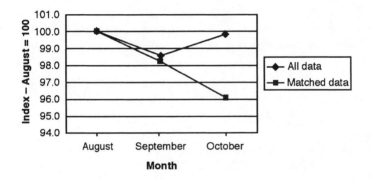

21" Televisions

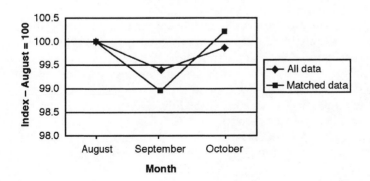

Cameras

Fig. 3.1   (cont.)

Table 3.3   **Average Prices for Recorded RPI Quotes and Scanner Unit Values (proportion of comparisons when the average for RPI quotes exceeded scanner unit values for individual product varieties (means in £s): August to October 1999**

	August	September	October
Dishwashers			
Mean of RPI quotes	339.8	347.4	355.9
Unit value	318.0	323.1	337.2
Proportion of RPI means > unit values	67	67	54
Washing machines			
Mean of RPI quotes	374.0	367.9	362.8
Unit value	348.8	337.0	342.8
Proportion of RPI means > unit values	74	71	67
14" televisions			
Mean of RPI quotes	134.9	134.7	140.6
Unit value	128.1	128.8	129.6
Proportion of RPI means > unit values	52	56	68
21" televisions			
Mean of RPI quotes	307.2	287.2	281.1
Unit value	287.6	271.7	285.4
Proportion of RPI means > unit values	57	69	54
Vacuum cleaners			
Mean of RPI quotes	135.7	131.8	128.0
Unit value	128.9	124.5	119.2
Proportion of RPI means > unit values	42	50	53
Cameras			
Mean of RPI quotes	65.0	71.4	66.0
Unit value	63.2	66.7	63.7
Proportion of RPI means > unit values	62	65	59

recorded by price collectors was higher than that for the scanner data unit values in more than 50 percent of cases for all items other than vacuum cleaners. This was most notably the case for washing machines, for which in 72 percent of cases the collected data produces a higher average. Looking at the average price for the whole product reinforces this point. In all cases, except in October for 21" televisions, the average recorded price was higher than the corresponding figure from scanner data.

However, further analysis indicates that in most cases the difference between price recorded by the price collector and the average unit value shown by the scanner data was caused by a relatively small number of abnormal high or low prices or unit values. This can be seen from the analysis given in table 3.4, which shows the deviation of the medians to be much lower than the deviation of the arithmetic mean values.

An indication of the dispersion in the absolute and percentage deviations is given by the coefficient of variation in table 3.5. As a measure of dispersion it is unaffected by the different means for the different products. The results are quite variable, showing substantial variations in price and unit

Table 3.4   **Absolute and Percentage Absolute Deviations between Averages for RPI Quotes and Scanner Data Unit Values, using Both Mean and Median Differences: Average of August to October 1999**

	Absolute Deviation (£s)		Percentage Absolute Deviation	
	Mean	Median	Mean	Median
Dishwashers	29.4	21.1	9.99	6.35
Washing machines	34.8	21.3	10.45	7.58
Vacuum cleaners	13.3	7.7	9.71	6.07
14" televisions	14.9	9.7	13.95	7.84
21" televisions	30.0	16.6	9.60	6.05
Cameras	9.2	5.9	16.10	10.36

Table 3.5   **Coefficients of Variation**

	Monetary Absolute Deviations	Percentage Absolute Deviations
Dishwashers	0.92	1.32
Washing machines	1.09	0.99
Vacuum cleaners	1.41	1.19
14" televisions	1.07	1.12
21" televisions	1.23	1.23
Cameras	1.04	1.04

value differences for vacuum cleaners, dishwashers, and 21" televisions, although with less variation for other products.

This work, of course, has practical applications in the sampling of items. It is clear that, if means can be influenced significantly by outliers, we need to look closely at the number of quotes sampled and whether they need to be increased for certain items to reduce this effect. Alternatively, the use of the geometric mean as an aggregator may be supported, given that it is less influenced by outliers than its arithmetic counterpart.

A corresponding analysis of monthly price changes indicates that there is no evidence of recorded price *changes* consistently exceeding unit value changes or vice versa; however, differences occur in (a) dishwashers, vacuum cleaners, and 14" televisions, for which changes in the prices recorded by price collectors are consistently higher than the changes shown by scanner data; and (b) cameras, for which, conversely, the changes shown by scanner data are higher.

In some instances, the divergences that occur in price and unit value trends may be due to the small number of price observations in the RPI for the particular model under investigation; in such circumstances, price can fluctuate wildly from one month to another with the introduction of sale prices and special offers. In other instances the difference is difficult to ex-

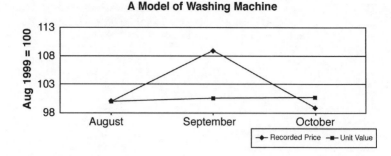

Fig. 3.2   Difference in price movement between scanner data and RPI data for a particular brand of washing machine: August to October 1999

plain but may be due to differences in the mix of outlets and, in particular, the changes that occur over time in market shares and the outlets making sales and therefore appearing with changing weights in the scanner data. This problem of lack of homogeneity was referred to in section 3.2.1. Despite these possible explanations, there yet remains a degree of mystery why some of the differences in price trends occur. This is best illustrated by reference to particular examples. The results for a specific model of washing machine are examined in detail in the paragraph that follows.

Although for washing machines as a whole no appreciable price trend differences were shown between RPI data and scanner data, one model stood out as being very different. The RPI average display price for this model increased by 9.4 percent between August 1999 and September 1999, compared with a much smaller increase of 1.5 percent in average unit value from scanner data before falling back to below its average August price. There was, therefore, a net drop in price over the two months compared with a net increase in price shown by the scanner data (see figure 3.2). Given the fact that there were twenty-six price quotes in the RPI sample, it is unlikely that sampling variability in the matched sample is a major factor. Reference to the outlet type given by the scanner data provides some insight, because this shows not only large differentials between outlet types for prices and price (unit value) movements over time (in scanner data terms unit revenue) but also large variations in the volumes of sales.

3.6   The Effect of Different Store Types

As we have said, one of the main differences between the scanner data and the RPI sample is the difference in the mix of store types. Table 3.6, which has been compiled from scanner data, suggests that, at an item level, there can be significant differences in both unit values and unit value changes for different store types.

For example, in October the average price of a particular brand of wash-

Table 3.6   **Effect of Shop Type on the Unit Value of One Brand of Washing Machine**

Store Type	August	Unit Value September	October	Percentage Change August to September
Multiple	301.2	304.9	303.3	1.2
Mass merchandiser	306.8	301.1	307.4	1.8
Independent	322.9	329.1	330.0	1.9
Catalog	384.5	388.1	386.7	0.5
All stores	316.8	321.4	320.8	1.5

ing machine varied from £301, in multiple chains of stores, to £384, for sales from mail-order catalogs. Additionally, the change in prices between August and September shows a large variation, with the smallest price rise being 0.5 percent, for mail-order catalogs, and the highest being 1.9 percent, for small independent stores.

Clearly differences in the mix of shops between scanner data and the RPI sample could produce significant differences in both the average price of items and the average price change. Unfortunately, this difference is difficult to test, because RPI quote data are not classified as finely as scanner data, although this is clearly an area that we need to investigate further.

For scanner data, clearly, the store mix is changing continually as sales fluctuate between the different sectors. It is important, therefore, that we fully understand the effects of these changes and how they fit into the conceptual basis of the RPI before scanner data can be used to provide weight data for index construction.

3.7   Using Scanner Data to Provide Explicit Weights for Aggregation Formulas

The calculation of indexes for items within the RPI is done using either a ratio of average or average of relatives formula (see the appendix). In neither case is any explicit weighting used in this calculation, and so the implicit assumption for the average of relatives (used in the RPI for these items) is that all quotes are equally important. This is clearly only truly accurate if the mix of quotes taken is representative of sales of brands and models for each item. An alternative approach would be to use the explicit weights available from the volumes of sales seen in scanner data. Table 3.7 shows a comparison of indexes of price changes using the ratio of averages and a Laspeyres-based weighted average using scanner data to provide weights.[4]

The comparisons show differences in all cases, with the possible excep-

---

4. See appendix.

Table 3.7   Comparison of Indexes Using Unweighted Ratio of Averages and a Weighted Laspeyres Calculation: August to October 1999

	August	September	October
Dishwashers			
Ratio of averages	100.0	99.2	97.2
Laspeyres	100.0	100.8	100.4
Washing machines			
Ratio of averages	100.0	103.3	99.7
Laspeyres	100.0	98.7	99.7
Vacuum cleaners			
Ratio of averages	100.0	102.1	101.6
Laspeyres	100.0	101.4	100.2
14" televisions			
Ratio of averages	100.0	100.9	100.4
Laspeyres	100.0	101.4	100.0
21" televisions			
Ratio of averages	100.0	100.2	94.6
Laspeyres	100.0	96.9	97.2
Cameras			
Ratio of averages	100.0	100.7	100.0
Laspeyres	100.0	99.2	97.9

tion of 14" televisions, and in some cases they are quite substantial—for example, 4.5 percentage points for washing machines in September. However, there appears to be no consistent pattern in the magnitude or direction of these differences. That there are differences should not be a surprise. Table 3.1 showed the degree of difference between the proportions of quotes for scanner data and RPI quotes, and it is these differences that are translating into differences in index calculations in the two cases. The reasons behind these differences are unclear, although it is likely that two particular aspects of the data collection contribute significantly. First, collectors are asked to select a variety that is "reasonably representative of the item as a whole." This is a very skilled judgment to make, and we cannot be certain that collectors are making the most appropriate choices in all cases. The second is that we endeavor to follow the same quotes over the period of a whole year. This means that, for a fast-moving technology, even if we start with a representative sample in January there is a real possibility that by August the items are no longer selling as well as at the start of the year and the sample is no longer representative of shopping patterns.

3.8   Conclusions and Implications for Sampling and the Collection of Price Data

The research described in this paper has raised a number of issues relating to current practices used in the sampling and collection of prices for the

U.K. RPI. It also points to a number of ways in which scanner data might be utilized to further ensure representativity of item and product varieties in the context of traditional forms of price collection in which prices are observed in shops. The research does not necessarily indicate that current sampling procedures lead to bias, but it does invite the prospect of additional controls and procedures to keep in check the potential for bias.

The starting point of any practical consideration must be whether the items indicated by scanner data truly represent the market they are chosen from. Do they cover a large proportion of the market? Do their changes in price give a true representation of the price changes in the goods they are chosen to represent? If the answer is yes, we can then make the following practical recommendations:

1. The introduction of some form of quota sampling based on scanner data is likely to help in providing a representative sample. In the current practice price collectors are given generic price descriptions and are asked to select for pricing the most representative product variety in the shop being visited. Using a quota sample would, for instance, provide a mechanism for ensuring a better representation of different brands.

2. As an alternative to a quota sample, scanner data could be used to postweight the quotes obtained by price collectors to produce a more representative final sample. Although this has many obvious problems, we will be exploring the principle further.

3. Deterioration in representativity during the life of the "representative" basket, even one that is fixed annually, can be quite marked for some items for which, for instance, the turnover of models is relatively high. In these cases scanner data may provide, at least in those areas where scanner data coverage is good, a useful check on representativity and indicate certain areas for more frequent updating of the representative basket by the introduction of planned "forced replacements." This could be done either by a change in the basket triggered by an algorithm based on scanner data or by perhaps the more practical alternative, prior agreement, in which case manufacturers or retailers warn us that changes are happening.

4. Where unplanned forced replacements continue to be necessary due to product varieties' disappearing from shops, scanner data may be helpful in choosing replacements by, for example, identifying replacements that are the closest in terms of characteristics to the disappearing model or with the use of hedonic regression identifying the most important characteristics that feature in purchasing decisions by consumers.

5. Scanner data by store type indicate that special care must be taken to ensure a proper spread of outlets in the RPI sample and that scanner data may be used for poststratification where there is reason to believe that the sample achieved under current RPI sampling practices is not totally self-weighting.

6. Where coefficients of variation suggest that outliers can have an undue influence, we need to reexamine the numbers of quotes taken to see if the situation can be improved by increasing the sample size.

The Office for National Statistics is looking at these issues in more detail as part of its longer-term methodological research program. Specifically, we are investigating the coverage, and quality, of the scanner data for the six items used in this report, to see whether our use of them as a benchmark is justified.

We are also starting practical work to see whether the construction, and use, of a quota sample is feasible in a live price collection. In particular, we are asking a sample of price collectors to try to select a complete basket of new goods for the six items in this study, using a quota sampling technique.

Appendix

Formulas of Elementary Aggregates and Index Formulations

$$\text{Laspeyres} = \frac{\sum P_t Q_0}{\sum P_0 Q_0}$$

where P_t = price at time t; Q_0 = quantity sold at time 0; and time 0 = the base month.

$$\text{Paasche} = \frac{\sum P_t Q_t}{\sum P_0 Q_t}$$

where P_t = price at time t; Q_t = quantity sold at time t; and time 0 = the base month.

$$\text{Fisher} = \sqrt{\frac{\sum P_t Q_0 \sum P_t Q_t}{\sum P_0 Q_0 \sum P_0 Q_t}} = \sqrt{\text{Laspeyres} \times \text{Paasche}}$$

where P_t = price at time t; Q_t = quantity sold at time t; and time 0 = the base month.

$$\text{Average of Relatives} = \frac{1}{n} \sum \frac{P_t}{P_0}$$

$$\text{Ratio of Averages} = \frac{\frac{1}{n} \sum P_t}{\frac{1}{n} \sum P_0}$$

References

Baxter, M., ed. 1998. *The Retail Prices Index: Technical manual.* London: The Stationary Office.

Bradley, R., B. Cook, S. G. Leaver, and B. R. Moulton. 1998. An overview of research on potential uses of scanner data in the U.S. CPI. In *Proceedings of the third International Working Group on Price Indices,* ed. Bert Balk, 169–88. Voorburg, the Netherlands: Statistics Netherlands.

Silver, M. 1995. Elementary aggregates, micro-indices, and scanner data: Some issues in the compilation of consumer price indices. *Review of Income and Wealth* 41:427–38.

4

Estimating Price Movements for Consumer Durables Using Electronic Retail Transactions Data

Robin Lowe and Candace Ruscher

4.1 Introduction

The emergence of electronic data records[1] that are kept by retailers, recording every transaction, provides new opportunities for price index makers. This paper compares the existing treatment for quality adjustment and sample maintenance for televisions in the Canadian Consumer Price Index (CPI) with what might be feasible using scanner data. Research has documented some of the costs and benefits in the use of scanner data for food items (see Reinsdorf 1996; Dalén 1997; Hawkes 1997; de Haan and Opperdoes 1997a,b; Scobie 1997). However, it stands to be of greater benefit for consumer durable products, especially those based on electronics: audio and visual equipment, cameras, and home computers (Silver 1995; Silver, Ioannides, and Haworth 1997). The discussion in this paper focuses on televisions, but the same approaches can probably apply to other durable goods.

The principal advantage of scanner data is that they record sales actually made, for an extensive array of products. Current practice for price index construction at Statistics Canada consists of selecting a small number of representative products and monitoring their prices. How many, if any, sales are made, however, is unknown; nor is anything known about the diversity of price changes in the group of products that the sampled products represent. The more complete records from scanner data should ensure that a more representative sample of products is monitored.

Robin Lowe and Candace Ruscher are in the Prices Division of Statistics Canada.

The views expressed in this chapter are those only of the authors and not necessarily those of Statistics Canada.

1. For simplicity, electronic data records will be called *scanner data* in the rest of the paper.

In current practice it usually happens that the exact item being observed becomes unavailable. For consumer durables this is almost inevitable because manufacturers routinely modify their products and introduce new ones, making existing ones obsolete. When this happens, a replacement must be made in the sample, and the comparison between the qualities of a replaced item and its replacement often triggers an adjustment to the index measurement. This is where one of the weaknesses of scanner data lies, because the larger number of records may preclude giving the same level of care to the quality adjustment process. A critical issue, then, is one of weighing the advantages of additional observations provided by the scanner data against the disadvantages of paying less attention to changes in the quality of the sampled items.

The first part of this paper describes the sample and the quality change evaluation process for televisions over the last nine years and identifies the main issues for improvement: the need to update the sample more quickly and to improve the quality adjustment procedure. It appears that these two problems are of similar magnitude and that an improvement of the sampling procedure would mitigate the effect of the weaknesses in the quality adjustment methods. The second part of the paper examines the results using scanner data for the period December 1997 to November 1999. Although the database could be used in a limited way—to evaluate quality differences periodically, or to assist sampling and weighting representative products—the attention is given to the use of these data to replace the existing methodology. We find that the breadth of the records identifies clearly different price movements for different sizes of televisions and provides the means to adjust for changes in purchase patterns. We find also, however, that it is difficult to compare qualities of products, even to identify similar or identical products, and that the results are very sensitive to this problem. A number of ways of dealing with it are tried, but none of the ways of handling the data seems entirely satisfactory without detailed examination of the microdata. Doing that examination as well as acquiring the data is costly, so it appears that a practical use of this source will involve using only a part of it, or using it in a limited way that only requires acquisition of the data occasionally.

4.2   Consumer Price Index Construction for Televisions

Televisions exhibit relatively uncommon price behavior, in that their prices have fallen steadily, both in nominal terms and as measured by price indexes. The available data set starts in June 1990, and figures are shown through November 1997. For most of this period there are two representative products—a 20" and a 27" color TV—but a television in the 32" to 36" range was added in June 1999. Deviations from the preferred specification are allowed; for example, 19" screens are permitted in the first representative product, and 25" to 28" screens are accepted in the second. Since the most common screen sizes are 20" and 27", they will be featured in the rest of the paper.

Over the study period, the total Canadian CPI sample averaged about 220 observations until early 1995, when it dropped to about 140—two price observations from each of about 70 outlets. Items were replaced, on average, about once a year, causing a quality change evaluation each time. Quality change adjustments were forced either because the existing item was replaced by a new variant of the model or because the outlet stopped selling that item altogether. There were no changes to the item selection initiated by the statisticians during the study period other than the addition of 32" televisions.

Routinely the specific items being surveyed have to be replaced in the sample. Comparisons between the replaced and replacing item may affect the index. There are two kinds of replacement. In the first, the replacement is directed; the old model has been updated, often with some minor changes, and the manufacturer has assigned a new model number. Often there may be no other changes to the product at all. The second kind of replacement occurs when the product is no longer available and there is no updated version available at that outlet. This may be because the manufacturer has stopped making that product or simply because the retailer is not selling it any more. In these cases, the price collector finds a replacement that may be quite different from the old item.

When the changes are minor, the price evaluators can value them quite easily. In most cases they have brochures from the manufacturers to help them assess changes in the specifications of models. Many times, a small change in a specification accompanies a model change—in the type of remote control supplied, in the warranty coverage, or in the number or placement of jacks, for example. In the second situation, in which the replacement is not a modification of the old item, it is more difficult to value the changes. The price collector is asked to find a similar item if possible, but one that is a volume seller. The volume seller requirement sometimes results in the selection of a model that is quite different from the previous one. Price evaluators have some guidelines for taking into account the price difference due to slightly different screen sizes, a change from mono sound to stereo sound, and other common improvements, so they can make reasonable comparisons in many cases. However, the comparison is complicated when it involves a change of manufacturer. Although it is recognized that manufacturers do vary in quality, it is difficult to compare and estimate by how much. A frequent shift in sourcing is a phenomenon particular to certain retail outlets. Most retailers carry certain manufacturers and change rarely. Some, however, switch manufacturers frequently, making the best buys they can each time.

For many replacements, the new item is linked into the index to show no change from the old one. To calculate a price ratio the current price is divided by a reference price. If, for example, the last report for item A was $20 in September, while the reference price was $10, and the first report for item B was $25 in October, the reference price would be changed to $12.50 so that the ratio remains the same. If the report for item B had been available in September at $25, the new item could have been substituted into the index calculations then. That method relies on the assumption that the ratio of prices reflects the ratio of qualities. However, because there is not usually a period of overlap, the method of linking from September to October relies on a further assumption, that prices have not changed between the two months. Thus the link is stretched across the two months, and the method is described as stretch-linked in this paper.[2]

The stretch-link method is the default in index calculations. However, in many cases it cannot be justified and the price evaluator imposes his own judgment. Sometimes the change in the product description, (a minor modification for example), is easy to assess, and the reference price will be adjusted for the value of the change independent of the ratio of prices. In some cases the evaluator may judge the value of the change as zero. Sometimes the ratio of prices may not reflect the ratio of qualities because one or other of the prices is out of line. This could be for any of several reasons. It can easily happen if the price of the old item had been discounted before its disappearance. It can also happen if prices generally are falling, and an old product remains in the sample with an unchanged price because it has become obsolete in the market, although still available. On the other hand, a new item might be introduced into the market at an unusually high price to attract the attention of those who will pay a premium for something new. Or the manufacturer may take the opportunity to adjust his price when he introduces a new product. Because a product usually remains in the sample as long as a price for it can be found, it is the price of the old item that is more likely to be out of line, but any of these conditions could hold. In all of these cases the evaluator must make the best judgment possible of the ratio of qualities. All cases in which the evaluator intercedes are called judgments in this paper. The judgment used might either raise or lower the index, depending on the conditions.

Analysis of the results of replacements in the index during the 1990s shows certain patterns (Lowe 1997). Overall the replacement was linked into the index to show no price change in slightly more than half the cases. There is a difference depending on how different in price the replacement was from the item it replaced. If the price of the new item was more than 10 percent different from the price of the old item, we call it a major change;

---

2. Some products, including televisions, are not surveyed every month, so the stretching can be for more than one month. Televisions are priced approximately every second month, so most stretch-links are for a two-month period.

otherwise it is a minor change. The figure of 10 percent is arbitrary, but it separates the small modifications from the rest. With that distinction we find that the evaluator used his judgment in over 60 percent of the minor changes. In a significant portion of these the editor judged that quality had not changed at all—that all the nominal price change was pure price change. On the other hand, for major changes, the evaluator only imposed a judgment 45 percent of the time, and even less often—less than one-third of the time—if the replacement was made by a different manufacturer. The single best improvement in quality change evaluation would be a better way to evaluate such large changes.

Given this program of quality assessment, these questions arise: what is its impact on the index, and what would be the result if different treatments were used? We have recalculated the index numbers for the study period using a number of scenarios reflecting different treatments of quality change.

4.2.1 Applying Different Assessments of Quality Change

The first scenario replicates current practice.[3] The second scenario uses stretch-links[4] for all replacements—an option that is easy to adopt. The difference between these two shows the effect of the evaluators' judgments. In order to see how these differences came about, we show the impact of large changes and small changes separately. The third scenario stretch-links all large price changes but keeps the existing results for small changes. The fourth scenario is the reverse—adjustments for large price changes are kept, but small changes are stretch-linked. Finally, the fifth scenario, a simplistic one, calculates the index with all quality changes ignored and all price changes accepted as pure price change. This is what would be obtained if all quality changes were ignored. It is also a measure of the movement through time of the unit values of the items in the sample.

The stretch-link method has been criticized as a default method. Other organizations have different methods for comparing items when replacements take place, and some differ from the stretch-link by the means they use to impute the movement between the two periods that an item and its replacement were in the sample. One method is to omit the records for those periods and estimate the movement on the remaining items that were in the sample in both periods. The difference between these methods amounts to the following. Assume there are ten items equally weighted in the sample, and one is replaced. Using common records only, the index movement between the two periods will be the average of the nine price ratios. Using the stretch-link method the movement will be the average of those nine plus an extra ratio of 1. Thus, if prices generally are rising, the stretch-link method

---

3. The first scenario does not recreate the historical indexes exactly for a number of reasons, including the fact that the regional strata were simplified for these calculations.

4. In earlier papers a stretch-link has been described sometimes as a splice, but splicing implies that both prices are available in the same period.

Table 4.1   Percentage Change in TV Index, Canada: June 1990 to November 1997

Scenario	All TVs	20" TV	27" TV	Difference between 27" TV and 20" TV
1 Current practice	−25.9	−22.1	−30.4	−8.3
2 All quality changes stretch-inked	−21.4	−19.0	−24.3	−5.3
3 Large price changes stretch-linked	−23.6	−20.7	−27.7	−7.0
4 Small price changes stretch-linked	−23.7	−20.4	−27.3	−6.9
5 All price changes treated as pure price changes	−24.4	−20.9	−28.8	−7.9
1a Current practice, most splices excluded	−26.9	−23.1	−31.4	−8.3
Difference between scenarios 1 and 2	4.5	3.1	6.1	

will tend to keep the index down, and if they are falling it will tend to keep it up. Scenario 1A in table 4.1 shows the result of replacing most stretch-links in our actual practice with the movement of common records instead of stretch-links.[5]

Table 4.1 shows the separate results for both common sizes of televisions, and for the two combined, for the whole study period. A large part of the drop in prices occurred between 1990 and 1992. The prices used in this study were exclusive of retail sales taxes, so the replacement of the manufacturers' sales tax by the goods and services tax probably accounted for some of this drop.

There are several things to note in table 4.1. First, however treated, prices for 20" TVs have fallen substantially less than prices for 27" TVs. This is true whatever method of handling quality change is used. In fact, the fastest rate of decline for 20" televisions is less than the slowest for the 27" size. On the other hand, the range of results from different treatments of quality change is only 3.1 percent for 20" televisions and 6.1 percent for 27" televisions. What evidence we have on sales indicates that there has been a substantial shift toward larger sizes, that continues toward larger sizes still, 32" to 35". This spread of price movements suggests that making sure the sample selection is representative is in the same order of importance as choosing the best quality adjustment technique.

Second, the impact of the judgments is 4.5 percent overall. When we look at the relative impact of large and small changes in scenarios 3 and 4 in table 4.1 we see that large and small changes had about equal effect. It was to be expected that the net impact of assessing small price changes was to lower the index, because these are mainly small modifications at little or no cost, but it was not obvious that the judgments on the larger price changes would

5. Those cases in which neither the price nor the quality changed were not regarded as quality changes, so they were not taken out of the sample for the calculation.

have the same impact. Since the judgments on large changes tended to lower the index, it must be suspected that the index would have been lower still if the large percentage of changes that were linked to show no price change had been replaced by some kind of judgment. Both this and the lack of adjustment in the sample for televisions of different sizes suggest that any error in this index is likely to be upward.

Third, it is curious that the simplistic approach, scenario 5, produces a result fairly close to the official index (scenario 1). This would not be the case for all time periods. Between 1990 and the end of 1991, the index under scenario 5 fell sharply compared to the official index, then rose since the end of 1995. They were virtually equal at the end of 1997. The periods (1990 to 1992, and 1992 onward) correspond to periods of weakness and recovery in the Canadian economy, and the result is consistent with consumers' trading down, then up, accordingly. This provides some validation of the changes in item selection that have occurred over the period, despite the limitations imposed by the specifications.

Finally, the computational practice of keeping the linked observation in the sample for the month in which it is linked has a fairly significant impact. Scenario 1A shows that the drag on indexes by stretch-linking was about 1 percent over the period, whereas the impact of quality adjustment was 4.5 percent. As prices were falling for this commodity, stretch-linking has kept the index higher. Preliminary testing on other commodities suggests that this may be a general result, particularly for durable goods whose prices are tending to decline.

4.3   Calculations Based on Scanner Data

4.3.1   Matched Records

We have sought scanner data from individual retailers as well as purchasing analyses from market research companies who also collect from retailers. Preliminary analysis of the market research data suggests that there may be differences between its behavior at the higher level of aggregation provided and reports from individual retailers, but it has been received too recently for extensive analysis to be done. The analysis presented here will be based on one seller's data. The emphasis is on the change in results from different applications rather than the absolute results. The data contain the number sold and average price for each identified product code by month and by store. The price is the actual transaction price before taxes. Data from stores were aggregated to create one average price and one total quantity for each product code for each month.

The product codes distinguish models to approximately the same level of detail as our official CPI survey—for example, a new production run under a different model number will carry a different product code in this data-

Table 4.2   **Chained Bimonthly Indexes, October–November 1999, All Sales**
                       (December 1997–January 1998 = 1)

Size	Laspeyres	Paasche	Fisher
13"	0.748	0.785	0.750
20"	0.767	0.772	0.770
27"	0.787	0.754	0.770
31"	0.751	0.710	0.730
35"	0.718	0.691	0.705
All	0.764	0.738	0.745

base. The number of product codes reporting sales in any month is about 200 for all stores together. The company carries only a few manufacturers, but it carries a full range of products from those manufacturers. The product code description provides enough information to identify the make and model, so by using brochures or consulting manufacturers, one can obtain the characteristics of each.[6] For eventual comparison with market research data, the results shown here are for sales aggregated over two-month periods, starting with December 1997–January 1998, which is used as the reference period in comparisons.

The range of models comprises six groups: 9", 13", 20" (19" to 21"), 27" (25" to 29"), 31/32", and 35/36". Indexes have been calculated for these specifications separately and grouped together.

Because there are numbers sold as well as prices for each period, indexes for each pair of periods can be weighted by sales in either period. The results of the chained Laspeyres, Paasche, and Fisher[7] indexes over the twelve two-month periods from December 1997–January 1998 to October–November 1999 are given in table 4.2.

As expected, except for 20" televisions, the larger the screen size, the greater the rate of decline. All of the index declines are substantial. One reason, which biases the measures downward, is the effect on the indexes of individual models at the beginning and the end of their market life. Typically prices fall at both those portions of their life. At the beginning, prices generally start high and drop as the market grows, and at the end, prices are often discounted to clear the stock. This behavior did not appear in the conventional surveys, partly because models at the beginning of their lives were rarely included in the sample, and partly because a direct comparison of the

6. The market research data provided have similar detail—quantities of individual models, and average price—but aggregated across all outlets reporting to their survey. Further, it has been aggregated over two-month periods: December to January, February to March, and so on.

7. If the quantities sold and average prices in successive periods are q, q' and p, p' respectively, the Laspeyres price index is $\Sigma qp'/\Sigma qp$, the Paasche index is $\Sigma q'p'/\Sigma q'p$, and the Fisher index is the geometric average of the two, $(\Sigma qp' \cdot \Sigma q'p'/\Sigma qp \cdot \Sigma q'p)^{1/2}$. Indexes for longer periods are calculated by chaining the period-to-period indexes.

price of models that disappeared, and their successors, usually produced an adjustment.

For many models, sales are small during these periods, so they should have little influence on the overall averages. However, for some of the most popular models, when one year's model is replaced by the next, sales can be high during the period over which the replacement occurs. Table 4.3 illustrates.

The first three index computations are based on the assumption that models 1 and 2 are not directly comparable. From February to August, and after October 1997, the movements of the three indexes—Laspeyres, Paasche, and Fisher—are identical because there are prices of one model only for all of them. Even in August, a true Paasche index cannot be calculated because there is no observed price for model 2 in July, and in November a true Laspeyres index cannot be calculated because there is no observed price for model 1 in that month. The three measures only differ between August and October, and they all show a sustained decline.

The last column in table 4.3 is based on recognizing that the two product codes describe identical models, so the sales data can be combined. The index is based on the weighted average price each month. This index shows some price drops during the overlap period, but by the end of the period shown the index is higher than in February 1997, as it should be because the identical model is selling for close to $900, compared to about $850 a year earlier.

If these prices had been collected and used in our conventional survey, model 1 would have been replaced by model 2 some time in the period. The evaluator should have judged that because the two models were of equal quality, all the change was price change, and a price increase would have been shown, from $828 to $883 if the replacement was made in August, $778 to $884 if in September, $732 to $863 if in October, or (most likely) from $697 to $852 if in November, when a price for the old model was no longer available. Depending on when the replacement was made, the index would differ through the replacement period, but in any case, it would finish the same by December.

Clearly, to avoid this ratcheting effect, one would like to treat these models as identical, but it is not very easy. Although the data for the two models are shown together in table 4.3, they would not appear in such an easy way to compare in the set of scanner data. The only identifying information is a unique code number to identify each model, and some description, which is not standardized. One has to know that these two models are identical ahead of time to treat them as such. Furthermore, pairs of models may not be identical, but very similar, and the same phenomenon of falling prices during the overlap may occur to lower the index. We need to identify and exclude that effect. One possibility is to exclude sales at the beginning and end of market runs, when their price movements may be abnormal.

Table 4.3   Monthly Chained Index Calculations When One TV Model Replaces an Identical One in the Market

1997–98	Model 1 Units Sold	Model 1 Average Price ($)	Model 2 Units Sold	Model 2 Average Price ($)	Combined Average Price of Models 1 and 2 ($)	Laspeyres	Paasche	Fisher	Based on Combined Average Price
February	91	846			846	1	1	1	1
March	99	850			850	1.005	1.005	1.005	1.005
April	66	850			850	1.004	1.004	1.004	1.004
May	73	845			845	0.999	0.999	0.999	0.999
June	68	844			844	0.998	0.998	0.998	0.998
July	53	828			828	0.979	0.979	0.979	0.979
August	85	778	15	883	794	0.920	0.920	0.920	0.938
September	63	732	73	874	808	0.873	0.891	0.882	0.955
October	17	697	79	863	833	0.849	0.875	0.862	0.985
November			87	852	852	0.838	0.864	0.851	1.007
December			114	845	845	0.832	0.857	0.844	0.999
January			68	884	884	0.870	0.896	0.883	1.045
February			55	904	904	0.889	0.917	0.903	1.068

Indexes (February 1997 = 1)

Table 4.4   **Indexes in October–November 1999 for 27" Televisions with Adjustments for Overlap (December 1997–January 1998 = 1)**

	Laspeyres	Paasche	Fisher
With no corrections	0.787	0.754	0.770
Data for first and last period excluded	0.793	0.767	0.783
Identical models grouped together	0.872	0.837	0.854

Another is to identify families of models that are identical or very similar and group their sales together. The results of both approaches when applied to 27" televisions are shown in table 4.4.

There are disadvantages of excluding data. One is that the exclusion of genuine sales is regrettable, and because model replacements tend to be grouped at two times of the year, the exclusions tend to occur together. A second is that the choice of period to exclude data is arbitrary. Furthermore, the difference it makes is not substantial.

Grouping similar models, however, makes a large difference. The groups were defined by the judgments made by price editors when they were faced with replacements in the course of regular surveying. Only those that were judged to be equal in quality were grouped together. There were only seven groupings over three manufacturers. It is likely that more groupings could be made, but there was no evidence to determine them.

4.3.2   Reducing the Database

One of the hoped-for advantages of using scanner data was that it could be analyzed without too much examination of microdata. It is clear that this is not the case. It will be necessary to examine and compare streams of data pertaining to different products.

In the initial analysis, all data that could be compared from one period to the next were used. This resulted in the exclusion of very little data. Models that had no sales in the second period in each comparison accounted for only about 1 percent of the revenue of each first period. Models that first appeared in the second period in each comparison accounted for about 1.5 percent of revenue in the second period. We do not, perhaps, need all the data. If the database can be trimmed of the sales of less important products, the number of products whose quality must be kept track of will be reduced. The results for 27" televisions from taking the products that account for the first 75 percent or 90 percent of sales in each period-to-period comparison are given in table 4.5.

To choose the data to be used in each period-to-period comparison, the products that could be matched were listed by revenue in descending order in each month. Then records were included by going down the list until the required percentage of sales, 75 percent or 90 percent, was reached.

The column "Number of Products Included" shows the number of differ-

Table 4.5   Indexes for 27" Televisions, October–November 1999 under Various Selections of Subsets (December 1997–January 1998 = 1)

Criteria for Selection	Laspeyres	Paasche	Fisher	Number of Products Included
On reported data				
All sales	0.787	0.754	0.770	99
90% of sales in first period	0.796	0.772	0.784	45
90% of sales in second period	0.797	0.761	0.779	54
75% of sales in first period	0.833	0.875	0.830	37
75% of sales in second period	0.813	0.772	0.792	34
On data with similar products grouped				
All sales	0.872	0.837	0.854	88
90% of sales in first period	0.892	0.875	0.883	37
90% of sales in second period	0.865	0.855	0.855	47
75% of sales in first period	0.925	0.920	0.922	28
75% of sales in second period	0.905	0.876	0.900	27

ent models included over the whole period from December 1997 to November 1999. In any matched pair of periods the number of products included is much less. The lower number of products for the grouped data is solely due to the replacement of several products by one in each group. Most of the saving in the number of products to consider comes from cutting the data to the first 90 percent of sales. The differences in the index calculation when excluding the bottom 10 percent are small.

The differences when including only the top 75 percent of sales are substantial, and it also matters whether we filter the data according to their value in the first period in each comparison or the second. For symmetry we could used the sales of the two periods combined to select data, but the consistent direction of the difference suggests something else at play. Selecting by the second-period sales leads to the inclusion of more new products, whose prices seem to be falling faster than those of the older products that are on the way out. We believe that by excluding the lesser sales we are avoiding somewhat the ratcheting problem when products are being replaced by similar products. However, not all replacements are by similar products, and some may argue that excluding a quarter of sales and waiting for new products to establish a large enough share of the market unnecessarily delays the price falls induced by their introduction. The share of the marginal product at the 75 percent sales total is about 4 percent in most periods. Most worrying is the fact that the choice of 75 percent or 90 percent or any other level is arbitrary, but it affects systematically the index measure.

4.3.3   Regression Approaches

The other way to adjust for the changing mix of quality in different models is to use multiple regression. The method and justification are widely available (see Silver and Heravi 1999 for an exposition and references). This method depends on transforming the description of each product sold into a list of its characteristics and regressing the price on the characteristics. Because manufacturers provide detailed specifications of their products, there is a wealth of description available.

The regressions are run for models of the following form:

$$\ln P_i = \mathbf{X}_{it}\boldsymbol{\beta}_t + u_{it}$$

where P_i is the price of model i in time t, $\mathbf{X}_{it}$ is a vector of characteristics describing model i in time t, $\boldsymbol{\beta}_t$ is a vector of parameters representing the implicit prices of the characteristics in time t, and u_{it} is an error term representing the factors not incorporated in the model.

Most of the characteristics are dichotomous variables representing the presence of a certain physical attribute or identification with a particular brand. Of the few that are not, the most significant variable is the screen area. A list of the characteristics collected is given in appendix A.

There is a high degree of correlation among the variables so that the list of significant variables can be reduced considerably, and the ones that remain must be considered as representatives for others. The most satisfactory model, based on relationships over the two-year period, depended on the following variables: size; size squared; whether the brand is Hitachi, Panasonic/JVC, RCA/Sanyo, Samsung, or Sony (Sony was the excluded option, being generally considered to command the highest prices); the incidence of a picture-in-picture feature, with one tuner, or two; the incidence of surround sound, either a basic or a more sophisticated version; and the number of S-video inputs, front and rear, front inputs being preferred.

Although the selection of significant characteristics was based on the two-year period, we can run a regression for each period separately. We then have a vector of implicit prices $\boldsymbol{\beta}_t$ (including a constant term) for each period. We can also calculate the average value for each characteristic in each period; for a continuous variable such as screen size it is the average screen size of all models sold, and for a dichotomous characteristic, such as picture-in-picture with two tuners, it is the percentage of models sold that had that that particular characteristic. Call this vector $\overline{X}_t$. (The incidence of the constant is 1.) Then we can estimate a price for period t using the average characteristics and implicit prices for period t as $\exp(\overline{X}_t\boldsymbol{\beta}_t)$. We can also estimate a price for period $t + 1$ using the prices for period $t + 1$ and the characteristics for period t. We can call this ratio of estimated prices a Laspeyres price index for $t + 1$ related to t. Similarly, we can calculate a Paasche index using the average characteristics in period $t + 1$. The implicit prices and the average values of physical characteristics are shown in appendix B.

Calculating Paasche and chained Laspeyres indexes on the implicit prices and characteristics weights, comparable to those from conventional price and quantity data, we get values of 0.898 and 0.922, respectively, and a chained Fisher index of 0.910, for October/November 1999, with December 1997/January 1998 = 1.

Another index estimate was run using the model derived in Moulton, Lafleur, and Moses (1998). That study ranged over a longer period and a wider range of products. In our data from one seller there was no variation in home delivery, console, or LCD display. However, to the extent that the North American market is unified, at least to the extent of the variety of products available a similar hedonic equation may apply.

The results for that model are, for Laspeyres, Paasche, and Fisher, respectively: 0.903, 0.934, and 0.918. Thus the two models produce similar results, with the Moulton model showing less decline, as should be expected. The main difference between the two models is that the one derived from this database uses a finer distinction of the varieties of surround sound and S-video inputs than the Moulton model could because it had to cover several more years. The other variable in the Moulton model, whether there was a universal remote control, was also coded to finer distinctions, but this variable proved not to be significant. Consequently, the refinement of these features, which made later products more attractive, could be picked up by one regression model but not the other.

These results seem plausible. They are at the high end of the range of results got from matching data, but it is recognized that the intervention in editing it has not been completed. Nevertheless, there are some drawbacks to using this method in regular production. First, the models are derived by examining the data after all the records are available. In running a monthly or bimonthly index one would want to be able to change the list of significant characteristics at the time the changes occur, rather than afterwards. Second, the high proportion of variance explained, around 90 percent on bimonthly data sets, is misleading. By far the most significant variable is screen size, which explains about 85 percent of price variation. It is not necessary to group all products together irrespective of size. The scanner data give us good information on total sales by size, so that if we had separate price indexes for each size category we could produce accurate indexes. However, if we stratify by size it is not nearly so easy to design reliable models. Third, some of the characteristics are given too much significance, whereas other changes cannot be captured. It will be remembered that close to half of the amount of quality change adjustment in the current procedure occurred because of small modifications to products. Most of these would not register in a regression model. On the other hand, some characteristics that can appear significant in the regression model were valued as insignificant in current production. For example, the variable S-video describes the existence of connections for a high-quality feed from another device. In products to which this has been added as an update from the previous version this improvement has been regarded as an insignificant quality change. However, for most of this period Sony made two series of televisions for each screen size, an S series and a V series, one substantially more expensive than the other but with generally similar characteristics. This particular characteristic is one that distinguishes the two series. Fourth, it is a lot of work to collect the characteristics on all the models to be used in the regression.

4.4   Costs

The cost savings in using scanner data are the field expenses currently incurred in collecting data and the processing and editing costs. The in-house costs would be replaced by the costs of collecting and processing the scanner data. The current sample includes three price observations from each of about seventy outlets. Given an average time per store of fifteen minutes and a driving distance of about ten kilometers, the annual cost, allowing for checking and overhead, would be on the order of $10,000 a year. Many of the prices are collected from outlets that provide many other prices as well, so unless the visit to the outlet can be avoided, which is possible only if all products were collected by scanner data, this is an overestimate of the field savings.

The collection costs from any individual company are relatively small, and once the processing has been set up to massage the data, collection and checking are straightforward. With a large number of retailers reporting, processing costs would not be insignificant, although they would probably still be no more than current processing costs. The major increase in costs would be with the editors. At present, although they have to keep up –to date with product developments across the whole field, they only have to evaluate between 100 and 200 quality changes, many of which are similar— the same model being replaced by another in different locations. To collect and codify thirty or more characteristics for all the models that may be sold and appear in the scanner data is a job several orders of magnitude higher. Thus, any method that depends on using all scanner data requires an increase in resources or a simpler approach.

4.5   Conclusion

The opportunities provided by the scanner data are extensive, but they pose new problems. The scanner data have to be managed carefully. There are challenging questions to answer concerning the choice of data to be included in the calculations, how to group together different products, and how to describe them.

One of the hoped-for advantages of using the scanner data was that because of the large amount of information, amounting to a census for the chosen source, little micro editing would be required. However, this has not happened. It is clear that the assumption underlying any use of matched samples—that relative prices reflect relative qualities—does not hold here. At the very least, replacements that are really continuations of the same product under a different brand name must be recognized. More generally, regression analysis might be applied if the characteristics can be obtained quickly enough. It is essential that products be classified effectively. A basic classification is into size categories, for each of which price measures should be developed separately.

The database from an individual retailer does not provide enough diversity to estimate regression models for televisions by size category with any degree of degree of reliability, but it may be possible from the market research company database. This will be the next step in the analysis. This database will also be analyzed for its behavior using matched records; because of the broader range of products and outlets, one would expect that the concentration of sales by product would be less. Whether or not the sensitivity to filtering data will be as great remains to be seen; the database provided includes some filtering already.

Because of the cost of collecting full descriptions of all products, it may be more practical to work with a subset. It would be easier to identify the main families of products that account for these sales and monitor their quality changes directly. The same applies to collecting the characteristics of products to be included in regression models. The drawback of this is that that method is a step back toward the position where new varieties of product are not included in the measurement soon enough. Whatever is chosen would be a compromise; at this stage we cannot yet estimate how big a compromise it would be.

References

Dalén, J. 1997. Experiments with Swedish scanner data. In *Proceedings of the third meeting of the International Working Group on Price Indices,* ed. Bert M. Balk, 163–68. Voorburg, the Netherlands: Statistics Netherlands.

de Haan, J., and E. Opperdoes. 1997a. Estimation of the coffee price index using scanner data: The choice of the microindex. *Proceedings of the third meeting of the International Working Group on Price Indices,* ed. Bert M. Balk, 191–202. Voorburg, the Netherlands: Statistics Netherlands.

———. 1997b. Estimation of the coffee price index using scanner data: Simulation of official practices. *Proceedings of the third meeting of the International Working Group on Price Indices,* ed. Bert M. Balk, 183–90. Voorburg, the Netherlands: Statistics Netherlands. Available at [file://www4.statcan.ca/secure/english/ottawagroup/toc3.htm].

Hawkes, W. J. 1997. Reconciliation of consumer price index trends with corresponding trends in average prices for quasi-homogeneous goods using scanner data. *Proceedings of the third meeting of the International Working Group on Price In-*

dices, ed. Bert M. Balk, 145–62. Voorburg: Statistics Netherlands. Available at [file://www4.statcan.ca/secure/english/ottawagroup/toc3.htm].

Lowe, R. 1997. Item selection and quality change in the Canadian CPI. *Proceedings of the third meeting of the International Working Group on Price Indices,* ed. Bert M. Balk, 275–90. Voorburg: Statistics Netherlands. Available at [file://www4.stat-can.ca/secure/english/ottawagroup/toc3.htm].

Moulton, B. R., T. J. Lafleur, and K. E. Moses. 1998. *Research on improved quality adjustment in the CPI: The case of televisions.* Washington, D.C.: U.S. Department of Labor, Bureau of Labor Statistics.

Reinsdorf, M. 1996. *Constructing basic components for the U.S. CPI from scanner data: A test using data on coffee.* Paper presented at NBER Conference on Productivity. 17 July, Cambridge, Massachusetts. Working Paper no. 277. Washington, D.C.: U.S. Bureau of Labor Statistics.

Scobie, H. 1997. Use of scanner data: The impact of new goods. Paper prepared for meeting of the Price Measurement Advisory Committee. 20–21 May, Ottawa, Canada.

Silver, M. 1995. Elementary aggregates, micro-indices, and scanner data: Some issues in the compilation of consumer price indices. *Review of Income and Wealth* 41 (4): 427–38.

Silver, M., and S. Heravi. 1999. The measurement of quality-adjusted price changes. *Proceedings of the fifth meeting of the International Working Group on Price Indices,* ed. Rosmundor Gudnason. Reykjavik, Iceland: Statistics Iceland. Available at [file://www4.statcan.ca/secure/english/ottawagroup/ottawa/list.htm].

Silver, M., C. Ioannides, and M. Haworth. 1997. Hedonic quality adjustments for non-comparable items for consumer price indices. *Proceedings of the third meeting of the International Working Group on Price Indices,* ed. Bert M. Balk, 203–14. Voorburg: Statistics Netherlands.

Appendix A

Characteristics Used in Regression Analysis

(Yes/no except where stated)

Brand	
Size	Screen size
Stereo	0 = mono, 1 = MTS
DBX	
SAP	
Comb filter	1 = 2 line, 2 = 2 line digital, 3 = 3 line digital, 4 = 3D y/c, 5 = advanced digital
Picture in picture	1 = 1 tuner, 2 = 2 tuner, 3 = twin view (side by side)
Surround sound with built-in speakers	1 = basic, 2 = 3D, surround sound, Dolby pro logic, 3 = advanced digital or digital theater sound (DTS)
Internal speaker on/off	

External speaker option	1 = for four-speaker surround sound
Type of speakers	0 = side, 1 = front, 2 = dome, 3 = vertical side firing
Number of speakers	number
Audio output	
Notch filter	
A/V program outputs	number
Audio inputs: rear	number
Audio inputs: front	number
RF inputs	number
S-video rear	number
S-video front	number
Fixed audio output	
Variable audio output	
Remote control	1 = TV only, 2 = basic universal, 3 = home theater universal, 4 = joystick universal
On-screen programming	1 = basic menu, 2 = icon or rolling icon, 3 = bitmat with pulldowns or presets
Channel guard	
Game and video guard	
TV lock	
Sleep timer	1 = limited preset times, 2 = 15- to 20-min. intervals up to maximum, 3 = program for any time
On/off timer	1 = yes, 2 = programming includes channel (e.g., two events), 3 = same as (2) but more times and days
Closed caption	
Auto channel programming	
Channel labeling	
Volume correction	1 = manual, set by channel; 2 = auto for ads and channels
Picture/color correction	
Headphone jack	
Favorite channel	1 = yes, 2 = pop-up screen, 3 = preview with picture-in-picture (PIP), 4 = view and hear with PIP and multiple screens
Xds	
Commercial skip	
Scan velocity modulation	
V-chip	
Component video in	
Wireless headphones	

Appendix B

Table 4B.1 Regression Results: Model Derived from Original Data

Period	Constant	Sam	Hit	Pan/J	RCA/	Size	Size^2	PIP1	PIP2+	Soun1	Soun2	SvidF	SvidR	Adj R^2	N
						Estimates of Parameters									
1	5.188		-0.288	-0.208	-0.315	0.035	6.97E-04	-0.027	0.081	-0.100	0.135	0.195	-0.060		
2	5.322		-0.313	-0.170	-0.313	0.018	1.10E-03	0.031	0.148	-0.135	0.179	0.151	-0.068		
3	5.177		-0.299	-0.199	-0.288	0.031	7.59E-04	-0.036	-0.060	-0.015	0.031	0.239	0.068		
4	5.079	-0.173	-0.386	-0.098	-0.355	0.025	1.02E-03	0.031	0.005	0.008	0.230	0.081	-0.095		
5	4.579	-0.194	-0.096	-0.013	-0.254	0.064	1.60E-04	0.046	-0.044	0.035	0.262	0.067	0.084		
6	5.191	-0.033	-0.226	0.076	-0.287	0.002	1.57E-03	0.025	-0.042	0.073	0.293	-0.060	-0.007		
7	4.968	-0.081	-0.288	0.017	-0.330	0.029	9.40E-04	0.093	-0.011	0.136	0.223	-0.022	0.036		
8	4.736	-0.025	-0.213	0.183	-0.128	0.039	6.23E-04	0.041	0.011	0.173	0.285	-0.010	0.070		
9	5.657	-0.397	-0.272	-0.158	-0.455	-0.001	1.20E-03	0.087	0.037	-0.006	0.087	0.156	0.133		
10	5.881	-0.303	-0.252	-0.106	-0.353	-0.029	1.81E-03	0.033	0.060	0.065	0.018	0.155	0.175		
11	5.411	-0.287	-0.336	-0.138	-0.542	0.009	1.17E-03	0.074	0.089	0.113	0.012	0.077	0.241		
12	5.908	-0.281	-0.304	-0.082	-0.350	-0.034	1.87E-03	0.061	-0.018	0.156	0.117	0.133	0.238		
						t-Statistics									
1	15.60		-2.39	-2.33	-3.47	1.20	1.07	-0.20	0.67	-0.91	1.18	1.72	-0.36	.952	37
2	21.00		-3.22	-2.53	-4.37	0.84	2.31	0.31	1.61	-1.49	2.24	1.86	-0.58	.963	45
3	15.30		-2.31	-2.41	-3.17	1.11	1.25	-0.30	-0.50	-0.13	0.31	2.31	0.48	.928	48
4	17.40	-1.16	-3.13	-1.38	-4.30	1.03	2.04	0.34	0.05	0.09	2.97	0.96	-0.71	.932	67
5	12.02	-1.14	-0.69	-0.13	-1.98	2.01	0.24	0.36	-0.32	0.27	2.34	0.60	0.46	.885	61
6	10.88	-0.49	-1.68	0.15	-2.43	0.75	1.17	0.73	-0.08	0.89	1.80	-0.15	0.15	.910	61
7	11.44	-0.16	-1.38	1.66	-0.98	1.17	0.92	0.35	0.08	1.34	2.59	-0.09	0.44	.887	53
8	19.91	-4.23	-1.91	-2.17	-5.42	-0.04	2.51	0.97	0.38	-0.07	0.94	1.91	1.08	.872	59
9	21.11	-3.23	-1.81	-1.51	-4.03	-1.32	4.13	0.42	0.71	0.84	0.19	2.00	1.51	.887	79
10	20.72	-3.10	-2.40	-2.04	-6.29	0.43	2.81	0.89	1.15	1.38	0.13	0.90	2.08	.910	83

(*continued*)

Table 4B.1 (continued)

Period	Constant	Sam	Hit	Pan/J	RCA/	Size	Size²	PIP1	PIP2+	Soun1	Soun2	SvidF	SvidR	Adj R^2	N
11	22.87	-3.27	-2.20	-1.40	-4.16	-1.62	4.60	0.72	-0.24	2.08	1.08	1.59	2.03	.927	81
12	22.87	-3.27	-2.20	-1.40	-4.16	-1.62	4.60	0.72	-0.24	2.08	1.08	1.59	2.03	.925	78

Period	Size	Size²	PIP1	PIP2+	Soun1	Soun2	SvidF	SvidR
			Weights for Physical Characteristics					
1	24.32	628.52	0.03	0.15	0.43	0.11	0.34	0.07
2	25.10	665.90	0.05	0.22	0.46	0.15	0.38	0.09
3	24.55	638.61	0.06	0.16	0.35	0.12	0.31	0.07
4	24.36	635.97	0.07	0.14	0.36	0.11	0.31	0.03
5	25.03	665.14	0.09	0.15	0.43	0.22	0.38	0.04
6	25.35	682.07	0.07	0.14	0.46	0.21	0.45	0.04
7	24.71	653.69	0.05	0.14	0.45	0.21	0.43	0.06
8	24.84	655.31	0.06	0.10	0.37	0.16	0.37	0.04
9	24.75	650.22	0.08	0.11	0.42	0.16	0.46	0.02
10	24.66	645.99	0.07	0.11	0.39	0.15	0.49	0.05
11	24.70	647.26	0.07	0.13	0.39	0.16	0.53	0.08
12	25.09	666.52	0.09	0.15	0.40	0.17	0.58	0.11

Notes: Sam = Samsung; Hit = Hitachi; Pan/J = Panasonic or JVC; RCA/ = RCA or Sanyo; Size = screen size in inches; PIP1 = picture-in-picture with one tuner; PIP2+ = picture-in-picture with two or more tuners; Soun1 = surround sound coded 1 (see Appendix A); Soun2 = surround sound coded 2 (see Appendix A); SvidF = number of S-type connections at front; SvidR = number of S-type connections at rear.

Table 4B.2   Using Moulton Model

Period	Constant	Sam	Hit	Pan/J	RCA/	Size	Size²	PIP1	PIP2+	SSound	Svideo	Remote	Adj R²	N
						Estimates of Parameters								
1	5.06		−0.18	−0.12	−0.22	0.04	4.35E-04	0.06	0.03	0.00	0.20	0.06		
2	5.36		−0.20	−0.10	−0.22	0.01	1.20E-03	0.07	0.12	−0.04	0.16	0.10		
3	5.16		−0.26	−0.15	−0.23	0.03	7.50E-04	0.00	−0.07	0.04	0.20	0.06		
4	5.17	−0.13	−0.26	−0.03	−0.27	0.01	1.16E-03	0.05	−0.02	0.10	0.14	0.15		
5	4.49	−0.24	0.00	−0.04	−0.30	0.08	−9.0E-05	0.11	0.01	0.06	0.17	−0.08		
6	5.47	−0.13	−0.11	0.06	−0.28	−0.02	1.86E-03	0.06	−0.02	0.06	0.10	0.19		
7	5.02	−0.15	−0.13	0.01	−0.32	0.03	8.45E-04	0.12	−0.02	0.12	0.12	0.08		
8	4.98	−0.13	−0.09	0.10	−0.19	0.02	8.55E-04	0.11	0.13	0.14	0.10	0.06		
9	5.76	−0.40	−0.23	−0.15	−0.43	−0.01	1.33E-03	0.08	0.05	0.02	0.18	0.07		
10	5.96	−0.32	−0.23	−0.11	−0.35	−0.04	1.91E-03	0.03	0.07	0.06	0.17	0.05		
11	5.59	−0.34	−0.32	−0.18	−0.55	−0.01	1.36E-03	0.06	0.12	0.07	0.15	0.08		
12	5.97	−0.32	−0.20	−0.11	−0.36	−0.03	1.88E-03	0.01	0.02	0.11	0.24	−0.05		
						t-Statistics								
1	14.78		−1.75	−1.68	−2.37	1.30	0.66	0.49	0.26	0.02	2.34	0.55	.949	37
2	19.33		−2.19	−1.58	−3.02	0.29	2.32	0.74	1.26	−0.48	2.33	1.08	.958	45
3	14.73		−2.24	−1.95	−2.40	0.93	1.20	0.03	−0.55	0.45	2.33	0.49	.928	48
4	14.69	−0.86	−2.15	−0.44	−3.07	0.31	1.90	0.56	−0.16	1.12	1.83	1.27	.923	67
5	9.94	−1.43	0.00	−0.39	−2.12	1.84	−0.11	0.80	0.05	0.47	1.58	−0.47	.875	61
6	12.84	−0.96	−0.88	0.75	−2.44	−0.61	2.54	0.50	−0.14	0.51	1.10	1.33	.895	61
7	9.68	−0.95	−0.80	0.09	−2.19	0.55	0.93	0.90	−0.10	0.82	0.96	0.50	.870	53
8	10.26	−0.87	−0.57	0.99	−1.36	0.54	1.07	0.93	0.97	1.19	0.93	0.40	.855	59
9	18.85	−4.49	−1.72	−2.23	−5.16	−0.42	2.63	0.90	0.53	0.25	2.52	0.74	.888	79
10	21.21	−3.68	−1.82	−1.92	−4.18	−1.54	4.24	0.41	0.89	0.86	2.73	0.67	.912	83
11	20.53	−3.74	−2.48	−2.79	−6.41	−0.22	3.09	0.73	1.56	0.92	2.29	0.90		
12	22.18	−3.76	−1.70	−2.05	−4.20	−1.55	4.38	0.17	0.31	1.57	3.91	−0.62	.923	78

(continued)

Table 4B.2 (continued)

Period	Size	Size2	PIP1	PIP2+	Ssound	Svideo	Remote
			Weights for Physical Characteristics				
1	24.32	628.52	0.03	0.15	0.43	0.41	0.73
2	25.10	665.90	0.05	0.22	0.46	0.47	0.76
3	24.55	638.61	0.06	0.16	0.35	0.39	0.68
4	24.36	635.97	0.07	0.14	0.36	0.34	0.71
5	25.03	665.14	0.09	0.15	0.41	0.42	0.78
6	25.35	682.07	0.07	0.14	0.43	0.49	0.83
7	24.71	653.69	0.05	0.14	0.41	0.48	0.80
8	24.84	655.31	0.06	0.10	0.33	0.41	0.81
9	24.75	650.22	0.08	0.11	0.39	0.48	0.73
10	24.66	645.99	0.07	0.11	0.38	0.54	0.72
11	24.70	647.26	0.07	0.13	0.39	0.61	0.72
12	25.09	666.52	0.09	0.15	0.40	0.69	0.74

Notes: Ssound = any surround sound; Svideo = any Svideo connection; Remote = universal remote; all other abbreviations, see notes to table 4B.1.

Roundtable Discussion

Dennis Fixler, John S. Greenlees, David Fenwick,
Robin Lowe, and Mick Silver

Dennis Fixler: These papers illustrate the way that scanner data can help statistical agencies improve the quality of their consumer price indexes. In particular, the papers highlight the enormous amount of information that is available and simultaneously illustrate the implementation difficulties that must be overcome with the use of scanner data.

It should be noted that these papers, and the other papers at the conference, focus on the scanner data collected at retail outlets. However, scanner data can also be collected at households—indeed, some of the firms providing the retail scanner data also have household-based databases. Given that the goal of using scanner data is to improve the quality of consumer price indexes, an examination of the household scanner data might prove useful.

The underlying issue addressed in these papers is whether scanner data can replace the price quotes collected by statistical agencies. The answer to this broad question is comprised of answers to a set of subsidiary questions. I shall address some of these questions.

1. *What kind of information is available with scanner data that is unavailable with the collected data or vice versa?* Clearly, the scanner data provide a greater number and scope of transactions for a particular product. For the Consumer Price Index (CPI) ready-to-eat breakfast cereal categories examined in the Richardson paper there are fifty-five collected price quotes, whereas the scanner data provide 80 thousand quotes. The attendant reduction in index variation is an obvious advantage of scanner data. However, the greater volume of data evidently does not include product characteristics. The Richardson paper points out that the U.S. CPI collection of product characteristics is much greater than that provided by scanner data.

In addition, the Lowe and Ruscher paper speaks of the need to look at brochures from manufacturers to obtain product characteristic data for the products in the scanner data set.

2. *How do unit values in the scanner data compare with the collected CPI data?* To some extent the answer depends on the time period being examined. In the case of a week in which a retailer does not change the price, the unit value should equal the collected price if the CPI collection occurs on a day within that week. However, it is not possible to use the weekly scanner data because there are too many missing observations; the Bureau of Labor Statistics (BLS) has decided that a month's worth of data must be used. Even at this frequency there is a need for imputing missing values. The result is that there is a considerable difference between the price measure in the scanner data and the transaction price collected by the CPI field economist. Table 2.3 in the Richardson paper shows a difference between the CPI cereal index and the amalgamated scanner index. Table 3.2 in the Fenwick, Ball, Morgan, and Silver paper presents a qualitatively equivalent finding for the United Kingdom. These findings may derive from the difference between transaction prices and unit values or from differences in weights and in the case of the CPI the inclusion of outlets that do not use scanner equipment. It would be interesting to examine the extent to which the difference in the price measures explains the differences in the indexes.

3. *What is the currency of the set of products? Is the age distribution of products in the CPI older than the average age in scanner data?* The advantage of scanner data is that whereas statistical agencies have to choose among different varieties of a given product to price, it is possible with scanner data to collect prices on all of them. Furthermore, the scanner data provide exact information about the sales attributable to the various varieties. Table 3.1 in the Fenwick, et al. paper shows that there can be a considerable difference in the items that are priced and in the number of price quotes collected for each item. These differences lead to some of the scanner data–based indexes moving quite differently from the corresponding component in the U.K. Retail Price Index (RPI).

4. *Are quality adjustments easier with scanner data?* One of the often-remarked limitations of current quality adjustment practices is that they are too reliant on subjective judgments. Such judgments come into play when a good that is being priced disappears and a replacement is selected. The immediate question is whether the replacement is a comparable (close) or noncomparable substitute. Only in the case of a noncomparable replacement will a quality adjustment be made. At first blush one might think that the Universal Product Code (UPC) based scanner data make such a question relatively easy to answer. Unfortunately that is not the case. Although distinct goods are assigned unique UPC codes, the assignments are made in such a way that the closeness of one number to another does not indicate

that the two goods are close substitutes. In fact, the UPC codes are not useful in making judgments about how products should be grouped.

When a noncomparable replacement is made, the analyst must determine the value of the difference between the new item and the replaced good, and it is here that subjective judgments can enter. However, scanner data do not help reduce this possibility. As mentioned earlier, the Lowe and Ruscher paper discusses how scanner data do not provide a set of recorded product characteristics that is sufficient to meet the needs of the quality adjustment practices. The U.S. CPI program also found that it collects a much more extensive set of product characteristics than is available with scanner data, as stated in the Richardson paper.

It should be noted that for the purposes of quality adjustment the attention does not have to be limited to data collected at cash registers—the typical source of scanner data. Some companies collect product varieties and prices for different products and sell them to marketing firms for use in planning product development, advertising, and so on. The U.S. CPI program is currently using data from such a company in their effort to develop a quality adjustment protocol for audio products.

5. *Can scanner data provide a better way for selecting items to be priced?* The answer seems to be yes; Fenwick et al. illustrate this point in their work comparing the number of quotes collected by top-selling items and the number of quotes used in the RPI. However, there can be too much data. The Lowe and Ruscher paper speaks of the advantages of reducing the scanner data set to those products that sell best; they show that such a decision requires the determination of a significant contribution to sales level as well as the determination of the relevant time period.

In sum, it does not appear that scanner data can generally replace the prices collected by statistical agencies. However, these papers show that the use of scanner data can help to improve the current computation of the CPI. The main advantage seems to be for item selection and maintaining the currency of the set of items being priced.

John S. Greenlees: The three papers by Lowe and Ruscher; Richardson; and Fenwick, Ball, Morgan, and Silver have presented valuable and sometimes fascinating empirical results.

All the papers highlight the potential benefits of scanner data. Those benefits are considerable. Not necessarily in order of importance, they include more up-to-date samples and weights; the use of superlative formulas, made possible by current-period sales information; and much lower index variance.

It is interesting, by the way, to note how this variance contrast is demonstrated in the papers. At the level of the individual products analyzed, such as breakfast cereal and televisions, the official Consumer Price Index (CPI) samples are so small that their sampling variances can explain even wide observed divergences between the CPI and scanner-based indexes. This makes it very difficult to determine whether there is an issue of bias in one or the other index.

Each of the papers also highlights the obstacles standing in the way of the use of scanner data. I believe it was John Astin, at a recent meeting of the Conference of European Statisticians, who said that within a few years the statistical agencies in many countries would be using scanner data to produce price indexes. I tend to agree with John, but there is a real question about how we can or will get there from here.

I will proceed by highlighting three issues, or themes, with illustrations from the three papers. The papers take different approaches and make different empirical uses of scanner data, but these issues arise in each. The emphasis will be on how I view these issues from my perspective in the U.S. CPI program.

1. *Sample representativeness.* The first major issue that has to be addressed by any statistical agency is the representativeness of the scanner data samples. This is the major emphasis of the paper by Fenwick et al.; they present very interesting comparisons of product samples between the U.K. Retail Price Index and their scanner data set. There are noticeable differences between the samples in item mix, average prices, and price changes. Given these differences, the authors recommend using scanner data for sample selection, as a resampling trigger, and for reweighting.

The Canadian authors, Lowe and Ruscher, focus their attention on analysis of quality change rather than on sample distribution, but their results nevertheless suggest that representativeness is an important issue. Lowe and Ruscher observe different rates of price change for 20" and 27" TVs, implying that there could be important effects of using the more up-to-date sample distributions taken from scanner data.

Finally, the Richardson paper also notes differences in coverage. Notably, scanner data cover weekends, unlike the CPI samples, but the scanner samples may not cover the universe of geography or outlet type appropriate to the CPI measurement objective. This is reflected in the differences between Richardson's indexes computed with scanner data only and his "amalgamated" indexes that combine scanner and CPI data. The New York cereal scanner data used thus far exclude mass merchandisers and wholesale clubs, so they could differ systematically from the universe of cereal outlets in terms of item mix or price change.

Mention of amalgamation raises another point with respect to index variance. Amalgamation is employed in the U.S. research effort as a means of eliminating potential bias, but it can come with a potentially significant cost in sampling error. A simple spreadsheet calculation can illustrate this point using sample sizes drawn from the Richardson paper for realism. Assume that the scanner index sample is 1,454 times as large as the regular CPI sample but that the underlying data are otherwise similar. Further assume that in construction of the amalgamated index the scanner index replaces 51/55 of the CPI sample and receives a corresponding share of the weight. In that case the amalgamated index will have a standard error about 27 percent as large as the CPI. Put another way, although the scanner index reduces the standard error by a factor of 38 compared to the CPI, the amalgamated index reduces the standard error by a factor of less than 4.

It seems to me that this issue of representativeness is absolutely crucial. Scanner data offer sizable payoffs as a means of evaluating and updating CPI item samples. It is equally important, however, to make sure that the scanner samples are representative.

In the U.S. context, I would also note that probability selection is inherent in our CPI for items as well as outlets, so some of the methods and solutions proposed by Fenwick may not be *directly* portable. For example, the use of scanner samples for postweighting or for quota sampling would be difficult, or at least complicated, to combine with our standard procedures for selecting and weighting items.

2. *Quality adjustment.* Quality adjustment is a second key issue with respect to scanner data. As noted, this is the focus of the Lowe and Ruscher paper. Scanner data, because of their volume and because of the way we receive and process them, do not lend themselves readily to the methods for comparison of old and new items that are presented in ordinary CPI samples at the time of item replacement (substitution). That is, the need to select and compare replacements when items disappear from shelves is a well-known problem in CPI construction. The problem may be even more severe for scanner data sets, however.

The purely mechanical processing of scanner data can implicitly treat all replacements using the often-criticized "linking" procedure. Tables 4.3 and 4.4 of the Lowe and Ruscher paper are very striking and suggest how the failure to compare the qualities of entering and exiting models can yield undesirable results. This is true even when the index is constructed with scanner data using monthly weights and the superlative Fisher formula.

A parallel issue is mentioned also by Richardson in his sections on imputation and item definition. It seems that we don't have a full solution for the quality adjustment issue yet, in these papers generally or in the U.S. CPI. More discussion of new and disappearing "items" (Universal Product Codes, or UPCs) in U.S. scanner data is in Ralph Bradley's paper presented at this conference (chap. 11 in this volume).

3. *Cost.* For the most part, the three papers do not discuss cost, but one point made in the Canadian paper is the relatively low marginal cost of CPI data collection—around $10,000 annually for televisions. Similarly, the marginal cost of collecting CPI cereal data in New York is probably only $100–200 per month, extremely small compared to the cost of scanner data. In the near term, therefore, the gains from scanner-based indexes likely will be confined to improved accuracy. Any resource savings will be small until

we learn how to employ scanner data to calculate large sections of the CPI. This is especially true if it will be necessary to maintain a direct-collection activity, either for amalgamation or for quality control purposes.

To conclude, I would like to emphasize again the value of the research presented at this conference. The authors have uncovered some issues, like quality adjustment, that may have been underappreciated when statistical agencies first set out to compute scanner-based indexes. I am sure that we will see much more research like this in the near future. Finally, these papers demonstrate that in addition to direct index construction there are many other important potential applications of scanner data, such as for hedonic regression estimation and for sample and weight evaluation.

David Fenwick: It is clear from studies of scanner data that the full potential to use these data in the construction of consumer price indexes has yet to be realized. I believe the reason for this is twofold: first, the lack of responsiveness of scanner data suppliers to the special needs of those who construct price indexes, and second, the limited knowledge of scanner data and a lack of appreciation of their detailed characteristics by price index statisticians. The former is the case not through a lack of dialogue; indeed, price index statisticians are greatly indebted to the main suppliers of scanner data for their cooperation and encouragement in piloting the use of scanner data for index construction. Rather, the lack of responsiveness is due to the new challenges of exploiting, at a micro level, scanner data that traditionally have been used for analysis only at a macro level. Similarly, the knowledge issue arises not through lack of awareness or effort but more through a growing realization that scanner data are a complex data set and that much greater knowledge is required to exploit for statistical purposes any data set that is essentially collected for nonstatistical—in this case, retail management—purposes. Both general points are well illustrated by the extraordinary effort that has been put into the construction of a price index for wheat in New York by the U.S. Bureau of Labor Statistics and for televisions by Statistics Canada. One is tempted to ask whether such efforts would be economic or feasible if applied to the construction of a national index covering all items or whether the vision is one of selective use of scanner data in those circumstances in which its advantages are particularly strong.

Examples of the way in which scanner data do not currently meet user needs include the following:

1. The limited coverage. For example, in the United States scanner data cover no more than 10 percent of transactions. The use of scanner data is uneconomic if price collectors still need to be sent into shops to collect prices for the remaining 90 percent.

2. The recording of average transaction value as opposed to display price. The former can include sale prices for soiled stock and give-aways

such as free videotapes given to customers who purchase a video recorder. It also includes the effect of outlet substitution that occurs when customers transfer their custom to cheaper outlets, something that should be included in a cost-of-living index but not in a "pure" price index such as the U.K.Retail Price Index.

3. The presentation of data, in particular coding. For example, the coding of shop type is not ideal for statistical purposes, and the European Union Classification of Individual Consumption According to Purpose [COICOP] classification for items in the Harmonised Index of Consumer Prices is not used.

There is clearly a challenge here for scanner data providers. For example, would it be possible for individual shop identifiers to be added to enable the monitoring of transaction values across a fixed sample of shops? Could another identifier be added so that shop-soiled or end-line stock can be excluded? Regardless of the answers to these questions, I also believe there is a challenge to price index statisticians, namely, whether some of the conventions used in the index materially affect the index, thus precluding the use of scanner data. For example, are trends in average transaction value materially different from trends in display prices? Have price statisticians collected the latter in the past simply because the transactions values would have been obtainable only at disproportionate cost and were therefore not a practical option?

The complexity of scanner data and the expertise required to manipulate them, the second point I mention in my opening paragraph, raise interesting questions about partnerships between collectors and users and the role of the former in educating the latter. From a user perspective I would certainly welcome more information from individual suppliers on the strengths and weaknesses of scanner data, their representativity, and relevant considerations that need to be taken into account when compiling a price index. For instance, the work reported in the Office of National Statistics (ONS) paper starts from the assumption that scanner data are representative of the consumer sales and can be used as a benchmark for quality control. Whether the latter assumption is a realistic one has yet to be proven, at least to me.

Against this background, what can reasonably be expected from scanner data over the next few years? At this point I should perhaps apologize if my remarks so far have appeared to be pessimistic. This is rather a reflection of the need I feel to throw out a few challenges. I do not take the view that there is no future in the use of scanner data for the construction of consumer price indexes. This would indeed be perverse, given the amount of time and effort we in ONS have devoted to research this area. Scanner data do have a lot of potential and I take the view that there are a number of uses to which such data can be put without delay. First, the research undertaken by ONS in conjunction the Cardiff Business School shows that there can be immediate gains for item and outlet selection by using scanner data to impose a form of quota sampling. Second, the use of hedonic regression, although in some instances still problematic for quality adjustment, can provide guidelines on relevant item characteristics to allow for when making forced replacements in connection with old items that have disappeared from the shelves.

Finally, what about the direct use of scanner data for price collection? Whether the potential to do so is universally fulfilled depends, in part, on whether the challenges I have laid down both to the data collector and to the data provider are met. Only history will be able to judge this, but I am clear in my own mind that there is potential for much greater exploitation of this very rich data source, both for construction of consumer price indexes by individual statistical offices and, equally important, for international price comparison exercises, a subject that I regret no time was available to debate.

Robin Lowe: We have seen in the foregoing papers a range of potential uses of scanner data in our programs and some of the difficulties in using them. I would like to address the issue of how the costs of acquiring the data may affect our programs.

We have acquired data through two sources, directly from retailers and (by purchasing it) from market research companies. Because the costs of capturing the data are hidden in our other activities, we have preferred until recently to deal with retailers directly. We can see the data in a more detailed form, so we can do our own editing. There do seem to be different reporting problems with different suppliers—in accuracy and in dealing with unusual sales and returns—so it is useful to be able to contact the original data source directly. Although the data we have bought appear to be plausible, data from different retailers have been combined before they reach us, and although we are sure they have been complied diligently, we have to accept this on faith. There has also been some loss of detail to preserve commercial confidentiality, which limits our analysis. At the moment, with the limited data we have been collecting for research, the data capture costs have been small, but if we were to collect for a large number of commodities more widely, they would become significant. Because the marginal costs of collecting prices for these products in our current surveys are relatively small we would not anticipate any savings in costs by moving to the use of scanner data; the justification for such a move would have to be in the improved indexes that result.

Cost considerations make it unlikely that we would move to using scanner data for everyday items like food, personal care items, and household supplies. These are relatively simple and cheap to survey, and there are not significant quality change problems; the main weakness in these surveys is a relative lack of diversity in the sample, but it does not appear to be serious compared to other products.

At the detailed level, we have a continuous problem in keeping our sample relevant. I suspect that if we did the kind of analysis shown in the U.K. paper—comparing the distribution of sales by model with the distribution of our sample—we would get similar results. There is inertia built into our sampling method so that the sample will always lag the latest distribution of sales. As we do not have a regular program of resampling, and we have no point-of-purchase survey to assist in item selection, using scanner data to postweight the sample or to guide sample selection is an attractive option. However, purchasing data occasionally for this purpose would be a straightforward extra cost because we would not be saving any of our current production costs. This is why we are presently concentrating on methods to replace completely our current surveys for certain commodities. At the moment, because of the kinds of statistical problems we have outlined here, we cannot justify doing that. However, it would be a pity if we had to ignore such a rich source of data, so I hope we will solve these problems and start working the use of scanner data into some durable goods before long.

Mick Silver: The papers by Richardson and by Fenwick, Ball, Morgan, and Silver are most welcome for their detailed matching of scanner against CPI data. Scanner data have many advantages, including their extensive coverage of transactions. Richardson notes the substantial reduction in standard errors: a factor of $\sqrt{80,000/55} = 38.1$. However, the fifty-five price quotes are outlet display prices against which there will be a large number of transactions. If, for example, only 100 transactions take place on average at that price in each outlet, the factor reduces to $\sqrt{80,000/5,500} = 3.81$.

In CPI practice, quality changes are controlled for by the price collector's comparing prices of "like" with "like." A problem arises when a variety becomes unavailable and only noncomparable replacements are available. Lowe and Ruscher provide an extensive account of the results from different imputation methods. They also compare the results with those from two different hedonic regression specifications that use scanner data as an alternative to CPI practice. The account is rigorous and extensive, so I extend the discussion here in a related area: that is, the use of hedonic regressions and scanner data to supplement current CPI practice to better serve, via an integrated approach, the needs of quality adjustment *and representativity.*

Price collectors collect prices on a variety of goods until they become unavailable. They hold on to the product variety until it dies: when few people purchase it, when it has unusual price changes, and when its quality features are quite different from newer models. The quality adjustment for these unpopular, unrepresentative varieties is thus more difficult. Endemic in the fixed basket and matched model approach is that CPIs become increasingly unrepresentative and quality adjustments more difficult. An integrated approach to quality adjustment and representativity, first, requires that switching between "old" and "new" varieties take place before a variety dies. Scanner data clearly show that models of, for example, television sets of different vintages coexist in the market. Scanner data or other market information may be available to identify when sales of the existing variety are falling and those of a newer one are picking up, so that price collectors can switch earlier. An integrated approach would, second, use scanner data on market sales and the results of hedonic regressions in the period immediately prior to item selection, to guide the initial selection of varieties. The hedonic regressions will help inform price collectors as to which brands and characteristics are salient in explaining price variation, thus ensuring their sample has a mix of such factors. The scanner sales data should help inform price collectors whether these brands and characteristics have a substantial presence in the market. Guidelines or even quota controls based on such information will help ensure representativity from the outset. However, under the integrated approach the selection of varieties is predicated on the hedonic characteristics. Consequently, any subsequent quality adjustment using hedonic regressions should be more satisfactory.

This use of hedonic regressions to supplement CPI practice includes, for example, the prediction of the replacement's prices in the base period by inserting its characteristics into a hedonic regression equation for that period. Silver and Heravi in this volume outline the use of hedonic regressions for predicting "missing" prices. Our concern is that the hedonic equations used for such adjustments relate closely to the samples of items being collected. For example, assume only Sony and Hitachi TVs exist in the market and surround sound is the only other explanatory variable in a hedonic regression. A subsequent quality adjustment from a "Sony" to a "Sony with surround sound" using the hedonic approach is easier because the sample was set up with this in mind. However, if a model with a new characteristic—say, a widescreen TV—is the only available replacement, then either a new regression on current data or an alternative imputation approach, as outlined in Lowe and Ruscher, is required. The integration of item selection and representativity with quality adjustment is not of course a panacea, but a recognition of a real dilemma and the need for a wider strategy.

II

Aggregation across Time

5

High-Frequency Substitution and the Measurement of Price Indexes

Robert C. Feenstra and Matthew D. Shapiro

5.1 Introduction

The availability of scanner data for a wide range of household products raises the possibility of improving the measurement of the Consumer Price Index (CPI). Scanner data have a number of potential advantages over price measurements based on survey sampling. Scanner data include the universe of products sold, whereas sampling techniques capture only a small fraction of the population. Scanner data are available at very high frequency, whereas the cost of survey sampling typically limits data to monthly or lower frequency. Finally, scanner data provide simultaneous information on quantities sold in addition to prices, whereas survey techniques typically collect separate data on price and quantity—typically at different frequencies and for different samples.

Ongoing research on using scanner data for measuring the CPI has attempted to mimic the CPI's monthly sampling frame and therefore abstracted from the high-frequency variation in prices and sales. Reinsdorf (1999), for example, uses either monthly unit values or the prices in the third week of each month to construct monthly price indexes for coffee. The collection of prices on a single day, which are then used to construct monthly indexes, corresponds to current practice at the Bureau of Labor Statistics (BLS). This practice has, of course, been constrained by the fact that prices

Robert C. Feenstra is professor of economics at the University of California, Davis, and a research associate of the National Bureau of Economic Research. Matthew D. Shapiro is professor of economics at the University of Michigan and a research associate of the National Bureau of Economic Research.

The authors thank Roger Betancourt, Erwin Diewert, Walter Oi, Marshall Reinsdorf, Julio Rotemberg, and Jack Triplett for very helpful comments.

are not sampled at frequencies greater than one month, but this constraint is no longer relevant with scanner data.

This paper takes a step toward using the higher-frequency data available from scanner data. It examines how consumer behavior at high-frequency—specifically, weekly purchases of canned tuna—affect the application of index number formulas that have typically been implemented for lower-frequency or time-average data.

Outside of price index research, it has been quite common to use the high-frequency variation in prices and sales available from scanner data. In the marketing literature, it is well recognized that a great deal of substitution occurs across weeks in response to changes in prices and advertising. For example, Van Heerde, Leeflang, and Wittink (2000) have found that store-level data for tuna and toilet tissue contain a dip in sales in the weeks following a promotion, a finding consistent with previous studies at the household level. There is also high substitution between different varieties of tuna, depending on whether they are on sale or not. Given this evidence, it would be highly desirable to construct weekly price indexes in a way that takes this behavior into account.

In order to construct "true" or "exact" price indexes, we need to have a well-specified model of consumer demand, which includes the response to sales and promotions. Betancourt and Gautschi (1992) present a model that distinguishes between *purchases* and *consumption* by individuals; in the presence of inventory behavior, these differ over time. Only *purchases* are observed when one uses data from retail outlets, as we do. Despite this, we show in section 5.2 that by using the Betancourt and Gautschi framework, one can still construct an exact price index that measures the true cost of living (COL) for an individual. This index must compare one planning horizon (e.g., a month or year) to another and cannot be constructed by comparing one week to the next.

In section 5.3, we introduce the data on canned tuna, which are drawn from the ACNielsen academic database. They consist of weekly data over 1993–94 for 316 varieties of tuna over 690 stores. In sections 5.4 and 5.5, we examine how several price indexes perform using these high-frequency price and quantity data. We construct two different types of weekly price indexes. The first, a *fixed-base* index, compares each week in 1993 to the modal price in 1992, using as weights the average 1992 sales at the modal price. We consider different formulas for the price index, including the Laspeyres, Geometric, and Törnqvist. The fixed-base Laspeyres index corresponds to the arithmetic average of price relatives traditionally used in the CPI. The fixed-base Geometric index corresponds to the "geometric mean" formula now used to produce the elementary price indexes for the majority of the CPI.[1]

---

1. The BLS uses unweighted averages for both the arithmetic and geometric means of price relatives. The goods to be averaged are probability-sampled using expenditure weights. Given that we will use the universe of observations, we use base-period expenditure weights rather than probability sampling.

The Törnqvist index uses changing expenditure weights to control for substitution among the goods. We calculate the fixed-base Törnqvist index using the average of the 1992 sales (at the modal price) and the current 1993 weekly sales as weights. Hence, it uses long-term (i.e., base period to present) price relatives. If we take one year as the planning horizon, then this formulation corresponds quite well to our theoretical model of section 5.2.

The second type of index we consider is *chained* formulas, which update the weights continuously and cumulate period-by-period changes in the price indexes to get long-term changes. The chained Törnqvist constructs the week-to-week Törnqvist using average sales in adjacent weeks and then cumulates these results.[2]

The fixed-base Törnqvist does not equal the chained Törnqvist in general, and for our sample of weekly tuna data, we find that the difference between these two indexes is rather large: the chained Törnqvist has a pronounced upward bias for most regions of the United States.[3] The reason for this is that periods of low price (i.e., sales) attract high purchases only when they are accompanied by advertising, and this tends to occur in the final weeks of a sale. Thus, the initial price decline, when the sale starts, does not receive as much weight in the cumulative index as the final price *increase,* when the sale ends. The demand behavior that leads to this upward bias of the chained Törnqvist—with higher purchases at the end of a sale—means that consumers are very likely purchasing goods for inventory accumulation. The only theoretically correct index to use in this type of situation is a fixed-base index, as demonstrated in section 5.3. Thus, our empirical results reinforce our theoretical results in showing the validity of fixed-base indexes when using high-frequency data.

In section 5.6, we directly investigate the extent to which the weekly purchases of tuna are consistent with inventory behavior. We find some statistical support for this hypothesis, more so in the Northern regions of the United States than in the South. We also find that advertising and special displays have a very pronounced impact on shopping patterns. Concluding remarks are given in section 5.7.

5.2   A Representative Consumer Model

The purchases of consumers from a retail outlet, as distinct from their consumption, have been modeled in a "household production" framework by Betancourt and Gautschi (1992). They have in mind any number of reasons why purchases differ from consumption, for example, because the individual must spend time to transform the former to the latter. Here we focus on the intertemporal decisions of a consumer purchasing a storable

2. Since Cobb-Douglas utility, which underlies the Geometric formula, implies constant expenditure shares, we do not compute a chained Geometric index.
3. An upward bias of the chained index with high-frequency data has also been noted by Triplett (1999, and also chapter 6 of this volume).

good, so that purchases and consumption differ due to inventory behavior. With this simplification, we initially summarize the two-stage decision problem presented by Betancourt and Gautschi and then show how even sharper results can be obtained by considering a single-stage decision problem.

Suppose the consumer is making the purchases q_t of a single brand of tuna, over the planning horizon $t = 1, \ldots, T$. Consumption of tuna over the same horizon is denoted by x_t, and the vectors of purchases and consumption are $\mathbf{q} = (q_1, \ldots, q_T)$ and $\mathbf{x} = (x_1, \ldots, x_T)$. Purchases and consumption are related; for example, we might specify that the sums of each over the horizon are equal. This would not allow for the decay of items (e.g., losing them), or any other reason that the consumer might limit purchases even when the item is on sale. We capture the general relationship between purchases and consumption by the constraints $f(\mathbf{q}, \mathbf{x}) < 0$, where f is a vector of quasi-convex functions. Given consumption $\mathbf{x}$, the individual then solves the first-stage problem:

$$(1) \qquad \min_{\mathbf{q} \geq 0} \sum_{t=1}^{T} p_t q_t \text{ subject to } f(\mathbf{q}, \mathbf{x}) \leq 0,$$

where the price of the item in period t is p_t, and the vector of prices is $\mathbf{p} = (p_1, \ldots, p_T)$. It is assumed that consumers know the future prices with perfect foresight. The constraint set represented by $f(\mathbf{q}, \mathbf{x}) < 0$ includes the feasibility constraints (e.g., that time t consumption cannot exceed time t purchases plus storage), the effect of depreciation during storage, and so on.

Denote the solution to equation (1) as the costs $C(\mathbf{p}, \mathbf{x})$. As usual, the derivative of this cost function with respect to prices gives the optimal level of purchases, $\mathbf{q}^* = C_p(\mathbf{p}, \mathbf{x})$. In the second stage, the consumer maximizes utility subject to the constraint that these costs do not exceed the available income I:

$$(2) \qquad \max_{\mathbf{q} \geq 0} U(\mathbf{x}, \mathbf{z}) \text{ subject to } C(\mathbf{p}, \mathbf{x}) \leq I,$$

where $\mathbf{z} = (z_1, \ldots, z_N)$ is a vector of consumption of all other goods, which we take as exogenous.[4] When N is chosen suitably large, this vector can include all goods that complement or substitute for canned tuna in all periods. Let us denote the optimal level of consumption obtained from equation (2) as $\mathbf{x}^* = g(\mathbf{p}, \mathbf{z}, I)$. Then it follows that optimal purchases can be obtained as $\mathbf{q}^* = C_p[\mathbf{p}, g(\mathbf{p}, \mathbf{z}, I)]$. This slightly complex formula for purchases does not show their relation to underlying utility, however, so we now consider a simpler derivation.

Consider combining equations (1) and (2) into a single-stage problem:

$$(3) \qquad \min_{\mathbf{q}, \mathbf{x} \geq 0} \sum_{t=1}^{T} p_t q_t \text{ subject to } f(\mathbf{q}, \mathbf{x}) \leq 0 \text{ and } U(\mathbf{x}, \mathbf{z}) \geq \overline{U},$$

---

4. Note that income I is *net* of the cost of purchasing the goods z.

where $\overline{U}$ is an exogenous level of utility. We can write the solution to equation (3) as an expenditure function, $E(\mathbf{p}, \mathbf{z}, \overline{U})$. Differentiating this function with respect to prices, and using the envelope theorem, we obtain optimal purchases $\mathbf{q}^* = E_p(\mathbf{p}, \mathbf{z}, \overline{U})$. These must equal purchases computed from our two-stage results above, so that $E_p(\mathbf{p}, \mathbf{z}, \overline{U}) = C_p[\mathbf{p}, g(\mathbf{p}, \mathbf{z}, E(\mathbf{p}, \mathbf{z}, \overline{U}))]$. Clearly, the single-stage problem gives a much simpler expression. In particular, the derivatives of the expenditure function are fully observable since they equal *purchases* rather than consumption. We might expect, therefore, that this information will be enough to "work back" and reveal enough properties of the expenditure function itself so as to construct a COL index—that is, that it will be valid to use the price and quantity of purchases to construct a COL index, representing the expenditures needed to achieve utility $\overline{U}$ at various prices. This type of result has been argued by Diewert (2000, section 9), using a household time-allocation model of Becker. We now show that this result holds in our model above, using some well-known propositions from the price index literature.

Let $\tau = 0,1$ denote two planning horizons, each of length T periods. For concreteness, we can say that the periods t denote weeks, and the planning horizons $\tau = 0, 1$ are years. We then consider the problem of a consumer's making weekly purchases in one year as compared to another. This formulation ignores the issue that at the end of the first year, the optimal purchases should depend on the prices in the beginning of the next year; by treating the two planning horizons as distinct, we are supposing that there is no overlap in the information used by the consumer to make decisions in one year versus the next. This is a simplification.

The price vectors $\mathbf{p}^\tau$ differ across the years, as do the exogenous variables $\mathbf{z}^\tau$ and the level of annual utility U^τ. We will specify that the expenditure function in year τ, $E(\mathbf{p}^\tau, \mathbf{z}^\tau, U^\tau)$, takes on a translog functional form over its price arguments:

(4)
$$\ln E = \alpha_0^\tau + \sum_{t=1}^{T} \alpha_t^\tau \ln p_t^\tau + \frac{1}{2} \sum_{s=1}^{T} \sum_{t=1}^{T} \gamma_{st} \ln p_s^\tau \ln p_t^\tau$$

where

(5)
$$\alpha_t^\tau = h_t(\mathbf{z}^\tau, U^\tau), \quad t = 0, 1, \ldots, T.$$

Without loss of generality we can suppose that $\gamma_{st} = \gamma_{ts}$ in equation (4). The functions $h_t(\mathbf{z}^\tau, u^\tau)$ in equation (5) are left unspecified, except for the requirement that the translog function is linearly homogeneous in prices, which is satisfied if

(6)
$$\sum_{t=1}^{T} \alpha_t^\tau = 1 \text{ and } \sum_{t=1}^{T} \gamma_{st} = \sum_{t=1}^{T} \gamma_{ts} = 0.$$

The first condition implies that the functions must sum to unity over $t = 1, \ldots, T$, for $\tau = 0,1$. Additional properties on these functions can be imposed to ensure that the expenditure function is increasing in utility and to obtain any desired properties with respect to the exogenous variables $\mathbf{z}^\tau$.

The formulation in equations (4)–(6) is quite general, and it is well known that the translog function provides a second-order approximation to an arbitrary function around a point (Diewert 1976). The form in which we have written the expenditure function emphasizes that changes in the exogenous variables $\mathbf{z}^\tau$ and U^τ in equation (5) act as *shift parameters* to the function in equation (4). For example, changes in the value of the function $\alpha_0^\tau = h_0(\mathbf{z}^\tau, U^\tau)$ have a neutral impact on the expenditure function in equation (4). More importantly, changes in value of α_t^τ, for $t = 1, \ldots, T$, have a *nonneutral* impact on the expenditure function in equation (4). The importance of this can be seen by differentiating the log of expenditure with respect to the log of prices $\mathbf{p}^\tau$, obtaining the share of annual expenditures spent on tuna in each week:

(7)
$$s_t^\tau \equiv \frac{p_t^\tau q_t^\tau}{\sum_{t=1}^T p_t^\tau q_t^\tau} = \alpha_t^\tau + \sum_{s=1}^T \gamma_{st} \ln p_s^\tau.$$

Thus, changes in annual utility or in the exogenous variables $\mathbf{z}^\tau$, which affect α_t^τ, clearly have an impact on the share of expenditure spent on tuna each period. For example, the consumption of more beef might shift demand away from tuna in some periods. Seasonal effects on demand are incorporated also, because α_t^τ can change exogenously over time.[5] In summary, the expenditure function in equations (4)–(6) encompasses a very wide range of demand behavior, across both products and time within the planning horizon.

We next need to specify how to measure the COL. Normally, the COL index is measured as the ratio of expenditure needed to obtain a fixed level of utility at two different prices. In our application, we have the utility levels U^0 and U^1 in the two years, so which should we choose? We follow Caves, Christensen, and Diewert (1982a,b) in considering a geometric mean of the ratio of expenditure levels needed to obtain each level of utility:

(8)
$$\text{COL} \equiv \left[\frac{E(\mathbf{p}^1, \mathbf{z}^1, U^1)}{E(\mathbf{p}^0, \mathbf{z}^1, U^1)} \frac{E(\mathbf{p}^1, \mathbf{z}^0, U^0)}{E(\mathbf{p}^0, \mathbf{z}^0, U^0)} \right]^{1/2}.$$

The first term on the right of equation (8) gives the ratio of annual expenditures need to obtain utility U^1, holding fixed the exogenous variable $\mathbf{z}^1$ but with prices changing. Of course, the consumer does not actually face the

---

5. Seasonal effects in tuna purchases are found by Chevalier, Kashyap, and Rossi (2000). By constructing the price index over the entire planning horizon, we are comparing one entire year of seasons with the next. This corresponds to the annual index, which compares a moving total of twelve months with twelve base year months, that has been proposed by Diewert (1999) to properly handle seasonal effects.

prices $\mathbf{p}^0$ with exogenous variables $\mathbf{z}^1$, so the expenditure level $E(\mathbf{p}^0, \mathbf{z}^1, U^1)$ is not observed. Similarly, the second term on the right side of equation (8) gives the ratio of annual expenditures needed to obtain utility U^0, holding fixed the exogenous variable $\mathbf{z}^0$ and with prices changing. Again, the expenditure $E(\mathbf{p}^1, \mathbf{z}^0, U^0)$ is not observed.

Despite the fact that equation (8) consists partially of unobserved information, this geometric mean can indeed be measured with data on purchases and prices:

THEOREM *(Caves, Christensen, and Diewert): If the annual expenditure function takes the form in equations (4)–(6), and purchases are optimally chosen so that equation (7) holds, then the COL in equation (8) can be computed as a Törnqvist index:*

$$(9) \qquad \text{COL} = \exp\left[\sum_{t=1}^{T} \frac{1}{2}(s_t^0 + s_t^1)\ln\left(\frac{p_t^1}{p_t^0}\right)\right].$$

We provide a brief proof in the appendix. This result of Caves, Christensen, and Diewert (1982a,b) demonstrates the generality of the Törnqvist index, in that it accurately measures the COL even when the "first-order" parameters α_i^τ of the translog function are changing. In a producer context, such changes capture nonneutral technical change, whereas in our consumer context these changes can capture change in prices of exogenous commodities, seasonal effects, and even the effects of advertising if it shifts α_i^τ.

Although our results so far were obtained for a single variety of tuna, purchased over time, they readily extend to multiple varieties. Thus, suppose that the price vectors $\mathbf{p}^0$ and $\mathbf{p}^1$ in equation (8) include the prices of $i = 1, \ldots, N$ varieties over $t = 1, \ldots, T$ periods. Then the COL is still measured with a Törnqvist index, defined over varieties and time:

$$(10) \qquad \text{COL} = \exp\left[\sum_{t=1}^{T}\sum_{i=1}^{N} \frac{1}{2}(s_{it}^0 + s_{it}^1)\ln\left(\frac{p_{it}^1}{p_{it}^0}\right)\right],$$

where the expenditure shares are $s_{it}^\tau \equiv p_{it}^\tau q_{it}^\tau / \sum_{t=1}^{T}\sum_{i=1}^{N} p_{it}^\tau q_{it}^\tau$. We shall refer to equation (10) as the "true" COL index, and contrast it with various other formulas traditionally used by the BLS. In order to implement any of these formulas, we need to decide what to use as the base period, when $\tau = 0$. We will be interested in focusing on the effects of sales on consumer purchases, so we will choose the base period prices as the *mode* prices for each item in an initial year (i.e., the typical nonsale prices). Correspondingly, the expenditure share in the base period will be constructed using the average quantity at the modal price. It follows that our base period prices and expenditure shares will not differ over weeks, so we rewrite these as p_{i0} and s_{i0}. Then we can also drop the superscript "1" for the current year and rewrite equation (10) simply as

(10′) $$COL = \exp\left[\sum_{t=1}^{T}\sum_{i=1}^{N}\frac{1}{2}(s_{i0} + s_{it})\ln\left(\frac{p_{it}}{p_{i0}}\right)\right].$$

In the next section, we use summary statistics to begin to investigate the frequency of sales and advertising in the data for canned tuna and the extent to which these affect demand. Price indexes are constructed in section 5.4, where we contrast equation (10′) with alternative formulas. Finally, in section 5.5 we directly test for the influence of inventory behavior on demand.

5.3 Tuna Data

The data we shall use are taken from the ACNielsen academic database. They include two years (1992–93) of weekly data, for 316 Universal Product Codes (UPCs) of canned tuna. There are ten market areas, with a total of 690 stores; the smallest market area is the Southwest (54 stores) and the largest is the Northeast (86 stores). The data are drawn from a random sample of the large-scale ACNielsen ScanTrack database. For each store, UPC product, and week, the database includes the value of sales, the quantity sold, and a host of marketing indicators. These indicators can be broken into two groups: advertising indicators (regarding whether there was a sale and what type of ads were used) and display indicators (regarding whether the product appeared in a special location within the store).

An example of the data for two actual products sold in one store, over the first six months of 1993, is shown in table 5.1. We define the "typical" price for a product as the mode price in each year, which was 66¢ for product A and $1.29 for product B in 1993, as indicated at the bottom of table 5.1. Both of these mode prices had fallen from the year before. We further define a "sale" as a week whose (average) price is at least 5 percent less than the annual mode price. The occurrences of sales are indicated in bold in table 5.1. In some cases, a sale coincides with an advertisement for the product,[6] and these cases are shown in italics. Notice that for both products, there are several instances in which the product first goes on sale *without* an advertisement, in which case the quantity does not increase by much, if at all. Following this, an ad occurs at the *end* of the sale, and this leads to a very marked increase in the quantity purchased. This particular pattern of purchases—which has a large increase at the end of the sale—is consistent with inventory behavior. When it occurs simultaneously with an ad, however, we will need to try to distinguish whether the behavior arises due to advance purchase and storage, or due to the information that consumers receive from the ad.

6. There are five different kinds of advertisements indicated in the database, such as featured ads, ads with coupons, etc., but we do not distinguish them. Similarly, there are a number of different kinds of displays, but we do not distinguish these in our analysis.

Table 5.1   **Data for Two Sample Products, January–June 1993**

	Product A			Product B		
Week Ending:	Quantity	Price	Ad	Quantity	Price	Ad
1/09/93	25	0.66	N	15	1.39	N
1/16/93	17	0.66	N	20	1.29	N
1/23/93	*150*	*0.59*	*Y*	14	1.29	N
1/30/93	*109*	*0.59*	*Y*	24	1.29	N
2/06/93	58	0.66	N	31	1.29	N
2/13/93	38	0.66	N	16	1.29	N
2/20/93	**7**	**0.33**	N	8	1.29	N
2/27/93	**5**	**0.33**	N	**15**	**1.19**	N
3/06/93	*213*	*0.49*	*Y*	**21**	**1.19**	N
3/13/93	43	0.66	N	*92*	*1.19*	*Y*
3/20/93	12	0.66	N	19	1.29	N
3/27/93	**5**	**0.33**	N	27	1.29	N
4/03/93	50	0.66	N	23	1.29	N
4/10/93	*231*	*0.49*	*Y*	22	1.29	N
4/17/93	15	0.66	N	15	1.29	N
4/24/93	18	0.66	N	28	1.39	N
5/01/93	**3**	**0.33**	N	12	1.39	N
5/08/93	**18**	**0.33**	N	8	1.39	N
5/15/93	*210*	*0.50*	*Y*	11	1.39	N
5/22/93	6	0.66	N	19	1.39	N
5/29/93	21	0.66	N	**18**	**1.19**	N
6/05/93	15	0.66	N	**43**	**1.19**	N
6/12/93	29	0.66	N	*81*	*1.19*	*Y*
6/19/93	6	0.66	N	13	1.39	N
6/26/93	4	0.66	N	15	1.39	N
Mode 92	20.6	0.79		17.7	1.39	
Mode 93	23.8	0.66		19.9	1.29	

Notes: Data in bold or in italics are on sale, with price more than 5 percent below the yearly mode. Data in italics *also* have an advertisement, as tends to occur in the final week of each sale. Demand is exceptionally high in these final weeks when the product is advertised.

In table 5.2 we report summary statistics of the data for three market areas: the Northeast (with eighty-six stores), Midwest (with fifty-seven stores) and Southwest (with fifty-four stores), for 1992 and 1993. All values reported are averaged across the product and stores in each region. First, we report the modal prices for each year, ranging from $1.30 (in the Midwest, 1992) to $1.73 (in the Northeast, 1993). For each product, we then measure its price each week relative to the mode for the year. Sales are defined as a week in which this "relative price" is less than 0.95.[7] The average value of

7. Out of 24,284 products in different stores in 1992, 86 percent of them had the mode price within one percent of the median price (this calculation gives 84 percent in 1993). Thus, we expect that using the median price rather than the mode price to define sales would lead to similar results.

Table 5.2   **Summary of Data for Three Regions**

	Northeast		Midwest		Southwest	
	1992	1993	1992	1993	1992	1993
Mode price ($)	1.69	1.73	1.30	1.32	1.56	1.59
Relative to mode						
Price	0.988	0.986	1.005	1.000	1.000	0.989
During weeks without sales						
No displays or ads						
Price	1.02	1.01	1.03	1.02	1.03	1.02
Quantity	0.98	0.99	0.98	0.98	0.98	0.99
With display, no ad						
Price	1.02	1.02	1.02	1.03	1.04	1.04
Quantity	1.84	1.72	1.50	1.66	1.69	1.67
With advertisement						
Price	1.01	1.01	1.02	1.04	1.03	1.04
Quantity	2.22	1.46	2.20	2.02	1.68	1.88
During weeks with sales						
No displays or ads						
Price	0.85	0.87	0.88	0.89	0.87	0.87
Quantity	1.94	1.79	1.97	1.40	1.87	2.09
With display, no ad						
Price	0.74	0.76	0.84	0.81	0.82	0.78
Quantity	7.20	7.94	5.93	6.41	6.77	5.64
With advertisement						
Price	0.66	0.68	0.76	0.75	0.73	0.70
Quantity	12.64	11.70	7.01	6.25	8.81	9.14
Frequency of no sale (%)	82.6	80.8	84.7	81.1	80.0	77.5
Frequency of sales (%)	17.4	19.2	15.3	18.9	20.1	22.5
Lasting one week	44.9	45.2	40.1	26.0	34.4	24.9
Lasting two weeks	19.1	15.1	16.5	15.2	22.1	15.6
Lasting three weeks	6.1	9.3	6.1	6.7	7.9	11.0
Lasting four weeks	5.6	9.6	7.0	9.2	7.5	15.6
More than four weeks	24.4	21.0	30.4	43.0	28.2	33.0
During weeks without sales						
Freq. of no displays or ads (%)	98.4	98.7	96.9	97.2	97.6	98.7
Freq. of displays, not ads (%)	1.0	0.8	2.2	2.1	1.3	0.9
Freq. of advertisements (%)	0.6	0.5	0.9	0.7	1.2	0.4
During weeks with sales						
Freq. of no displays or ads (%)	78.2	80.7	81.6	86.9	81.0	85.2
Freq. of displays, not ads (%)	3.4	2.9	7.0	5.3	2.6	1.9
Freq. of advertisements (%)	18.4	16.4	11.3	7.8	16.4	12.9
Freq. of ads during sales (%)						
For sales of one week only	71.7	65.1	56.9	62.1	59.7	67.4
At start (for sales > one week)	26.4	16.1	10.6	5.9	27.2	11.2
At end (for sales > one week)	19.2	14.4	20.4	18.1	24.1	18.1

this relative price and the unit value (constructed as the sales-weighted average of the relative prices) are reported in the second and third rows. Naturally, the unit values are below the average relative prices, indicating that consumers purchase more when prices are low. Following this, we report average prices (relative to the mode) and quantities (relative to the mean quantity at the mode price), during weeks with and without sales. Three cases are distinguished: (i) no display or ad; (ii) a display but no ad; (iii) an advertisement (with or without a special display).

In weeks without sales, having either a display or an advertisement is seen to increase the quantity purchased by 1.5 to 2 times. Surprisingly, about the same impact is obtained from having a sale in the *absence* of both displays and ads. Larger impacts are obtained when either of these features accompanies a sale, and the combination of a sale and advertisement increases the quantity purchased by six to thirteen times. Generally, sales occur in 15–23 percent of the weeks, and of these, somewhere between one-quarter and one-half of the sales last only one week or last more than four weeks. Less than 1 percent of weeks without sales have ads, but 8–18 percent of the weeks with sales also have ads. At the bottom of table 5.2 we report the frequency of such ads during sales: for sales lasting only one week, 57–67 percent have ads; for sales lasting longer, 6–27 percent have an ad in the first week, and 14–24 percent have an ad in the last week. In the Midwest, we are much more likely to see an ad at the end of a sale than at the beginning, but the reverse holds in the Northeast, and there is no consistent pattern in the Southwest.

5.4   Formulas for Price Indexes

The individual tuna varieties (i.e., UPC codes) are denoted by the subscript i within each store. We will be using the modal price in 1992 as a "base period" price p_{i0}, and let q_{i0} denote the mean quantity purchased at that price in 1992. Then the Laspeyres index from the base period to the week t in 1993 is

$$(11) \qquad P_t^L \equiv \frac{\sum_i q_{i0} p_{it}}{\sum_i q_{i0} p_{i0}} = \sum_i w_{i0} \left(\frac{p_{it}}{p_{i0}} \right),$$

where the equality in equation (11) follows by defining the base period expenditure shares, $w_{i0} \equiv p_{i0} q_{i0} / \sum_i p_{i0} q_{i0}$.

We will refer to equation (11) as a fixed-base Laspeyres index. It can be distinguished from the chained Laspeyres, which is constructed by first taking the week-to-week index,

$$(12) \qquad P_{t-1,t}^L \equiv \sum_i w_{i0} \left(\frac{p_{it}}{p_{it-1}} \right),$$

using the same base period weights. The chained Laspeyres is then constructed by simply cumulating these week-to-week indexes:

(13) $$CP_t^L \equiv CP_{t-1}^L \cdot P_{t-1,t}^L, \quad \text{with } CP_0^L \equiv 1.$$

It is well known that the chained Laspeyres has an upward bias, because it does not satisfy the "time reversal" test.[8] For this reason BLS generally uses fixed-base formulas, constructed over the "long-term relatives" p_{it}/p_{i0}. We will be constructing the chained Laspeyres for comparison purposes.[9]

An alternative to using the arithmetic mean in equation (11) is to use a weighted geometric mean of the prices for individual products. This results in the fixed-base Geometric index,

(14) $$P_t^G = \exp\left[\sum_i w_{i0} \ln\left(\frac{p_{it}}{p_{i0}}\right)\right].$$

Note that the fixed-base Geometric formula in equation (14) would be identical to a chained version (constructed by defining a week-to-week geometric index $P_{t-1,t}^G$ and then cumulating). For this reason, we do not construct the chained Geometric.

The Laspeyres and Geometric indexes presume, respectively, zero and unit elasticity of substitution among varieties. To provide a better approximation to changes in the COL under more general assumption, we consider the superlative Törnqvist functional form. The fixed-based Törnqvist index is defined as

(15) $$P_t^T = \exp\left[\sum_i \frac{1}{2}(w_{i0} + w_{it}) \ln\left(\frac{p_{it}}{p_{i0}}\right)\right],$$

where $w_{it} \equiv p_{it}q_{it}/\sum_{i \in I_k} p_{it}q_{it}$ is the expenditure share of product i in week t.[10] It is important to compare this formula to the true COL index in equation (10′), which is also a Törnqvist formula: the only difference is that equation (10′) is aggregated over varieties *and* time, whereas equation (15) is aggregated only over varieties, for a single week. If we average equation (15) over all the weeks in a year, then we would expect the result to be quite close to that calculated from equation (10′).[11] Thus, an average of the Törnqvist in-

---

8. Denoting any price index by $P(\mathbf{p}_{t-1}, \mathbf{p}_t)$, the "time reversal" test is satisfied if $P(\mathbf{p}_{t-1}, \mathbf{p}_t)P(\mathbf{p}_t, \mathbf{p}_{t-1}) = 1$. That is, when prices change from $\mathbf{p}_{t-1}$ to $\mathbf{p}_t$ and then back to $\mathbf{p}_{t-1}$, we want the two-period chained index to be unity. However, this test is not satisfied for the Laspeyres formula in equation (12): it can be shown that $P^L(\mathbf{p}_{t-1}, \mathbf{p}_t)P^L(\mathbf{p}_t, \mathbf{p}_{t-1}) \geq 1$, so the index is upward biased.

9. An alternative formula for the chained Laspeyres would be to use the period $t-1$ weights in equation (12), so it becomes $\sum_i w_{it-1}(\mathbf{p}_{it}/\mathbf{p}_{it-1})$, which would then be cumulated as in equation (13). Results for this index are reported in note 13.

10. Note that the *fixed-base* formula does include current data in the expenditure weight.

11. There is not an exact equality between taking a weighted average of (15) over all weeks in the year, versus computing (10′) directly, because calculating a Törnqvist index in two stages is not the same as calculating it directly in one stage. This is shown by Diewert (1978), who nevertheless argues that "approximate" consistency between one-stage and two-stage Törnqvist indexes will obtain.

dexes in equation (15) appears to be quite close to the true COL index in equation (10').

An alternative formulation of the Törnqvist is to first construct it on a week-to-week basis:

$$(16) \qquad P^T_{t-1,t} = \exp\left[\sum_i \frac{1}{2}(w_{it} + w_{it-1})\ln\left(\frac{p_{it}}{p_{it-1}}\right)\right]$$

The chained Törnqvist is then obtained by cumulating equation (16):

$$(17) \qquad CP^T_t \equiv CP^T_{t-1} \cdot P^T_{t-1,t}, \quad \text{with } CP^T_0 \equiv 1.$$

The chained Törnqvist in equation (17) will generally *not* equal the fixed-base Törnqvist in equation (15), and, therefore, we expect that the average values of the chained Törnqvist over a year might differ substantially from the exact index in equation (10'). Thus, we do not have the same justification for equation (17) as for the fixed-base index in equation (15), which we expect to be close to equation (10').[12]

5.5 Calculation of Price Indexes

We calculated the Laspeyres-ratio, Geometric, and Törnqvist indexes for 1993, using as the base period the mode price in 1992 and the average sales at that price. As an initial example, we show this calculation for the sample data over January–June 1993 in table 5.1, with results in table 5.3. Any of the fixed-base indexes have nearly the same values in the first week of January and last week of June, because the prices for the two products were identical in those weeks (66¢ for product A and $1.29 for product B, respectively). The chained indexes, however, do not satisfy this property. The chained Laspeyres ends up with a value of 1.28, rising some 37 percent from its value in the first week of January. This is entirely due to the fact that the Laspeyres index does not satisfy "time reversal," so that when one product goes on sale and its price falls temporarily, the index does not return to its former value when the sale ends.

More surprisingly, the chained Törnqvist index shows an even greater upward bias, ending with a value of 1.45, which is nearly twice the value of the chained Laspeyres! The chained Törnqvist index does satisfy "time reversal" provided that the weekly expenditures are consistent with the maximization of a static (i.e., weekly) utility function. However, this assumption is violated in the data for these two sample products: in periods when the prices are low, but there are no advertisements, the quantities are not high (see table 5.1). Because the ads occur in the final period of the sales, the

---

12. Alterman, Diewert, and Feenstra (2000, chap. 4, Propositions 1,2) have identified some conditions under which a fixed-base Törnqvist index between two dates, and the chained index between the same dates, will be similar in magnitude. Since these indexes do not coincide in our data, the conditions they identify are not satisfied.

Table 5.3   Price Indexes Constructed over Two Sample Products,
                   January–June 1993

Week Ending	Fixed-Base Laspeyres	Chained Laspeyres	Fixed-Base Geometric	Fixed-Base Törnqvist	Chained Törnqvist
1/09/93	0.934	0.934	0.931	0.927	0.927
1/16/93	0.891	0.894	0.890	0.894	0.885
1/23/93	*0.856*	*0.856*	*0.851*	*0.812*	*0.830*
1/30/93	*0.856*	*0.856*	*0.851*	*0.826*	*0.830*
2/06/93	0.891	0.897	0.890	0.886	0.886
2/13/93	0.891	0.897	0.890	0.883	0.886
2/20/93	**0.724**	**0.718**	**0.675**	**0.736**	**0.688**
2/27/93	**0.681**	**0.684**	**0.643**	**0.720**	**0.641**
3/06/93	*0.764*	*0.821*	*0.756*	*0.709*	*0.769*
3/13/93	*0.848*	*0.930*	*0.848*	*0.850*	*0.889*
3/20/93	0.891	0.977	0.890	0.897	0.947
3/27/93	**0.724**	**0.782**	**0.675**	**0.777**	**0.856**
4/03/93	0.891	1.094	0.890	0.884	1.044
4/10/93	*0.805*	*0.982*	*0.790*	*0.729*	*0.857*
4/17/93	0.891	1.118	0.890	0.893	1.015
4/24/93	0.934	1.170	0.931	0.945	1.071
5/01/93	**0.768**	**0.936**	**0.706**	**0.820**	**0.968**
5/08/93	**0.768**	**0.936**	**0.706**	**0.722**	**0.968**
5/15/93	*0.851*	*1.123*	*0.830*	*0.743*	*1.240*
5/22/93	0.934	1.272	0.931	0.954	1.433
5/29/93	**0.848**	**1.163**	**0.848**	**0.848**	**1.277**
6/05/93	**0.848**	**1.163**	**0.848**	**0.850**	**1.277**
6/12/93	*0.848*	*1.163*	*0.848*	*0.850*	*1.277*
6/19/93	0.934	1.280	0.931	0.949	1.452
6/26/93	0.934	1.280	0.931	0.955	1.452
Averages					
Base 92	0.848	0.997	0.835	0.842	1.015
Base 93	0.951	1.116	0.941	0.946	1.144

Notes: Data are for the two products in table 5.1. Data in bold or in italics had one product on sale, with price more than 5 percent below the yearly mode. Data in italics *also* have an advertisement for that produce, as tends to occur in the final week of each sale. Demand is high in these final weeks when the product is advertised, so the largest increases in the indexes— especially the chained indexes—follow these weeks.

price increases following the sales receive much greater weight than the price decreases at the beginning of each sale. This leads to the dramatic upward bias of the chained Törnqvist. When averaged over all the weeks, the chained Törnqvist gives a value of 1.015 relative to the 1992 modal prices and 1.144 relative to the 1993 model prices; both of these are substantially higher than the fixed-base Törnqvist and the other indexes.

The question arises as to whether this is a general feature of the data on canned tuna. To determine this, we report in table 5.4 the values of prices indexes in 1993 computed for each store and then averaged over the weeks in 1993 and over the ten regions of the United States. The prices indexes are computed using either the modal prices in 1992 as the base or the modal

Table 5.4   Price Indexes Constructed over Complete Sample (average values over 1993)

	True COL Index	Fixed-Base Laspeyres	Chained Laspeyres	Fixed-Base Geometric	Fixed-Base Törnqvist	Chained Törnqvist
East Northeast						
1992 base	0.950	1.009	1.144	1.002	0.967	0.980
1993 base	0.940	0.991	1.127	0.987	0.959	0.986
Northeast						
1992 base	0.937	0.987	1.204	0.976	0.941	1.006
1993 base	0.930	0.972	1.193	0.966	0.932	0.991
Northwest						
1992 base	0.921	0.995	1.184	0.978	0.940	1.075
1993 base	0.954	1.007	1.224	0.996	0.971	1.097
West Northwest						
1992 base	0.977	1.013	1.118	1.002	0.978	0.998
1993 base	0.954	0.985	1.095	0.975	0.956	0.974
Midwest						
1992 base	0.970	1.004	1.145	0.998	0.972	0.956
1993 base	0.958	0.983	1.108	0.978	0.960	0.956
Upper Midwest						
1992 base	0.937	0.958	1.033	0.949	0.951	0.995
1993 base	0.985	0.999	1.081	0.997	1.000	1.037
South Southeast						
1992 base	0.949	0.972	1.036	0.965	0.955	0.993
1993 base	0.988	1.006	1.072	1.001	0.994	1.034
South Southwest						
1992 base	0.970	1.006	1.104	0.997	0.978	0.976
1993 base	0.971	0.994	1.093	0.989	0.980	0.979
Southeast						
1992 base	0.985	0.989	1.017	0.985	0.978	0.972
1993 base	1.000	1.007	1.043	1.005	0.998	0.994
Southwest						
1992 base	0.964	1.029	1.204	1.017	0.983	1.138
1993 base	0.945	0.998	1.192	0.991	0.961	1.123
Total United States						
1992 base	0.956	0.996	1.119	0.987	0.964	1.007
1993 base	0.962	0.994	1.122	0.989	0.971	1.014

prices in 1993. In the first column of table 5.4, we report the true COL index from equation (10′), constructed relative to each base, and averaged over all stores in each region. The values for this index show the drop in the COL (or, conversely, the welfare gains) from having items periodically on sale during 1993. We are interested in comparing this true index to the others, so as to determine their bias.

From table 5.4, we see that the fixed-base Laspeyres is always higher than the true index and that the chained Laspeyres is considerably higher still.[13]

13. When instead we use the alternative formula for the chained Laspeyres, described in note 8, then the upward bias of the index is much worse. This is because the weight w_{t-1} is much higher as the end of the sale than at the beginning, so the price *increase* at the end of the sale is given a much greater weight than the price *decrease* at the beginning. (This problem is amelio-

Both of these are above the chained and fixed-base Törnqvist, respectively. In addition, the chained Törnqvist exceeds its fixed-base counterpart in many regions of the country: the upward bias of the chained Törnqvist is most apparent in the Northwest and Southwest and occurs in seven out of the ten regions (all except the Midwest, South Southwest, and Southeast). On the other hand, the average of the fixed-base Törnqvist over the stores and weeks is quite close to the average of the true COL index over stores in each region. This result was expected, because the COL index itself was a Törnqvist index computed over product varieties and time, as in equation (10′), whereas our fixed-base Törnqvist has been computed over product varieties and then averaged across weeks. Thus, they differ only in their respective weights.

The difficulty with using the true COL index in equation (10′) in practice is that it compares one planning horizon (e.g., a year) to another, whereas the BLS may very well need to report price indexes at higher frequency (i.e., monthly). The fixed-base Törnqvist more than meets this requirement, because it constructed at weekly intervals. Furthermore, as we have shown, the average of the fixed-base Törnqvist is empirically quite close to the COL index. These results, therefore, lend support to fixed-base Törnqvist, even when applied to high-frequency scanner data. Conversely, the upward bias of the chained Törnqvist makes it highly inappropriate to use at high frequency, and it appears that this bias is due to inventory behavior. To confirm this, it would be desirable to have some independent evidence on such behavior, as we explore econometrically in the next section.

5.6 Estimation of Inventory Behavior

To determine how demand for tuna responds to prices, we need to adopt a specific functional form. The static constant elasticity of substitution (CES) specification of the utility function leads to a demand curve for a variety of tuna, as follows:

$$(18) \qquad x_{it} = \left(\frac{p_{it}}{P_t} \right)^{-\rho}$$

where x_{it} is consumption (relative to some base), p_{it} is the price of a variety i, and P_t is the price index for tuna at time t.

We have experimented with developing a full-blown model of inventory behavior for consumers, but it quickly gets very complicated. Simple models have the following implications:

---

rated in the chained Törnqvist, because the weights are averaged over two periods.) For example, this alternative formula for the chained Laspeyres, then averaged over all weeks in 1993 and stores in a region, equals 20.6 for the Northeast, 2.1 for the Midwest, and 3.1 for the Southwest. In one extreme case (a store in the East Northeast), the week-to-week Laspeyres calculated as in note 8 typically exceeds 1.2, so that the chained Laspeyres rises from unity to $1.2^{52} > 10,000$ during the 1993 year!

1. Consumers buy for future consumption when goods are on sale.
2. Consumers will buy more when the next sale is more distant.
3. If there is a cost of storage, consumers will defer purchases for storage until the last period of the sale.
4. Sales are asymmetric: Consumers might want to sell back some of their inventory when prices are unusually high (a negative sale), but they cannot.

To make this concrete, consider the following formulation. Suppose that there is a per-period storage cost of s units of tuna. This would include depreciation or loss in storage, the shadow price of shelf space in the pantry, and interest.[14] Suppose that there is a sale—defined as a substantially lower than normal price, perhaps accompanied by an advertisement. The consumer expects the next sale to be H periods in the future. Then a consumer will purchase now to fulfill future demand. The shadow price of consumption h periods ahead for a variety i put into storage at the time of the sale t is $p_{it}(1 + s)^h$. Assuming that the cost of storage (s) and that the time to the next sale (H) are not too high, the consumer will purchase sufficient quantity for all future needs until the next sale. Hence, quantity sold at the time of the sale will be

$$(19) \qquad q_{it} = \sum_{h=0}^{H} \left(\frac{p_{it}(1 + s)^h}{P_t} \right)^{-\rho} = \left(\frac{p_i}{P_t} \right)^{-\rho} \left(\frac{1 - (1 + s)^{-\rho(H+1)}}{1 - (1 + s)^{-\rho}} \right).$$

If the shadow price $p_{it}(1 + s)^h$ exceeds some future price $p_{i,t+H'}$ prior to the next sale, then the process is truncated at H'. If s is small, then the term in the power of H simplifies to be simply $(H + 1)$ itself, since by L'Hospital's rule:

$$(20) \qquad \lim_{s \to 0} \left(\frac{1 - (1 + s)^{-\rho(H+1)}}{1 - (1 + s)^{-\rho}} \right) = H + 1.$$

In order to estimate equation (19), we take natural logs and make use of equation (20). We include both current prices and leads and lags up to length L, obtaining the estimating equation:

$$(21) \qquad \ln q_{it} = \beta_0 + \sum_{\ell=-L}^{L} \beta_{1\ell} \ln p_{it+\ell} + \sum_{\ell=-L}^{L} \beta_{2\ell} \ln P_{t+\ell} + \beta_3 \ln(1 + H_{\text{own},it})$$

$$+ \beta_4 \ln(1 + H_{\text{any},t}) + \varepsilon_{it}$$

where q_{it} are weekly sales measured relative to the quantity at the mode price; p_{it} is the price in that week relative to its mode for the year; P_t is the fixed-base Törnqvist index for that store; $H_{\text{own},it}$ is the number of weeks to the next sale of this product i; and $H_{\text{any},t}$ is the number of weeks to the next

---

14. There is a problem with units of measurement: depreciation and loss is in units of tuna, whereas interest and storage costs are in units of the numeraire.

sale in that store of any variety of canned tuna. The inclusion of leads and lags for p_{it} and P_t (up to length L) allows for intertemporal substitution in consumption, as potentially distinct from inventory behavior. Note that the variables $\ln(1 + H_{\text{own},it})$ and $\ln(1 + H_{\text{any},t})$ are nonzero *only* when it is the last week of a sale; otherwise, they are not relevant to the inventory problem.

Estimates of equation (21) for each region of the United States, over all weeks in 1993, are reported in table 5.5. In the first set of estimates for each region we report the coefficients of equation (21), along with their standard errors. In the second set of estimates, we extend equation (21) to allow for indicator variables indicating whether that variety of tuna had a special display or was advertised, and also an interaction term between advertising and the price of that variety relative to its mode. There are nearly 50,000 observations or more for each region, which pools over weeks, stores, and varieties of tuna.[15]

Estimation is by ordinary least squares, including fixed effects for each store, as recommended by Betancourt and Malanoski (1999).[16] We do not report the coefficients on the store fixed effects, and we also do not report the coefficients on the lead and lag values of p_{it} and P_t. The inclusion of these leads and lag often increased the (absolute) values of the concurrent price elasticities, and the leads and lags themselves were sometimes significant although not always of positive sign.[17] Most importantly, the inclusion of the leads and lag of prices has little impact on the coefficients on the inventory terms $\ln(1 + H_{\text{own},it})$ and $\ln(1 + H_{\text{any},t})$: the estimates reported in table 5.5 are for a single lead and lag, $L = 1$, but similar results are obtained for $L = 0$ or $L = 2$. Coefficients on $\ln(1 + H_{\text{own},it})$ and $\ln(1 + H_{\text{any},t})$ that are significantly different from zero at the 5 percent level are indicated in bold.

Strong evidence of inventory behavior is found for the Northeast regions, at the top of table 5.5: the East Northeast has a coefficient of 0.35 on $\ln(1 + H_{\text{own},it})$, whereas the Northeast has a coefficient of 0.33 on $\ln(1 + H_{\text{any},t})$. To interpret these, we can measure the total "inventory effect" on demand during the last week of a sale as

(22) $\text{Inventory Effect} = \hat{\beta}_3 \overline{\ln(1 + H_{\text{own},it})} + \hat{\beta}_4 \overline{\ln(1 + H_{\text{own},it})}.$

Note that the sample average value of $\ln(1 + H_{\text{own},it})$ when this variable is positive is 2.4 (so the next sale of each product is 10 weeks away), and the

---

15. In some cases the value of $H_{\text{own},it}$ could not be measured, because the next sale of that variety was after the end of the sample, so these observations were omitted. Less frequently, the value of $H_{\text{any},t}$ could not be measured because the next sale of any variety was after the end of the sample; these values of $H_{\text{any},t}$ were set equal to zero.

16. We considered using an instrumental variables estimator to take into account less than perfect foresight for H, but we obtained inadequate first-stage fits.

17. Betancourt and Gautschi (1992) show generally that for retail purchases (as contrasted with consumption) there is a tendency to obtain complementarity rather than substitution in demand. This might explain the cross-price elasticities that were sometimes significantly negative.

Table 5.5 Regression Results over 1993 Sample (dependent variable: Log of quantity [relative to mode])

Log Relative Price	Log Price Index	Log (Weeks to Own Next Sale)	Log (Weeks to Any Next Sale)	Display	Ad	Log Relative Price $*$ Ad	R^2	N
East Northeast								
−3.82	0.85	**0.34**	**−0.08**				0.23	115,434
(0.04)	(0.03)	**(0.01)**	**(0.04)**					
−2.25	0.84	**0.11**	**−0.11**	1.08	0.66	−1.15	0.29	115,434
(0.04)	(0.03)	**(0.01)**	**(0.04)**	(0.02)	(0.02)	(0.06)		
Northeast								
−3.37	0.76	**0.03**	**0.33**				0.22	120,554
(0.03)	(0.03)	**(0.01)**	**(0.03)**					
−2.31	0.81	−0.01	**0.22**	0.71	0.46	−0.71	0.26	120,554
(0.04)	(0.03)	(0.01)	**(0.03)**	(0.01)	(0.02)	(0.06)		
Northwest								
−2.85	0.66	0.01	**0.14**				0.26	57,168
(0.04)	(0.04)	(0.02)	**(0.04)**					
−2.42	0.67	0.01	0.07	0.58	0.33	−0.20	0.28	57,168
(0.05)	(0.04)	(0.02)	(0.04)	(0.03)	(0.02)	(0.06)		
West Northwest								
−2.57	0.79	0.01	0.05				0.15	79,488
(0.04)	(0.06)	(0.02)	(0.04)					
−2.32	0.85	0.01	0.04	0.57	0.41	0.34	0.18	79,488
(0.05)	(0.06)	(0.02)	(0.04)	(0.01)	(0.02)	(0.07)		
Midwest								
−2.26	0.56	−0.01	**0.10**				0.09	48,537
(0.06)	(0.06)	(0.03)	**(0.05)**					
−1.74	0.57	−0.01	**0.02**	0.70	0.40	−0.10	0.13	48,537
(0.07)	(0.06)	(0.03)	**(0.05)**	(0.02)	(0.03)	(0.10)		
Upper Midwest								
−2.21	0.38	**0.15**	0.19				0.08	46,906
(0.06)	(0.06)	**(0.03)**	(0.05)					
−1.34	0.48	−0.01	**0.12**	0.50	0.59	−1.03	0.12	46,906
(0.07)	(0.06)	(0.03)	**(0.05)**	(0.02)	(0.03)	(0.11)		
South Southeast								
−2.04	0.40	−0.02	**0.18**				0.10	59,340
(0.06)	(0.06)	(0.03)	**(0.05)**					
−1.68	0.44	0.01	−0.003	0.51	0.20	−0.71	0.11	59,340
(0.07)	(0.06)	(0.03)	(0.05)	(0.02)	(0.02)	(0.09)		
Southeast								
−2.06	0.27	**0.09**	**−0.09**				0.06	66,689
(0.07)	(0.09)	**(0.02)**	**(0.04)**					
−1.43	0.29	**0.07**	**−0.12**	0.46	0.46	−0.27	0.08	66,689
(0.08)	(0.09)	**(0.02)**	**(0.04)**	(0.02)	(0.02)	(0.11)		
Southwest								
−3.26	0.62	−0.03	**0.15**				0.24	57,121
(0.05)	(0.05)	(0.02)	**(0.05)**					
−2.48	0.70	**−0.05**	0.06	0.52	0.51	−0.62	0.26	57,121
(0.05)	(0.05)	**(0.02)**	(0.05)	(0.03)	(0.03)	(0.09)		

Table 5.5   (continued)

Log Relative Price	Log Price Index	Log (Weeks to Own Next Sale)	Log (Weeks to Any Next Sale)	Display	Ad	Log Relative Price * Ad	R^2	N
Total United States								
−3.08	0.73	**0.13**	0.00				0.17	728,122
(0.01)	(0.01)	**(0.006)**	(0.01)					
−2.19	0.78	**0.08**	**−0.06**	0.67	0.45	−0.78	0.20	728,122
(0.02)	(0.01)	**(0.006)**	**(0.01)**	(0.006)	(0.007)	(0.02)		

Notes: Coefficients on weeks to next sale that are significantly different from zero at the 5 percent level are indicated in bold. Standard errors are shown in parentheses. Regressions also included fixed effects by store, and lag and lead prices.

average value of $\ln(1 + H_{any,t})$ when this variable is positive is 1.2 (so the next sale of any product is 2.3 weeks away).

Using the coefficients in table 5.5, for the East Northeast the "inventory effect" is $\exp(0.35 * 2.4 - 0.08 * 1.2) = 2.2$, indicating that the quantity demanded during the last week of a sale is more than twice as high as average. For the Northeast region, the "inventory effect" equals $\exp(0.03 * 2.4 + 0.22 * 1.2) = 1.4$, so demand is 40 percent higher at the end of sale. Other regions that show particularly strong inventory behavior are the Upper Midwest, for both inventory variables, and most regions of the South, for the variable reflecting sales in other varieties.

However, when we add the indicator variables for displays and advertising, along with the interaction between advertising and price, then the magnitude of inventory behavior is substantially reduced in all regions. In the cases in which there is still some evidence of inventory behavior—such at the East Northeast and Southeast—a positive coefficient on one of the inventory variables is offset by a negative coefficient on the other. Indeed, when advertising is included then the only region that retains significant evidence of inventory behavior (without an offsetting negative effect) is the Northeast. As an example, in one store in that region a certain tuna product fell in price from $1.59 to 88¢ in one week and sales went from about 100 cans average to 20,000 in that week! This is the largest demand response in our data set and almost surely indicates that the purchases were for inventory. At the same time, we cannot rule out that some portion of the increased demand was in response to the advertised price of 88¢. Generally, when we take into account displays and advertising in table 5.5, the extent of inventory behavior is reduced markedly.[18]

Although these inventory regressions provide some direct evidence of in-

18. We have also re-estimated (15) while *excluding* all one-week sales. This allows us to determine what inventory behavior is associated with multi-week sales. Generally, the coefficients we obtain on $\ln(1 + H_{own,it})$ and $\ln(1 + H_{any,t})$ are lower than those reported in Table 5, which combines the one-week and multi-week sales.

ventory behavior, we also wish to know whether this can explain the upward bias in the chained Törnqvist index. To this end, in figure 5.1 we graph the "inventory effect" against the index bias, measured as the difference between the chained Törnqvist and the true COL index (where both of these are averaged over all weeks in 1993, and using the modal price in 1993 as the base). The "inventory effect" in equation (22) is measured using the coefficients on the first row for each region in table 5.5; that is, ignoring the advertising and display variables. The means for $\ln(1 + H_{own,it})$ and $\ln(1 + H_{any,t})$ in equation (22) are now computed over the entire sample (i.e., for both positive and zero observations). This will capture not only the average value of these variables when positive but also the number of times that sales occur. We graph the average "inventory effects" against the index bias for the ten regions in figure 5.1 and for the 580 individual stores over which equation (22) could be estimated in figure 5.2.

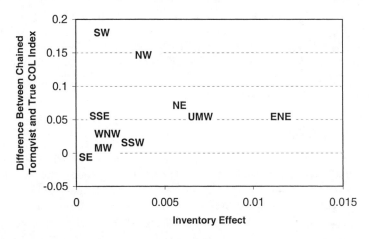

Fig. 5.1   Index bias and inventory effect: Regions

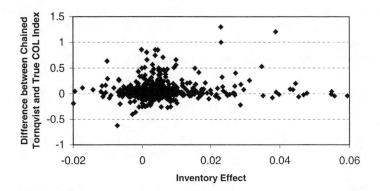

Fig. 5.2   Index bias and inventory effect: Stores

In figure 5.1, there is only a weak positive relation between the "inventory effect" and the index bias; the correlation between these variables is 0.05. The Southwest and Northwest have the highest bias of the chained Törnqvist index, and these both have coefficients of about 0.15 on $\ln(1 + H_{any,t})$ in table 5.5: although these effects are significant, they are not the largest coefficients that we find on inventory behavior. Conversely, the East Northeast region is shown as having the highest "inventory effect" in figure 5.1, and although it has a nonnegligible bias of the chained Törnqvist index in table 5.4, this bias is not the largest across regions.

However, when we look across individual stores in figure 5.2, the evidence for a positive relationship between inventory behavior and index bias is more apparent. The correlation between these two variables is 0.12, which is significantly different from zero at the 1 percent level (with $N = 580$). Thus, there are some stores that display both strong inventory behavior and a pronounced upward bias of the chained Törnqvist index. The three stores shown in figure 5.2 whose index bias exceeds unity are all in the Northeast and East Northeast regions; and in addition, twenty out of the top twenty-five stores with highest "inventory effects" are also in these two regions. Generally, the shopping patterns of the Northeast regions show marked inventory behavior and an upward bias of the chained Törnqvist, supporting the idea that such behavior causes the upward bias.

5.7   Conclusions

The data on tuna show substantial high-frequency variation in price and substantial response of consumer demand to this variation in price, suggesting inventory behavior. A true COL index in this context, as derived in section 5.2, must compare all prices over one planning horizon to all prices in another, (e.g., it must compare one year to the next). This differs from the conventional approach taken at the BLS, which is to compute price indexes in each month. Averaging over a month, as the BLS does, is a step toward aligning price measurement with the consumption rather than the shopping period. However, the month might not be the correct planning horizon. Moreover, even if it were, the results of section 5.2 show that the arithmetic average of prices is not the correct summary statistic to input into a COL index.

We find that the fixed-base Törnqvist, computed weekly and then averaged over a year, can adequately measure the true COL index (which is itself a Törnqvist formula). That is, the fixed-base Törnqvist captures the reduction in the COL that arises when consumers economize by substituting toward goods whose price is low. Conversely, the chained Törnqvist gives too much weight to price increases that follow the end of sales, and it is upward biased.

The upward bias of the chained Törnqvist can be explained by purchases for storage rather than consumption. During sales, some of the increase in demand corresponds to purchases for storage, as supported by our regression results. In particular, we find that purchases are increasing in time to the next sale. This finding is consistent with a forward-looking consumer engaging in storage. This evidence of forward-looking behavior is somewhat undermined by accounting for advertisements. Nevertheless, we find a link between inventory behavior—especially in the Northeast—and the upward bias of the chained Törnqvist. It follows that the chained approach is to be avoided when using high-frequency scanner data, and a fixed-base Törnqvist (or the true COL index) should be used instead.

Appendix
Proof of Theorem

Taking the log of equation (8), we obtain

$$\ln(\text{COL}) = \frac{1}{2}[\ln E(p^1, z^1, U^1) - \ln E(p^0, z^1, U^1) + \ln E(p^1, z^0, U^0)$$

$$- \ln E(p^0, z^0, U^0)]$$

$$= \frac{1}{2}\left[\sum_{t=1}^{T}(\alpha_t^1 + \alpha_t^0)\ln\left(\frac{p_t^1}{p_t^0}\right) + \sum_{s=1}^{T}\sum_{t=1}^{T}\gamma_{st}\ln p_s^1 \ln p_t^1 - \sum_{s=1}^{T}\sum_{t=1}^{T}\gamma_{st}\ln p_s^0 \ln p_t^0\right]$$

$$= \frac{1}{2}\left[\sum_{t=1}^{T}(\alpha_t^1 + \alpha_t^0)\ln\left(\frac{p_t^1}{p_t^0}\right) + \sum_{s=1}^{T}\sum_{t=1}^{T}\gamma_{st}(\ln p_s^1 + \ln p_t^0)(\ln p_t^1 - \ln p_t^0)\right]$$

$$= \frac{1}{2}\left[\sum_{t=1}^{T}(s_t^1 + s_t^0)\ln\left(\frac{p_t^1}{p_t^0}\right)\right]$$

where the second line follows when we use the translog formula in equations (4) and (5), the third line follows from simple algebra, and the final line follows from the share formula in equation (7).

References

Alterman, William F., W. Erwin Diewert, and Robert C. Feenstra. 2000. *International price indexes and seasonal commodities.* Washington, D.C.: U.S. Department of Labor, Bureau of Labor Statistics.

Betancourt, Roger R., and David Gautschi. 1992. The demand for retail products and the household production model: New views on complementarity and substitution. *Journal of Economic Behavior and Organization* 17:257–75.

Betancourt, Roger R., and Margaret Malanoski. 1999. An estimable model of supermarket behavior: Price, distribution services, and some effects of competition. *Empirica* 26:55–73.

Caves, Douglas W., Laurits R. Christensen, and W. Erwin Diewert. 1982a. The economic theory of index numbers and the measurement of input, output, and productivity. *Econometrica* 50 (11): 1393–414.

———. 1982b. Multilateral comparisons of output, input, and productivity using superlative index numbers. *Economic Journal* 92 (March): 73–86.

Chevalier, Judith A., Anil K. Kashyap, and Peter E. Rossi. 2000. Why don't prices rise during periods of peak demand? Evidence from scanner data. NBER Working Paper no. 7981. Cambridge, Mass.: National Bureau of Economic Research.

Diewert, W. Erwin. 1976. Exact and superlative index numbers. *Journal of Econometrics* 4:115–45.

———. 1978. Superlative index numbers and consistency in aggregation. *Econometrica* 46 (4): 883–900.

———. 1999. Index number approaches to seasonal adjustment. *Macroeconomic Dynamics* 3:48–68.

———. 2000. The Consumer Price Index and index number purpose. Discussion Paper no. 00-02. University of British Columbia, Department of Economics. Available at [http://web.arts.ubc.ca/econ/diewert/hmpgdie.htm], forthcoming in *Journal of Economic and Social Measurement.* Reinsdorf, Marshall B. 1999. Using scanner data to construct CPI basic component indexes. *Journal of Business and Economic Statistics* 17 (2): 152–60.

Triplett, Jack. 1998. Elementary indexes for a consumer price index, In *Proceedings of the fourth meeting of the International Working Group on Price Indices,* ed. Walter Lane, 176–97. Washington, D.C.: U.S.Department of Labor, Bureau of Labor Statistics.

van Heerde, Harald J., Peter S. H. Leeflang, and Dick R. Wittink. 2000. The estimation of pre- and post-promotion dips with store-level scanner data. *Journal of Marketing Research* 37 (3): 383–95.

Comment   Marshall B. Reinsdorf

Overview

This paper provides a thoughtful treatment of one of the challenges that arise in using scanner data to produce price indexes. Scanner data sets are generally highly disaggregated, with weekly observations on a large number of varieties of each item in a large number of stores. Products at this level of disaggregation are often so similar that they are highly substitutable for one another, but the item that these authors consider, canned tuna fish, has the distinction of exhibiting high substitution across time. In particular, temporary price reductions have a large effect on the timing of purchases of tuna because it has a low cost of storage.

Marshall B. Reinsdorf is an economist at the U.S. Bureau of Economic Analysis.

The views expressed in this comment are those of the author and should not be attributed to the Bureau of Economic Analysis.

Fortunately, Feenstra and Shapiro recognize that the static model under-lying standard cost-of-living (COL) index theory is unsuitable when many purchases are for storage rather than current consumption. They therefore consider a model in which purchases are for inventory, and consumption decisions are subject to an inventory constraint. The authors refer to this as a "household production" model, but it differs from the usual household production function setup because additional inputs, such as the con-sumer's time, are not required to produce the consumption good. The two-stage model can therefore be simplified into a more useful one-stage model, in which purchases from different weeks are effectively substitutes in a util-ity function that covers the entire planning period.

To estimate a COL index for this model, the authors specify an interval of one year for the planning period and a translog functional form for the expenditure function. A COL index for the year can then be calculated as a Törnqvist index that in effect treats purchases from different weeks as in-puts into the household production process for the year.

Cost-of-living indexes for ten regions of the United States and the United States as a whole that compare all of 1993 to the modal prices of 1992 and 1993 average about 0.96, compared with fixed-base Laspeyres indexes, which aver-age around 1. Although this indicates substantial substitution, the tendency of tuna fish to experience large swings in prices and quantities led me to an-ticipate an even larger difference. Furthermore, the authors find that a fixed-base Törnqvist index, which would be more practical for statistical agencies to calculate, is on average less than 1 percent higher than the "true" COL in-dex. Since the fixed-base Törnqvist index ignores substitution between weeks, this result suggests that allowing only for substitution between varieties and stores captures about three-quarters of the gains from substitution.

Substitution between weeks has another effect besides causing upward bias in the annual average of direct Törnqvist indexes: it makes weeks non-separable from each other. If current quantities have stable relationships to current prices, a chained Törnqvist index can be expected to agree closely with a direct Törnqvist index. For a storable commodity like tuna, on the other hand, sensitivity of current quantities to past (or expected future) prices is likely to cause chained indexes to "drift." Indeed, the empirical re-sults in the paper show substantial upward drift for chained Törnqvist in-dexes and very large drift for chained Laspeyres indexes.

Variability in expenditure shares due to advertisements and in-store dis-plays also contributes to the drift that is observed for the chained indexes. Advertisements and in-store displays cause large increases in quantities that consumers buy, especially when they occur in conjunction with a sale. Moreover, in some regions they tend to occur in the last week of sales that last longer than one week, causing the chained Törnqvist index to give more weight to the reversion of the sale price to the regular price than to the re-duction to the price.

The final major section of the paper seeks empirical evidence on inventory behavior by examining the effect of the length of time until the next sale on the quantity sold. In many of the regions that the authors examine, consumers do seem to stock up more during a sale when the next sale is further away. Furthermore, a positive relationship exists between the inventory effect at the store level (which partly reflects the frequency of sales in the store) and the upward drift of chained Törnqvist indexes. Nevertheless, the addition of variables for the presence of advertisements and displays leaves only the Northeast with a significant effect of time-until-the-next-sale.

Discussion

Accounting for substitution between weeks by means of a Törnqvist index covering the entire planning interval is a clever and useful solution to the problem of how to treat storable commodities in a COL index. Research on more detailed models of inventory behavior would, however, be valuable. The authors obtain their eminently practical solution from a simplified model. In particular, some consumption in a planning interval is likely to be from inventories carried over from previous planning intervals, and some purchases are likely to be intended for carry-over to the next planning interval. Ignoring this allows the authors to force an essentially dynamic problem back into the framework of static COL index theory.

In addition, the empirical finding that advertising and in-store displays have large effects on purchases suggests that imperfect information plays an important role in this retail market. A model of inventory management behavior under imperfect information would therefore capture an important feature of this market that is beyond the scope of the model in the present paper.

Imperfect information may also be the basis for an alternative theory of how to aggregate prices from adjacent weeks for a single product. The simple technique of aggregating prices from adjacent weeks by means of unit values is justified if consumers regard purchases in those weeks as perfect substitutes for each other. However, perfect substitutability implies that all sales occur at the lowest price, making aggregation unnecessary. To be logistically consistent, therefore, an approach that treats purchases at varying prices in adjacent weeks as perfect substitutes requires a model in which consumers do not acquire complete information.

Turning to the findings in this paper on high frequency chaining, the conclusion that high-frequency chaining must be avoided for products like tuna fish is worth emphasizing. Nonseparabilities and consumers' responses to promotional information are likely to make the data behave as if preferences were unstable from week to week. Chained indexes can be expected to perform poorly under this circumstance. Indeed, in a footnote the authors report that chained Laspeyres indexes grow by factors of 2 to 20, even though the fixed-base Laspeyres indexes are around 1. Even the chained

Törnqvist index, a formula that usually performs well, exhibits upward drift of three or four percent at the national level and up to 15 percent in the regions.

Finally, I have three minor quibbles with this paper. First, the index formula that the authors call "chained Laspeyres"—equation (12)—is mislabeled because it holds constant relative expenditures rather than quantities. To keep quantities constant in a chained index, expenditure weights must be adjusted in proportion to the price change that has occurred since the base period. The Bureau of Labor Statistics, for example, updates each quote's expenditure weight in this way. The authors omit this updating step in their calculations of the chained Laspeyres index because it renders the comparison with the fixed-base Laspeyres index uninteresting: Unless the chained index includes observations absent from the fixed-base index, no discrepancy can exist between the indexes. The authors' "alternative chained Laspeyres index" has a formula that is consistent with its label, however, and it should be compared to the authors' chained Törnqvist index.

Second, I would have liked to see a discussion of the importance and treatment of missing values. Scanner data sets omit products that no one buys in a week, and in very disaggregated data, exit and entry of products is common. Consequently, missing values are often a problem in store-level scanner data. If products that exit or enter command sizable portions of total expenditures when they are present, a researcher may choose to use chained indexes because they can include prices for products that exit or enter. I presume that the chained indexes in this paper differ from their fixed-base counterparts only because of their functional form and not because they include prices for products that exit or enter. Statistics on product exit and entry are also important because they can indicate the presence of a potential source of bias. In particular, Feenstra (1994) shows that coverage of a diminished portion of consumers' expenditures on an item biases a price index upward compared to a true COL index.

Third, I think the regression analysis should include checks for some covariances of the error terms. In particular, store effects or manufacturers' advertising campaigns may cause positive cross-sectional covariances in errors. In addition, unusually high sales in the recent past may tend to depress current sales. Evidence of this would be an additional indication of inventory behavior.

Reference

Feenstra, Robert C. 1994. New product varieties and the measurement of international prices. *American Economic Review* 84 (March): 157–77.

6

Using Scanner Data in Consumer Price Indexes
Some Neglected Conceptual Considerations

Jack E. Triplett

6.1 Introduction

New data present not only opportunities, but also new problems. They often require new statistical techniques to explore them and new analytical tools to understand what they are telling us. This chapter explores some problems that arise in using scanner data in the consumer price index (CPI).

6.2 Cost-of-Living Index Theory and Scanner Data

The theory of the cost-of-living index (COLI) provides a way to reason about practical decision making in the CPI (Triplett 2001). However, for scanner data we need first to consider some aspects of COLI theory that are normally left unstated or are presently undeveloped.

One area in which COLI theory is undeveloped is the distinction between consumption periodicity and acquisition periodicity. Standard COLI theory rests on a theory of consumption behavior and not on a theory of acquisition behavior. Accordingly, the standard COLI relates solely to consumption periodicity. One usually assumes in the standard COLI theory that consumption periodicity and acquisition periodicity are the same, that is, that price changes have exactly the same effect on consumption and on purchases. In the long run, this may be acceptable, but empirically consumption periodicity and acquisition periodicity are not equal.

Durable goods provide a well-known example. Acquisition periodicity is very long for durable goods, although consumption periodicity for the services of durable goods may be quite short. High-frequency data (time use or

Jack Triplett is a visiting fellow in the economic studies program at the Brookings Institution.

actual consumption studies) can capture consumption of services from durables by individual households, but it is well known that high-frequency expenditure data are unlikely to capture acquisitions.

The distinction between consumption periodicity and acquisition periodicity arises in storable nondurable goods as well. Walter Oi, in discussion at the conference, gave Tabasco sauce as an example of a commodity that is purchased infrequently. For nondurable goods, the wedge between acquisition periodicity and consumption periodicity involves storage costs, as well as search and information costs. Household search and shopping behaviors matter, and not just *consumption* behavior.

Because the standard COLI theory implicitly assumes that consumption periodicity and acquisition periodicity are the same, it ignores search, information, and shopping costs. However, those costs are part of the total cost of consumption. The shorter the period during which prices and quantities are observed—high-frequency data—the smaller the linkage between purchases and consumption.

The economic behavior recorded in high-frequency price and quantity data will be dominated by acquisition periodicity, *which a theory of consumption behavior in response to changes in relative prices does not address.* Toilet paper and soft drinks are frequently on sale. Consumers know they are frequently on sale and can plan their acquisitions accordingly. Surely sale prices for storable commodities affect the timing—and location—of acquisitions far more than they influence the quantity of consumption. To confront the household behavior recorded in high-frequency data requires a theory that adequately describes search, storage, shopping, and other household activities that drive a wedge between acquisition periodicity and consumption periodicity.

Applying the standard COLI paradigm to CPI component indexes for storable nondurables like toilet paper and soft drinks, or for many of the other commodities available in scanner data—and indeed for the CPI price index for bananas—may be instructive and enlightening. I have in mind contributions such as that by Diewert (1995). However, because the standard theory is a theory of consumption, not of acquisition, it is incomplete.[1] Applying the theory to data on acquisitions may yield misleading conclusions. In this, I agree with Pollak (1998) that we need a more elaborate COLI theory for guidance, perhaps building on the neglected work of Baye (1985).

Readers who are familiar with the international literature on CPIs may have noted already that many statistical agencies have recognized pragmatically the problems posed by consumption periodicity and acquisition periodicity and have sought to define them away by saying that their CPIs are

---

1. Moreover, adding to the standard consumption model tastes over different retail outlets, in parallel with tastes for different commodities, does not make the problem more tractable. See section 6.4.

indexes not of consumption prices but of acquisition prices. In the same breath, they often also state that their CPIs are not COLIs. They do not, however, escape the problems described in the next two sections.

6.3   Cost-of-Living Index Theory and Aggregation Questions

Cost-of-living index theory is, partly, a theory of commodity aggregation. The theory tells us how to aggregate commodities (i.e., don't use fixed consumption weights to form intertemporal comparisons).

Other aggregations exist in price and quantity data that are assumed away in the theory's simplifying assumptions. One aggregates, inevitably, over time. High-frequency price collections may show price variations that are invisible in lower-frequency collections. Some studies have endorsed unit values to reduce high-frequency price variation, but this implicitly assumes that the high-frequency variation represents simply noise in the data and is not meaningful in the context of a COLI. That is debatable. We need to develop a theory that confronts the data, not truncate the data to fit the theory.

Conventional price and quantity data are also aggregations over people. Cost-of-living index theory rests on a theory of an individual consumer's behavior.

Scanner data are, in general, less aggregated. However, scanner data are typically disaggregated by store, not by individual consumers, so they are still aggregations over individuals. Any aggregation over consumers poses knotty questions (Pollak 1989), which scanner data do not circumvent. Indeed, scanner data on prices charged and quantities sold *by stores* may exacerbate the consumer aggregation problem, as suggested below.

Statistical agencies now collect the prices *offered by retailers,* and they aggregate them, or their price relatives, across stores. Cost-of-living index theory requires the *prices paid by consumers* and assumes that one price prevails (perhaps because search theory was not a prominent part of economics before Stigler [1961]). Accordingly, there is no store aggregation problem. The average price across retail outlets—strictly speaking, the average price change—is the price that is deemed relevant to the theory.

It is well established, however, that prices vary across stores at any instant of time, even for precisely defined commodities, and the variation does not seem fully accounted for by differences in retailing services. Variability in store prices presents both opportunities and problems. In some of the existing empirical work using scanner data, researchers have reaggregated the store data into unit values, partly to reduce the size of the database (for example, Reinsdorf's [1999] study of coffee prices). However, if households shift their purchases across stores in response to sale prices, special promotions, and so forth, one does not want to aggregate across stores; household search and shopping behavior is a serious topic for investigation. In any

Table 6.1   Numerical Example of Semihigh Frequency Data

| | Observation Period (Month) | | | |
	1	2	3	4
A. The Data				
Actual price observations ($\cent$)				
Store 1	49	99	33	49
Store 2	99	49	99	99
Hypothetical quantities				
Store 1	300	100	350	300
Store 2	50	250	50	50
Hypothetical revenue ($; price × quantity)				
Store 1	147.00	99.00	115.50	147.00
Store 2	49.50	122.50	49.50	49.50
Hypothetical revenue shares (w_i)				
Store 1	0.75	0.45	0.70	0.75
Store 2	0.25	0.55	0.30	0.25
B. Weighted CPI Basic Component Calculations				
Chained Laspeyres	1.000	1.636	2.071	2.774
Chained Paasche	1.000	0.747	0.332	0.440
Chained Fisher	1.000	1.105	0.830	1.104
Chained geometric mean	1.000	1.418	1.280	1.688
Chained unit value	1.000	1.127	0.735	1.000

Source: Actual price observations from extract from unpublished Canadian CPI data from Schultz (1994)

case, unit values across stores are not the prices actually faced by households and do not represent the per-period price in the COLI, even if the unit values are grouped by type of retail outlet.[2]

These several aggregations—across time, across people, and across retail outlets—cause analytical difficulties that the standard theory does not address. High-frequency collection of price and quantity data from retailers, feasible with scanner information, may result in statistics that describe the behavior of no consumer. The following section demonstrates.

6.4 Some Interpretive Examples with High-Frequency Price and Quantity Data

The price information in table 6.1 is an extract of data from Schultz (1994), which were used in Triplett (1998). They are actual monthly prices in one city for a particular size and brand of soft drink, collected for the Canadian CPI. Since they are monthly, they are only medium-frequency, not high-frequency, data. Scanner data in principle yield even higher fre-

2. For a contrary position, see Balk (1999) and Diewert (1995).

quency price and quantity data, which might magnify substantially the effects in this example.

The quantity data in table 6.1 are hypothetical, put together only on the hypothesis that periodic sales of soft drinks "work," in the sense that they result in larger quantities of soft drinks sold in any store that is offering a temporary sale price than otherwise. Although the quantity data are hypothetical, I interpret the paper by Feenstra and Shapiro (chap. 5 in this volume) as showing that my quantity data are indeed realistic as a description of what actual scanner data will show. The hypothetical quantity data in table 6.1 are designed to encompass consumer preferences for store 1, which always sells more for any particular price than store 2, along the lines suggested by Diewert (1995).

Note that in period 4 the prices return to exactly their values in period 1. For heuristic reasons, the hypothetical quantity data also return to their exact period 1 values when the prices return to their initial values.

Section B of table 6.1 shows that chained versions of standard price index formulas behave perversely, in the sense that none recovers the initial period's level when the prices and quantities return (in period 4) to their initial period levels. As this example suggests, chaining is part of the "problem" with high-frequency data, as is the common presumption that the price indexes should necessarily be time reversible. These topics are not explored here.

Applying the conventional theory of consumption to the quantity changes for store 1 shown in table 6.1 implies that this store's customers gorge themselves on soft drinks during the sale month and go thirsty in non-sale months, and similarly for store 2's customers. However, the quantity changes in these data are unlikely to represent changes in *consumption* of soft drinks in response to sale prices. Instead, at least two things are driving the data: Households switch stores in response to sales, and they stock up on soft drinks when they are on sale, consuming the sale-price soft drinks in other periods when they do not buy them.

Thus, I speculate that some households exhibit shopping and inventory behavior, although others may not. In these circumstances, what are households' acquisition prices for soft drinks? Their consumption prices? Consumption prices are relevant for the COLI, the former for CPIs of those countries that refer to their indexes as non–cost-of-living acquisition price indexes (such as Australia and the European Union's Harmonized Indexes, or HICP). Both acquisition prices and consumption prices depend on household shopping and inventory behaviors. Section B of table 6.2 lists some possibilities.

One type of household doesn't shop and doesn't inventory: call it the habit purchaser. The prices this household faces (and the period-to-period price relatives) are given by lines (1a) and (1b).

For the habit purchaser household, and only for the habit purchaser, the price changes Statistics Canada (or the Bureau of Labor Statistics [BLS])

Table 6.2   Price Changes Faced by Different Consumer Types

	Observation Period (Month)			
	1	2	3	4
A. The Data				
Actual price observations, soft drink, Canadian city				
Store 1	49¢	99¢	33¢	49¢
Store 2	99¢	49¢	99¢	99¢
B. Prices and Price Index Relatives for Different Consumer Types				
1a. The habit purchaser (store 1)	49¢	2.02 (99/49)	0.33 (33/99)	1.48 (49/33)
1b. The habit purchaser (store 2)	99¢	0.49 (49/99)	2.02 (99/49)	1.00 (99/99)
2a. The shopper	49¢	1.00 (49/49)	0.67 (33/49)	1.48 (49/33)
2b. The shopper, with assumed 15¢ search costs	49¢	1.31 (64/49)	0.98 (48/49)	1.94 (64/33)
3. The inventory/shopper (store 1)	49¢	(no purchase)	0.67 (33/49)	(no purchase)

Source: Actual price observations from extract from unpublished data from Schultz (1994).

collects from the stores match exactly both acquisition prices and consumption prices. The habit-purchaser households may vary their consumption of soft drinks in response to price changes (they drink more fruit juice in months when soft drinks are not on sale), matching the behavior that is embodied in COLI theory, but they do nothing more. If store quantities actually measure purchases (and therefore consumption) by habit-purchaser households, then conventional price index calculations on store price and quantity data measure lower-level COLIs, along the lines developed in Diewert (1995). I have no data, but I presume that these households do not account for much of the variation in store quantities that typical scanner data show result from soft drink sales.

Next is the "shopper" household. This household switches stores, only buying at the sale price, and it consumes all that it purchases in each period. If the household ignores switching and shopping costs, then the acquisition prices it faces are given by line (2a). As with the habit purchaser, the acquisition price for the shopper is also the household's consumption price. This household never pays the nonsale price, so only the sales prices are relevant. This household's price index is an index of the minimum prices prevailing in each period. In the second period, for example, when prices in store 1 and store 2 just reverse themselves, this shopper household faces no change in price.[3]

---

3. Note that the unit value index in table 6.1 does not represent the acquisition price index for this shopper, essentially because this shopper has no preferences between the two stores, and I have built store preferences into the quantity data used in table 6.1. This is an artifact of the hypothetical data, but not an unreasonable one. Unit values across stores do not in general correspond to the prices that are relevant for COLI theory, nor do they represent acquisitions prices.

However, the price changes collected by Statistics Canada or the BLS do not measure changes in the prices that the shopper household faces, nor do store-level scanner data. As table 6.1 shows, weighted Laspeyres, Fisher, geometric mean, and unit value indexes of store prices all rise between periods 1 and 2, but the shopper household's price index is unchanged (as is, coincidentally, the ratio of unweighted average prices [RA]). For the third period, the shopper household's price index falls by one-third, which is more than any of the weighted indexes in table 6.1 (ignoring the Paasche formula), because for the shopper household the price rise in store 2 is irrelevant.

A variant is the shopper household that considers switching and shopping costs before changing stores. Acquisition costs for this household are given by line (2b). In this case, none of the store prices or their changes measure acquisition costs directly, nor do they measure consumption prices. For example, in the second period, this household experiences a price increase because obtaining the 49¢ soft drink from store 2 entailed a 15¢ switching cost. Collecting scanner data by retail outlet does not provide the relevant measure of price change faced by this household, nor does the collection methodology of the BLS or Statistics Canada. Shopping and switching costs are outside the domain of the CPI.

The final case is the inventory shopper. This shopper knows that soft drinks are frequently on sale and follows the rule: Stock up when they are on sale and consume from inventory when they are not. Although I have no data, I presume that this household type accounts for a large amount of the quantity variation when soft drinks go on sale. Line (3) shows acquisition prices faced by the inventory shopper. A similar inventory shopper exists for store 2, but the data are omitted from the table.

The inventory shopper makes no purchases during months 2 and 4, in which soft drinks are not on sale in this household's favorite store. The household's acquisition price is not defined in those months.

What about this household's consumption price? One could elaborate on inventory, storage, and capital costs and calculate a user cost equation for consumption of soft drinks from inventory. Or one could assert that the household should charge itself the opportunity cost (the nonsale price?) for consumption out of inventory. However, the point is that it is not obvious how the inventory purchaser should be treated in scanner data for a COLI or in scanner data for a non–cost-of-living "acquisitions" price index.

The COLI, or the CPI, should be viewed as the average of the indexes across households. If these five household types were equally distributed across the population, one could average the price relatives from table 6.2, making some rule to allow for the inventory shoppers' consumption. I have not presented that "democratic" CPI in table 6.2. Such a democratic CPI, calculated on actual data, is unlikely to resemble any of the commonly used index number formulas in table 6.1.

What is to be concluded from these examples? First, explorations of scanner data, and indeed of methods for calculating component indexes of the CPI, have mostly employed standard index number formulas from the existing price index literature, applied to store data. Theoretical analyses of price index basic components also follow the standard index number commodity substitution paradigm. This is understandable, since it is a relatively new topic. This empirical and theoretical work assumes, implicitly, that scanner data are measuring the commodity substitution behavior that is incorporated in the usual COLI theory.

The examples in table 6.2 suggest that conventional index number approaches only capture acquisition and consumption prices for the household that doesn't shop and doesn't inventory (the habit purchaser). No index number formula, *applied to period-to-period store prices,* can solve the problem that such prices are not the period-to-period transactions prices for the shopper households or for households that inventory storable commodities. Moreover, it is hard to see how an index number formula, no matter how ingenious, can deal with the zeros in the inventory purchasers' transactions for periods when the soft drink is not on sale. An index number formula cannot solve the problem that we are collecting, in the CPI and in scanner data, prices from sellers. To understand household behavior with respect to periodic sale prices, we need prices paid by buyers.

Second, price indexes calculated using scanner data seem always to differ from the CPI. It is not clear why. However, it is also not clear that we have been addressing the problems posed by high-frequency data with the right theoretical tools, and the right tools are always necessary to an understanding of any economic phenomenon. Much more work needs to be done on the theoretical and practical frameworks for using scanner data in the CPI.

6.5   Classifications

In their chapter in this volume, Hawkes and Piotrowski point out that ACNielsen and BLS classifications diverge. Their table 1.4 points out that to ACNielsen ice cream is a frozen food, whereas to BLS it is a dairy product. From a conceptual point of view, what commodity classification is appropriate for the CPI?

Classifications are not just definitions. Classifications group data. It is not generally recognized that economic theory exists that can guide thinking about how economic classifications should be devised. A review of the theory of economic classifications—including classifications for the CPI— is Triplett (1990).

The conceptual approach to economic classifications, as developed in my 1990 paper, has transformed thinking about industry classification systems (see "Preface" to U.S. Office of Management and Budget 1998; Kort 2001).

However, I have to say that the use of economic theory has had no impact whatever on classification systems used for consumer price indexes, despite the fact that the CPI is the economic statistic that is probably most closely aligned with a concept from economic theory, by which I mean the theory of the COLI.

One reason, no doubt, is the inevitable lag between ideas and implementations (although the implementation lag was short for industrial classifications). Additionally, empirical implementation of an economic concept for CPI classification is harder than for industry classification systems, partly because there is more than one way to proceed and partly because the empirical knowledge is scant for implementation of the theoretical principle.

For CPI classifications, economic theory tells us that we should look for separable "branches" of the utility or the consumer cost function. The basic references are Pollak's (1989) paper on the subindex of the COLI and Blackorby and Russell (1978). This classification concept is very hard to implement empirically, partly because separability is a mathematical condition that is not very intuitive. Triplett (1990) also discusses chains of close substitutes.[4]

In any case, the appropriate COLI classification concept is drawn from consumer demand theory. In the language used in Triplett (1990), CPI classifications are "product" grouping systems. Theoretical classifications for a COLI do not depend on supply conditions; production conditions determine industry classification systems, not CPI classifications.

Nielsen and BLS seem both to have used some sort of supply-side reasoning about classifications. Nielsen classifies ice cream according to the way it is handled, transported, and stored; for the CPI, what is important is how the product is used, not how it is produced. The BLS classifies ice cream according to one of its major ingredients, dairy products (even, I gather, when the ice cream contains no dairy product!). Classification by materials inappropriately applies a supply-side criterion; a demand-side criterion is appropriate for CPI classifications. Thus, the Neilsen and the BLS classifications are both inappropriate for a COLI.

I do not have any empirical data on which to rely, but my intuition suggests that ice cream belongs in a "dessert" branch. Of course, practicality considerations ought to enter as well. For efficient collection of prices, one ought to be able to find products that are grouped together in CPI food index components in the same part of the grocery store, which might force modification of the theoretical principle (perhaps in Neilsen's direction).

As a final point on this important question of classifications for CPIs, users of the CPI should know of a proposal that is currently being consid-

4. Hicksian aggregation also figures in the theoretical literature, and (implictly) in deflation practices for national accounts.

ered by the international group that is writing an international manual for consumer price indexes, because it seems a wholly inappropriate way to proceed. They propose to use the classification of consumer expenditures that was published in the 1993 system of national accounts (SNA93; Inter-Secretariat Working Group on National Accounts 1993). This classification system is called COICOP (Classification of Individual Consumption by Purpose). COICOP was plucked out of the air by a small group of people who did not even consult with consumer price index experts to see if their classification system reflected CPI practice or accumulated wisdom. Constructing a classification with neither theory nor practice is the very worst methodology.

The right way to proceed is, surely, to use economic theory and empirical analysis to determine the appropriate classifications in the CPI. Because these will also be classifications for grouping consumption expenditures, the same classifications should be used in the consumption portions of national accounts.

As developed in SNA93, COICOP was not very detailed (it did not distinguish anything more detailed than "food," for example), so little harm was done in practice. More recently, however, COICOP was elaborated with more detail, but without any use of economic principles for classifications, so far as I know. The classification system for international CPIs should not be developed in the same way the COICOP system was developed for national accounts. Economic principles should be employed for CPI classifications.

It is also worth noting that classifications of consumption in the U.S. CPI and in the U.S. national accounts do not agree. This is a source of serious problems for economists who wish to analyze consumer behavior, and it should receive attention from both agencies. However, a new and improved classification should also incorporate economic theory, to the extent possible with available knowledge. The United States should not just adopt COICOP, without evidence that it meets the conceptual principles of economic classifications for consumption and the CPI.

Classifications should get more attention from economists. The classifications that are chosen by some public or private statistical agency provide the indivisible units of economic analysis.

6.6   Conclusions

Using scanner data in the CPI is a more complicated matter than it may appear. For one thing, our theoretical tools (mainly the existing corpus of COLI theory) are not fully adequate for the economic behaviors—search, shopping, and inventory behaviors—that are incorporated into high-frequency data. For another, aggregations over time, over households, and over stores—present in existing CPI data—are not lessened with scanner data, and their effects may be more severe with high-frequency data than with the lower-frequency data with which we have long worked. Additionally, the quantity changes that are apparent in high-frequency store data are likely to reflect inventory and shopping behavior in response to sale prices more than changes in consumption. As a result, acquisitions and consumption periodicities differ, and the period-to-period store prices (the output of scanner data) diverge from households' acquisitions and consumption prices in ways that depend on their inventory and shopping behaviors, as shown by the lines in table 6.2.

Classifications also matter. We need better classifications in the CPI in order to have CPI component indexes that are suitable for economic analysis. Collecting and processing scanner data may reduce collection costs, but scanner data will greatly increase index editing and analysis costs. As these latter problems loom larger, there is more need to think hard about the grouping of the data, because inappropriate groupings may increase the editing and processing costs unduly, as well as create groupings that are inappropriate for economic analysis.

References

Balk, Bert. 1999. On the use of unit value indices as consumer price subindices. In *Proceedings of the fourth meeting of the International Working Group on Price Indices,* ed. Walter Lane, 112–20. Washington, D.C.: U.S. Department of Labor.

Baye, Michael R. 1985. Price dispersion and functional price indices. *Econometrica* 53 (1): 213–23.

Blackorby, Charles, and Robert R. Russell. 1978. Indices and subindices of the cost-of-living and the standard of living. *International Economic Review* 19 (1) : 229–40.

Diewert, W. Erwin. 1995. Axiomatic and economic approaches to elementary price indexes. NBER Working Paper no. 5104. Cambridge, Mass.: National Bureau of Economic Research, May.

Inter-Secretariat Working Group on National Accounts. 1993. *System of national accounts 1993.* Brussels/Luxembourg, New York, Paris, Washington, D.C.: Commission of the European Communities, International Monetary Fund, Organisation for Economic Cooperation and Development, United Nations, and World Bank. Available from United Nations Publications.

Kort, John R. 2001. The North American industry classification system in BEA's economic accounts. *Survey of Current Business* 81 (5): 7–13.

Pollak, Robert A. 1989. *The theory of the Cost of Living Index.* New York: Oxford University Press.

———. 1998. The Consumer Price Index: A research agenda and three proposals. *Journal of Economic Perspectives* 12 (1): 69–78.

Reinsdorf, Marshall. 1999. Using scanner data to construct CPI basic component indexes. *Journal of Business and Economic Statistics* 17 (2): 152–60.

Schultz, Bohdan J. 1994. Choice of price index formula at the microaggregation level: The Canadian empirical evidence. In *International Conference on Price In-*

dices, Papers and Final Report: First Meeting of the International Working Group on Price Indices. Ottawa, Canada: Statistics Canada, November, 93–127. Available at http://www4.statcan/ca/secure/english/ottawagroup/toc1.htm

Stigler, George J. 1961. The economics of information. *The Journal of Political Economy* 69 (3): 213–25.

Triplett, Jack E. 1990. The theory of industrial and occupational classifications and related phenomena. *Bureau of the Census 1990 Annual Research Conference Proceedings.* Washington, D.C.: U.S. Department of Commerce, August, 9–25.

———. 1998. Elementary indexes for a consumer price index. In *Proceedings of the fourth meeting of the International Working Group on Price Indices,* ed. Walter Lane, 176–97. Washington, D.C.: Department of Labor.

———. 2001. Should the Cost-of-Living Index provide the conceptual framework for a consumer price index? *The Economic Journal* 111 (June): 312–35.

U.S. Office of Management and Budget. 1998. *North American industry classification system: United States, 1997.* Washington, D.C.: Executive Office of the President, Office of Management and Budget.

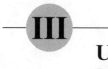

III

Using Price Data to Study
Market Structure

What Can the Price Gap between Branded and Private-Label Products Tell Us about Markups?

Robert Barsky, Mark Bergen, Shantanu Dutta,
and Daniel Levy

7.1 Introduction

The magnitude of marginal costs and markups over marginal cost are empirical questions of considerable general interest in economics. Microeconomists are interested in markups because they bear on such questions as the relevance of alternative models of imperfect competition, the welfare consequences of market power, and the benefits of new product introduction. In recent macroeconomic research as well, markups play a central role (see, e.g., Hall 1986, 1988). Although macroeconomic discourse most often focuses on the cyclicality rather than the level of markups, the degree of cyclicality is often limited by the absolute size of the markup (Rotemberg and Saloner 1986).

Robert Barsky is professor of economics at the University of Michigan and a research associate of the National Bureau of Economic Research. Mark Bergen is associate professor of marketing and logistics management at the Carlson School of Management, University of Minnesota. Shantanu Dutta is associate professor of marketing at the University of Southern California. Daniel Levy is associate professor of economics at Bar-Ilan University and Emory University.

The authors are grateful to the paper's discussant, Julio Rotemberg, for his insightful comments, which played a fundamental role in the restructuring and strengthening of the argument. Susanto Basu and Matthew Shapiro provided numerous valuable suggestions and essential advice. The authors would also like to thank Ning Liu for her outstanding research assistance under a very tight schedule, Owen Beelders, Ernie Berndt, Hashem Dezhbakhsh, Jim Hess, Kai-uwe Kuhn, Jim Levinsohn, Peter Rossi, and Steve Salant for many helpful discussions, Robert Feenstra for comments, Steve Hoch for providing us with his survey data on national brand/private-label quality differences, and Jong Kim for his help with computations. They thank the participants of the NBER-CRIW conference, the 2001 Midwest Marketing Camp, and seminar participants at the University of Michigan and the University of Minnesota. Finally, the authors thank both the Kilts Center for Marketing, Graduate School of Business, University of Chicago, and Dominick's for providing us with the data. The usual disclaimers apply.

The estimation of markups is difficult because marginal cost is not directly observable. There are essentially two ways in which inference about markups and marginal cost is approached in the econometric literature. One approach is via the cost function, which is either inferred directly from engineering data or estimated from cross-sectional or time series market data. The other is to estimate consumer demand functions and compute the markup based on estimated demand elasticities, in combination with a model of market equilibrium.

This paper takes a quite different approach to measurement of marginal costs and markup ratios. We argue that the price of a "private-label" equivalent or near-equivalent product provides valuable information about the marginal cost of the nationally branded product. In particular, because the private-label version would not sell at a price less than its marginal cost, the ratio of the price of the branded product to that of the private-label one serves as a lower bound on the markup ratio. The high relative price of national brands is thus indicative of substantial markups over marginal cost.

Underlying our approach is the notion that private-label products are more or less physically identical to nationally branded products, but the branded product commands a higher market price due to characteristics not related to marginal costs of either manufacturing or retail handling. Many of the promotional expenses that vertically differentiate the branded product from its private-label counterpart appear largely as sunk, or at least fixed, costs. Essentially the same is true of expenditure on research and development. To the extent that marginal costs of private-label goods diverge from those of the branded versions, we present evidence that suggests that manufacturing costs for the private labels are if anything higher on the margin than those for the corresponding brands.

Informed by the above considerations and in possession of data on both retail prices and the retailer's margins over wholesale, we take the wholesale price of the private-label product as an upper bound for the marginal manufacturing cost of its branded counterpart. The presumption that retailers' margins must at least cover marginal handling costs allows inference about the contribution of the retail channel to full marginal cost. We present several ratios that, under reasonable assumptions, bound the true marginal cost of manufacturing and selling the branded product from above as well as below.

We emphasize the lower-bound measure of the true markup. To briefly summarize our main results, markups computed in this manner are consistent with, but on the high side of, those found in previous studies, for the few products for which such studies exist. Markups for national brands sold in supermarkets are large. Lower bounds on markup ratios measured this way range from 3.44 for toothbrushes and 2.23 for soft drinks to about 1.15–1.20 for canned tuna and frozen entrees, with the majority of categories falling in the range 1.40–2.10.

The ratio of brand to private-label retail prices has on occasion been used in the literature as a measure of the markup. The texts by Scherer (1980) and Carlton and Perloff (1994) present some informally collected data of this sort. A recent paper by Nevo (1997) computes the retail price ratio as a check on structural estimation of markups on breakfast cereals and finds a markup ratio of about 1.30, very much in accord with the estimates from the structural approach. Our data indicate, in accord with results from previous studies, that retailers earn higher margins on private labels than on national brands. This suggests that the retailer's margin on the branded variety is most likely the best indicator of actual marginal handling cost at the retail level. If this is the case, ratios of retail prices understate national brand markups over the "true" marginal cost of providing goods to the consumer.

We apply our approach to products in the grocery industry, in which there are many private-label or "store brand" products in a wide variety of categories.[1] We compute our markup ratios using scanner data from the Chicago area supermarket chain Dominick's Finer Foods. The Dominick's data include both retail prices and the retailer's "margin" (and hence, implicitly, wholesale prices) for both national brands and the store brand. This allows us to decompose ratios of the retail prices into a manufacturer's markup and a retailer's markup on wholesale prices—an exercise that will prove to be important in our efforts to bound the "true" markup from above and below. The product descriptions are sufficiently detailed that we are able to identify many pairs of national brand and private-label offerings that are comparable in both quality and package size.

The paper is structured as follows. In the next section we present our conceptual framework. In subsection 7.2.1, we present a simple vertical differentiation model emphasizing the role of sunk advertising costs, consumer heterogeneity, and competition for "niche" in carving out a role for private labels and determining the size of the equilibrium markup. In section 7.2.2, we highlight the role of retail stores and point out how advertising and competition between retailers leads to an inverse relation between wholesale and retail margins. In section 7.2.3, the most critical part of the analytical section, we develop a set of inequalities involving the various price ratios and show how we can bound the true markup both above and below.

In section 7.3 we answer some possible objections about the comparability of national brand and private-label products. Evidence suggests that to the extent that there are differences, they point in the direction that prices

1. Fitzell (1998) recounts that private labels go back to the late nineteenth century and gradually developed from the sale of bulk commodity staples. From the beginning, the main focus of private-label manufacturers has been on packaged goods—packaged teas, sugar, flour, spices, and so on. Early in the twentieth century, private-label manufacturers expanded their activity by offering canned vegetables and fruits, frozen foods, and bakery and dairy products as well. Later, the private-label industry expanded to include paper products, detergents, deli items, soft drinks, health and beauty care products, and more recently even "untouchable" products such as cosmetics, baby food, natural health products, and gourmet delicacies.

of private-label products *overestimate* the marginal cost of national brands—suggesting that our assumptions are in fact conservative. In section 7.4 we introduce the data and discuss measurement methods. In section 7.5 we present five different but related markup ratios, covering both the wholesale and retail levels, for over 230 comparable nationally branded-private-label product pairs representing nineteen categories. Computing the lower bound on markup ratios developed in section 7.2, we document that the markups for national brands are large. In section 7.6 we briefly discuss our findings, linking the variation in the magnitude of the markup ratios to the materials share in production cost. We conclude the paper in section 7.7.

7.2   Inferring Marginal Cost and Markups From Private Labels: Theory

7.2.1   Vertical Differentiation and the Coexistence of Brands and Private Labels

We begin with a very stylized example of a market with two firms, best thought of as integrated manufacturers and sellers, one producing a branded product, the other offering a physically identical unbranded product. This example is an adaptation of Tirole (1989, 296–98), which in turn follows Shaked and Sutton's (1982) model of vertical differentiation and price competition. Following Sutton (1991), we regard "perceived quality" as a function of the stock of past advertising A ("brand capital"). No horizontal differentiation is possible. The two firms both produce at the constant unit cost c. Under conditions that guarantee that the market will support both the branded and the private-label product, we derive product prices (and thus margins) as well as profits for the two firms.

Firm 1 enters the game with a stock of "brand equity" $A = \overline{A}$, which can be thought of as the return to past expenditure on advertising. Firm 2 has no brand equity: $A_2 = 0$. Although all consumers prefer the branded product at the same price, willingness to pay for the characteristics associated with the branding differs across individuals. Let this heterogeneity, which we might associate either with taste or with income differences, be parameterized by $\theta \sim U(\theta_0, \theta_1)$, where $\theta_0 \geq 0$, and $\theta_1 = \theta_0 + 1$. The utility of a type θ consumer is $U = \theta(1 + A) - p$ if the consumer purchases one unit of the good with brand equity A at price p, and 0 otherwise. The type θ consumer is thus indifferent between the branded and the private-label good when $\theta(1 + \overline{A}) - p_1 = \theta - p_2$.

When we use a result from Tirole (1989), demands for the two firms as a function of the prices p_1 and p_2 are then

$$D_1(p_1, p_2) = \theta_1 - \frac{p_1 - p_2}{\overline{A}}, \text{ and } D_2(p_1, p_2) = \frac{p_1 - p_2}{\overline{A}} - \theta_0.$$

As $\overline{A}$ becomes large, the products become less and less substitutable, and the relative demand less and less price-sensitive.

Nash equilibrium occurs when firm i maximizes $(p_i - c)D_i(p_i, p_j)$ with respect to $p_j (i, j = 1, 2)$. The prices, quantities demanded, and profits in the Nash equilibrium are

$$p_1 = c + \frac{2\theta_1 - \theta_0}{3}\overline{A} \quad p_2 = c + \frac{\theta_1 - 2\theta_0}{3}\overline{A} < p_1$$

$$D_1 = \frac{2\theta_1 - \theta_0}{3} \quad D_2 = \frac{\theta_1 - 2\theta_0}{3}$$

$$\pi_1 = \frac{(2\theta_1 - \theta_0)^2 \, \overline{A}}{9} \quad \pi_2 = \frac{(\theta_1 - 2\theta_0)^2 \, \overline{A}}{9}$$

Thus, the qualitative results are as follows:

- Firm 1, the nationally branded incumbent, charges a higher price than the private-label firm 2. However, both charge above marginal cost.
- The excess of price over marginal cost, and the profits of both the brand and the private-label producer, are increasing in the degree of heterogeneity in the population and in firm 1's stock of brand capital.[2]
- Both firms make some profit, although the national brand makes more.

7.2.2   Adding the Retail Sector

The stylized model above illustrates the role of brand capital and heterogeneous tastes for "perceived quality" in providing a market niche for private labels, and their effect on markups, quantity sold, and profits. However, we must now add a specific role for retailers, which are obviously central to our empirical analysis of the supermarket data. Lal and Narasimhan (1996) construct a model along the lines of the above example, but with two manufacturing firms, two retailers, and a composite outside good. Their model is intended to explain why under some conditions a manufacturer's advertising can "squeeze," that is, lower the retail margin while simultaneously increasing the wholesale margin, a point stressed previously by Steiner (1993).

Stores carry many products, and on any given purchase occasion a typical consumer buys only a subset of the products. Retailers, Lal and Narasimhan (1996) hypothesize, therefore tend to compete more aggressively based on the prices of a selected set of well-recognized nationally branded items by advertising these prices to consumers. Since the contribution to profit from any customer is the sum of revenue from advertised and unadvertised items, the intensity of retail competition, as is evident from the

---

2. That the margin of the private-label supplier is increasing in firm 1's stock of brand equity reflects the "principle of maximal differentiation," which is not entirely robust (Tirole 1989).

prices of these items, increases with the amount the consumer will expend on the unadvertised items once at the store. This aggressiveness therefore translates into lower retail margins on these selected items since the retailers expect that consumers, once inside a store, will also buy non-advertised products on which the retailers receive high margins. Manufacturers who, via advertising, have established a stock of well-recognized products, are able to charge high prices to retailers. The higher margin earned by retailers on their private-label products compared with national brands is an important feature of the data we examine.

If the retail level of the channel is very competitive, retail margins are not likely to be much larger than handling costs. Many authors (such as Levy et al. 1998; Levy, Dutta, and Bergen 2002) suggest that the retail grocery industry is indeed very competitive. Retail margins on branded products are in fact very small for most product groups in our data set.

7.2.3   Lower Bounds for Markups: Algebra[3]

The "ideal" measure of the markup ratio—that which measures the extent to which quantity consumed falls short of the first best optimum—is the price paid by the consumer relative to the full marginal cost of supplying an extra unit. Denote the marginal production cost faced by the brand manufacturer as c_b^p and the marginal cost the retailer faces in stocking and selling the branded product—the "marginal handling cost"—as c_b^h.[4] The "full" marginal cost of providing a unit of the branded product is thus

$$(1) \qquad c_b = c_b^p + c_b^h.$$

Consequently, we define the *true markup* as

$$(2) \qquad \mu^* \equiv \frac{p_b^r}{c_b^p + c_b^h},$$

where p_b^r denotes the retail price of the branded product. In this subsection, we show how to bound this ideal measure in terms of quantities that we are able to observe directly in the data on retail price and store margins.

In line with evidence presented in section 7.3, we postulate that the marginal production cost of the private label (denoted by g) is not less than that of the brand, that is,

$$(3) \qquad c_b^p \leq c_g^p.$$

Because the manufacturer of the private label will not normally sell at a wholesale price less than its marginal production cost, we have

---

3. This section owes a major debt to our discussant, Julio Rotemberg.

4. Note that we do not make the assumption that c_b^p and c_b^h are constant unit costs. We do not need this assumption in our empirical work, because we are using price data to make bounding arguments rather than to arrive at point estimates of marginal costs. In particular, if there are fixed costs in production or selling that must be covered, the wholesale price and the retail price will overestimate marginal costs.

(4) $$c_g^p \leq p_g^w$$

Combining equations (3) and (4), we have

(5) $$c_b^p \leq p_g^w.$$

Thus, the wholesale price of the private label is an upper bound on the marginal manufacturing cost of the brand.

Likewise, the retailer's margin on the branded product should at least cover the marginal handling costs. Letting

(6) $$m_b^r \equiv p_b^r - p_b^w,$$

where p_b^w denotes the wholesale price of the branded product, we have

(7) $$c_b^h \leq m_b^r.$$

The degree to which m_b^r overstates marginal handling costs depends on the ability of the brand manufacturer to extract, on the margin, the rents associated with its brand equity. In the limit, the brand manufacturer extracts all of the rents, and m_b^r equals the retailer's true marginal handling cost.[5] However, since we are seeking *lower bounds* for the "true" markup, the logic of our argument does not in any way depend on such an assumption. Our bounds will of course be tighter if the marginal profit earned by the store on brand name goods is small. This is normally the case in practice since, as we will see in section 7.5, for all but a few product categories the observed m_b^r—which must be the sum of true marginal handling cost and the store's marginal profit—is itself small.

Adding equations (5) and (7), we see that

(8) $$c_b \equiv c_b^p + c_b^h \leq p_g^w + m_b^r.$$

Define a new ratio $\hat{\mu}$ as

(9) $$\hat{\mu} \equiv \frac{p_b^r}{p_g^w + m_b^r} = \frac{p_b^r}{p_g^w + p_b^r - p_b^w},$$

where the latter equality follows from equation (6). Recalling the definition of the unobservable "true" markup as $\mu^* \equiv p_b^r / c_b^p + c_b^h$ from equation (2), the inequality in equation (8) implies that

(10) $$\hat{\mu} \leq \mu^*.$$

Equation (10) is the result most central to our empirical analysis because it implies that $\hat{\mu}$ is a lower bound on the "true" or "ideal" markup. Moreover,

5. There exist some handling cost data in marketing studies that focus on direct product profitability issues. Although we have not yet obtained these cost data, they would allow us to see just how conservative our assumptions about handling costs are. Because our primary focus in this paper is on constructing a lower bound on the "ideal" markup, the main thrust of the paper would remain unchanged. See Chen et al. (1999) and Marsh Super Study Special Report (*Progressive Grocer,* December 1992 and January 1993) for details. We thank Jim Hess for informing us about the existence of such data.

it shows how to construct a lower bound on the markup ratio using data directly available in the Dominick's data set. We will refer to the ratio $\hat{\mu}$ as our *preferred lower-bound markup* because, as we show immediately below, it is a tighter lower bound for μ^* than is the ratio of the retail prices.

7.2.4   Relationship of μ and to Retail and Wholesale Price Ratios

It is interesting to compare the preferred markup measure $\hat{\mu}$ to the retail price ratio p_b^r/p_g^r and to the wholesale price ratio p_b^w/p_g^w—the former because retail prices are available in a wide variety of data sets (whereas data on retailer's margins are less common), and the latter because it is a lower bound for the *manufacturer's* markup over marginal production cost; that is, p_b^w/p_g^w $\leq p_b^w/c_b^p$. Let $m_g^r \equiv p_g^r - p_g^w$. As section 7.5 shows, in the data it is almost always the case that

$$(11) \qquad\qquad m_b^r \leq m_g^r,$$

that is, the retailer earns less revenue net of the wholesale price from selling a unit of the national brand than from selling a unit of the comparable private label. When equation (11) holds, we can see, by combining equations (8) and (11), and using equations (5) and (7), that

$$(12) \qquad\qquad c_b \equiv c_b^p + c_b^h \leq c_b^p + m_b^r \leq p_g^w + m_g^r = p_g^r.$$

The retail price of the private label is an upper bound for the full marginal cost of the brand; it is, however, a less tight upper bound than the preferred marginal cost measure that appears in the denominator of $\hat{\mu}$. Hence, the markup measure based on retail prices, $\mu^r \equiv p_b^r/p_g^r$, is a lower bound for the true markup μ^* and understates μ^* to a greater extent than does $\hat{\mu}$.

Finally, it is easy to see that the markup measure based on wholesale prices, $\mu^w \equiv p_b^w/p_g^w$, satisfies $\mu^w \geq \hat{\mu}$. Recall that $\hat{\mu} \equiv p_b^r/p_g^w + m_b^r$. To go from $\hat{\mu}$ to μ^w, we subtract m_b^r from both the numerator and the dominator. Since markup ratios exceed unity, the subtraction has a larger percentage effect on the denominator than the numerator. It is not, however, possible to say that μ^w is unambiguously an upper bound for μ^*, because we don't know the extent to which p_g^w and m_b^r exceed, respectively, the true marginal production cost and marginal handling cost of the national brand.

In summary, we report five markup ratios:

1. $\hat{\mu} \equiv p_b^r/p_g^w + m_b^r$, the "preferred" lower-bound measure of the full markup on the brand,
2. $\mu^r \equiv p_b^r/p_g^r$, the lower-bound measure of the full markup based on retail prices,
3. $\mu^w \equiv p_b^w/p_g^w$, the lower-bound measure of the manufacture's markup ratio based on wholesale prices,
4. $\mu_b \equiv p_b^r/p_b^w \equiv m_b^r/p_b^w + 1$, the "retailer's markup" ratio on the brand, and finally,
5. $\mu_g \equiv p_g^r/p_g^w \equiv m_g^r/p_g^w + 1$, the "retailer's markup" ratio on the private label.

Table 7.1   **Notation Used in Deriving the Lower Bounds for Markups**

c_b^p	Marginal production cost of the branded product
c_g^p	Marginal production cost of private label
c_b^h	Retailer's "marginal handling cost" of the branded product
c_b	The "Full" marginal cost of providing a unit of the branded product
p_b^r	Retail price of the branded product
p_g^r	Retail price of private label
p_g^w	Wholesale price of private label
p_b^w	Wholesale price of the branded product
m_b^r	Retailer's margin on branded product
m_g^r	Retailer's margin on private label
μ^*	The "true" or the "ideal" markup
$\hat{\mu}$	The "preferred" lower bound on the "true" markup
μ^r	The lower-bound markup based on retail prices
μ^w	The lower-bound markup based on wholesale prices
μ_b	The retailer's markup on the branded product
μ_g	The retailer's markup on private label

The first three ratios, along with the "true" underlying markup ratio $\mu^* \equiv p_b^r / c_b^p + c_b^h$, satisfy the inequalities

$$\mu^r \leq \hat{\mu} \leq \mu^w$$

and

$$\mu^r \leq \hat{\mu} \leq \mu^*.$$

In table 7.1, we summarize the algebraic notation used in this section for deriving the lower bounds on the markup ratio.

7.3   Branded and Private-Label Products: Issues of Comparability

In section 7.2, we established algebraic conditions under which the ratios we report can be considered lower bounds on the true markup. The usefulness of our arguments depends, however, on the maintained hypothesis that neither the marginal production cost nor the marginal handling cost of the branded product exceeds that of the private-label version. The appropriateness of this assumption is an empirical question whose answer may differ across product categories. In this section we consider three potential objections to the approach in this paper:

- Private-label goods are inferior products produced at lower cost using cheap, low-quality inputs (the "physical quality" objection).
- Differences in production technique, scale, and factor prices make variable costs in the manufacturing process noncomparable even when the final outputs are comparable (the "production method" objection).
- Even if the private-label product is *physically* comparable to the nationally branded version, the activities of advertising and otherwise

promoting the national brand (and perhaps also expenditures on research and development) may create additional marginal costs for national brands (the "marketing cost" objection).

All three of these objections concern the comparability of the national brand and the store brand versions, and all potentially call into question the supposition that marginal production and marketing costs for the private-label product are at least as great as those for their branded counterparts. In the three subsections that we follow, we take up these objections in turn.

7.3.1   Physical Quality

This subsection has two purposes. First, it presents evidence that private-label products are not in general of lower physical quality than the corresponding national brands. For the purposes of this paper, this is of interest not in and of itself, but because a finding of low quality in tests by quality control managers and consumer organizations might indicate the use of lower quality inputs, and hence lower marginal cost.

Second, although private-label products are not in general physically inferior, there is some evidence of variation in the relative quality of brands and private labels across product categories. Thus we discuss in this section our efforts to weed out categories in which there are in fact problems of comparability that make it difficult to construct matching pairs of physically identical products.

Branded and private-label versions of a product cannot be *economically identical,* as that would violate the law of one price. The first objection from the earlier list concerns possible differences in the quality of the *physical* product and not differences in "perceived quality" associated with sunk advertising costs, as discussed by Sutton (1991). Further, because the relevant concern is with differences in marginal costs, it is in fact not necessary that the private-label product be of equal physical quality in all respects. Superior designs or propriety formulas that do not affect marginal cost do not pose a problem. We focus on "quality" to the extent that low quality of the private-label product is suggestive of the use of lower cost inputs. We identify product categories in which this appears to be an issue, and we avoid these in the empirical work reported in sections 7.4 and 7.5.

Hoch and Banerji (1993) note the absence of a secondary data source on private-label quality comprehensive enough to cover all the SAMI (Selling Areas Marketing, Inc.) product categories. For example, *Consumer Reports* does not have quality ratings for all the products included in our data set. Therefore, it undertook a survey of quality assurance managers at the fifty largest supermarket chains and grocery wholesalers in the United States (according to *Thomas Food Industry Register*). These experts typically have a graduate education in food science and wide experience testing numerous product categories. For each of the original SAMI categories the managers

Table 7.2   **Product Quality Ratings by Category**

Product Category	Quality Rating of Private Label
Analgesics	4.8
Toothbrushes	4.7
Frozen Juices	4.7
Cereals	4.7
Oatmeal	4.7
Crackers	4.6
Cheeses	4.6
Frozen Entrees	4.6
Canned Tuna	4.5
Fabric Softeners	4.5
Bottled Juices	4.5
Laundry Detergents	4.4
Snack Crackers	4.4
Cookies	4.3
Grooming Products	4.3
Dish Detergents	4.2
Toothpaste	4.2
Canned Soup	4.1
Bathroom Tissues	4.1
Soft Drinks	4.0

Source: Hoch and Banerji (1993), unpublished data.

Notes: Quality ratings range from 1 to 5. "1" means that the private label is much worse in quality than the corresponding national brand, while "5" means that the private-label quality is fully comparable to that of national brand.

were asked: "How does the quality of the best private-label supplier compare to the leading national brands in the product category?" The respondents gave a rating on a five-point scale: a "1" suggests that private labels are much worse in quality than the national brands, whereas a "5" suggests that the private-label quality is fully comparable to that of the national brand.[6] In table 7.2, we report the means of these survey-based quality ratings for each of the categories that we examine in the Dominick's data.

Hoch and Banerji's (1993, 62) own evaluation of the evidence is that "the overriding sentiment of these experts was that quality of the best private label was quite close to that of the national brands." This is consistent with industry observers (e.g., Quelch and Harding 1996; Fitzell 1998) who suggest that although over the long haul private-label products have not consistently exhibited the uniformly high quality standards as national brands, in

6. Hoch and Banerji contacted each of these managers by telephone to solicit their participation and followed up with a questionnaire. Thirty-two people (64 percent) returned the survey, resulting in twenty-five usable sets of responses (50 percent). The experts received a one-page set of instructions explaining what is meant by each question and how to use the scales. They were instructed to evaluate "objective" quality rather than quality as perceived by customers.

recent years private-label products have significantly improved in quality and packaging enhancements, making them comparable to the national brands. The quality comparability of private-label products in these categories is further reinforced by a survey that asks consumers about their perceptions of the quality premium that national brands offer relative to private labels (Sethuraman and Cole 1997). This study finds that consumers are willing to pay a price premium for national brands even though they are aware that the price premiums do not reflect corresponding quality differences.

It is important to stress that the label "Dominick's Finer Foods" is in itself a kind of branding that differentiates the supermarket chain's products from true generics. The very particular sort of branding practiced by Dominick's and other supermarket chains makes no attempt to provide the utility-yielding associations that are the object of much national advertising. It may, however, do a very good job of assuring physical quality. According to Fitzell (1998), private-label owners do not compromise on quality because they cannot really afford to put a store name or their own brand name on a product that may be considered inferior. Use of a name such as Dominick's serves a bonding function: if one good (or the services of one store) proves to be inferior or unpalatable, there is a spillover on the credibility of all goods and all stores carrying that label.

Finally, we can use Hoch and Banerji's private-label quality ratings along with other information to identify categories in which quality differences are more likely so that we can learn whether or not the quality differences are likely to indicate lower variable costs for the private-label version. To that end we undertook further study of the two product categories that were ranked lowest by Hoch and Banerji's survey and that are also included in the Dominick's data: bathroom tissue and soft drinks.

Bathroom Tissue

This was one of the lowest-rated categories in terms of quality comparability. Thus the higher markups may, in this category, represent true input quality differences and therefore differences in marginal costs. There exists a recent *Consumer Reports* article on bathroom tissue as well as recent academic paper by Hausman (1999) on the category. Both of these, as well as a survey of consumer perceptions by Sethuraman and Cole (1997), reinforced the belief that this category does indeed have significant quality variation. The *Consumer Reports* article reported studies of many products that ranged broadly from Ultra Plush Charmin to low-quality private-label products and Scott tissue. Hausman (1999) echoes the claim that some brands are of low quality whereas others are of high quality. Consistent with this, Sethuraman and Cole (1997) find that consumers rate bathroom tissue as one of the two product categories for which the quality gap as perceived by consumers is highest. Further, Hausman (1999) suggests that this is due to real differences in input quality in the pulp used to make the paper, which is likely to lead to higher costs for higher-quality branded manufacturers in this category. We thought this might allow us to compare the private-label Scott, but Scott turns out to have many more sheets per role than the private label, making it possible that Scott faces higher costs because of the additional sheets, even if the input costs are the same or lower. In the end this additional information led us to drop the bathroom tissue category from this paper (although the price ratios in this category averaged above 2.0). We were not able to find national brand/private label pairs that were of comparable quality and for which we were confident that the private-label product was not cheaper to produce on the margin.

Soft Drinks

According to our quality experts, soft drinks are one of the least comparable categories in terms of quality based on quality control manger's perceptions. To the degree that the quality differences relate to cost savings for the private label, this would inflate our markup estimates. However, to the degree that the differences in quality are in terms of taste or other inputs into the syrup, they are unlikely to lead to substantial differences in variable costs. We include soft drinks in this paper because knowledge of the nature of soft drink production and distribution suggests that the sources of quality differences were not likely to be related to the marginal costs faced by soft drink manufacturers. In this category the majority of the costs are bottling and distribution. The cost of the syrup is only a very small portion of the cost of producing soft drinks (Levy and Young 2001).

7.3.2   Production Methods, Scale, Factor Prices, and Other Cost Differences

Even if the final products are physically identical, marginal manufacturing costs may differ because of differences in production technology, scale, or the prices paid for labor or materials. We report here some observations concerning differences between national brand manufacturers and manufacturing firms that supply output for sale under private labels—referred to in the industry as "co-packers."

We interviewed a number of industry experts on private labels. Their general sense was that for products of equal quality, the variable costs of producing private labels were likely to be at least as high as, and probably higher than, the corresponding costs for national brands. The general tenor of the responses we received is captured by the following comment from the vice-president of a major private-label food broker: "National brands should be able to physically produce at a lower cost. . . . [T]hey are able to negotiate lower prices on components and vertically integrate to carry out processes themselves rather than having to buy at higher marginal cost."

Below we describe in more detail the nature of manufacturing by co-packers and its implications for marginal costs.

Types of Private-Label Manufacturers

As spelled out on the web page of the Private Labels Manufacturers Association, private-label manufactures fall into four categories:

1. Large national brand manufacturers that utilize excess plant capacity to supply store brands
2. Small, quality manufacturers that specialize in particular product lines and concentrate on producing store brands almost exclusively. Often, these companies are owned by corporations that also produce national brands.
3. Major retailers and wholesalers that own their own manufacturing facilities and provide store brand products for themselves
4. Regional brand manufacturers that produce private-label products for specific markets

In general, private-label manufacturers are smaller, more regional, and more fragmented than their national brand counterparts. Indeed, according to Fitzell (1998), as private-label manufacturing evolved in the United States, the trend has been more toward smaller manufacturers and processors. As a result, the national brand business, with its high costs of product development and marketing, was left to the larger manufacturers. For example, some of the producers for TOPCO (which handles distribution for what is perhaps the largest private-label program in the country) are large enough to produce and market products successfully under their own brands. In many cases, however, it turns out that they are small or medium-sized producers that lack the necessary financial strength or organizational structure to market their own brand products effectively when facing strong national competitors (Fitzell 1998).

We interviewed at some length a production manager at a large branded manufacturer in the consumer packaged goods industry. Although he preferred to remain anonymous, he expressed the belief that everything he shared with us is common knowledge in the industry.

This manager noted that at one time or another, most co-packers produce for branded manufacturers. To that end, private-label manufacturers would have access to the same equipment and techniques as manufacturers of the brand because they must meet the quality standards of the national brand manufacturers for which they produce. Further, he said, branded manufacturers supply some of the equipment for their co-packers. These observations are also found in the Federal Trade Commission complaint against the proposed merger of General Mills with Ralcorp, which was at the time (1997) both the fifth largest supplier of ready-to-eat breakfast cereal for sale under a national brand name and the largest producer of private-label cereals.

Our interviewee described three major considerations determining relative production cost, which he called *throughput, crewing,* and *wage rates. Throughput* appears to be industry terminology for number of units produced per hour, and *crewing* apparently refers to labor intensity. It is not clear that these are entirely separate considerations from the point of view of microeconomic theory, but we will try to stick as closely as possible to the terminology used by the interviewee.

The manager contended that throughput for branded manufacturers is significantly higher than for co-packers, whereas crewing is indicative of greater automation and lower labor intensity in production of branded products. First and foremost, private-label manufacturers are smaller in scale. Second, private-label manufacturers, by the nature of their business, need to be more flexible with respect to the quantities they produce. They often supply multiple private labels, and uncertain demand calls for a degree of flexibility that limits their ability to benefit from large-scale production runs and the economies of scale of the brand manufacturer. This leads to lower line speeds and lower throughput for private-label manufacturers.

As to crewing, branded product factories have greater automation than private-label factories, an observation that the manager regarded as central to his belief that brand manufacturers produce at a lower variable cost. Relative to the private-label manufacturers, branded firms have fewer employees and more equipment per unit of output. Wage rates, on the other hand, work in the opposite direction: here, brand manufacturers are at a cost disadvantage. They are more likely to use union workers, which raises cost, in terms of wages and benefits. This is closely related to the "large firm effect" on wages in the academic literature (Brown and Medoff 1989). The manager's sense was that the throughput advantage roughly offset the wage disadvantage for an equal crew size. However, the branded manufacturer had a sufficiently lower labor intensity—a crewing advantage—that more than offset the higher wages.

The value of size for national brands has been noted in academic studies as well. For example, Schmalensee (1978) has shown that national brands benefit from the substantial economies of scale in production and advertising that accrue through national distribution in the cereal category. Likewise, Brown and Medoff (1991) have shown that larger buyers receive substantial quantity discounts on their purchases, although this advantage is again offset to a greater or lesser extent by higher wage costs.

In sum, industry experts as well as academic articles regard the preponderance of the evidence as indicating that marginal costs for private-label products are at least as high as—and in many cases higher than—marginal costs for the national brands with which they are paired. This conclusion supports our use of wholesale prices of private-label goods as *upper bounds* for the marginal manufacturing cost of the corresponding brand name products.

7.3.3   The Marketing Cost Issue

A third potential difference between national brands and private labels concerns costs of product introduction and marketing. Industry sources indicate that in general private-label manufacturers do far less in terms of research and development (R&D), advertising, trade promotion, and consumer promotion than national brands. For example, Fitzell (1998) states that national brand businesses have high costs of product development and marketing.

This leaves us with the remaining question of how large these costs are and whether they are fixed or variable costs in nature. We argue that R&D is a sunk cost and that national advertising expenditure constitutes predominantly a fixed cost, much but not all of which can be regarded as sunk in the sense of Sutton (1991). This leaves trade promotion spending and consumer promotion spending as possible variable cost differences we must consider. Notice that the largest effect of both trade promotions and consumer promotions is the reduced price the manufacturer receives from the promotions. Thus, they aren't marginal cost differences but adjustments to the prices the manufacturer receives that we must consider. There are additional costs of implementing the promotional programs that we should also consider.

Research and Development

Research and development is one area in which private labels and national brands differ substantially. For example, according to Fitzell (1982), R&D expenditures of private-label manufacturers usually are substantially lower than the expenditures of the national brand manufacturers. The managers of national brands see these kinds of expenditures as critical to maintaining their brand equity. Clearly R&D spending for new product development is not marginal for products being sold in grocery chains. According to Monroe (1990), as well as many other authors, R&D costs do not vary with the (sales) activity and are not easily traceable to a product or segment, and therefore they should be treated as fixed from our perspectives.

Advertising

Advertising spending is another major difference between national brands and private labels. National brands invest large amounts of money in advertising. For example, in the survey of Leading National Advertisers in *Advertising Age* magazine (2000), it is reported that advertising spending for major brands is substantial. Further, many brands have been investing substantially on advertising for many years. Indeed, according to Quelch and Harding (1996), it took decades of advertising by the strongest national brands to build their consumer equities. As another example, it seems that restrictions on television advertising may help explain the strength of private labels in Europe relative to the United States because "regulated television markets mean that cumulative advertising for brand names does not approach the U.S. levels" (Quelch and Harding 1996).

This has not been true for most private labels because their owners could not afford the expense of building their own brand equity by adopting multimillion-dollar advertising campaigns (Fitzell 1998). In the case of the specific retailer we are studying, we know that it did not invest anywhere near the amounts spent by the national brand manufacturers of comparable products, even on a per-unit sold or sales basis, on advertising to build brands.

The question, then, is whether it is more reasonable to treat advertising expenditures by manufacturers as a fixed cost or variable cost. If we suppose for a moment that the branded variant is heavily advertised but the private-label version is not, the average cost of a unit sold (which includes costs incurred by the "marketing department" in addition to those of the "production department") would be higher for the branded product. The question, put differently, then becomes whether advertising should be seen as a marginal cost as opposed to a fixed or sunk cost.

The best evidence we could find on this question in the literature is from the Cox Annual Survey of Promotional Practices (1996). It surveys consumers, packaged goods manufacturers, and grocery retailers on issues of promotion practice and usage. The particular survey was conducted in 1995 and its participants included 34 percent larger firms (i.e., those with annual sales of $1 billion or more) and 66 percent smaller firms (i.e., those with annual sales of less than $1 billion).

When asked about the share of national advertising programs designed to support and build brand equity, consumer and trade promotions, and the like, the survey participants state that they view their advertising expenses as mostly aimed at building brand equity, which is more of a fixed or long-run cost. According to the survey results, the packaged goods manufacturers believe that at least 66 percent of their advertising spending is meant to build their brand equity only. Of the remaining 34 percent, 14 percent of their advertising spending is devoted to both brand equity and consumer promotions, 7 percent to both brand equity and trade promotions, and the remaining 13 percent to brand equity, trade, and consumer promotions. It follows that up to 80 percent of advertising is related to brand equity. Morton and Zettelmeyer (2000) also emphasize the difference in fixed costs between national and store brands. The advertising required to support national brands, they argue, implies that national brand manufacturers have substantially higher average costs than their marginal costs of production. This is consistent with the idea that advertising by national brands may be viewed as a fixed, rather than variable, cost.

Trade Promotions

Manufacturers also invest heavily in trade promotions. In the Cox survey they report some industry averages on how firms in the grocery industry allocate their promotional dollars. It looks to be about 50 percent trade promotions, 25 percent national advertising, and 25 percent consumer promotions. Thus, trade promotions are the largest component of manufacturer spending. Private-label manufacturers do not undertake nearly as much trade spending, so this is another major difference between national brands and private labels.

Fortunately the Dominick's data already incorporate some of the trade spending in its wholesale prices, so we have already taken part of manufacturer's trade promotion spending into account in our measurement of national brand markups. It is likely that there are trade promotions that are not captured by the wholesale prices in our data. These are most likely lumpy payments such as slotting allowances, cooperative advertising allowances, and various case discounts and spiffs the manufacturer gives to the retailer. To the degree that they are lumpy and not incorporated into the wholesale price that retailers are using in their pricing decisions, however, it is not clear that these expenses are truly variable. Thus, these unreported trade expenditures may not be as relevant as the trade promotions incorporated into the data we use in this paper. However, to the degree that the unreported trade spending is variable, and substantial, our measure of markups will be overstated.

Consumer Promotions

This is also a major difference between national brands and private labels. Private labels tend not to use coupons or promote to consumers, as discussed by Slade (1998), whereas branded manufacturers spend, on average, 25 percent of their promotional expenses on consumer promotions. That is about on par with the amount spent on national advertising.

These activities are likely to be either reductions in the price manufacturers receive (as with redeemed coupons) or variable expenses to run the promotion. Although scanner data sets often include some measures of usage of manufacturers' coupons, that is not true in this data set. To give the reader some sense of how important these may be by category, we report the percentage of sales made using a coupon for all product categories we study in table 7.3.

In summary, we believe there is enough evidence to suggest that using private-label product prices to infer national brand costs is a reasonable assumption in this industry. There is reason to believe, therefore, that this measure of markup can be appropriate for at least some categories and products in this industry. Further, since the private label will have some

Table 7.3   **Manufacturer Coupon Usage by Product Category**

Product Category	% Sales with Manufacturers Coupon
Analgesics	10.6
Toothbrushes	12.5
Frozen Juices	1.7–5.9
Cereals	16.5
Oatmeal	9.9
Crackers	0.8–5.3
Cheeses	2.6–6.6
Frozen Entrees	2.5–16.5
Canned Tuna	0.6
Fabric Softeners	14.2–16.3
Bottled Juices	0.7–2.1
Laundry Detergents	14.0
Snack Crackers	6.4
Cookies	3.9
Grooming Products	9.4
Dish Detergents	12.3
Toothpastes	13.6
Canned Soup	6.5
Bathroom Tissues	4.8
Soft Drinks	2.2

Source: Supermarket Business, 16th Annual Product Preference Study (1993).

markup, and the nationally branded products have advantages on size and scale in production, packaging, and negotiation on input prices, we believe that private-label product prices provide a conservative measure of these costs.

7.4   Data

We use scanner data from Dominick's Finer Food (DFF), which is one of the largest retail supermarket chains in the larger Chicago metropolitan area, operating ninety-four stores with a market share of about 25 percent. Large multistore U.S. supermarket chains of this type made up about $310,146,666,000 in total annual sales in 1992, which was 86.3 percent of total retail grocery sales (*Supermarket Business* 1993). In 1999 the retail grocery sales had reached $435 billion (Chevalier, Kashyap, and Rossi 2000). Thus the chain we study is a representative of a major class of the retail grocery trade. Moreover, Dominick's-type multistore supermarket chains' sales constitute about 14 percent of the total retail sales of about $2,250 billion in theUnited States. Since retail sales account for about 9.3 percent of the gross domestic product (GDP), our data set is a representative of as much as 1.28 percent of the GDP, which seems substantial. Thus the market we are studying has a quantitative economic significance as well.

The original Dominick's data—which have been used also by Chevalier, Kashyap, and Rossi (2000); Müller et al. (2001); Dutta, Bergen, and Levy (2002); and Levy, Dutta, and Bergen (2002)—consist of up to 400 weekly observations of actual transaction prices in twenty-nine different categories, covering the period from 14 September 1989 to 8 May 1997. The length of individual product price time series, however, varies depending on when the data collection for the specific category began and ended. Note that Dominick's Universal Product Code–level database does not include all products the chain sells. The database we use represents approximately 30 percent of Dominick's revenues (Chevalier, Kashyap, and Rossi 2000). The data come from the chain's scanner database, which contains actual retail transaction prices of the products along with the profit margin the supermarket makes on each one of them. From the information on retail prices and the profit margin, we have constructed the weekly time series of wholesale prices.

The retail prices are the actual transaction prices: the prices customers paid at the cash register each week. If the item was on sale, then the price data we have reflect the sale price. Although the retail prices are set on a chain-wide basis at the corporate headquarters of Dominick's, there may still be some price variation across the stores depending on the competitive market structure in and around the location of the stores (Levy et al. 1998). According to Chevalier, Kashyap, and Rossi (2000), Dominick's maintains three such price zones. Thus, for example, if a particular store of the chain is located in the vicinity of a Cub Food store, then the store may be designated a "Cub-fighter" and, as such, it may pursue a more aggressive pricing policy in comparison to the stores located in other zones. In the analysis described below we have used all the data available from all stores by properly aggregating them across the stores. Note that our retail prices reflect any retailer's coupons or discounts but, as mentioned above, do not include manufacturer coupons.

The wholesale prices, which measure the direct cost to the retailer, are computed by combining the retail price data with the information provided by the retailer on its weekly gross margins for each product and using the relation wholesale price = (1 – gross margin percent) multiplied by the retail price. The wholesale prices DFF uses for computing its gross margin series are constructed by the retailer as a weighted average of the amount the retailer paid for all its inventory. For example, a profit margin of 25.3 means that DFF makes 25.3 cents on the dollar for each item sold, which yields a cost of good sold of 74.7 cents. If the retailer bought its current stock of Kellogg's Corn Flakes, 18-oz., in two transactions, then its wholesale price is computed as the average of these two transaction prices (no FIFO [First In,

First Out] or LIFO [Last In, First Out] accounting rules are used in these computations).[7]

For the purpose of this study, we went through DFF's entire data set and identified pairs of national brand and private-label products. Of the approximately 350 pairs we were able to locate in the twenty-nine product categories, we have eliminated a portion of them because of substantial size differences. For example, if, say, in the cereals category we compare Kellogg's corn flakes to DFF's corn flakes, but the national brand comes in a 32-oz. box (which is a family size) and DFF's product comes in an 18-oz. box, then the two products are not really comparable because they are targeted to two different kinds of customers, and computing prices per ounce would not necessarily eliminate this fundamental problem. Other pairs were eliminated because many non-private-label brands did not really qualify as national brand products because these products are marketed only regionally (and some even locally only) or they did not have substantial market share. Still other pairs were eliminated because of our uncertainty about equality of their quality. Finally, we have imposed a minimum on the length of the weekly time series for them to be informative.

Thus, the results we report in this paper are for national brand/private-label product pairs, such that (a) the national brand product is clearly marketed nationally; (b) the national brand product is widely recognized; (c) the national brand product has a nontrivial market share; (d) the national brand/private-label product pair is comparable in size, quality, and packaging; and (e) the price time series for the product pairs are available for at least a twenty-four-week period for each of the three price zones.

The product pairs that pass these criteria represent nineteen categories, which include analgesics, bottled juices, cereals, cheeses, cookies, crackers, canned soups, dish detergent, frozen entrees, frozen juices, fabric softeners, grooming products, laundry detergent, oatmeal, snack crackers, toothbrushes, toothpastes, soft drinks, and canned tuna. In the case of the soft

---

7. Thus, the wholesale costs in the data do not correspond exactly to the replacement cost or the last transaction price. Instead we have the average acquisition cost (ACC) of the items in inventory. So the supermarket chain sets retail prices for the next week and also determines AAC at the end of each week, t, according to the formula

$$AAC(t+1) = (\text{Inventory bought in } t) \text{ Price paid } (t)$$

$$+ [\text{Inventory, end of } t-1 - \text{sales}(t)] \, AAC(t).$$

There are two main sources of discrepancy between replacement cost and AAC. The first is the familiar one of sluggish adjustment. A wholesale price cut today only gradually works itself into AAC as old, higher-priced inventory is sold off. The second arises from the occasional practice of manufacturers of informing the buyer in advance of an impending temporary price reduction. This permits the buyer to completely deplete inventory and then "overstock" at the lower price. In this case AAC declines precipitously to the lower price and stays there until the large inventory acquired at that price runs off. Thus, the accounting cost shows the low price for some time after the replacement cost has gone back up.

drinks category, it should be noted that most of the nationally branded products included in this category are handled by their manufacturers through various direct store delivery arrangements.[8] Thus, the "handling costs" of these nationally branded products are incurred by their manufacturers.[9] Therefore, to get a markup ratio, in this case, we would take the ratio of the retail price of the nationally branded product over our estimate of the marginal cost of the branded product, calculated as the sum of the wholesale price of the private-label product and our estimate of the retailer handling cost. We, however, choose to treat the soft drink products and the rest of the products in an identical fashion by using the same formula for measuring the markup ratio. Therefore, by including in the denominator of the markup ratio the retailer's margin on the nationally branded product, we are overestimating the retailer's handling cost by counting the retailer's profit as part of the marginal cost. The resulting markup measure for the soft drink products will, therefore, be even more conservative than for the rest of the categories.

To compute the average markup figures for each category, which we report in figures 7.1–7.6, we had to compress the data by using three different weighted-averaging procedures. First, we have computed the weighted average of all weekly price series across all the chain's stores to get a single weekly wholesale and retail price series for each of the national brand and private-label products chosen for the analysis. The purpose of the weighing procedure we have implemented is to ensure that the price series coming from the stores that sell proportionally more than others receive higher weight. This averaging was done by weighing the national brand and private-label price series from each store according to the store's sales share in the total DFF sales where the sales are measured by the weekly sales figures of the specific national brand and private-label products, respectively. Since the scanner database does not include information on the quantities purchased at the wholesale level, we used the retail sales figures as its proxy. This procedure likely introduces a noise in the generated series because the retail sales are more spread over time in comparison to wholesale purchases, which occur with lower frequency. The noise, however, will mostly

8. Most big retail supermarket stores use some kind of dedicated warehouse channel distribution system for their product replenishment. However, for a number of reasons, the retailers often find it preferable to obtain some products directly from the suppliers or manufacturers who deliver them directly to the store, rather than via their normal warehouse channel. The products handled through such direct store delivery mechanisms usually are high-volume, fast-moving, or perishable products. See Levy et al. (1998) for further details on direct store delivery arrangements at multiproduct retail settings.

9. In the remaining ten categories, which include bath soap, beer, cigarettes, front-end candies, frozen dinners, paper towels, refrigerated juices, shampoos, soaps, and bathroom tissues, we were unable to find comparable national brand/private-label pairs. That is, in these categories we were unable to find any national brand/private-label product pair that met all five criteria listed above.

affect the weekly volatility properties of the price series, but the average values are unlikely to be affected from this procedure in a significant way.

Next, we computed the weighted average weekly values of the above across-store weighted averaged series by taking each price series for the sample period it was available and computing its weekly average value by weighing each weekly observation according to the share of that week's quantity sold in the total quantity sold over the entire sample period. As before, the purpose of this weighing is to give higher weight to observations (i.e., weeks) that represent higher sales volume measured in terms of products' quantity (such as ounces). In each case the prices of national brand products were weighed using the sales volume of that specific national brand product, whereas the price series of the private-label products were correspondingly weighed by sales volume of the private-label products. These series were then used to compute various markup measures reported in tables 7A.1–7A.19.

It should be noted that an alternative way of computing these weekly average markup values for each national brand/private-label product pair is to first compute weekly markup series for the entire sample period covered by each product pair and then compute their weekly weighted average using the procedure outlined above. The calculations performed using this procedure have yielded similar quantitative results in terms of the average markup figures. The procedure we use, however, has the advantage that first computing the markup ratios and then averaging them over time (instead of first averaging them over time and then computing the markup ratios) makes it possible to explore the time series variability in each individual markup series and perhaps also to provide some measure of over-time variability associated with the markup.

Finally, we have taken the above-calculated average markup figures for each product pair and computed the average markup for each of the nineteen product categories included in our sample. As before, these category averages were also calculated as weighted averages. However, unlike the previous steps, here the weighing was done according to the share of the *dollar* value of the sales for each product pair in the *dollar* value of the total sales in the category. For example, if in the analgesics category we have twenty-four national brand/private-label product pairs, to compute the category average markup, we took the markup figures for the twenty-four product pairs (listed in table 7A.5) and computed their weighted average, where the weights are the ratios of the total dollar sales of the pair to the total dollar sales in the category. The weights here use dollar sales rather than unit sales in order to avoid the problem of "adding apples to oranges." The resulting category averages figures are reported in figures 7.1–7.6 and in the bottom rows of tables 7A.1–7A.19.

Along with the average markup ratio measures we also report their interquartile ranges. The interquartile range figures reported for individual product pairs within each category (tables 7A.1–7A.19) are computed by using the weekly time series of the corresponding markup ratios and determining the range in which 50 percent of these weekly markups fall for each product pair. The interquartile range figures reported for category averages (see the bottom rows in tables 7A.1–7A.19) are computed by considering the average weekly markups for each product pair and determining the range in which 50 percent of them fall for each category.

In the individual category tables (tables 7A.1–7A.19), we identify each national brand/private-label product pair by the name of the branded products because the private-label equivalents of the nationally branded products listed in these tables are always the Dominick's store brand products. Note also that in these tables some brand names appear more than once. This is because they refer to different sizes. For example, in the analgesics category reported in table 7A.5, Advil (with the corresponding private-label product) is listed three times because it comes in three different sizes ("counts" or number of tablets): 10, 50, and 100.

7.5   Empirical Findings

In this section we report computations of the five markup ratios derived in section 7.2.3. Our primary objective is to offer the tightest possible lower bound on μ^*, the "ideal" full markup ratio for the nationally branded product. Our second goal is to provide a sense of the quantitative relationships between the five markup ratios that we derived in section 7.2.3. These ratios offer insight into the anatomy of $\hat{\mu}$; and because they have interpretations as markups at specific stages of the production and distribution processes, they are of interest in their own right.

In section 7.5.1, we report the results for category averages. We begin with the "bottom line," the "preferred" measure $\hat{\mu}$, our tightest lower bound on μ^*. We then move on to μ^w, the ratio of the wholesale prices, which usually exceeds $\hat{\mu}$ and is a lower bound on the manufacturer's markup. Next, we discuss μ_b and μ_g, the retailer's markups over wholesale price for branded and private-label products, respectively. These provide the link from μ^w to the more commonly observed markup ratio computed using retail prices, μ^r, which is the last of the five ratios that we report. Finally, we close the section with the presentation of a graph that shows $\hat{\mu}$ flanked by μ^w and μ^r and thus offers an empirical counterpart to the bounding inequalities derived in section 7.2.3.

In section 7.5.2 we focus in more detail on selected product categories. The category of ready-to-eat breakfast cereals, in particular, has been the object of several studies in the econometric literature, and we are able to compare our results with available structural estimates. Finally, examining closely several product pairs in representative categories, we obtain some insight into within-category variation of the markups.

7.5.1   Results for Category Averages

The "Preferred" Lower-bound Markup Measure $\hat{\mu}$

In figure 7.1 we report our "preferred" lower-bound markup measure labeled $\hat{\mu}$ in section 7.2.3. The figure shows that in four product categories—

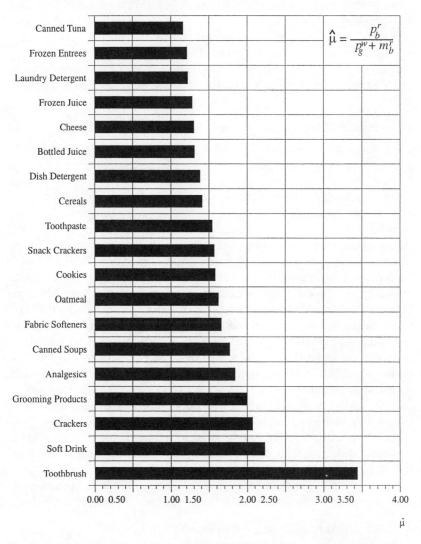

$$\hat{\mu} = \frac{p_b^r}{p_g^w + m_b^r}$$

μ

Fig. 7.1   Markup Ratio for Branded Products: "Preferred" Lower Bound (Measure a)

toothbrushes, soft drinks, crackers, and grooming products—the mean lower-bound markup ratio $\hat{\mu}$ is on the order of 2.0 or higher. In three categories—analgesics, canned soups, and fabric softeners—$\hat{\mu}$ averages between 1.60 and 2.00, whereas in six categories—oatmeal, cookies, snack crackers, toothpaste, cereals, and dish detergent—mean $\hat{\mu}$ falls approximately in the range 1.40–1.60. For the remaining six categories—bottled juice, cheese, frozen juice, laundry detergents, frozen entrees, and canned tuna—the average lower-bound markup ratio is less than 1.40. The categories with smallest $\hat{\mu}$ are canned tuna (1.16), frozen entrees (1.21), and laundry detergents (1.22).

Figure 7.1 provides a good deal of evidence that nationally branded products are sold at a substantial markup. In more than half of the categories, the average lower-bound on the markup ratio is at least 1.40. Since the measure we report here is conservative, true markup ratios are likely to be even higher.

Manufacturer's Markup: Lower Bound Based on Wholesale Prices

As discussed in sections 7.2 and 7.3, μ^w—the ratio of the wholesale prices—provides a lower bound for the brand manufacturer's markup. In figure 7.2 we present average μ^w by category along with our preferred lower bound, $\hat{\mu}$. A comparison of the two lower-bound measures indicates that with the exception of the toothbrush and crackers categories, the two markup ratios, μ^w and $\hat{\mu}$, are of similar magnitude. For ten categories—fabric softeners, oatmeal, toothpaste, cereal, dish detergent, bottled juice, cheese, laundry detergent, frozen entrees, and canned tuna—the difference between the two measures is less than 0.1. For seven categories—soft drinks, grooming products, analgesics, canned soups, cookies, snack crackers, and frozen juice—the difference between the two measures is between 0.10 and 0.20. Nationally branded products that have a large manufacturer's markup according to μ^w also have large full markups according to $\hat{\mu}$. This should not be surprising, as we obtained $\hat{\mu}$ from μ^w by adding m_b^r—the retailer's margin on the brand—to both the numerator and the denominator of μ^w, and as we show immediately below, with a few exceptions, the retail margins on branded products are quite small. This conclusion also holds, for the most part, within individual categories, as tables 7A.1–7A.19 indicate.

As we move down the list to categories with lower markup ratios, the gap between the two markup measures becomes particularly small, a direct result of the algebraic relationship between $\hat{\mu}$ and μ^w. Thus, although the conservative treatment of the retailer's handling cost embodied in $\hat{\mu}$ is theoretically appealing, its actual quantitative significance is not overwhelming.

Retailer's Markups on Private Labels and National Brands

In figure 7.3 we report the retailer's markup—the ratio of retail price to wholesale price—for the private-label (μ_g) and nationally branded products

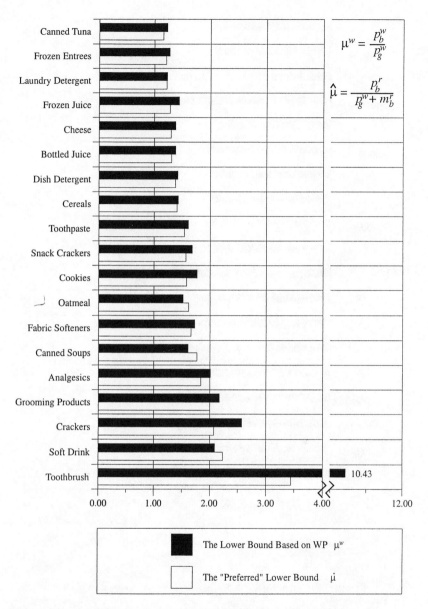

Canned Tuna
Frozen Entrees
Laundry Detergent
Frozen Juice
Cheese
Bottled Juice
Dish Detergent
Cereals
Toothpaste
Snack Crackers
Cookies
Oatmeal
Fabric Softeners
Canned Soups
Analgesics
Grooming Products
Crackers
Soft Drink
Toothbrush

$$\mu^w = \frac{P_b^w}{P_g^w}$$

$$\hat{\mu} = \frac{P_b^r}{P_g^w + m_b^r}$$

10.43

0.00   1.00   2.00   3.00   4.00   12.00

■ The Lower Bound Based on WP μ^w

☐ The "Preferred" Lower Bound $\hat{\mu}$

Fig. 7.2   National Brand Markup: The Preferred" Lower Bound (Measure a) vs. the Lower Bound Based on Wholesale Prices (Measure c)

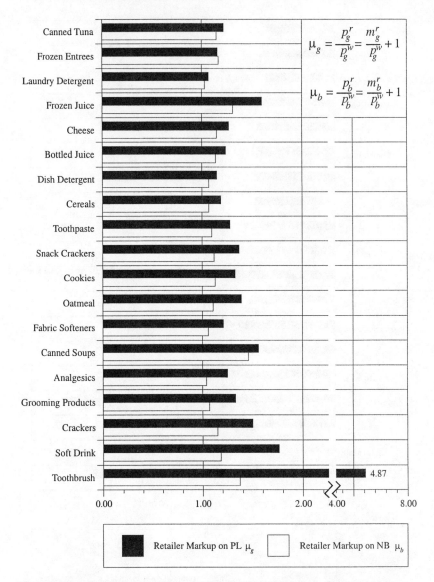

$$\mu_g = \frac{p_g^r}{p_g^w} = \frac{m_g^r}{p_g^w} + 1$$

$$\mu_b = \frac{p_b^r}{P_b^w} = \frac{m_b^r}{P_b^w} + 1$$

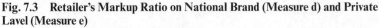

Fig. 7.3 Retailer's Markup Ratio on National Brand (Measure d) and Private Lavel (Measure e)

(μ_b), by category. According to the figure, for all but three products, the retailer's markup ratios for the nationally branded products are all less than 1.20. The exceptions are canned soups (1.46), toothbrushes (1.37), and frozen juice (1.31). Moreover, the retailer's markups on nationally branded products are small both in comparison to $\hat{\mu}$ and μ^w (see figure 7.4 for a comparison of μ_b with μ^w) and in comparison to retailer's markup on the private

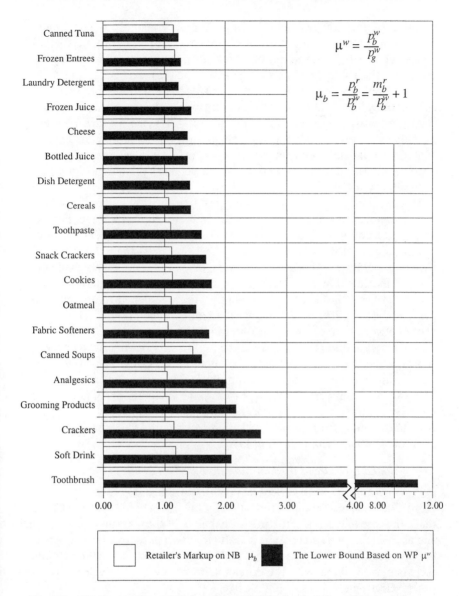

Fig. 7.4 The Lower Bound Markup Based on Wholesale Prices (Measure c) vs. Retailer's Markup on NB (Measure d)

label. Specifically, in all but one category (frozen entrees), retail markups are higher for private labels than for national brands. Second, in all but one category (frozen juice), the retail markups for nationally branded products are lower than the manufacturers' markups.

According to figure 7.3, the retailer's markup ratios for nationally branded products range from 1.03 for laundry detergent to 1.46 for canned soups. For more than one-third of categories—grooming products, analgesics, fabric softeners, toothpaste, cereal, dish detergents, and laundry detergents—the average retailer's markup ratio on the brand is less than 1.10.

In contrast, the retailer's markup ratios for private-label products are substantially higher. Omitting the puzzling case of the toothbrush category (with a measured retailer's markup ratio of 4.87), the average retailer's markup on the private-label version ranges from 1.07 for laundry detergents to 1.76 for soft drinks. Only in the categories of laundry detergents, dish detergents, cereals, and frozen entrees are the retailer's private-label markup ratios less than 1.20.

Thus we find clear evidence that retailers' markups are higher for private labels than national brands. This fact is well known in the trade. For example, according to Morton and Zettelmeyer (2000), retailers "achieve higher price-cost margins [on private-label products] than those earned with national brands. Industry observers, the popular press and academic work all indicate that this effect can be quite large." According to Hoch and Banerji (1993), "Industry sources suggest that retailer gross margins on private labels are 20% to 30% higher than on national brands." This divergence between retailers' margins on branded and private-label products is associated with differences between the profitability of American and European supermarkets. "In European supermarkets, higher private-label sales result in higher average pretax profits. U.S. supermarkets average only 15% of sales from private labels, they average 2% pretax profits from all sales. By contrast, European grocery stores such as Sainsbury's, with 54% of its sales coming from private labels, and Tesco, with 41%, average 7% pretax profits" (Quelch and Harding 1996).

Lower-Bound Measure of the Full Markup Based on Retail Prices

Previous authors, such as Scherer (1980), Carlton and Perloff (1994), and Nevo (2001), have focused on the ratio of retail prices μ^r. Although we have made the case that $\hat{\mu}$ is a better measure than μ^r of the markup paid by consumers over full marginal cost, it is useful to report μ^r as well, both for comparison with these previous studies and because retail prices are becoming increasingly available with the development of new technologies in computers, electronic scanners, and the like.

Figure 7.5 shows the markup ratios for national brands based on the retail prices of nationally branded products and private labels, μ^r, along with our preferred lower bound, $\hat{\mu}$. The markup ratio figures computing using the retail prices range from a high of 2.33 for toothbrushes to a low of 1.14 for canned tuna. The majority of the markups are below 1.4, the only exceptions being crackers (2.00), grooming products (1.75), analgesics (1.63), fabric softeners (1.52), and cookies (1.49), as well as the aforementioned

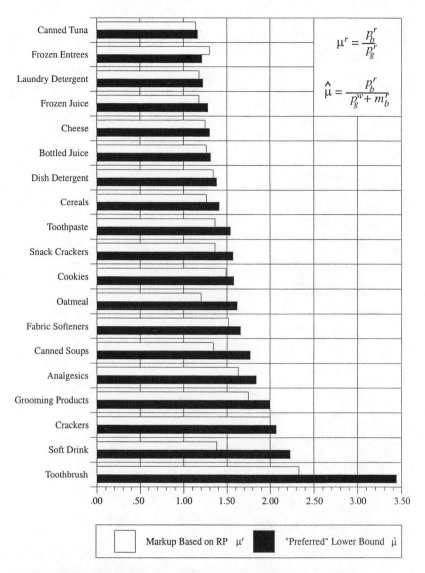

$$\mu^r = \frac{p_b^r}{p_g^r}$$

$$\hat{\mu} = \frac{p_b^r}{p_g^w + m_b^r}$$

Legend: Markup Based on RP μ^r (white) · "Preferred" Lower Bound $\hat{\mu}$ (black)

Fig. 7.5   National Brand Markup: The "Preferred" Lower Bound (Measure a) vs. the Lower Bound Measure Based on Retail Price (Measure b)

toothbrushes (2.33). This is in general true within the individual categories as well, again with the exception of the above categories. Recall that μ^r underestimates the full markup to a greater extent than does $\hat{\mu}$, because μ^r treats the handling cost more conservatively by using as its proxy the retailer's margin on the private-label product.

Summary

To further explore the relationship between our preferred lower-bound ratio and the lower-bound ratios computed using the wholesale and the retail prices, we plot the three lower-bound series together in figure 7.6. As the figure demonstrates, the lower-bound ratio calculated using the wholesale price usually exceeds our "preferred" lower bound, whereas the lower-bound ratio calculated using the retail price typically falls below the pre-

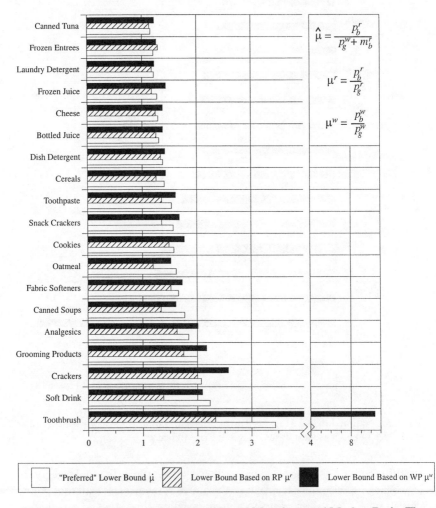

Fig. 7.6   Lower Bounds on the National Brand Manufacturers' Markup Ratio: The "Preferred" Lower Bound (Measure a), the Lower Bound Based on Wholesale Price (Measure c), and the Lower Bound Based on Retail Price (Measure b)

ferred lower bound. The figure also indicates that the three lower-bound measures attain values that are closer to each other as the markups' size decreases.

7.5.2   Detailed Results for Some Selected Categories and Products

In tables 7A.1–7A.19, we report detailed tabulations of all five markup ratios derived in section 7.2.3, for each national brand/private-label pair for all nineteen product categories included in our data set.

Among the nineteen categories, the toothbrush category (table 7A.1) attains the highest average value of our preferred lower-bound markup ratio, with a category average of 3.44. Within the category, four types of Crest toothbrush (of different size and strength) attain a markup ratio in the range of 5.48–5.80, and two types of Reach toothbrush attain markup values of 4.36 and 4.56. The results for the remaining products in this category suggest more moderate market power, with markup ratios in the range of 1.56 for Johnson and Johnson waxed mint dental floss and 1.49 for the Pepsodent toothbrush.

The manufacturers' lower-bound markup ratios calculated using the wholesale prices attain even higher values. For example, for the four Crest and two Reach toothbrushes, μ^w falls in the range of 13.00–19.84. Overall, the category average of these markup figures is 10.43. The reasons for these very high measured markup figures, unique to the toothbrush category, remain a mystery.

The figures in the last two columns of table 7A.1 suggest that the retailer's markup on private-label products in this category far exceeds its markup ratio on the corresponding nationally branded product by nearly an order of magnitude. For example, for the highest markup brand, the Crest toothbrush, the retailer's markup ratio is only 1.14, whereas the markup ratio on the corresponding private label is 7.03. Overall, the retailer's average markup ratio for nationally branded products in this category equals 1.37, whereas the average markup ratio for private-label products equals 4.87.

Finally, the lower-bound markup ratios calculated using the retail prices are more moderate, although for the top four products the ratio still exceeds 3.00, and for another two products it is close to 3.00. The category average for this ratio is 2.33.

For the remaining eighteen categories we find more moderate markup figures. Nevertheless, in most categories they are quite substantial. For example, for the analgesics category, reported in table 7A.5, the average of our preferred lower-bound markup ratio is 1.84. Several products in this category have especially high markup ratios. For example, the preferred lower bound on the markup ratio for children's Anacin-3 tablets is 4.99 (column [1]). Four other products with especially high markup ratios are Panadol children's tablets, with the lower-bound markup ratio of 3.91, followed by

Tylenol extra- strength caplets, with 2.53; Tylenol tablets (regular), with 2.44; and Bayer children's aspirin, with a markup ratio of 2.28.[10]

Turning to the manufacturers' markup ratios calculated using the wholesale prices (column [2]), we find that they are quantitatively very similar to the values of $\hat{\mu}$, with the exception of children's Anacin-3 tablets, with a manufacturer's lower-bound markup ratio of 7.62, and Panadol children's tablets, with a manufacturer's lower-bound markup ratio of 6.73. Further, as we move down the list from the highest preferred lower bound to the lowest, the discrepancy between the two ratios essentially disappears, as expected. Overall, the lower-bound manufacturers' markup ratios calculated using wholesale prices are high. For example, the figures in the table indicate that for seven of the twenty-four products in this category, the manufacturers' lower-bound markup ratio exceeds 2.00, and for another ten products the ratio exceeds 1.7. Only for two products, both Tylenol extra-strength tablets (different sizes), is μ^w below 1.2. Overall, the average manufacturer's lower-bound markup ratio for this category equals 2.01.

The figures in the third column of table 7A.5, which measure the lower bound on the full markup using retail prices, are smaller than the first two ratios, as predicted by the inequalities derived in section 7.2.3. Still, the markup ratios we obtain for the analgesics category are large. For example, of the twenty-four products, for three products—children's Anacin-3 tablets, Panadol children's tablets, and Tylenol extra-strength caplets—the markup ratio calculated using only the retail prices exceeds 2.0; for ten other products the ratio exceeds 1.6, and for another eight products the markup ratio exceeds 1.3. The average markup ratio using retail prices for the analgesics category equals 1.63.

Finally, the retailer's markup on the national brand systematically exceeds its markup on the private label. For example, for twenty-three of the twenty-four products (Bayer children's aspirin being the only exception), the retailer's markup on nationally branded products in this category is less than 1.15, with an overall average of only 1.04. In contrast, the markup ratio on the private label is substantially higher, averaging 1.25.

Next, consider the cereals category. According to table 7A.12, all of the markup figures we find in this category are smaller than those we reported for the analgesics category. As the figures in the first column of the table suggest, here the preferred lower-bound markup ratio falls in the range 1.27–1.57, with an average of 1.41, again suggestive of very substantial market power. Total raisin bran attains the highest lower-bound value with 1.57, followed by Kellogg's corn flakes, with 1.54, and Post raisin bran and Kellogg's Nut & Honey, each with a lower-bound markup ratio of 1.41.

The manufacturers' markup figures reported in the second column of

---

10. Ernie Berndt noted that the extraordinarily high markups on children's medicine might possibly be explained by parents' risk aversion regarding their children's health.

table 7A.12 are only slightly higher than the preferred lower-bound figures. For example, for Total raisin bran, the lower bound on the manufacturer's markup ratio equals 1.61, in comparison to the preferred lower bound of 1.57. The manufacturers' markup and the preferred markup figures are equally close for the remaining products of the category. Overall, cereal manufacturers on average mark up their branded product prices to 1.43 of their marginal cost.

According to the third column of table 7A.12, the markup ratios we obtain using retail prices average 1.26 for the cereals category. Total raisin bran still attains the highest value with 1.46, and Kellogg's corn flakes' markup ratio is a distant second with a value of 1.23. Finally, comparing the retailer's markup ratio on branded products to its markup ratio on private labels, we again find that the latter, 1.19 on average, exceeds the former, 1.07 on average.

It is instructive to compare our markup figures in this category to existing econometric estimates. The category of breakfast cereals has been a subject of several recent studies, such as those by Hausman (1997) and Nevo (2001). Nevo presents estimates of price-marginal cost margins under different assumptions on market structure and finds that they range from about 1.3 to as high as 2.0, very much consistent with the lower-bound measures reported here.

As a final example, consider the crackers category, in which we were able to find ten matching pairs of national brand and private-label products. According to table 7A.3, our preferred lower-bound markup figures are relatively high, with the highest ratio for Nabisco premium saltines (2.84), and the lowest for Salerno graham crackers (1.34); the overall category average is 2.07. For four branded products, two Nabisco Premium saltines (different sizes) and two Salerno saltines (also different sizes), the ratio exceeds 2.00. Only for two products is the lower-bound markup ratio less than 1.40.

The manufacturers' lower-bound markup ratios (second column of table 7A.3) substantially exceed the preferred lower-bound figures. For example, the category average of the manufacturers' lower-bound markup equals 2.57, which is about 25 percent higher than the preferred lower bound. Further, for Nabisco Premium saltines, the manufacturer's lower-bound markup ratio is 4.22, about 50 percent higher than the corresponding preferred lower bound.

It turns out that in the crackers category we obtain especially high markup figures even if we consider the lower bound on the full markup ratio calculated using only the retail prices. For example, according to table 7A.3 (column [3]), the category average of this markup ratio is 2.00, which is the second highest (the toothbrush category being first) among all nineteen categories included in our study. Individual product markup ratios calculated using the retail prices range from the highest ratio of 3.12 for Nabisco premium saltines to 1.20 for Salerno graham crackers.

Finally, if we consider the retailer's markup on the nationally branded and private-label products, we find that, as before, the retailer's markup on the private label is systematically higher than its markup on the nationally branded product, with an average of 1.50 in contrast to 1.15, a difference of about 20 percent.[11]

Next, consider some specific products that stand out in other categories. In the canned soup category (table 7A.6), the only nationally branded product with a preferred lower-bound markup ratio in excess of 2.00 is Campbell's tomato soup, with a ratio of 2.61. The remaining products in this category attain a markup value of less than 2.00. In the cookies category (table 7A.9), two brand-name products, Nutter Butter peanut butter and Cameo crème sandwich, attain a "preferred" lower-bound markup ratio of about 2.70, and another ten products attain markup values exceeding 1.40. In the snack cracker category (table 7A.10), Nabisco Ritz cracker attains the highest preferred lower-bound markup ratio, 1.74, followed by Nabisco Ritz Bits, with a ratio of 1.58.

In the soft drinks category (table 7A.2), we find that Coca-Cola Classic and Pepsi cola attain preferred lower-bound markup values of 3.83 and 2.36, respectively. Other branded products with particularly high lower-bound markup ratios in the soft drink category are Schweppes ginger ale, with 3.52; Snapple strawberry and Snapple pink lemonade, with 2.88 and 2.47, respectively; Diet Pepsi, with 2.28; and Seagrams ginger ale, with 2.18. Diet Coke attains a more moderate lower-bound markup ratio of 1.69.

Finally, the nationally branded products attaining the highest preferred lower-bound markup ratios in the remaining categories include Motts apple juice in the bottled juice category, Minute Maid pink lemonade in the frozen juice category, Crest Regular in the toothpaste category, Kraft soft Philly cream cheese in the cheese category, Dawn lemon in the dish detergent category, L.C. Baked cheese ravioli in the frozen entrees category, Bounce single scented in the fabric softener category, Trac II Plus cart 10 in the grooming products category, ultra Ivory Snow in the laundry detergent category, quick Quaker oats in the oatmeal category, and Chicken of the Sea lite tuna in water in the canned tuna category.

7.6   The Role of the Materials Share

It might be worthwhile to hypothesize as to the determinants of cross-category and within-category variation in the magnitude of markup ratios. Consider first the within-category variation. In most categories, we find

11. Slade (1998) assumes a 20 percent retail markup for saltine crackers in her study of price adjustment costs at several Pennsylvania grocery stores. This is equivalent to a retailer's markup ratio of 1.20. The average retailer's markup ratio on the nationally branded product we report is 1.15, with the interquartile range of (1.12–1.17) indeed very close to what Slade assumes.

that more heavily branded and well-known products achieve higher markups. For example, Kellogg's corn flakes, Nabisco Premium saltine crackers, Crest toothpaste, Coca-Cola Classic, Motts apple juice, Nutter Butter peanut butter, Nabisco Ritz crackers, Kraft cream cheese, Dawn lemon dish detergent, Bounce single scented fabric softener, and so on, which have the highest markups within respective categories, all are heavily advertised and widely recognized nationally branded products.

Perhaps a more interesting issue is the variation in markup ratios across product categories. Basu and Fernald (1997) and Rotemberg and Woodford (1996) provide the following formula linking the gross output markups that are the focus of this paper to the value added markups, via products material share:

$$\mu^v = \frac{\mu(1 - s)}{1 - \mu s},$$

where μ^v denotes the markup on real value added, s denotes the intermediate inputs share in total revenue, and μ denotes the gross output markup. The formula implies that if the value added markup is to be finite, the gross output markup must not exceed $1/s$.

Nevo (2001), using data from the Annual Survey of Manufacturers over the period 1988–92, provides materials share figures for ready-to-eat cereals (SIC [Standard Industrial Classification] 2043) and for the food industry overall (SIC 20). For cereals, he reports a materials share of 26.5 percent, which from the above formula implies that the gross output markup should not exceed $1/0.265 = 3.77$. Indeed, according to our findings (see figure 7.1), the preferred lower-bound markup ratio for the cereals category equals 1.41, well below the upper bound imposed by the above formula.

For the entire food industry, Nevo reports a materials share of 63.4 percent. This imposes an upper bound of 1.58 on the gross output markup ratio. Twelve of the nineteen categories we study would be classified as food. These are soft drinks, crackers, canned soups, oatmeal, cookies, snack crackers, cereals, bottled juice, cheese, frozen juice, frozen entrees, and canned tuna. Of these twelve categories, the numerical values of the preferred markup ratios for the last eight categories fall below 1.58. For two additional categories (oatmeal and canned soups), the markup ratio is only slightly higher than 1.58. For only two categories (crackers and soft drinks) does the markup ratio substantially exceed 1.58. This suggests that materials share in these two categories must be smaller than 26.5 percent, which seems reasonable. Moreover, the interquartile ranges we report indicate that the great majority of the products in each one of the twelve categories satisfy this constraint.

Finally, without having actual data on the cost shares of intermediate inputs used by manufacturers of individual food categories, we strongly suspect that the products with the lowest markup ratios, such as canned tuna, frozen entrees, cheese, frozen juice, and bottled juice, also have the highest share of materials.[12]

7.7 Concluding Remarks

In this paper we study the size of markups for nationally branded products sold in a large U.S. retail supermarket chain. Our approach, which we hope will serve as a complement to more structural econometric approaches, treats the wholesale price of a comparable private-label product as an upper bound on the marginal costs faced by the brand manufacturer. Using scanner data from a large Midwestern chain, we have computed various upper- and lower-bound markup ratios for over 230 products in nineteen categories. We found that markup ratios measured this way range from 3.44 for toothbrushes and 2.23 for soft drinks to about 1.15–1.20 for canned tuna and frozen entrees, with the majority of categories falling in the range 1.40–2.10. Lower bounds on manufacturers' markups are even higher. Thus, the data indicate that markups on nationally branded products sold in U.S. supermarkets are large.

Our approach offers several benefits. Because it involves only a simple computation (once the data have been assembled), the method permits calculation of markups for a large variety of products. It is transparent and intuitive, and it offers a benchmark comparison for more structural approaches.

Particularly in light of the importance of markups in recent macroeconomic discourse, one might ask whether the finding of high markups for heavily advertised differentiated products generalizes to the economy at large. In this direction, it is worth noting that many "commodity" products such as automotive parts, personal computers and their components, and many other producers' goods come in both branded and nonbranded (OEM or Original Equipment Manufacturer) versions, and that the price gap for those products is comparable to that for the supermarket goods we have studied. This is also true for other consumer goods sold outside the supermarket industry, home and office supply products being one example.

Appendix

In this appendix we present detailed results for each pair of national brand and private-label products, for each of the nineteen product categories in-

---

12. We are grateful to Susanto Basu for calling our attention to the above formula and its implications.

cluded in our data set. The results are reported in separate tables, tables 7A.1 through 7A.19, by categories.

In these tables, columns (1)–(5) correspond to the five markup measures we report in the paper, as follows:

1. Column (1) corresponds to the markup measure (a), $\hat{\mu}$, which is our "preferred" lower bound on the full markup.
2. Column (2) corresponds to the markup measure (c), μ^w, which provides a lower bound on manufacturers' markup by using wholesale prices.
3. Column (3) corresponds to the markup measure (b), μ^r, which provides a lower bound on the full markup by using retail prices.
4. Column (4) corresponds to the markup measure (d), μ_b, which is the retailer's markup on the nationally branded product.
5. Column (5) corresponds to the markup measure (e), μ_g, which measures the retailer's markup on private label product.

In each table, the figures in parentheses indicate the interquartile range. The sample size numbers, which are listed in the last column of each table, report the number of weekly time series observations of price and cost data used in calculating the various markup measures for the corresponding national brand/private-label product pair. See text for more details.

Table 7A.1   Toothbrush

Product Pair	Full Markup: "Preferred" Lower Bound ($\hat{\mu}$)	Manufacturer's Markup: Lower Bound based on Wholesale Price (μ^w)	Lower Bound for Full Markup Based on Retail Price (μ^r)	Retailer's Markup on National Brand (μ_b)	Retailer's Markup on Private Label (μ_g)	Sample Size
Crest toothbrush #5 soft	5.80 (4.55, 6.35)	19.84 (8.64, 41.23)	3.33 (2.88, 3.75)	1.14 (1.12, 1.16)	7.03 (3.26, 13.17)	170
Crest toothbrush #1 medium strong	5.75 (4.68, 6.40)	23.70 (8.64, 41.23)	3.34 (2.88, 3.75)	1.14 (1.12, 1.16)	8.01 (3.26, 13.17)	170
Crest toothbrush #2 medium strong	5.57 (4.55, 6.35)	19.26 (8.64, 39.86)	3.31 (2.88, 3.75)	1.14 (1.12, 1.16)	6.65 (3.26, 13.17)	170
Crest toothbrush #6 soft	5.48 (4.55, 6.35)	16.20 (8.64, 38.91)	3.28 (2.88, 3.75)	1.14 (1.12, 1.16)	5.78 (3.26, 13.17)	170
Reach between soft	4.56 (3.79, 5.19)	17.97 (8.27, 34.60)	2.92 (2.59, 3.32)	1.21 (1.20, 1.22)	7.70 (3.26, 13.17)	170
Reach between medium	4.36 (3.79, 5.13)	13.00 (8.96, 29.79)	2.92 (2.52, 3.32)	1.21 (1.20, 1.22)	5.77 (3.26, 13.17)	170
J&J floss waxed mint	1.56 (1.54, 1.63)	2.05 (2.02, 2.24)	1.54 (1.50, 1.75)	1.41 (1.41, 1.45)	1.90 (1.87, 1.94)	164
J&J floss waxed regular	1.55 (1.54, 1.63)	2.05 (2.02, 2.25)	1.52 (1.49, 1.71)	1.42 (1.41, 1.45)	1.92 (1.87, 1.94)	163
J&J floss unwaxed regular	1.55 (1.53, 1.64)	2.04 (2.00, 2.26)	1.51 (1.49, 1.71)	1.42 (1.41, 1.45)	1.93 (1.90, 1.94)	164
Pepsodent toothbrush medium	1.50 (1.37, 1.73)	3.33 (1.96, 7.39)	1.17 (1.00, 1.43)	2.04 (1.97, 2.02)	5.65 (3.26, 13.17)	170
Pepsodent toothbrush soft perfect	1.49 (1.34, 1.76)	3.16 (1.93, 7.85)	1.16 (1.00, 1.43)	1.95 (1.95, 2.00)	5.52 (2.92, 13.17)	170
Weighted average	3.44 (1.55, 5.57)	10.43 (2.05, 19.26)	2.33 (1.51, 3.31)	1.37 (1.14, 1.42)	4.87 (1.93, 7.03)	

Notes: Column one corresponds to markup measure (a), column two to markup measure (b), column three to markup measure (c), column four to markup measure (d), and column five—to markup measure Figures in the parentheses indicate the inter-quartile range. See text for details.

Table 7A.2   **Soft Drink**

Product Pair	Full Markup: "Preferred" Lower Bound ($\hat{\mu}$)	Manufacturer's Markup: Lower Bound based on Wholesale Price (μ^w)	Lower Bound for Full Markup Based on Retail Price (μ^r)	Retailer's Markup on National Brand (μ_b)	Retailer's Markup on Private Label (μ_g)	Sample Size
Coca-Cola classic	3.83 (1.84, 2.55)	2.35 (2.10, 3.07)	1.38 (1.20, 1.89)	1.15 (1.03, 1.24)	1.91 (1.41, 2.10)	389
Schweppes ginger ale	3.52 (1.07, 2.14)	2.17 (1.69, 2.96)	1.30 (1.11, 1.71)	1.15 (0.96, 1.26)	1.74 (1.41, 2.05)	390
Snapple strawberry kiwi	2.88 (1.49, 1.75)	2.36 (2.13, 2.72)	1.02 (1.22, 1.51)	1.20 (1.47, 1.68)	2.88 (2.55, 3.05)	108
Snapple pink lemonade	2.47 (1.49, 1.75)	2.26 (2.13, 2.74)	1.06 (1.22, 1.51)	1.27 (1.47, 1.68)	2.83 (2.55, 3.05)	122
Pepsi cola n/r	2.36 (1.90, 2.73)	2.23 (2.19, 3.21)	1.38 (1.22, 1.89)	1.18 (1.03, 1.18)	1.83 (1.41, 2.10)	390
Pepsi diet n/r	2.28 (1.86, 2.69)	2.25 (2.15, 3.14)	1.41 (1.22, 1.90)	1.14 (1.03, 1.18)	1.78 (1.40, 2.09)	390
Seagrams ginger ale 1	2.18 (1.81, 2.48)	2.47 (2.48, 2.91)	1.37 (1.25, 1.68)	1.21 (1.07, 1.39)	2.13 (2.03, 2.30)	75
Pepsi cola	2.07 (1.70, 2.23)	2.07 (1.87, 2.25)	1.53 (1.42, 1.71)	1.06 (1.02, 1.15)	1.42 (1.38, 1.46)	222
Schweppes lime seltzer	2.06 (1.47, 2.61)	1.97 (1.48, 2.55)	1.23 (1.20, 1.20)	1.20 (1.01, 1.37)	1.88 (1.63, 2.15)	36
Seagrams tonic 1 liter	2.05 (1.78, 1.89)	2.52 (2.43, 2.70)	1.44 (1.32, 1.59)	1.26 (1.32, 1.35)	2.20 (2.13, 2.28)	125
Barq's root beer	1.95 (1.63, 2.26)	2.00 (1.86, 2.48)	1.39 (1.12, 1.80)	1.26 (1.03, 1.30)	1.76 (1.45, 2.04)	364
Schweppes tonic n/r	1.94 (1.36, 2.25)	2.28 (1.75, 2.73)	1.36 (1.19, 1.51)	1.37 (1.06, 1.47)	2.09 (1.87, 2.39)	388
Schweppes diet tonic	1.93 (1.36, 2.23)	2.29 (1.75, 2.73)	1.35 (1.19, 1.51)	1.37 (1.06, 1.47)	2.10 (1.87, 2.39)	388
Royal Crown cola	1.89 (1.46, 2.48)	1.88 (1.75, 2.85)	1.19 (1.11, 1.61)	1.32 (1.03, 1.26)	1.75 (1.40, 2.05)	389
A&W root beer regular	1.86 (1.30, 2.13)	1.78 (1.49, 2.54)	1.16 (1.02, 1.51)	1.14 (1.02, 1.26)	1.68 (1.40, 2.02)	389
Minute Maid fruit punch	1.80 (1.66, 1.97)	2.33 (2.01, 2.62)	1.48 (1.25, 1.75)	1.18 (1.15, 1.30)	1.97 (1.79, 2.32)	86
A&W root beer	1.79 (1.73, 2.01)	1.80 (1.77, 2.07)	1.68 (1.60, 1.98)	1.01 (0.99, 1.07)	1.09 (1.08, 1.12)	253
New York seltzer cola	1.77 (1.16, 2.04)	2.66 (1.23, 3.26)	1.70 (1.19, 1.95)	1.35 (1.36, 1.36)	2.03 (1.40, 2.34)	34
Snapple kiwi strawberry s	1.75 (1.40, 1.74)	2.38 (2.12, 2.74)	1.29 (1.22, 2.37)	1.47 (1.48, 1.74)	2.93 (2.80, 3.05)	36
Sunkist orange	1.75 (1.17, 2.17)	1.46 (1.40, 2.46)	1.10 (1.00, 1.48)	1.64 (1.03, 1.32)	1.79 (1.45, 2.05)	390
Schweppes ginger ale	1.73 (1.29, 2.10)	2.06 (1.60, 2.67)	1.31 (1.14, 1.47)	1.49 (1.21, 1.68)	2.06 (1.80, 2.43)	340
Canada Dry ginger ale	1.72 (1.34, 1.93)	2.36 (1.76, 2.50)	1.48 (1.27, 1.52)	1.47 (1.30, 1.55)	2.09 (1.81, 2.43)	305
A&W root beer sugar free	1.70 (1.25, 2.08)	1.72 (1.44, 2.54)	1.18 (1.06, 1.51)	1.19 (1.02, 1.26)	1.67 (1.41, 2.02)	389
Diet Coke	1.69 (1.84, 2.53)	2.25 (2.12, 3.03)	1.42 (1.21, 1.89)	1.14 (1.03, 1.24)	1.80 (1.40, 2.09)	389

(*continued*)

Table 7A.2 (continued)

Product Pair	Full Markup: "Preferred" Lower Bound ($\hat{\mu}$)	Manufacturer's Markup: Lower Bound based on Wholesale Price (μ^w)	Lower Bound for Full Markup Based on Retail Price (μ^r)	Retailer's Markup on National Brand (μ_b)	Retailer's Markup on Private Label (μ_g)	Sample Size
Canada Dry tonic water	1.69 (1.39, 1.90)	2.42 (1.80, 2.55)	1.48 (1.29, 1.59)	1.47 (1.30, 1.50)	2.11 (1.91, 2.39)	355
Minute Maid orange	1.69 (1.38, 2.12)	1.72 (1.45, 2.11)	1.67 (1.50, 2.01)	1.08 (1.01, 1.12)	1.09 (1.08, 1.13)	52
Ocean Spray kiwi strawberry	1.67 (1.60, 1.79)	2.66 (2.49, 2.96)	1.54 (1.48, 1.68)	1.56 (1.52, 1.64)	2.74 (2.22, 3.05)	73
Crystal Light kiwi strawberry	1.65 (1.55, 1.75)	2.54 (2.36, 2.80)	1.39 (1.34, 1.59)	1.54 (1.47, 1.65)	2.89 (2.55, 3.05)	81
Pepsi cola cans	1.63 (1.66, 2.06)	1.65 (1.64, 2.09)	1.58 (1.50, 2.01)	1.05 (1.00, 1.04)	1.09 (1.07, 1.10)	202
Fruitopia pink lemonade	1.61 (1.58, 1.65)	2.43 (2.45, 2.54)	1.42 (1.31, 1.51)	1.56 (1.51, 1.65)	2.81 (2.80, 3.05)	102
Sunkist orange	1.58 (1.59, 1.79)	1.62 (1.66, 1.85)	1.53 (1.60, 1.81)	1.03 (1.03, 1.06)	1.10 (1.08, 1.12)	254
Barq's diet root beer	1.56 (1.71, 2.29)	2.12 (1.92, 2.40)	1.27 (1.03, 1.40)	1.06 (1.02, 2.19)	1.86 (1.57, 2.12)	62
Royal Crown cola	1.56 (1.54, 1.87)	1.65 (1.62, 2.08)	1.30 (1.31, 1.71)	1.12 (1.10, 1.18)	1.42 (1.38, 1.46)	222
Minute Maid orange	1.55 (1.47, 1.72)	1.81 (1.62, 2.03)	1.23 (1.11, 1.34)	1.19 (1.14, 1.26)	1.76 (1.40, 2.02)	137
Seagrams ginger ale	1.44 (1.46, 1.96)	1.99 (1.74, 2.39)	1.37 (1.12, 1.79)	1.33 (1.09, 1.40)	1.88 (1.57, 2.12)	177
Barq's root beer	1.40 (1.74, 2.38)	2.20 (1.99, 2.49)	1.22 (1.03, 1.40)	1.06 (1.02, 1.21)	1.97 (1.79, 2.12)	56
Barq's root beer	1.36 (1.32, 1.49)	1.48 (1.44, 1.64)	1.01 (0.96, 1.12)	1.19 (1.14, 1.27)	1.75 (1.41, 2.01)	31
Seagram's lemon lime	1.04 (1.43, 1.65)	1.75 (1.67, 2.00)	1.31 (1.12, 1.20)	1.29 (1.18, 1.39)	1.81 (1.64, 2.12)	50
Weighted average	2.23 (1.56, 2.13)	2.09 (1.72, 2.29)	1.38 (1.19, 1.48)	1.18 (1.14, 1.37)	1.76 (1.70, 1.99)	

Notes: See table 7A.1.

Table 7A.3   Crackers

Product Pair	Full Markup: "Preferred" Lower Bound ($\hat{\mu}$)	Manufacturer's Markup: Lower Bound Based on Wholesale Price (μ^w)	Lower Bound for Full Markup Based on Retail Price (μ^r)	Retailer's Markup on National Brand (μ_b)	Retailer's Markup on Private Label (μ_g)	Sample Size
Nabisco premium saltines	2.84 (2.62, 3.12)	4.22 (3.71, 4.51)	3.12 (2.27, 3.86)	1.17 (1.14, 1.18)	1.63 (1.36, 1.81)	125
Nabisco premium saltines	2.30 (2.14, 2.43)	2.75 (2.50, 3.08)	2.32 (2.14, 2.61)	1.15 (1.11, 1.17)	1.35 (1.20, 1.57)	82
Salerno saltines	2.11 (2.05, 2.23)	2.47 (2.34, 2.68)	2.11 (1.89, 2.40)	1.13 (1.10, 1.16)	1.34 (1.20, 1.57)	82
Salerno saltines	2.03 (1.72, 2.42)	2.97 (2.47, 3.51)	2.39 (1.90, 2.98)	1.28 (1.17, 1.36)	1.63 (1.36, 1.81)	125
Nabisco premium saltines	1.83 (1.60, 2.04)	2.08 (1.77, 2.39)	1.44 (1.20, 1.65)	1.16 (1.13, 1.18)	1.68 (1.58, 1.71)	372
Honey Maid grahams	1.67 (1.55, 1.69)	1.81 (1.65, 1.82)	1.45 (1.37, 1.42)	1.11 (1.10, 1.12)	1.38 (1.32, 1.42)	90
Keebler graham crackers	1.58 (1.48, 1.69)	1.70 (1.58, 1.83)	1.39 (1.27, 1.50)	1.12 (1.10, 1.13)	1.37 (1.32, 1.42)	380
Nabisco graham crackers	1.52 (1.43, 1.64)	1.63 (1.50, 1.76)	1.31 (1.22, 1.41)	1.10 (1.10, 1.12)	1.37 (1.32, 1.42)	380
Salerno saltines	1.37 (1.24, 1.56)	1.52 (1.34, 1.77)	1.14 (1.00, 1.30)	1.27 (1.17, 1.36)	1.67 (1.59, 1.71)	372
Salerno graham crackers	1.34 (1.26, 1.41)	1.42 (1.32, 1.50)	1.20 (1.12, 1.23)	1.15 (1.14, 1.18)	1.37 (1.32, 1.41)	380
Weighted average	2.07 (1.52, 2.11)	2.57 (1.63, 2.75)	2.00 (1.31, 2.32)	1.15 (1.12, 1.17)	1.50 (1.37, 1.63)	

Notes: See table 7A.1.

Table 7A.4   Grooming Products

Product Pair	Full Markup: "Preferred" Lower Bound (μ)	Manufacturer's Markup: Lower Bound Based on Wholesale Price (μ^w)	Lower Bound for Full Markup Based on Retail Price (μ^r)	Retailer's Markup on National Brand (μ_b)	Retailer's Markup on Private Label (μ_g)	Sample Size
Trac II plus cartridge 10	2.30 (2.13, 2.45)	2.43 (2.22, 2.60)	2.04 (1.88, 2.16)	1.04 (1.04, 1.04)	1.24 (1.24, 1.26)	80
Slim twin disposabl	2.29 (1.78, 2.57)	2.86 (2.47, 3.18)	1.77 (1.68, 1.89)	1.18 (1.12, 1.17)	1.89 (1.91, 1.93)	211
~Slim twin cartridge	1.96 (1.94, 1.97)	2.04 (2.02, 2.05)	1.70 (1.69, 1.72)	1.04 (1.04, 1.04)	1.24 (1.24, 1.25)	73
Good News pivot plus	1.63 (1.35, 2.02)	1.77 (1.41, 2.27)	1.55 (1.23, 1.95)	1.09 (1.09, 1.11)	1.25 (1.24, 1.27)	100
Good News pivot plus	1.47 (1.30, 1.42)	1.55 (1.33, 1.50)	1.35 (1.17, 1.38)	1.08 (1.07, 1.10)	1.24 (1.24, 1.24)	115
Weighted average	2.00 (1.63, 2.29)	2.17 (1.77, 2.43)	1.75 (1.55, 1.77)	1.07 (1.04, 1.09)	1.33 (1.24, 1.25)	

Notes: See table 7A.1. The symbol "~" is an internal code used by Dominick's to identify discontinued products.

Table 7A.5   **Analgesics**

Product Pair	Full Markup: "Preferred" Lower Bound ($\hat{\mu}$)	Manufacturer's Markup: Lower Bound Based on Wholesale Price (μ^w)	Lower Bound for Full Markup Based on Retail Price (μ^r)	Retailer's Markup on National Brand (μ_b)	Retailer's Markup on Private Label (μ_g)	Sample Size
Anacin-3 children's tablets	4.99 (4.90, 5.03)	7.62 (7.41, 7.84)	3.77 (3.65, 3.94)	1.09 (1.08, 1.10)	2.20 (2.18, 2.20)	40
Panadol children's tablets	3.91 (3.84, 3.93)	6.73 (6.75, 7.25)	3.51 (3.51, 3.78)	1.14 (1.14, 1.16)	2.20 (2.18, 2.20)	43
Tylenol extra strength caplet	2.53 (2.24, 2.76)	2.81 (2.38, 3.08)	2.23 (1.91, 2.46)	1.06 (1.05, 1.06)	1.33 (1.29, 1.35)	392
Tylenol tablets regular	2.44 (1.66, 3.29)	2.50 (1.68, 3.37)	1.92 (1.40, 2.42)	1.02 (1.01, 1.02)	1.30 (1.23, 1.38)	392
Bayer children's aspirin	2.28 (2.16, 2.36)	3.23 (3.04, 3.36)	1.81 (1.72, 1.91)	1.23 (1.22, 1.25)	2.19 (2.18, 2.20)	43
Tylenol infant drops	1.94 (1.87, 1.91)	2.09 (2.01, 2.05)	1.71 (1.67, 1.68)	1.07 (1.07, 1.08)	1.31 (1.30, 1.31)	114
~Excedrin IB caplets	1.91 (1.78, 1.98)	2.04 (1.86, 2.14)	1.78 (1.63, 1.89)	1.07 (1.06, 1.07)	1.22 (1.22, 1.23)	89
~Excedrin IB tablets 50	1.86 (1.69, 1.97)	1.97 (1.77, 2.11)	1.68 (1.54, 1.84)	1.06 (1.06, 1.07)	1.24 (1.22, 1.26)	67
Advil	1.84 (1.68, 1.91)	1.91 (1.73, 1.98)	1.62 (1.49, 1.69)	1.04 (1.03, 1.05)	1.22 (1.21, 1.24)	349
Tylenol extra strength gelcaps	1.82 (1.55, 2.09)	1.86 (1.57, 2.13)	1.69 (1.45, 1.93)	1.02 (1.02, 1.03)	1.12 (1.11, 1.13)	365
Motrin IB gelcaps	1.79 (1.68, 1.82)	1.86 (1.74, 1.88)	1.60 (1.53, 1.61)	1.04 (1.04, 1.05)	1.21 (1.20, 1.21)	134
Aleve caplets	1.79 (1.67, 1.85)	1.86 (1.72, 1.94)	1.61 (1.50, 1.69)	1.05 (1.04, 1.05)	1.21 (1.20, 1.22)	145
~Excedrin IB tablets 50	1.79 (1.65, 1.95)	1.89 (1.72, 2.08)	1.63 (1.47, 1.80)	1.06 (1.06, 1.08)	1.24 (1.22, 1.26)	109
Tylenol extra strength tablets	1.79 (1.53, 1.85)	1.81 (1.55, 1.87)	1.56 (1.37, 1.60)	1.01 (1.01, 1.02)	1.18 (1.12, 1.21)	349
Advil	1.69 (1.57, 1.85)	1.72 (1.58, 1.90)	1.56 (1.43, 1.72)	1.02 (1.01, 1.03)	1.13 (1.12, 1.13)	365
Children's chewable fruit Tylenol	1.67 (1.60, 1.79)	1.83 (1.72, 2.00)	1.40 (1.32, 1.53)	1.13 (1.12, 1.14)	1.47 (1.44, 1.49)	71
Children's chewable grape Tylenol	1.66 (1.54, 1.79)	1.82 (1.66, 2.00)	1.39 (1.30, 1.53)	1.13 (1.12, 1.14)	1.47 (1.44, 1.49)	68
Advil	1.59 (1.41, 1.69)	1.61 (1.42, 1.71)	1.46 (1.29, 1.55)	1.02 (1.02, 1.02)	1.12 (1.12, 1.13)	39
Motrin IB caplets	1.53 (1.47, 1.55)	1.55 (1.48, 1.57)	1.42 (1.35, 1.43)	1.02 (1.02, 1.03)	1.12 (1.12, 1.12)	248
~Excedrin IB caplets	1.46 (1.28, 1.51)	1.48 (1.29, 1.54)	1.36 (1.19, 1.42)	1.03 (1.03, 1.04)	1.13 (1.12, 1.13)	75
~Excedrin IB tablets 100	1.44 (1.38, 1.49)	1.47 (1.40, 1.52)	1.35 (1.29, 1.39)	1.03 (1.03, 1.04)	1.13 (1.13, 1.13)	95
Advil caplets	1.41 (1.37, 1.47)	1.42 (1.37, 1.49)	1.28 (1.24, 1.35)	1.02 (1.01, 1.02)	1.12 (1.12, 1.12)	245
Tylenol extra strength tablets	1.18 (1.12, 1.19)	1.18 (1.12, 1.20)	1.02 (0.98, 1.04)	1.03 (1.03, 1.03)	1.19 (1.17, 1.20)	239
Tylenol extra strength tablets	1.17 (1.11, 1.19)	1.18 (1.12, 1.20)	1.02 (0.98, 1.04)	1.03 (1.03, 1.03)	1.19 (1.17, 1.19)	238
Weighted average	1.84 (1.56, 1.92)	2.01 (1.58, 2.06)	1.63 (1.40, 1.75)	1.04 (1.02, 1.07)	1.25 (1.13, 1.32)	

Notes: See table 7A.1. The symbol "~" is an internal code used by Dominick's to identify discontinued products.

Table 7A.6   Canned Soup

Product Pair	Full Markup: "Preferred" Lower Bound (μ)	Manufacturer's Markup: Lower Bound Based on Wholesale Price (μ^w)	Lower Bound for Full Markup Based on Retail Price (μ^r)	Retailer's Markup on National Brand (μ_b)	Retailer's Markup on Private Label (μ_g)	Sample Size
Campbell's tomato	2.61 (1.22, 1.69)	1.76 (1.30, 2.03)	1.37 (1.09, 1.22)	1.73 (1.10, 1.44)	1.58 (1.40, 2.17)	377
Progresso zesty minestrone	1.78 (1.63, 1.73)	2.07 (1.87, 2.02)	1.82 (1.67, 1.88)	1.20 (1.19, 1.22)	1.35 (1.28, 1.38)	114
Rokeach vegetable	1.67 (1.61, 1.81)	2.32 (2.09, 2.55)	1.92 (1.65, 2.06)	1.45 (1.22, 1.43)	1.75 (1.58, 1.88)	372
Home Cookin' tomato	1.57 (1.43, 1.74)	2.09 (1.80, 2.57)	1.81 (1.60, 1.90)	1.48 (1.44, 1.55)	1.86 (1.50, 2.17)	321
Campbell's vegetable beef	1.54 (1.42, 1.61)	1.59 (1.62, 1.98)	1.58 (1.49, 1.65)	1.31 (1.27, 1.34)	1.29 (1.38, 1.61)	377
Campbell's cream of celery	1.53 (1.11, 1.32)	1.73 (1.16, 1.52)	1.21 (1.04, 1.16)	1.36 (1.30, 1.47)	1.87 (1.40, 1.87)	377
Campbell's broccoli cheese	1.46 (1.16, 1.28)	1.63 (1.22, 1.42)	1.49 (1.15, 1.37)	1.34 (1.29, 1.43)	1.45 (1.39, 1.54)	246
Chunky chicken noodle	1.41 (1.62, 1.83)	2.26 (2.05, 2.50)	2.00 (1.98, 2.19)	1.30 (1.28, 1.37)	1.46 (1.25, 1.61)	321
Healthy Request Vegetable	1.41 (1.38, 1.49)	1.66 (1.55, 1.83)	1.52 (1.38, 1.77)	1.35 (1.27, 1.41)	1.48 (1.45, 1.54)	182
Campbell's chicken with rice	1.40 (1.16, 1.30)	1.58 (1.23, 1.48)	1.23 (1.07, 1.22)	1.38 (1.29, 1.44)	1.72 (1.35, 1.96)	377
Swan chicken broth	1.39 (1.17, 1.34)	1.61 (1.30, 1.70)	1.11 (1.11, 1.25)	1.55 (1.53, 1.68)	2.24 (1.78, 2.24)	269
Campbell's chicken and stars	1.37 (1.13, 1.28)	1.52 (1.19, 1.42)	1.30 (1.12, 1.27)	1.35 (1.29, 1.41)	1.50 (1.35, 1.56)	377
Chunky vegetable	1.34 (1.19, 1.27)	1.47 (1.34, 1.49)	1.36 (1.29, 1.41)	1.49 (1.44, 1.61)	1.60 (1.45, 1.70)	321
Chunky vegetable	1.25 (1.23, 1.32)	1.33 (1.30, 1.43)	1.23 (1.20, 1.36)	1.24 (1.23, 1.29)	1.33 (1.31, 1.38)	216
Progresso vegetable	1.25 (1.21, 1.28)	1.35 (1.30, 1.41)	1.28 (1.22, 1.39)	1.31 (1.29, 1.34)	1.39 (1.32, 1.45)	115
Progresso chicken noodle	1.24 (1.20, 1.30)	1.30 (1.26, 1.39)	1.24 (1.21, 1.40)	1.17 (1.19, 1.23)	1.23 (1.19, 1.26)	217
Progresso chicken rice with vegetables	1.24 (1.20, 1.29)	1.29 (1.25, 1.38)	1.23 (1.19, 1.40)	1.16 (1.18, 1.22)	1.23 (1.19, 1.25)	217
Campbell's bean with bacon	1.23 (1.20, 1.31)	1.38 (1.34, 1.48)	1.05 (1.03, 1.12)	1.44 (1.38, 1.49)	1.88 (1.75, 1.96)	82
Chunky chicken noodle	1.23 (1.19, 1.29)	1.28 (1.24, 1.36)	1.23 (1.19, 1.34)	1.17 (1.17, 1.22)	1.22 (1.19, 1.26)	216
Chunky minestrone	1.22 (1.21, 1.29)	1.29 (1.26, 1.40)	1.23 (1.20, 1.36)	1.24 (1.23, 1.30)	1.31 (1.24, 1.35)	215
Chunky chicken rice	1.21 (1.21, 1.29)	1.26 (1.26, 1.36)	1.22 (1.19, 1.34)	1.17 (1.17, 1.20)	1.32 (1.19, 1.25)	215
Home Cookin' minestrone	1.19 (1.21, 1.27)	1.25 (1.26, 1.36)	1.19 (1.20, 1.34)	1.25 (1.24, 1.29)	1.32 (1.24, 1.35)	216
Progresso minestrone soup	1.19 (1.18, 1.29)	1.27 (1.25, 1.41)	1.26 (1.26, 1.41)	1.31 (1.27, 1.35)	1.31 (1.24, 1.35)	217
Weighted average	1.77 (1.23, 1.53)	1.61 (1.29, 1.73)	1.34 (1.23, 1.52)	1.46 (1.24, 1.44)	1.56 (1.31, 1.72)	217

Notes: See table 7A.1.

Table 7A.7 **Fabric Softeners**

Product Pair	Full Markup: "Preferred" Lower Bound (μ)	Manufacturer's Markup: Lower Bound Based on Wholesale Price (μ^w)	Lower Bound for Full Markup Based on Retail Price (μ')	Retailer's Markup on National Brand (μ_b)	Retailer's Markup on Private Label (μ_g)	Sample Size
Bounce single scented	1.96 (1.95, 1.95)	2.01 (2.00, 2.00)	1.89 (1.88, 1.88)	1.03 (1.03, 1.03)	1.09 (1.09, 1.09)	29
~Downy regular refill	1.78 (1.58, 1.63)	1.89 (1.67, 1.71)	1.58 (1.42, 1.44)	1.08 (1.07, 1.10)	1.28 (1.29, 1.29)	40
~Downy regular refill	1.77 (1.57, 1.62)	1.87 (1.67, 1.71)	1.57 (1.42, 1.44)	1.08 (1.07, 1.10)	1.28 (1.29, 1.29)	46
~Downy sunrise refill	1.76 (1.57, 1.63)	1.87 (1.67, 1.71)	1.57 (1.42, 1.44)	1.08 (1.08, 1.10)	1.28 (1.29, 1.29)	55
~Downy sunrise refill	1.75 (1.57, 1.61)	1.86 (1.67, 1.70)	1.56 (1.42, 1.44)	1.08 (1.08, 1.10)	1.28 (1.29, 1.29)	52
Downy ultra refill breeze	1.54 (1.40, 1.71)	1.58 (1.43, 1.77)	1.45 (1.31, 1.66)	1.05 (1.04, 1.05)	1.14 (1.14, 1.15)	209
Downy ultra refill spring	1.53 (1.40, 1.71)	1.57 (1.43, 1.76)	1.45 (1.31, 1.62)	1.05 (1.04, 1.05)	1.14 (1.14, 1.15)	209
Downy ultra refill	1.51 (1.31, 1.60)	1.59 (1.34, 1.69)	1.41 (1.15, 1.50)	1.09 (1.09, 1.10)	1.25 (1.26, 1.29)	182
~Downy ultra refill	1.50 (1.31, 1.61)	1.58 (1.34, 1.69)	1.39 (1.15, 1.51)	1.09 (1.09, 1.10)	1.25 (1.26, 1.29)	176
Bounce	1.48 (1.39, 1.71)	1.52 (1.43, 1.81)	1.37 (1.29, 1.64)	1.04 (1.04, 1.05)	1.16 (1.16, 1.16)	52
Downy ultra refill breeze	1.47 (1.33, 1.63)	1.50 (1.35, 1.68)	1.44 (1.29, 1.67)	1.05 (1.04, 1.05)	1.09 (1.08, 1.11)	209
Downy ultra refill spring	1.46 (1.33, 1.63)	1.49 (1.35, 1.66)	1.44 (1.29, 1.61)	1.05 (1.04, 1.05)	1.09 (1.08, 1.11)	209
Weighted average	1.66 (1.49, 1.77)	1.73 (1.55, 1.87)	1.52 (1.42, 1.57)	1.06 (1.05, 1.08)	1.21 (1.12, 1.28)	

Notes: See table 7A.1. The symbol "~" is an internal code used by Dominick's to identify discontinued products.

Table 7A.8   Oatmeal

Product Pair	Full Markup: "Preferred" Lower Bound (μ)	Manufacturer's Markup: Lower Bound Based on Wholesale Price (μ^w)	Lower Bound for Full Markup Based on Retail Price (μ^r)	Retailer's Markup on National Brand (μ_b)	Retailer's Markup on Private Label (μ_g)	Sample Size
Quick Quaker oats	2.20 (1.63, 2.06)	1.77 (1.78, 2.38)	1.19 (1.24, 1.55)	1.12 (1.12, 1.14)	1.65 (1.63, 1.66)	184
Quick Quaker oats	1.43 (1.35, 1.53)	1.47 (1.38, 1.57)	1.27 (1.19, 1.32)	1.08 (1.07, 1.08)	1.25 (1.25, 1.25)	184
Quaker instant	1.37 (1.41, 1.77)	1.41 (1.46, 1.89)	1.20 (1.24, 1.58)	1.11 (1.08, 1.10)	1.29 (1.29, 1.30)	184
Quaker instant raisin	1.36 (1.44, 1.76)	1.40 (1.48, 1.89)	1.18 (1.24, 1.58)	1.10 (1.07, 1.09)	1.29 (1.29, 1.30)	184
Quaker instant maple	1.34 (1.42, 1.76)	1.37 (1.47, 1.89)	1.16 (1.24, 1.58)	1.11 (1.07, 1.09)	1.29 (1.29, 1.30)	184
Weighted average	1.62 (1.36, 1.43)	1.52 (1.40, 1.47)	1.20 (1.18, 1.20)	1.11 (1.10, 1.11)	1.39 (1.29, 1.29)	

Notes: See table 7A.1.

Table 7A.9   Cookies

Product Pair	Full Markup: "Preferred" Lower Bound (μ)	Manufacturer's Markup: Lower Bound Based on Wholesale Price (μ^w)	Lower Bound for Full Markup Based on Retail Price (μ^r)	Retailer's Markup on National Brand (μ_b)	Retailer's Markup on Private Label (μ_g)	Sample Size
Nutter Butter peanut butter	2.71 (2.66, 2.78)	3.37 (3.28, 3.49)	2.71 (2.62, 2.79)	1.11 (1.11, 1.12)	1.40 (1.37, 1.43)	262
Cameo creme sandwich	2.70 (2.66, 2.78)	3.38 (3.29, 3.47)	2.70 (2.62, 2.73)	1.12 (1.11, 1.12)	1.40 (1.38, 1.43)	233
Famous Amos chocolate chip with raisins	1.70 (1.64, 1.79)	1.93 (1.83, 2.03)	1.64 (1.50, 1.67)	1.16 (1.14, 1.18)	1.38 (1.37, 1.42)	169
Almost Home chocolate	1.67 (1.58, 1.72)	1.81 (1.70, 1.88)	1.49 (1.34, 1.62)	1.12 (1.10, 1.15)	1.36 (1.35, 1.40)	89
Famous Amos chocolate chip	1.66 (1.58, 1.77)	1.88 (1.77, 2.03)	1.61 (1.50, 1.67)	1.18 (1.16, 1.19)	1.38 (1.37, 1.42)	169
Almost Home oatmeal	1.64 (1.56, 1.72)	1.78 (1.67, 1.88)	1.43 (1.32, 1.54)	1.12 (1.12, 1.12)	1.39 (1.37, 1.42)	43
Keebler sugar wafers-vanilla	1.62 (1.63, 1.70)	1.75 (1.74, 1.83)	1.41 (1.40, 1.40)	1.12 (1.10, 1.10)	1.39 (1.37, 1.44)	10
Salerno vanilla wafer	1.59 (1.46, 1.64)	1.73 (1.56, 1.80)	1.42 (1.28, 1.50)	1.15 (1.13, 1.17)	1.40 (1.38, 1.42)	357
~Archway chocolate chip	1.48 (1.41, 1.50)	1.56 (1.50, 1.60)	1.29 (1.24, 1.34)	1.11 (1.13, 1.13)	1.35 (1.34, 1.38)	53
Salerno mint cream pie	1.41 (1.37, 1.50)	1.52 (1.47, 1.62)	1.44 (1.39, 1.49)	1.18 (1.15, 1.20)	1.24 (1.25, 1.25)	96
~Archway fat free apple pie	1.40 (1.28, 1.54)	1.46 (1.32, 1.61)	1.40 (1.22, 1.56)	1.09 (1.09, 1.10)	1.14 (1.12, 1.19)	62
Salerno royal graham	1.39 (1.35, 1.44)	1.47 (1.44, 1.52)	1.28 (1.30, 1.30)	1.14 (1.13, 1.17)	1.31 (1.32, 1.32)	80
Famous Amos chocolate cream	1.32 (1.40, 1.58)	1.37 (1.49, 1.67)	1.22 (1.29, 1.50)	1.08 (1.10, 1.16)	1.23 (1.22, 1.26)	94
Super Mario chocolate	1.31 (1.27, 1.38)	1.40 (1.33, 1.46)	1.17 (1.11, 1.18)	1.17 (1.15, 1.19)	1.40 (1.38, 1.42)	61
Mini chocolate chip	1.30 (1.24, 1.38)	1.34 (1.25, 1.46)	1.03 (0.88, 1.18)	1.07 (1.01, 1.15)	1.40 (1.39, 1.42)	99
Archway fat free fig bars	1.29 (1.15, 1.47)	1.31 (1.16, 1.52)	1.19 (1.05, 1.34)	1.06 (1.06, 1.07)	1.18 (1.16, 1.20)	90
Salerno chocolate grahams	1.28 (1.22, 1.35)	1.34 (1.27, 1.41)	1.18 (1.11, 1.20)	1.15 (1.12, 1.17)	1.31 (1.32, 1.32)	74
Honey Maid chocolate	1.22 (1.20, 1.26)	1.25 (1.23, 1.29)	1.19 (1.18, 1.24)	1.11 (1.10, 1.12)	1.17 (1.16, 1.18)	43
Salerno butter	1.21 (1.31, 1.52)	1.28 (1.41, 1.71)	1.07 (1.22, 1.39)	1.18 (1.18, 1.25)	1.43 (1.37, 1.45)	147
Archway chocolate chip	1.18 (1.14, 1.31)	1.22 (1.17, 1.37)	1.07 (1.00, 1.14)	1.19 (1.17, 1.19)	1.37 (1.36, 1.42)	215
Famous Amos chocolate chip	1.17 (1.20, 1.29)	1.20 (1.24, 1.33)	1.09 (1.20, 1.24)	1.06 (1.10, 1.13)	1.19 (1.18, 1.20)	172
Weighted average	1.58 (1.29, 1.64)	1.77 (1.34, 1.78)	1.49 (1.18, 1.44)	1.13 (1.11, 1.16)	1.33 (1.24, 1.40)	

Notes: See table 7A.1. The symbol "~" is an internal code used by Dominick's to identify discontinued products.

Table 7A.10   Snack Crackers

Product Pair	Full Markup: "Preferred" Lower Bound ($\hat{\mu}$)	Manufacturer's Markup: Lower Bound Based on Wholesale Price (μ^w)	Lower Bound for Full Markup Based on Retail Price (μ^r)	Retailer's Markup on National Brand (μ_b)	Retailer's Markup on Private Label (μ_g)	Sample Size
Nabisco Ritz	1.74 (1.64, 1.78)	1.92 (1.78, 1.98)	1.50 (1.41, 1.50)	1.13 (1.12, 1.13)	1.45 (1.40, 1.52)	41
~Nabisco Ritz bits	1.58 (1.53, 1.64)	1.70 (1.63, 1.78)	1.36 (1.21, 1.43)	1.12 (1.12, 1.14)	1.41 (1.38, 1.46)	204
Nabisco Ritz	1.54 (1.40, 1.70)	1.62 (1.45, 1.82)	1.33 (1.22, 1.53)	1.08 (1.09, 1.11)	1.32 (1.26, 1.35)	197
Nabisco cheese nips	1.51 (1.44, 1.53)	1.66 (1.56, 1.66)	1.35 (1.25, 1.34)	1.17 (1.15, 1.18)	1.44 (1.39, 1.52)	87
Sunshine cheez-it	1.50 (1.38, 1.68)	1.64 (1.47, 1.85)	1.35 (1.22, 1.44)	1.17 (1.13, 1.19)	1.43 (1.38, 1.52)	236
Town House cheddar jalapeño	1.46 (1.43, 1.49)	1.59 (1.55, 1.64)	1.30 (1.28, 1.36)	1.17 (1.17, 1.18)	1.44 (1.42, 1.43)	25
Keebler club	1.34 (1.23, 1.50)	1.40 (1.26, 1.61)	1.20 (1.09, 1.31)	1.15 (1.11, 1.14)	1.31 (1.26, 1.35)	197
Weighted average	1.57 (1.46, 1.58)	1.68 (1.59, 1.70)	1.36 (1.30, 1.36)	1.12 (1.12, 1.17)	1.37 (1.32, 1.44)	197

Notes: See table 7A.1. The symbol "~" is an internal code used by Dominick's to identify discontinued products.

Table 7A.11 Tooth Paste

Product Pair	Full Markup: "Preferred" Lower Bound ($\hat{\mu}$)	Manufacturer's Markup: Lower Bound Based on Wholesale Price (μ^w)	Lower Bound for Full Markup Based on Retail Price (μ^r)	Retailer's Markup on National Brand (μ_b)	Retailer's Markup on Private Label (μ_g)	Sample Size
*Crest regular	2.15 (2.05, 2.26)	2.22 (2.20, 2.27)	1.61 (1.59, 1.61)	1.03 (1.00, 1.05)	1.42 (1.41, 1.47)	75
*Aqua Fresh	2.03 (2.04, 2.27)	2.16 (2.16, 2.35)	1.65 (1.71, 1.71)	1.10 (1.03, 1.07)	1.41 (1.41, 1.42)	25
Aqua Fresh	2.00 (2.06, 2.06)	2.05 (2.07, 2.07)	1.49 (1.47, 1.47)	1.03 (1.01, 1.06)	1.41 (1.41, 1.41)	38
Arm & Hammer dental	1.75 (1.85, 1.90)	1.92 (2.04, 2.09)	1.59 (1.68, 1.72)	1.11 (1.09, 1.11)	1.34 (1.34, 1.34)	44
Arm & Hammer dental	1.67 (1.57, 1.85)	1.78 (1.66, 2.02)	1.50 (1.40, 1.68)	1.09 (1.09, 1.10)	1.29 (1.28, 1.29)	248
~Colgate tartar gel	1.61 (1.62, 1.68)	1.70 (1.71, 1.80)	1.56 (1.53, 1.65)	1.08 (1.08, 1.10)	1.18 (1.17, 1.21)	107
Arm & Hammer dental	1.59 (1.57, 1.71)	1.71 (1.69, 1.87)	1.49 (1.48, 1.66)	1.11 (1.12, 1.14)	1.29 (1.29, 1.29)	211
*Crest tartar gel	1.38 (1.31, 1.56)	1.41 (1.34, 1.61)	1.24 (1.18, 1.39)	1.06 (1.06, 1.09)	1.21 (1.18, 1.24)	349
*Colgate tartar regular	1.38 (1.30, 1.45)	1.41 (1.32, 1.51)	1.22 (1.15, 1.39)	1.06 (1.05, 1.09)	1.22 (1.18, 1.23)	359
*Colgate tartar gel	1.36 (1.31, 1.52)	1.40 (1.34, 1.58)	1.23 (1.15, 1.39)	1.06 (1.06, 1.09)	1.20 (1.18, 1.24)	349
*Crest tartar regular	1.36 (1.29, 1.42)	1.39 (1.33, 1.46)	1.22 (1.18, 1.32)	1.06 (1.06, 1.09)	1.21 (1.18, 1.23)	357
~Colgate tartar gel	1.34 (1.32, 1.37)	1.39 (1.36, 1.41)	1.24 (1.21, 1.28)	1.08 (1.08, 1.08)	1.21 (1.20, 1.21)	35
Pepsodent with floride	1.32 (1.32, 1.51)	1.51 (1.61, 1.95)	1.45 (1.60, 1.80)	1.44 (1.34, 1.55)	1.45 (1.41, 1.48)	73
Close-Up tartar control	1.20 (1.20, 1.34)	1.23 (1.21, 1.40)	1.15 (1.13, 1.34)	1.12 (1.10, 1.15)	1.19 (1.18, 1.23)	359
Weighted average	1.54 (1.36, 1.75)	1.61 (1.40, 1.92)	1.36 (1.23, 1.56)	1.10 (1.06, 1.11)	1.28 (1.21, 1.41)	

Notes: See table 7A.1. The symbol "~" is an internal code used by Dominick's to identify discontinued products.

Table 7A.12   Cereals

Product Pair	Full Markup: "Preferred" Lower Bound (μ)	Manufacturer's Markup: Lower Bound Based on Wholesale Price (μ^w)	Lower Bound for Full Markup Based on Retail Price (μ^r)	Retailer's Markup on National Brand (μ_b)	Retailer's Markup on Private Label (μ_g)	Sample Size
Total raisin bran	1.57 (1.39, 1.53)	1.61 (1.42, 1.57)	1.46 (1.30, 1.39)	1.05 (1.04, 1.05)	1.15 (1.15, 1.17)	88
Kelloggs corn flakes	1.54 (1.52, 1.80)	1.50 (1.59, 1.93)	1.23 (1.29, 1.65)	1.21 (1.06, 1.10)	1.28 (1.24, 1.32)	333
Post raisin bran	1.41 (1.44, 1.72)	1.45 (1.48, 1.80)	1.33 (1.34, 1.65)	1.06 (1.04, 1.06)	1.15 (1.14, 1.16)	334
Kelloggs nut and honey	1.41 (1.32, 1.50)	1.45 (1.34, 1.54)	1.28 (1.22, 1.39)	1.04 (1.04, 1.06)	1.17 (1.13, 1.19)	229
Kelloggs raisin bran	1.39 (1.38, 1.63)	1.41 (1.40, 1.67)	1.28 (1.27, 1.52)	1.03 (1.04, 1.05)	1.15 (1.14, 1.16)	334
W.C. raisin bran	1.38 (1.32, 1.41)	1.44 (1.37, 1.46)	1.36 (1.32, 1.38)	1.09 (1.07, 1.11)	1.15 (1.14, 1.15)	76
Apple cinnamon Cherrios	1.35 (1.37, 1.56)	1.38 (1.41, 1.61)	1.23 (1.29, 1.49)	1.02 (1.05, 1.07)	1.16 (1.13, 1.18)	239
Kelloggs low fat granola with raisins	1.33 (1.27, 1.38)	1.38 (1.29, 1.46)	1.22 (1.15, 1.17)	1.09 (1.08, 1.08)	1.23 (1.21, 1.23)	28
Honey nut Cheerios	1.27 (1.37, 1.57)	1.29 (1.40, 1.61)	1.14 (1.30, 1.48)	1.02 (1.04, 1.06)	1.16 (1.13, 1.18)	239
Weighted average	1.41 (1.35, 1.41)	1.43 (1.38, 1.45)	1.26 (1.23, 1.33)	1.07 (1.03, 1.09)	1.19 (1.15, 1.17)	

Notes: See table 7A.1.

Table 7A.13   Dish Detergents

Product Pair	Full Markup: "Preferred" Lower Bound (μ)	Manufacturer's Markup: Lower Bound Based on Wholesale Price (μ^w)	Lower Bound for Full Markup Based on Retail Price (μ^r)	Retailer's Markup on National Brand (μ_b)	Retailer's Markup on Private Label (μ_g)	Sample Size
Dawn lemon	1.80 (1.91, 2.03)	1.92 (2.07, 2.21)	1.80 (1.83, 2.13)	1.08 (1.07, 1.09)	1.16 (1.10, 1.23)	90
Sunlight automatic	1.64 (1.63, 1.72)	1.70 (1.69, 1.77)	1.61 (1.56, 1.66)	1.06 (1.04, 1.07)	1.12 (1.11, 1.13)	183
Palmolive automatic	1.53 (1.40, 1.69)	1.58 (1.44, 1.73)	1.48 (1.37, 1.63)	1.05 (1.04, 1.07)	1.12 (1.11, 1.14)	264
Joy lemon	1.47 (1.41, 1.51)	1.53 (1.47, 1.58)	1.42 (1.28, 1.56)	1.09 (1.09, 1.09)	1.18 (1.10, 1.24)	63
Lemon Dawn	1.31 (1.33, 1.42)	1.33 (1.36, 1.46)	1.21 (1.24, 1.35)	1.04 (1.05, 1.08)	1.16 (1.13, 1.19)	142
Sunlight automatic	1.31 (1.27, 1.35)	1.35 (1.30, 1.39)	1.30 (1.25, 1.31)	1.09 (1.08, 1.09)	1.13 (1.11, 1.15)	318
Sunlight automatic	1.31 (1.27, 1.35)	1.35 (1.30, 1.39)	1.30 (1.25, 1.31)	1.09 (1.08, 1.09)	1.13 (1.11, 1.15)	320
Dial automatic	1.29 (1.26, 1.35)	1.31 (1.30, 1.39)	1.14 (1.19, 1.22)	1.05 (1.07, 1.08)	1.21 (1.16, 1.24)	97
Sunlight automatic gel	1.17 (1.05, 1.40)	1.18 (1.05, 1.43)	1.11 (0.92, 1.45)	1.06 (1.05, 1.07)	1.16 (0.99, 1.23)	82
Palmolive automatic gel	1.12 (1.09, 1.18)	1.14 (1.11, 1.21)	1.07 (1.03, 1.15)	1.11 (1.11, 1.11)	1.18 (1.17, 1.19)	86
Weighted average	1.38 (1.29, 1.53)	1.42 (1.31, 1.58)	1.34 (1.14, 1.48)	1.07 (1.05, 1.09)	1.15 (1.13, 1.18)	

Notes: See table 7A.1.

Table 7A.14   Bottled Juice

Product Pair	Full Markup: "Preferred" Lower Bound ($\hat{\mu}$)	Manufacturer's Markup: Lower Bound Based on Wholesale Price (μ^w)	Lower Bound for Full Markup Based on Retail Price (μ^r)	Retailer's Markup on National Brand (μ_b)	Retailer's Markup on Private Label (μ_g)	Sample Size
Motts apple	1.61 (1.09, 2.16)	2.09 (1.17, 3.19)	2.09 (1.55, 2.97)	1.57 (1.30, 1.86)	1.43 (1.35, 1.52)	80
Seneca apple	1.60 (1.22, 1.38)	1.86 (1.32, 1.56)	1.39 (1.09, 1.28)	1.30 (1.29, 1.36)	1.67 (1.59, 1.74)	59
Northern cranberry apple	1.44 (1.39, 1.57)	1.49 (1.43, 1.64)	1.41 (1.33, 1.54)	1.08 (1.08, 1.08)	1.15 (1.14, 1.16)	68
Northern cranberry raspberry	1.44 (1.39, 1.57)	1.50 (1.45, 1.64)	1.41 (1.35, 1.54)	1.08 (1.07, 1.09)	1.15 (1.14, 1.16)	68
Flavor fresh apple	1.43 (1.39, 1.47)	1.57 (1.51, 1.64)	1.13 (1.10, 1.16)	1.21 (1.19, 1.23)	1.67 (1.66, 1.68)	53
Ocean Spray ruby red grapefruit	1.40 (1.40, 1.44)	1.43 (1.42, 1.46)	1.24 (1.23, 1.27)	1.04 (1.04, 1.04)	1.20 (1.21, 1.21)	41
~Tree Top apple	1.40 (1.17, 1.40)	1.53 (1.22, 1.51)	1.16 (0.96, 1.17)	1.21 (1.15, 1.21)	1.58 (1.48, 1.58)	391
Musselman apple	1.38 (1.31, 1.43)	1.46 (1.38, 1.53)	1.13 (1.10, 1.16)	1.16 (1.14, 1.17)	1.49 (1.49, 1.51)	55
Ocean Spray cranapple drink	1.35 (1.31, 1.48)	1.40 (1.33, 1.55)	1.31 (1.25, 1.45)	1.08 (1.08, 1.09)	1.16 (1.15, 1.17)	134
Ocean Spray cranraspberry drink	1.34 (1.30, 1.48)	1.39 (1.33, 1.55)	1.30 (1.25, 1.45)	1.09 (1.08, 1.09)	1.16 (1.15, 1.17)	134
~Minute Maid natural apple	1.34 (1.26, 1.44)	1.39 (1.30, 1.52)	1.05 (0.96, 1.15)	1.12 (1.11, 1.13)	1.50 (1.48, 1.53)	151
Ocean Spray pink grapefruit	1.33 (1.31, 1.42)	1.39 (1.36, 1.50)	1.28 (1.26, 1.38)	1.13 (1.12, 1.14)	1.22 (1.21, 1.24)	173
~Northland cranberry	1.32 (1.31, 1.35)	1.35 (1.35, 1.39)	1.38 (1.38, 1.42)	1.08 (1.07, 1.08)	1.06 (1.06, 1.06)	48
Northland cranberry	1.31 (1.32, 1.35)	1.34 (1.35, 1.38)	1.38 (1.38, 1.42)	1.09 (1.08, 1.10)	1.06 (1.06, 1.06)	48
Ocean Spray grapefruit	1.31 (1.22, 1.35)	1.35 (1.26, 1.41)	1.24 (1.15, 1.30)	1.12 (1.12, 1.15)	1.23 (1.21, 1.24)	339
Ocean Spray cranberry	1.22 (1.23, 1.30)	1.23 (1.24, 1.32)	1.21 (1.22, 1.30)	1.04 (1.04, 1.04)	1.06 (1.06, 1.06)	48
Speas Farm apple	1.21 (1.24, 1.40)	1.30 (1.35, 1.53)	1.08 (1.11, 1.24)	1.34 (1.19, 1.36)	1.63 (1.52, 1.68)	109
Welch's grape	1.20 (1.14, 1.22)	1.22 (1.16, 1.24)	1.20 (1.14, 1.21)	1.10 (1.09, 1.11)	1.13 (1.13, 1.13)	58
Sunsweet prune juice	1.16 (1.10, 1.23)	1.21 (1.12, 1.30)	1.13 (1.11, 1.18)	1.23 (1.21, 1.24)	1.31 (1.24, 1.38)	391
~Veryfine ruby red grapefruit	1.15 (1.12, 1.23)	1.18 (1.14, 1.26)	1.15 (1.05, 1.17)	1.15 (1.13, 1.16)	1.18 (1.21, 1.24)	90
~Veryfine cranberry	1.11 (1.11, 1.18)	1.12 (1.12, 1.20)	1.16 (1.15, 1.23)	1.09 (1.09, 1.09)	1.06 (1.06, 1.06)	47
Del Monte prune	1.01 (1.01, 1.12)	1.01 (1.02, 1.15)	1.08 (1.06, 1.13)	1.36 (1.23, 1.31)	1.25 (1.25, 1.26)	39
Weighted average	1.31 (1.21, 1.40)	1.38 (1.23, 1.49)	1.26 (1.13, 1.38)	1.14 (1.08, 1.21)	1.24 (1.15, 1.49)	

Notes: See table 7A.1. The symbol "~" is an internal code used by Dominick's to identify discontinued products.

Table 7A.15   Kraft Cheese

Product Pair	Full Markup: "Preferred" Lower Bound ($\underline{\mu}$)	Manufacturer's Markup: Lower Bound Based on Wholesale Price (μ^w)	Lower Bound for Full Markup Based on Retail Price (μ^r)	Retailer's Markup on National Brand (μ_b)	Retailer's Markup on Private Label (μ_g)	Sample Size
Soft philly cream	1.55 (1.43, 1.71)	1.82 (1.60, 2.07)	1.50 (1.32, 1.71)	1.25 (1.23, 1.28)	1.52 (1.43, 1.61)	392
Light natural shredded mozzarella	1.34 (1.27, 1.47)	1.45 (1.34, 1.61)	1.28 (1.20, 1.43)	1.18 (1.18, 1.21)	1.34 (1.32, 1.37)	237
Sliced muenster resealable	1.32 (1.28, 1.36)	1.40 (1.35, 1.46)	1.28 (1.23, 1.36)	1.18 (1.17, 1.19)	1.29 (1.26, 1.30)	27
Light natural swiss chunks	1.30 (1.23, 1.38)	1.37 (1.28, 1.47)	1.24 (1.17, 1.31)	1.15 (1.15, 1.18)	1.27 (1.26, 1.30)	163
Grated parmesan	1.28 (1.25, 1.34)	1.31 (1.28, 1.38)	1.25 (1.21, 1.33)	1.09 (1.08, 1.10)	1.14 (1.12, 1.15)	392
Sliced swiss	1.27 (1.21, 1.34)	1.33 (1.24, 1.41)	1.19 (1.13, 1.28)	1.14 (1.13, 1.16)	1.28 (1.26, 1.30)	198
Shredded mild cheddar	1.24 (1.18, 1.40)	1.32 (1.21, 1.53)	1.17 (1.09, 1.36)	1.19 (1.18, 1.23)	1.34 (1.33, 1.38)	309
Mild colby	1.22 (1.14, 1.34)	1.29 (1.17, 1.43)	1.11 (1.03, 1.25)	1.18 (1.18, 1.23)	1.37 (1.34, 1.43)	175
Shredded mozzarella	1.16 (1.13, 1.32)	1.22 (1.16, 1.42)	1.08 (1.05, 1.25)	1.17 (1.18, 1.23)	1.33 (1.32, 1.37)	392
Finely shredded	1.15 (1.16, 1.28)	1.19 (1.20, 1.36)	1.08 (1.11, 1.23)	1.18 (1.18, 1.20)	1.30 (1.28, 1.33)	80
~Shredded mozzarella	1.14 (1.11, 1.21)	1.16 (1.13, 1.25)	1.14 (1.13, 1.21)	1.13 (1.13, 1.14)	1.15 (1.15, 1.16)	48
Weighted average	1.30 (1.16, 1.32)	1.38 (1.22, 1.40)	1.25 (1.11, 1.28)	1.15 (1.14, 1.18)	1.27 (1.27, 1.34)	

Notes: See table 7A.1. The symbol "~" is an internal code used by Dominick's to identify discontinued products.

Table 7A.16   **Frozen Juice**

Product Pair	Full Markup: "Preferred" Lower Bound ($\hat{\mu}$)	Manufacturer's Markup: Lower Bound Based on Wholesale Price (μ^w)	Lower Bound for Full Markup Based on Retail Price (μ^r)	Retailer's Markup on National Brand (μ_b)	Retailer's Markup on Private Label (μ_g)	Sample Size
Minute Maid pink lemonade	2.26 (1.97, 2.20)	3.67 (3.12, 3.89)	1.87 (1.92, 2.00)	1.33 (1.31, 1.43)	2.64 (2.33, 2.63)	36
Welch's 100% white grape	1.78 (1.74, 1.81)	2.23 (2.19, 2.33)	1.60 (1.56, 1.70)	1.27 (1.26, 1.30)	1.76 (1.72, 1.80)	104
Minute Maid lemonade	1.76 (1.49, 1.75)	2.37 (1.95, 2.68)	1.35 (1.12, 1.48)	1.48 (1.42, 1.52)	2.50 (2.30, 2.80)	396
Minute Maid pink lemonade	1.68 (1.50, 1.75)	2.33 (1.96, 2.65)	1.32 (1.13, 1.49)	1.49 (1.42, 1.51)	2.54 (2.32, 2.82)	394
~Minute Maid orange	1.52 (1.44, 1.67)	2.11 (1.84, 2.56)	1.27 (1.13, 1.31)	1.50 (1.45, 1.59)	2.60 (2.21, 3.33)	396
Minute Maid grapefruit	1.37 (1.30, 1.39)	1.50 (1.40, 1.53)	1.29 (1.19, 1.31)	1.24 (1.22, 1.24)	1.44 (1.37, 1.55)	115
Minute Maid orange juice	1.34 (1.28, 1.40)	1.43 (1.35, 1.50)	1.31 (1.24, 1.37)	1.17 (1.16, 1.19)	1.28 (1.25, 1.33)	396
Welch's cranberry raspberry	1.34 (1.27, 1.42)	1.44 (1.35, 1.55)	1.36 (1.32, 1.43)	1.21 (1.20, 1.22)	1.28 (1.25, 1.33)	111
Dole pineapple orange	1.31 (1.25, 1.37)	1.43 (1.35, 1.53)	1.27 (1.24, 1.34)	1.29 (1.27, 1.32)	1.46 (1.40, 1.50)	195
Minute Maid orange	1.21 (1.20, 1.37)	1.28 (1.26, 1.52)	1.08 (1.09, 1.36)	1.21 (1.22, 1.34)	1.45 (1.32, 1.55)	396
Tropicana orange	1.20 (1.15, 1.30)	1.26 (1.19, 1.38)	1.18 (1.12, 1.26)	1.20 (1.18, 1.22)	1.28 (1.25, 1.33)	395
Welch 100% grape	1.19 (1.17, 1.24)	1.26 (1.23, 1.33)	1.20 (1.17, 1.30)	1.27 (1.27, 1.30)	1.35 (1.32, 1.37)	195
Minute Maid orange with calcium	1.19 (1.16, 1.38)	1.27 (1.22, 1.55)	1.18 (1.14, 1.36)	1.30 (1.25, 1.32)	1.43 (1.32, 1.52)	114
Tree Top apple	1.19 (1.12, 1.28)	1.29 (1.17, 1.44)	1.20 (1.14, 1.36)	1.42 (1.32, 1.45)	1.55 (1.36, 1.73)	396
Welch's white grape	1.16 (1.13, 1.23)	1.26 (1.22, 1.38)	1.10 (1.09, 1.17)	1.56 (1.43, 1.62)	1.76 (1.72, 1.80)	104
Citrus Hill orange	1.16 (1.10, 1.21)	1.20 (1.12, 1.25)	1.17 (1.11, 1.25)	1.20 (1.17, 1.22)	1.23 (1.22, 1.25)	43
Tropicana Season's Best orange	1.15 (1.11, 1.27)	1.20 (1.15, 1.38)	1.02 (1.03, 1.30)	1.21 (1.26, 1.36)	1.44 (1.32, 1.55)	395
Tree Top apple	1.14 (1.06, 1.25)	1.27 (1.12, 1.45)	1.26 (1.20, 1.38)	1.83 (1.57, 1.91)	1.85 (1.74, 1.93)	33
Welch's grape juice	1.13 (1.09, 1.22)	1.19 (1.15, 1.37)	1.03 (1.04, 1.19)	1.47 (1.47, 1.59)	1.73 (1.67, 1.80)	396
Minute Maid pink grapefruit	1.08 (1.03, 1.16)	1.13 (1.04, 1.27)	1.21 (1.14, 1.33)	1.52 (1.52, 1.57)	1.41 (1.36, 1.47)	148
Weighted average	1.28 (1.16, 1.44)	1.44 (1.26, 1.80)	1.18 (1.17, 1.31)	1.31 (1.21, 1.49)	1.60 (1.38, 1.80)	

Notes: See table 7A.1. The symbol "~" is an internal code used by Dominick's to identify discontinued products.

Table 7A.17   Laundry Detergents

Product Pair	Full Markup: "Preferred" Lower Bound (μ)	Manufacturer's Markup: Lower Bound Based on Wholesale Price (μ^w)	Lower Bound for Full Markup Based on Retail Price (μ^r)	Retailer's Markup on National Brand (μ_b)	Retailer's Markup on Private Label (μ_g)	Sample Size
Ultra Ivory Snow	1.78 (1.69, 1.81)	1.82 (1.72, 1.87)	1.62 (1.50, 1.66)	1.03 (1.02, 1.03)	1.15 (1.15, 1.17)	182
Era heavy duty liquid	1.67 (1.46, 1.89)	1.70 (1.50, 1.93)	1.60 (1.44, 1.78)	1.03 (1.01, 1.05)	1.10 (1.09, 1.11)	166
Woolite liquid	1.56 (1.50, 1.65)	1.67 (1.60, 1.78)	1.42 (1.35, 1.55)	1.11 (1.10, 1.13)	1.30 (1.30, 1.32)	293
Solo heavy duty liquid	1.44 (1.41, 1.49)	1.47 (1.43, 1.53)	1.40 (1.36, 1.46)	1.05 (1.04, 1.06)	1.10 (1.09, 1.11)	168
~Ultra Tide with bleach	1.44 (1.39, 1.53)	1.47 (1.41, 1.56)	1.34 (1.31, 1.40)	1.04 (1.04, 1.04)	1.14 (1.11, 1.17)	212
Non-phosphate concentrated All	1.43 (1.35, 1.51)	1.45 (1.37, 1.55)	1.41 (1.32, 1.56)	1.03 (1.01, 1.04)	1.05 (1.05, 1.06)	108
Woolite liquid	1.41 (1.32, 1.66)	1.45 (1.35, 1.74)	1.30 (1.24, 1.57)	1.06 (1.05, 1.07)	1.18 (1.18, 1.19)	108
Tide with bleach ultra	1.30 (1.35, 1.39)	1.31 (1.37, 1.40)	1.26 (1.30, 1.34)	1.02 (1.02, 1.03)	1.07 (1.07, 1.07)	50
~Ultra Tide with bleach	1.26 (1.28, 1.36)	1.27 (1.29, 1.37)	1.22 (1.24, 1.32)	1.01 (1.02, 1.02)	1.05 (1.05, 1.07)	217
Non-phosphate Wisk heavy duty liquid	1.10 (1.15, 1.38)	1.10 (1.15, 1.40)	1.07 (1.12, 1.39)	1.00 (1.01, 1.02)	1.04 (1.03, 1.05)	148
Ultra Wisk with bleach	1.05 (1.15, 1.28)	1.05 (1.16, 1.29)	1.01 (1.12, 1.23)	1.02 (1.02, 1.03)	1.07 (1.06, 1.07)	99
Ultra Bold	1.05 (1.02, 1.07)	1.05 (1.02, 1.07)	1.02 (1.00, 1.05)	1.02 (1.02, 1.03)	1.05 (1.04, 1.06)	197
~Ultra Surf liquid	1.03 (1.07, 1.19)	1.03 (1.07, 1.20)	1.02 (1.03, 1.18)	1.04 (1.03, 1.03)	1.06 (1.05, 1.07)	99
Solo heavy duty liquid	1.03 (0.95, 1.14)	1.03 (0.95, 1.14)	1.02 (0.93, 1.14)	1.03 (1.03, 1.03)	1.04 (1.04, 1.05)	37
Era heavy duty liquid	1.02 (0.93, 1.12)	1.02 (0.93, 1.13)	1.01 (0.91, 1.12)	1.03 (1.02, 1.03)	1.04 (1.04, 1.05)	36
Weighted average	1.22 (1.05, 1.44)	1.23 (1.05, 1.47)	1.18 (1.02, 1.41)	1.03 (1.02, 1.04)	1.07 (1.05, 1.14)	

Notes: See table 7A.1. The symbol "~" is an internal code used by Dominick's to identify discontinued products.

Table 7A.18   Frozen Entrees

Product Pair	Full Markup: "Preferred" Lower Bound ($\hat{\mu}$)	Manufacturer's Markup: Lower Bound Based on Wholesale Price (μ^w)	Lower Bound for Full Markup Based on Retail Price (μ^r)	Retailer's Markup on National Brand (μ_b)	Retailer's Markup on Private Label (μ_g)	Sample Size
Lean Cuisine baked cheese ravioli	1.36 (1.43, 1.64)	1.47 (1.58, 1.92)	1.44 (1.72, 2.02)	1.11 (1.20, 1.22)	1.17 (1.13, 1.20)	39
Mrs. Belgo's cheese ravioli	1.32 (1.27, 1.41)	1.40 (1.33, 1.51)	1.45 (1.30, 1.55)	1.17 (1.17, 1.17)	1.15 (1.13, 1.19)	38
Mrs. Belgo's meat ravioli	1.32 (1.27, 1.41)	1.40 (1.33, 1.51)	1.45 (1.30, 1.55)	1.17 (1.17, 1.17)	1.15 (1.13, 1.19)	37
Stouffer's cheese ravioli	1.20 (1.17, 1.40)	1.26 (1.21, 1.59)	1.31 (1.19, 1.77)	1.18 (1.22, 1.28)	1.17 (1.13, 1.20)	39
Ore-Ida cheese tortellini	1.10 (1.10, 1.22)	1.12 (1.12, 1.27)	1.15 (1.14, 1.38)	1.14 (1.14, 1.19)	1.14 (1.09, 1.17)	38
Italia meat tortellini	1.09 (1.18, 1.31)	1.14 (1.26, 1.44)	1.30 (1.33, 1.67)	1.27 (1.20, 1.33)	1.13 (1.09, 1.17)	38
Italia cheese ravioli	1.04 (1.01, 1.10)	1.05 (1.01, 1.12)	1.11 (1.00, 1.18)	1.19 (1.17, 1.22)	1.15 (1.13, 1.20)	39
Italia meat ravioli	1.03 (0.99, 1.09)	1.03 (0.99, 1.12)	1.10 (0.99, 1.18)	1.19 (1.18, 1.22)	1.15 (1.13, 1.20)	39
Weighted average	1.21 (1.06, 1.32)	1.27 (1.08, 1.40)	1.30 (1.13, 1.44)	1.17 (1.15, 1.19)	1.16 (1.14, 1.16)	

Notes: See table 7A.1.

Table 7A.19   Canned Tuna

Product Pair	Full Markup: "Preferred" Lower Bound ($\hat{\mu}$)	Manufacturer's Markup: Lower Bound Based on Wholesale Price (μ^w)	Lower Bound for Full Markup Based on Retail Price (μ^r)	Retailer's Markup on National Brand (μ_b)	Retailer's Markup on Private Label (μ_g)	Sample Size
Lite tuna in water	1.53 (1.46, 1.60)	1.78 (1.66, 1.85)	1.43 (1.23, 1.63)	1.24 (1.21, 1.25)	1.55 (1.35, 1.70)	129
Lite tuna in water	1.50 (1.40, 1.58)	1.91 (1.59, 1.83)	1.46 (1.23, 1.67)	1.26 (1.22, 1.32)	1.61 (1.36, 1.70)	140
Lite tuna in water	1.48 (1.33, 1.53)	1.94 (1.55, 1.81)	1.51 (1.22, 1.67)	1.32 (1.25, 1.43)	1.65 (1.34, 1.82)	66
Chunk light in water	1.10 (1.03, 1.18)	1.11 (1.04, 1.21)	1.09 (1.02, 1.19)	1.12 (1.09, 1.17)	1.14 (1.12, 1.20)	267
Chunk light in water	1.09 (1.07, 1.14)	1.10 (1.07, 1.16)	1.06 (1.04, 1.12)	1.08 (1.04, 1.10)	1.11 (1.05, 1.17)	106
Solid white	1.07 (1.00, 1.21)	1.08 (1.00, 1.25)	1.08 (1.01, 1.22)	1.21 (1.15, 1.21)	1.20 (1.17, 1.23)	198
Weighted average	1.16 (1.09, 1.50)	1.23 (1.10, 1.91)	1.14 (1.08, 1.46)	1.15 (1.12, 1.26)	1.22 (1.14, 1.61)	

Notes: See table 7A.1.

References

Basu, Susanto, and John Fernald. 1997. Are apparent productive spillovers a figment of specification error? *Journal of Monetary Economics* 36 (1): 165–88.

Bils, Mark J. 1986. The cyclical behavior of marginal cost and price. *American Economic Review* 77:838–57.

Brown, Charles, and James Medoff. 1989. The employer size-wage effect. *Journal of Political Economy* 97 (October): 1027–59.

———. 1991. Cheaper by the dozen. Harvard Institute of Economic Research Working Paper no. 1557. Cambridge, Mass.: Harvard Institute of Economic Research.

Carlton, Dennis W., and Jeffrey M. Perloff. 1994. *Modern industrial organization.* New York: Harper Collins.

Chen, Yuxin, James D. Hess, Ronald T. Wilcox, and Z. John Zhang. 1999. Accounting profits versus marketing profits: A relevant metric for category management. *Marketing Science* 18 (3): 208–29.

Chevalier, Judith, Anil K. Kashyap, and Peter E. Rossi. 2000. Why don't prices rise during periods of peak demand? Evidence from scanner data. NBER Working Paper no. 7981. Cambridge, Mass.: National Bureau of Economic Research.

Cox Eighteenth Annual Promotional Practice Survey. 1996. Atlanta, Ga.: Cox Communications and Donnelly Marketing, Inc.

Dutta, Shantanu, Mark Bergen, and Daniel Levy. 2002. Price flexibility in channels of distribution: Evidence from scanner data. *Journal of Economic Dynamics and Control* 26:1845–1900.

Fitzell, Philip. 1982. *Private labels: Store brands and generic products.* Westport, Conn.: AVI Publishing.

———. 1998. *The explosive growth of private labels in North America.* New York: Global Books.

Hall, Robert E. 1986. Market structure and macroeconomic fluctuations. *Brookings Papers on Economic Activity,* Issue no. 2:285–322. Washington, D.C.: Brookings Institution.

———. 1988. The relation between price and marginal cost in U.S. industry, *Journal of Political Economy* 96:921–47.

Hausman, Jerry A. 1997. Valuation of new goods under perfect and imperfect competition. In *The economics of new goods,* ed. Timothy Bresnahan and Robert J. Gordon, 209–37. Studies in Income and Wealth, vol. 58. Chicago: University of Chicago Press.

Hausman, Jerry A., and Gregory K. Leonard. 1999. The competitive effect of a new product introduction: A case study. MIT, Department of Economics. Working Paper.

Hoch, Steve. 1995. How should national brands think about private labels? University of Chicago, Department of Marketing, Graduate School of Business. Working Paper.

Hoch, Steve, and Shumeet Banerji. 1993. When do private labels succeed? *Sloan Management Review* 34 (summer): 57–67.

Hoch, Steve, J. S. Kim, Alan Montgomery, and Peter Rossi. 1995. Determinants of store-level price elasticity. *Journal of Marketing Research* 32 (February): 43–75.

Lal, Rajiv, and Chakravarthi Narasimhan. 1996. The inverse relationship between manufacturer and retailer margins: A theory. *Marketing Science* 15 (2): 132–51.

Levy, Daniel, Shantanu Dutta, and Mark Bergen. 2002. Heterogeneity in price rigidity: Evidence from a case study using micro-level data. *Journal of Money, Credit, and Banking,* forthcoming.

Levy, Daniel, Shantanu Dutta, Mark Bergen, and Robert Venable. 1998. Price adjustment at multiproduct retailers. *Managerial and Decision Economics* 19:81–120.

Levy, Daniel, and Andrew Young. 2001. "The real thing": Nominal price rigidity of the nickel Coke, 1886–1959. Department of Economics, Bar-Ilan University and Department of Economics, Emory University. Working Paper.

Monroe, Kent B. 1990. *Pricing: Making profitable decisions.* 2d ed. New York: McGraw-Hill.

Morton, Feona Scott, and Florian Zettelmeyer. 2000. The strategic use of store brand in retailer-manufacturer bargaining. University of California, Berkeley, Department of Marketing, Haas School of Business. Working Paper.

Müller, Georg, Mark Bergen, Shantanu Dutta, and Daniel Levy. 2001. Price rigidity during holiday periods: The role of price adjustment costs. University of Minnesota, Department of Marketing, Carlson School of Management and Bar-Ilan University, Department of Economics. Working Paper.

Nevo, Aviv. 1997. Demand for ready to eat cereal and its implications for price competition, merger analysis, and valuation of new brands. Ph.D. diss., Harvard University.

———. 2001. Measuring market power in the ready-to-eat cereal industry. *Econometrica* 69 (2): 265–306.

Quelch, John A., and David Harding. 1996. Brand versus private labels: Fighting to win. *Harvard Business Review* reprint 96109 (Jan.–Feb.): 99–109.

Rotemberg, Julio, and G. Saloner. 1986. A supergame-theoretic model of business cycle and price wars during booms. *American Economic Review* 76 (June): 390–407.

Rotemberg, Julio, and Michael Woodford. 1996. Imperfect competition and the effects of energy price increases on economic activity. *Journal of Money, Credit, and Banking* 28 (4): 549–77.

Scherer, F. M. 1980. *Industrial market structure and economic performance,* 2nd ed. Boston: Houghton Mifflin.

Schmalensee, Richard. 1978. Entry deterrence in the ready to eat breakfast cereal industry. *Bell Journal of Economics* 9:305–27.

Sethuraman, Raj, and Catherine Cole. 1997. Why do consumers pay more for national brands than for store brands? Marketing Science Institute Report no. 97-126. Cambridge, Mass.

Shaked, A. and J. Sutton. 1982. Relaxing price competition through product differentiation. *Review of Economic Studies* 49:3–13.

Slade, Margaret E. 1998. Optimal pricing with costly adjustment: Evidence from retail-grocery prices. *Review of Economic Studies* 65:87–107.

Steiner, Robert L. 1993. The inverse association between the margins of manufacturers and retailers. *Review of Industrial Organization* 8:717–40.

Supermarket Business. 1993. Fourth annual consumer expenditures study: From recession to reality. 49 (9): 35–56.

Sutton, John. 1991. *Sunk cost and market structure.* Cambridge, Mass.: MIT Press.

Tirole, Jean. 1989. *The theory of industrial organization.* Cambridge, Mass.: MIT Press.

Comment   Julio Rotemberg

This is an excellent paper, which contains a trove of interesting data on prices and costs. The thorough comparison between retail and wholesale prices of both nationally advertised brands and comparable products sold under private labels that the authors carry out turns out to convey important lessons for many issues in economics.

The authors focus on a very important magnitude, which they call the "ideal" markup. This is the ratio of the price paid by consumers for a nationally advertised good and the marginal cost of both producing the good and delivering it to the consumer. The gap between this price and this marginal cost gives the answer to a standard microeconomics question. This is the extent to which the sum of consumer and producer surplus increases when the final price is reduced sufficiently that the quantity sold increases by one unit. This magnitude is also a critical ingredient in macroeconomics because it answers the question of whether producers would continue to be willing to sell and distribute their goods if, either because prices are rigid or for some other reason, price falls by some percentage relative to this marginal cost.

Once one has the retail price of a good, one can obtain this gap if one knows how much it costs to produce an additional unit and how much it costs to deliver it to a customer. The paper's solution to these hard measurement problems is attractive on a number of counts. The authors suppose that Dominick's acquisition price of a private-label good that is similar to a nationally branded good is generally no smaller than the marginal cost of producing and delivering to the supermarket an additional unit of the branded good. They also suppose that the supermarket's margin between the price it pays for the branded good and the price at which it sells the good is no smaller than the supermarket's own marginal cost of distributing the good. Thus, the sum of the private label's wholesale price and the margin on branded goods is an underestimate of the full marginal cost of delivering an additional unit to the consumer, and the ratio of the price to this sum is an underestimate of the markup they seek to measure.

Although no assumption that simplifies calculations so much can be valid 100 percent of the time, I find this approach very compelling. Although one might initially suspect that private-label goods are cheaper to manufacture than branded goods so that their low wholesale price is not informative, many of Dominick's private-label goods proudly proclaim in their package their similarity in content and appearance to well-publicized branded goods. Indeed, one thing I would have liked to see is more soft information from the authors about the relative appearances of the pairs of goods they consider. Broad surveys that show that good private-label goods

Julio Rotemberg is the William Ziegler Professor of Business Administration at Harvard Business School and a research associate of the National Bureau of Economic Research.

are quite often of high quality and not cheap to manufacture are in some ways less compelling than particular comparisons for the goods in their sample because private-label goods vary a great deal in quality.

Interestingly, the magnitude that seems harder to measure in this study is the price paid by consumers, because the retail price the authors measure does not include coupons and rebates. Still, it is quite clear that some consumers pay the full retail price for branded goods at least some of the time, so that the authors have a valid measurement of a particular ratio between price and marginal cost. What is less clear is the fraction of the economy that involves the high markups they find in their analysis because, even within this sector, many transactions involve smaller markups.

For macroeconomics, the ratios they consider matter because they measure how much price can be squeezed relative to marginal cost while maintaining an incentive to sell. The authors' calculation essentially supposes that the retail margin cannot be squeezed, so that the entire ability to absorb lower prices falls on the manufacturer. I see the ratio of wholesale prices charged by branded goods and private-label goods as, in some ways, a more direct measurement of the extent to which manufacturers of branded goods would continue to deliver products even if their prices fell. It is thus good to see these numbers reported as well, and it is interesting that they are similar to those of their ideal markup.

Let me close by offering some thoughts on the microeconomic implications of this paper's findings. The first is that it is far from clear that the ideal markup the authors compute says much about the extent to which branded goods' prices are too high from a social point of view. It is true that lower prices would increase producer and consumer surplus, if advertising and research and development (R&D) expenditures were held constant. However, firms would almost certainly not hold these expenditures constant if they were forced by an omniscient planner to lower their prices. It is more likely that such a squeezing of margins would lower the manufacturer's incentive to carry out R&D and advertising. The resulting fall in R&D could be costly, particularly because the fact that private labels free-ride on branded products by copying their designs suggests that the incentives for R&D in this industry may actually be too low. If advertising expenditures are socially useful—as they can be, for example, in the model of Becker and Murphy (1993)—reductions in these expenditures could be deleterious as well.

Once one focuses on R&D and advertising expenditures, the natural question that poses itself is whether the ratio of these expenditures to other costs is of the same order of magnitude as the ratio of branded wholesale prices to private-label wholesale prices. If this is the case, one could conclude that these high markups are simply necessary to cover these additional costs. This in no way reduces the interest in the paper's finding that these markups are high, although it would suggest that rents in these industries are dissipated in a relatively straightforward way.

The paper also contains a second set of fascinating facts that raise important microeconomics issues. In particular, the paper shows that the ratios of the four prices considered here for each pair of goods (i.e., the retail and wholesale prices for both members of each pair) vary quite dramatically across goods, even within narrow product categories. Trying to understand some of these variations seems extremely worthwhile. Indeed, some of the relative prices reported here seem to cry out for explanation. This seems particularly true of the "negative" margin between the retail and the wholesale price of certain soft drinks. This almost makes one worry about the authors' ability to measure the amount that Dominick's actually paid for its products.

One source of variation in the ratio of branded to private-label retail prices is obviously the extent to which branded products are seen as superior by customers (and this may explain the huge markups in toothbrushes). Open questions fall into two categories, however. The first is whether other ratios, such as the ratios of wholesale prices or the difference in branded and private-label retail margins, are also explainable in these terms or whether they hinge on variables related to the manufacturing industry's structure. The other is whether any of these ratios, including the ratio between the retail prices of the products in each pair, are related to the extent to which there is price discrimination in each product.

Reference

Becker, Gary S., and Kevin M. Murphy. 1993. A simple theory of advertising as a good or bad. *The Quarterly Journal of Economics* 108 (4): 941–64.

The Long Shadow of Patent Expiration
Generic Entry and Rx-to-OTC Switches

Ernst R. Berndt, Margaret K. Kyle, and Davina C. Ling

8.1 Introduction

In 2001 and 2002, a number of the United States' best-selling prescription pharmaceuticals—Prilosec, Prozac, Pepcid, and Claritin, for example—faced patent expiration. What should we expect to happen as these products approach the end of their patent product life cycle? Will switches from prescription (Rx) to nonprescription over-the-counter (OTC) status occur, and, if so, what will be their effects on average prices and utilization? Does the Rx-to-OTC switch significantly mitigate the effects of Rx patent expiration on branded pharmaceutical sales?

In this paper we address a number of issues surrounding the economic behavior of pioneer branded pharmaceutical firms facing Rx patent expiration and the consequences of generic Rx entry. We integrate retail scanner transactions data with wholesale sales records and data on marketing efforts. We focus on three main sets of issues: (a) pricing and marketing strategies by branded pioneer drug manufacturers on their Rx drugs before

Ernst R. Berndt is the Louis B. Seley Professor of applied economics in the Alfred P. Sloan School of Management, Massachusetts Institute of Technology, and director of the Program on Technological Progress and Productivity Measurement at the National Bureau of Economic Research. Margaret K. Kyle is assistant professor of strategy at the Graduate School of Industrial Administration at Carnegie Mellon University. Davina C. Ling is a postdoctoral fellow in health care policy and international health at Harvard University.

Research support from the National Science Foundation (to Berndt) and the MIT Program on the Pharmaceutical Industry (to Berndt and Kyle) is gratefully acknowledged, as is data support from Information Resources Inc., J&J•Merck Consumer Products, IMS Health, and Merck & Co. The authors thank Steve Morgan, Robert Feenstra, Richard Frank, Robert Pindyck, and an anonymous referee for comments on an earlier version of this paper. The views expressed in this paper are those of the authors only and do not necessarily reflect those of any institutions with which they are related, or of any research sponsor.

and after patent expiration; (b) the impact of generic Rx entry on the price, utilization, and revenues of the Rx molecule after patent expiration; and (c) the effects of Rx-to-OTC switches on cannibalization of same-brand Rx sales and on total (Rx plus OTC) brand sales. Although the first two sets of issues can be addressed using traditional data sources for pharmaceuticals, the third set of issues requires use of OTC data, data now available from scanned retail transactions.

To assess the more general impacts of generic Rx entry and Rx-to-OTC switches on prices and utilization, it is necessary to construct aggregate price indexes that incorporate these introductions of new goods. In this context, alternative ways of introducing new goods into price indexes have been proposed by Feenstra (1994, 1997) and by Griliches and Cockburn (1994). In this paper we compare these two price index approaches in terms of their data and modeling requirements, robustness of empirical results, and plausibility of empirical findings.

As best we can determine, the research we report here is the first systematic empirical examination of the interactions between Rx and OTC versions of "sunset" branded pharmaceuticals as they face Rx patent expiration.[1] In this study we focus on the U.S. market segments for antiulcer and heartburn drugs, which are large and in the last decade have experienced both patent expiration and extensive OTC introductions. We examine how the various product life cycle forces have operated in this market segment over the last decade. Our research integrates data from various sources, such as prescription drug sales data from IMS Health, as well as scanner OTC retail transactions data from Information Resources Inc. (IRI).

8.2 Background

In 1977 SmithKline introduced a pharmaceutical product branded Tagamet (a histamine$_2$-receptor antagonist, chemical name cimetidine) into the U.S. market. Tagamet promotes the healing of ulcers by blocking receptors on parietal cells that stimulate acid production, thereby reducing the secretion of stomach acid. The introduction of Tagamet marked the beginning of a new medical era in which ulcers were treated pharmacologically on an outpatient basis, rather than on the traditional inpatient basis, which had involved more costly hospitalizations and surgeries.

In the following years, a number of additional new histamine$_2$-receptor antagonist (hereafter, H$_2$) launches occurred, first involving Zantac (ranitidine, introduced by Glaxo in 1983), then Pepcid (famotidine, by Merck in 1986), and finally Axid (nizatidine, by Eli Lilly in 1988). Since their introductions, the four H$_2$s have expanded medical uses far beyond just the treatment of existing ulcers. For example, over the last two decades the Food and

---

1. For earlier empirical research on Rx-to-OTC switches, see Temin (1992).

Drug Administration (FDA) has approved use of the H$_2$s for the treatment of hypersecretory conditions and gastroesophageal reflux disease ("GERD," a common but severe form of heartburn); for the prevention of stress ulcers; for long-term maintenance therapy for the prevention of duodenal and gastric ulcer recurrence; and for the treatment and prevention of episodic heartburn, acid indigestion, and sour stomach. The H$_2$s have also been often prescribed to offset stomach-related side effects from other medications, as well as from anesthesia and radiological and chemotherapy treatments.[2]

Aided by patent protection, the widespread utilization of the H$_2$s resulted in spectacular revenue growth for their manufacturers. In the early to mid-1990s, for example, not only was Zantac the number one dollar sales volume prescription drug in the United States, but Tagamet was typically in the top ten, and Pepcid and Axid were also usually among the fifty or so best-selling prescription drugs.

The H$_2$s revolutionized medical treatments for gastrointestinal disorders. However, they soon faced forces of creative destruction in the form of a new and sometimes superior generation of drugs for the treatment of ulcers and GERD, namely the proton pump inhibitors (PPIs).[3] The more potent PPIs suppress acid secretion by directly inhibiting the acid-producing pump system of the parietal cell, have very few side effects, and have convenient once-a-day dosing.

The first PPI on the U.S. market was Prilosec (omeprazole, renamed Prilosec in 1990 after initially being branded Losec by Merck in 1989); then came Prevacid (lansoprazole, by TAP-Abbott in May 1995), Aciphex (rabeprazole, by Janssen in August 1999), and Protonix (pantoprazole, by Wyeth Ayerst in May 2000). Concerned about safety and risks from long-term use of the potent Prilosec, initially the FDA only approved its use for short-term treatment. However, after reviewing long-term use evidence, in March 1995 the FDA permitted Prilosec to remove the "black box" warning in its product labeling regarding possible risks from long-term use, and in June 1995 the FDA explicitly granted long-term maintenance use approval for Prilosec.

Although the H$_2$s provide effective treatments for many individuals, in some cases the PPIs are even better. For example, at the time of its obtaining initial marketing approval in May 1995, the manufacturer of Prevacid was permitted by the FDA to claim superiority over ranitidine (then the most prescribed H$_2$) for the treatment of heartburn (Electronic Orange Book 2000).

With long-term safety issues settled, and superiority over the H$_2$s estab-

2. For more detailed discussions of the H$_2$ market up until 1994, see Berndt et al. (1995, 1997).

3. A London Business School case study dealing with how the H$_2$ manufacturers could respond to competition from the new PPIs is that by Dell'Osso (1990). Also see Perloff and Suslow (1994).

lished, the PPIs were marketed intensively beginning in the mid-1990s. Remarkably, sales of the PPIs exceeded even those of the record-setting H_2s. By 1997, for example, Prilosec had overtaken Zantac as the United States' (and the world's) largest revenue prescription drug, and by 1999, Prevacid ranked not far behind.[4]

In addition to intense rivalry from the next-generation PPIs, the H_2s also faced imminent loss of patent protection. Tagamet's patent was the first to expire, on 17 May 1994, and after considerable litigation, Zantac's market exclusivity was terminated in late July 1997.

In this context, one specific provision of the Waxman-Hatch Act of 1984 was particularly important to the H_2 prescription drug manufacturers in the 1990s. This provision granted pioneer manufacturers an additional three years of limited market exclusivity, if they obtained FDA approval for a new presentation and indication for the chemical entity.[5] As early as a decade before its anticipated patent expiration, SmithKline discussed with the FDA the possibility of its seeking and gaining approval for an OTC version of Tagamet for the treatment of heartburn.[6] By timing the OTC launch to coincide approximately with the pioneer Rx patent expiration date, SmithKline could potentially benefit from an additional three years of market exclusivity on the OTC version of Tagamet, thereby offsetting somewhat its loss of post–patent expiration Rx sales. Consumers, not just branded manufacturers, might also enjoy welfare gains from Rx-to-OTC switches. Specifically, provided the OTC drug is safe, consumers could benefit by having access to an effective medication without incurring the time and dollar costs of obtaining a physician's prescription (Rx).[7]

This provision of the Waxman-Hatch Act created clear incentives for SmithKline, the manufacturer of the pioneer H_2 Tagamet, to be the first to switch from Rx to OTC. However, the later H_2 Rx entrants (Zantac, Pepcid,

---

4. That Prilosec even made it to the market was remarkable, since its Swedish developers nearly terminated research on it several times, viewing its research program as a likely failure. For a history of its development, see Eliasson and Eliasson (1997).

5. See Section 505 of the Federal Food, Drug, and Cosmetics Act, 21 USC Section 355 (c)(3)(B)(iii). Empirical analyses of the effect of the Waxman-Hatch Act include those by Grabowski and Vernon (1992); Caves, Whinston, and Hurwitz (1991); and Frank and Salkever (1997). For a historical overview of FDA regulation of the drug industry prior to 1980, see Temin (1980).

6. For a Harvard Business School case study discussion of the race to develop and launch the first OTC H_2 in the United States, see King et al. (2000).

7. For discussions of possible benefits and costs to consumers, manufacturers, and insurance providers from the Rx-to-OTC switch, see Hesselgrave ("Will Managed Care Embrace Rx-to-OTC Switches?" *Drug Topics,* 2 June 1997), Jaroff ("Fire in the Belly, Money in the Bank," *Time,* 6 November 1995, 56–58), McCarthy (1999), Tanou and Burton ("More Firms 'Switch' Prescription Drugs to Give Them Over-the-Counter Status," *Wall Street Journal,* 29 July 1993, B1), and Temin (1983, 1992). More general discussions of consumers' response to drug prices, and the factors affecting substitution between Rx and OTC drugs, are found in, inter alia, Leibowitz (1989); Leibowitz, Manning, and Newhouse (1985); O'Brian (1989); Phelps and Newhouse (1974); and Stuart and Grana (1995).

and Axid) also had incentives to launch OTC versions of their Rx products, particularly if late OTC entry meant forgoing potentially large OTC sales. For the later Rx entrants, OTC entry could possibly occur even *prior to* their own Rx patent expiration. All H_2 manufacturers realized that the order of exit from patent protection in the Rx market need not be the same as the order of entry into the OTC market, nor would first-mover advantages in the Rx market necessarily transfer to the OTC environment.[8]

Moreover, in implementing an Rx-to-OTC switch, pharmaceutical firms had to consider two possible offsetting forces. Branded Rx manufacturers needed to account for the possible cannibalization of sales of their branded Rx product that could result by introducing a same-brand OTC variant. On the other hand, positive spillovers could result from increased brand awareness when both OTC and Rx same-brand products were marketed simultaneously. Would positive spillover or negative cannibalization effects dominate?[9]

Two of the four H_2 brands (Tagamet and Zantac) lost patent protection in the 1990s, and the other two brands (Axid and Pepcid) lost patent protection in 2001. All four have implemented Rx-to-OTC switches. Thus the variation among the H_2s, over time, should enable us to quantify the importance of the various factors affecting sales of these molecules. Moreover, Prilosec, currently the best-selling drug in the world, is scheduled to lose U.S. market exclusivity and face generic competition some time in 2002, although ongoing litigation currently leaves the precise date of Prilosec patent expiration uncertain. Thus an examination of the recent historical record involving the H_2s could yield insights into what developments to expect in the market for the PPIs as patent protection ends and, possibly, as Rx-to-OTC switches occur for the PPIs as well.

The remainder of this chapter continues as follows. In section 8.3 we review conceptual bases that provide hypotheses involving pricing and marketing as Rx brands face Rx generic competition. Then in section 8.4 we describe alternative methodologies for incorporating generic and OTC products ("new goods") into various aggregate price indexes. In section 8.5 we discuss data sources and the construction and interpretation of various

8. On first-mover advantages and their rationale in the market for pharmaceuticals, see Bond and Lean (1977), Berndt et al. (1995, 1997), King (2000), and King et al. (2000). The theoretical foundations and empirical evidence on first-mover advantages in other markets are discussed in, among others, Robinson, Kalyanaram, and Urban (1994); Samuelson and Zeckhauser (1988); Schmalensee (1982); and Urban et al. (1986).

9. It is interesting to note that when joining up with or creating joint ventures with the more retail-oriented consumer product companies, the Rx drug manufacturers also created cannibalization possibilities for the traditional antacids used to treat heartburn. For example, for SmithKline Beecham, OTC Tagamet competed with its OTC antacid products, Tums and Gaviscon. For Glaxo Wellcome, pairing with Warner-Lambert meant that OTC Zantac would compete with OTC Rolaids. Finally, for the J&J•Merck joint venture, the OTC Pepcid would compete with OTC Mylanta and Imodium. Ling (1999) provides an empirical analysis of the interactions among the incumbent OTC antacid and the newer OTC H_2 products.

price and quantity measures, first for prescription drugs and then for OTCs. With this as background, in section 8.6 we present a number of stylistic facts that appear to characterize these markets in anticipation of and following Rx patent protection, and we provide some preliminary evidence on our hypotheses. We discuss our price index results in section 8.7. Finally, in section 8.8 we summarize and conclude.

8.3   Conceptual Foundations and Testable Hypotheses

The existing literature in economics and marketing provides a conceptual basis for a number of hypotheses. We first address pricing by branded Rx firms in response to generic competition. Frank and Salkever (1992, 1997) demonstrate that under certain conditions, a profit-maximizing branded pioneer may not lower (and may even increase) price in response to generic competition. The branded firm must be able to segment its market into sets of brand-loyal consumers, who will continue to purchase the product, and price-sensitive consumers, who will migrate to the lower-cost generics.[10] Other things being equal, the larger the brand-loyal segment is relative to the price-sensitive segment, the greater the branded pioneer's post–patent expiration price. The magnitude and speed of the price response by the branded pioneer following patent expiration is, however, an empirical issue. We hypothesize that branded firms will not lower Rx prices following patent expiration.[11]

Economic theory provides some very useful general guidance and intuition on marketing efforts by branded firms. In particular, as enunciated by Dorfman and Steiner (1954), for profit-maximizing firms facing downward-sloping demand curves and having market power such as that provided by patent protection, the optimal ratio of marketing expenditures to revenues turns out to be equal to the ratio of two elasticities; that is,

$$(1) \qquad \frac{\$ \text{ Marketing}}{\$ \text{ Sales}} = \frac{\varepsilon_M}{\varepsilon_P},$$

where ε_M is the elasticity of demand with respect to marketing efforts, and ε_P is the absolute value of the price elasticity of demand.[12]

There is considerable evidence that early in the product life cycle phar-

10. On this, also see Scherer (1993, 2000), Griliches and Cockburn (1994), and Ellison et al. (1997).

11. Empirical evidence presented in Frank and Salkever (1997) and Berndt, Cockburn, and Griliches (1996) is consistent with the Frank-Salkever segmented market hypothesis. Related econometric evidence from Berndt, Griliches, and Rosett (1993) suggests that over the 1986–91 time period, prices of older drugs increased more rapidly than those of newer products.

12. The original Dorfman-Steiner formulation was in the context of static optimization. Extensions to dynamic optimization are presented in Schmalensee (1972). Most of the intuition generalizes to the dynamic environment. For additional discussions, see Hurwitz and Caves (1988) and Leffler (1981).

maceutical marketing efforts involving physician detailing and medical journal advertising provide long-lived benefits in the form of additional current and future sales; that is, evidence suggests that up to the mature phase of the product life cycle, ε_M is positive and significant. Moreover, ε_M is larger in the long run than over the short term. The substantial amount of marketing commonly observed at the time of initial product launch is of course consistent with large and long-lived sales impacts from such marketing efforts (see, e.g., Berndt et al. 1995, 1997; Perloff and Suslow 1994; King 2000).

However, as patent expiration approaches, one expects that branded manufacturers anticipate a decline in ε_M, because lower-priced generic entrants could instead capture a large portion of sales from additional marketing (on this, see also Ellison and Ellison 2000). If this is true, branded manufacturers would reduce their current marketing-to-sales ratio in anticipation of patent expiration. Notice that if marketing efforts were not long-lived, one might instead expect them to occur unabated until the day of patent expiration. Once patent expiration actually occurs, not only would ε_M likely fall further, but it is also reasonable to expect that price competition would intensify, increasing ε_P, the denominator of the right side of equation (1), and thereby further reducing the ratio of marketing-to-sales. We hypothesize, therefore, that the pioneer's marketing-sales ratio will fall as patent expiration approaches, and it may even approach zero after patent expiration occurs. Because any single generic entrant finds it difficult to appropriate any sales benefits from marketing of the molecule, for generic firms we expect ε_M to be very small. The intense price competition among generics implies a large ε_P. Hence, we hypothesize that generic manufacturers will have marketing-sales ratios close to zero, where marketing efforts consist of physician detailing and medical journal advertising.[13]

8.4   Alternative Procedures for Incorporating New Goods into Price Indexes

For the purpose of assessing impacts of generic Rx entry and Rx-to-OTC new product introductions, it is useful to construct price indexes aggregated up to the level of a molecule (including both generic and brand Rx), or a brand level (including both Rx and OTC versions). Theoretical and empirical discussions of alternative methodologies for constructing an aggregate price index over generic and brand Rx drugs are found in Feenstra (1997)

---

13. Generic firms may, however, engage in other marketing efforts for which the benefits are more easily internalized. Generic firms market very differently from brand firms. Instead of engaging in detailing and journal advertising, generic firms tend to have home office major account representatives for particular customers, such as drugstore chains, staff model managed care organizations, and mass merchandisers such as Wal-Mart. Unfortunately, we have no data on these types of marketing efforts.

and in Griliches and Cockburn (1994; hereafter GC).[14] Griliches and Cockburn assume a uniform distribution of reservation prices across heterogeneous consumers between the brand and generic prices at the time of patent
expiration, and they thereby obtain an average reservation price midway between the brand and generic price. Their price index method employs post–
generic entry data only. Feenstra's method involves inferring the elasticity
of substitution from aggregate expenditure variations pre– and post–patent
expiration, and it has the benefit of not requiring estimation of a reservation
price. In this chapter, in addition to examining these issues in the more general context of Rx-to-OTC switches (not just brand-generic drugs after
patent expiration), we will assess the sensitivity of alternative price index
calculations to the choice of functional form, to the complexity of modeling requirements, and to the inclusion of nonprice regressors.

Both the Feenstra and GC procedures are based on the economic theory
of consumer demand. In the context of the Rx drug market, principal-agent
issues involving physicians and patients, as well as moral hazard considerations resulting from the presence of insurance coverage, complicate matters
considerably. Price comparisons between OTC and Rx versions of the same
molecule are also more complex to interpret when the Rx version is covered
by insurance whereas the OTC is not. Thus, although we make no attempt
to incorporate such complications here, we caution that many of the traditional relationships between welfare calculations and price index movements are unlikely to hold in the Rx and OTC markets.

Following Feenstra's notation, we denote total expenditures on a molecule by E, price by P, the change operator by Δ, and the positive price elasticity of demand by η. Since $\Delta E = -(\eta - 1)\,\Delta P$, it follows that

$$(2) \qquad \Delta P = \frac{-\Delta E}{(\eta - 1)},$$

where $\eta > 0$. Feenstra's insight is that if data on ΔE were available and if η
were known, then one could simply use equation (2) to obtain an estimate
of ΔP consistent with consumer preferences, without requiring knowledge
of the reservation price of the generic drug. Feenstra suggests estimating η
simultaneously with parameters of the price index P, as described below.

Assuming that different molecules are imperfect substitutes, Feenstra
specifies a simple log-log demand equation for molecule i having the form

$$(3) \qquad \ln Q_i^t = \alpha_i - \eta_i \ln P_i^t + \sum_{i \neq j} \beta_j \ln P_j^t + \delta_i \ln I^t + \varepsilon_i^t,$$

for periods $t = 0, 1, \ldots, T$, where Q_i and P_i are quantity (in grams) and price
per gram of the ith molecule, P_j is the price of imperfect substitutes for the
ith molecule, I is total expenditures across the various molecules, and ε_i is a

---

14. Feenstra's (1997) work builds on that in Feenstra (1994) and Feenstra and Shiells (1997).

random disturbance term. When i and j are substitutes, the β_j are positive. Also, as long as i is not an inferior good, we expect the δ_i to be positive.

To incorporate brand-generic substitutability within a given molecule, Feenstra assumes the existence of a unit expenditure function that is weakly separable from other molecules (and other goods) and that is consistent with aggregation of tastes over heterogeneous consumers. When a constant elasticity of substitution (CES) unit expenditure assumption is assumed (which can be derived from a linear random utility model in which each consumer has differing additive utility over the varieties available), Feenstra shows that the exact price index in period t (after the generic is introduced) relative to time period 0 (just prior to the generic introduction) is

$$(4) \qquad P_i^t = \left(\frac{p_{ib}^t}{p_{ib}^0}\right)(1 - s_{ig}^t)^{1/(\sigma_i - 1)}$$

where p_{ib} is the per gram price of the branded version of molecule i, s_{ig} is the revenue share of the generic, and σ_i is the elasticity of substitution between generic and branded versions of molecule i, with $\sigma_i > 1$. The elasticity of substitution σ_i is obtained by estimating parameters in the equation

$$(5) \qquad \ln\left(\frac{s_{ig}^t}{s_{ib}^t}\right) = \alpha_i + (\sigma_i - 1)\ln\left(\frac{p_{ib}^t}{p_{ig}^t}\right) + u_i^t$$

where s_{ib} is the brand revenue share, p_{ig} is the per gram price of the generic version of molecule i, and u_i is a random disturbance term. Feenstra also derives estimating equations in the case of a translog unit expenditure functional form. To save on space, we do not discuss translog forms further here; their extension is straightforward.

Notice that in order that the area above price but under the demand curve (consumers' surplus) be finite, it is required that the σ_i elasticities of substitution between brand and generic versions of a molecule be greater than 1. In the current context, since there are only two goods (brand and generic drugs), and quantity demanded is homogeneous of degree zero in prices, this elasticity of substitution restriction is tantamount to requiring demands to be own-price elastic. Intuitively, when the price of good i increases with p_j fixed, eventually as quantity demanded of good i approaches zero, the proportional decline in quantity of good i must be greater than its price increase, else the demand curve would not intersect the vertical price axis (the reservation price would not be finite). When $\sigma_i > 1$, the CES function satisfies this condition globally. However, if any of the elasticities of substitution σ_i are less than or equal to unity, at any positive price the amount of consumers' surplus (and the reservation price) will be infinite. It is worth emphasizing that both the GC and Feenstra approaches to aggregate price index construction in the context of the introduction of a new good share this substitution elasticity constraint.

To implement the CES framework empirically, Feenstra substitutes equation (4) into equation (3), normalizes a "real" expenditure index relative to the price of the branded drug,

$$\tilde{Q}_i^t = \frac{E_i^t/E_i^0}{p_{ib}^t/p_{ib}^0},$$

and then obtains an estimating equation nonlinear in the parameters, of the form

$$(6) \qquad \ln \tilde{Q}_i^t = \alpha_i - \eta_i \ln \frac{p_{ib}^t}{p_{ib}^0} + \left(\frac{1-\eta_i}{\sigma_i - 1}\right) \ln(1 - s_{ig}^t)$$

$$+ \sum_{i \neq j} \beta_{ij} \left[\ln \frac{p_{jb}^t}{p_{jb}^0} + \frac{\ln(1 - s_{jg}^t)}{\sigma_j - 1} \right] + \delta_i \ln I^t + \varepsilon_i^t,$$

where $i \neq j$. Notice that estimation of the within-molecule and between-molecule substitution elasticities is accomplished using data from both the pre– and post–generic entry time periods.

The alternative, simpler methodology suggested by GC is to estimate within-molecule brand-generic substitutability employing only post–generic entry data, using data on, for example, the CES revenue share equation (5). These elasticity estimates are then inserted into equation (4) to obtain exact price indexes.

Feenstra (1997) argues that his approach has two advantages over that of GC. First, it makes use of a longer time series of data, and, second, it is more robust empirically to the choice of functional form when applied to monthly October 1984–September 1990 U.S. data on two anti-infective drugs. We assess both procedures here in a rather different context—the H_2 market for two types of new goods, generic and OTC drugs, based on data primarily from the 1990s. Specifically, we first consider construction of aggregate price indexes with generic entry into the Rx H_2 market, and then we aggregate further to consider the impacts of OTC entry in the total H_2 market (Rx brand, Rx generic, and OTC), using monthly data from the time period January 1989–December 1998.

8.4.1   Rx H_2 Market Only, Brands, and Generic Entry

Of the four molecules in the Rx H_2 market, two (cimetidine and ranitidine) experienced generic entry during the 1989–99 time period analyzed. We therefore specify two estimable equations embodying both within- (brand-generic) and between-molecule (cimetidine, ranitidine, Pepcid, and Axid) substitutability, based on a CES unit expenditure function. We also experiment with introducing additional explanatory variables into the molecule demand equations (e.g., marketing efforts), but only in a preliminary way, because an extensive demand analysis is beyond the scope of the current study.

The relatively simple equations take the form

$$(7) \quad \ln \tilde{Q}_i^t = \alpha_i - \eta_i \ln \frac{p_{ib}^t}{p_{ib}^0} + \left(\frac{1-\eta_i}{\sigma_i-1}\right) \ln(1 - s_{ig}^t) + \beta_{ij} \left[\ln \frac{p_{jb}^t}{p_{jb}^0} + \frac{\ln(1 - s_{jg}^t)}{\sigma_j - 1}\right]$$

$$+ \beta_{ik} \ln\left(\frac{p_{kb}^t}{p_{kb}^0}\right) + \beta_{il} \ln\left(\frac{p_{lb}^t}{p_{lb}^0}\right) + \delta_i \ln I^t + \varepsilon_i^t$$

where i = cimetidine (brand name Tagamet) or ranitidine (brand name Zantac); j, k, and l denote the other H_2-antagonist molecules; and I^t is total expenditures on all four molecules (both brand and generic, where applicable).

Assuming a CES unit expenditure assumption, for the GC framework the two estimating equations have the considerably simpler form

$$(8) \quad \ln\left(\frac{s_{ig}^t}{s_{ib}^t}\right) = \alpha_i + (\sigma_i - 1) \ln\left(\frac{p_{ib}^t}{p_{ig}^t}\right) + u_i^t$$

where i = cimetidine or ranitidine, b refers to the Rx brand, and g refers to the Rx generic. Although in principle equation (8) could be generalized to incorporate data on relative brand-generic marketing efforts, in fact generics' traditional marketing efforts are essentially zero.

8.4.2   Total H_2 Market with OTC Entry

The exact price indexes obtained for the cimetidine and ranitidine Rx H_2 molecules can now be employed in a larger context in which aggregate molecule price indexes are constructed consistent with imperfect substitutability between OTC and Rx versions of the same H_2 molecule. Recall that during our 1989–99 sample period, all four H_2 Rx drugs implemented same-brand introductions of OTC versions.

With a CES unit expenditure function defined over Rx and OTC versions of the same H_2 molecule in the Feenstra approach, the four estimating equations take the form

$$(9) \quad \ln \tilde{Q}_i^t = \alpha_i - \eta_i \ln \frac{p_{ir}^t}{p_{ir}^0} + \left(\frac{1-\eta_i}{\sigma_i-1}\right) \ln(1 - s_{ic}^t)$$

$$+ \sum_{i \neq j} \beta_{ij} \left[\ln \frac{p_{jr}^t}{p_{jr}^0} + \frac{\ln(1 - s_{jc}^t)}{\sigma_j - 1}\right] + \delta_i \ln I_{rc}^t + \varepsilon_i^t.$$

Here, p_{ir} is the estimated price index of the Rx version of the molecule i (as calculated in section 8.5.1 below) when i = cimetidine or ranitidine, but p_{ir} is the price index of the branded Rx version of molecule i when i = Pepcid or Axid, because Rx Pepcid and Rx Axid did not lose patent protection and thus did not face generic entry during the 1989–98 time period of our study. The revenue share of the OTC version of the molecule i is s_{ic}, and in this broader context σ_i is the elasticity of substitution between Rx and OTC versions of molecule i, $\sigma_i > 1$. The index j denotes the imperfect substitutes for molecule i. Hence, p_{jr} is the estimated price index of the Rx version of the molecule j, as calculated in section 8.5.1, when j = cimetidine or ranitidine. However, p_{jr} is the price index of the branded Rx version of molecule j if j = Pepcid or Axid. The revenue share of the OTC version of molecule j is s_{jc}, and σ_j is the elasticity of substitution between Rx and OTC versions of molecule j. The total expenditure across the Rx and OTC versions of the molecules is I_{rc}, and ε_i is a random disturbance term. These four equations are nonlinear in the parameters and contain numerous cross-equation restrictions.

With the GC approach based on the CES unit expenditure function, the four estimating equations take the relatively simple form

$$(10) \qquad \ln\left(\frac{s_{ic}^t}{s_{ir}^t}\right) = \alpha_i + (\sigma_i - 1)\ln\left(\frac{p_{ir}^t}{p_{ic}^t}\right) + u_i^t,$$

where the notation is the same as above. Below we undertake empirical analyses of equations (9) and (10), adding measures of relative cumulative marketing efforts as additional demand-shifters.

8.5   Data Sources, Descriptions, and Interpretations

Our framework requires integrating data from a number of diverse sources, which we now briefly summarize. We begin with prescription drugs and then discuss the OTCs.

8.5.1   Prescription Drug Markets

Quantity shipped, revenue, and marketing data for antiulcer and heartburn prescription drugs are taken from IMS Health, monthly from January 1988 through June 1999. IMS Health's Retail Perspective™ tracks monthly shipments from manufacturers and wholesalers to retail warehouses and outlets. The data on revenues include those to manufacturers and wholesalers but not to the retail outlets (which add retail margins). Although revenues are net of chargebacks (discounts given purchasers and channeled through wholesalers), rebates (payments made to providers who often do not take title to the pharmaceuticals, e.g., managed care organizations) are not included in the IMS revenue data, nor are prompt payment discounts. The exclusion of rebates from the revenue data implies an overstatement of manufacturers' Rx revenues and prices. The extent of this bias is unknown, because data on rebates tend to be highly proprietary. In spite of this drawback in the IMS data, however, most branded and generic pharmaceutical companies purchase and utilize the IMS data for their internal research. Industry officials have indicated to us that although the absolute prices and revenues are likely to be upward biased, there is no reason to believe any bias carries over to *relative* prices and revenues.

Information on quantity shipped and revenue is at the level of presentation, for example, thirty-tablet bottles of 150 milligram (mg) strength tablets. We convert these presentational sales measures into quantity or unit data by using the recommended daily dosage for active duodenal ulcer treatment as the transformation factor. The resulting quantity data can then be interpreted as the hypothetical patient days of therapy per month were all patients taking the recommended active duodenal ulcer daily dosage.[15] Data on recommended daily dosages are taken from the *Physicians' Desk Reference* (2000). Price per day of therapy is then computed as revenues divided by the quantity of therapy days in that month. Further details on price, quantity, and revenue measurement are found in the data appendix of Berndt et al. (1997).

The price and quantity data we employ only cover Rx sales into drugstores. Drugstore sales constitute on average about 70–80 percent of sales in all outlets but exclude sales to hospitals, long-term care facilities, and mail-order distributors (IMS Health 1998). Because hospital usage and marketing differ considerably from the outpatient environment, we confine our attention here to transactions occurring in the traditional retail sector.

To measure marketing efforts involving visits by pharmaceutical sales representatives ("detailers") to physicians' offices, we employ IMS Health data from its Office Contact Report™. Basing its data on a panel of about 3,800 physicians who report the number of visits and minutes spent with detailers discussing particular products, IMS extrapolates monthly detailing efforts by drug to the national level. Using an estimated cost per detailing visit, IMS also estimates total detailing expenditures.

Medical journal advertising pages and expenditures are estimated by IMS in its National Journal Audit™. This audit includes journal pharmaceutical advertising directed to practitioners in all types of medical practice, including pharmacists, nurses, podiatrists, and dentists, as well as medical and osteopathic practitioners. Based on circulation, the number of square inches, pages of advertisements, and copy characteristics such as premium positioning and the number of colors in each advertisement, IMS uses standard rate sheets from over 300 major medical journals to estimate total dollars of journal advertising, monthly, by drug. Further details on these marketing measures can be found in the data appendix of Berndt et al. (1997) and in IMS Health (1998).

The Rx H_2 antagonists have been marketed not only to physicians but also, more directly, to consumers. In the context of Rx-to-OTC switches, direct-to-consumer (DTC) marketing of Rx products permits manufacturers to build up consumer brand awareness in anticipation of the future launch of OTC variants. In the mid-1980s Tagamet Rx had a "Tommy Tummy"

15. The transformation factors are: Tagamet (cimetidine), 800 mg/day; Zantac (ranitidine), 300 mg/day; Pepcid, 40 mg/day; Axid, 300 mg/day; Prilosec, 20 mg/day; Prevacid, 30 mg/day; and Propulsid, 40 mg/day. Since Propulsid never had FDA approval for active duodenal ulcer treatment, we use the recommended daily dosage for treatment of nocturnal GERD.

DTC marketing campaign, and later in the early 1990s Glaxo launched an extensive TV and print DTC campaign for Zantac. In 1997 the FDA clarified regulations on the content of DTC ads. Increases in DTC marketing of Rx drugs were steady during the 1990s.[16]

Data on DTC marketing of Rx brands from Leading National Advertisers (LNA)/Media Watch Multi-Media Service is published on a quarterly basis by Competititve Media Reporting. This service reports Rx brand advertising expenditure estimates in ten major media: consumer magazines, Sunday magazines, newspapers, outdoor advertising, network television, spot television, syndicated television, cable television, network radio, and national spot radio. The LNA/Media Watch Multi-Media Service includes only brands of companies spending a total of $25,000 or more year-to-date in the ten media measured. The data we employ are taken from Class D21X, which reports advertising expenditures by company and then lists brands for each company. Currently our DTC data are available only through 1998:4. To transform the quarterly data into monthly periodicity, we employ the Stata command "ipolate."[17] The monthly expenditure data are then deflated by the Bureau of Labor Statistics' Advertising Agency Producer Price Index to convert them into constant-dollar figures.[18]

8.5.2   Over-the-Counter Drug Markets

Quantity and revenue data for the OTC H_2 market are taken from InfoScan™, based on store-level optical scanner data purchased and collected from multiple retail outlets by IRI.[19] These scanner data are collected weekly from more than 29,000 chain drugstores, mass merchandisers, food stores, and chain convenience stores located in major metropolitan areas and rural areas. They are then projected to national levels for these chains. The IRI data provide detailed information on sales, pricing, and promotion on a stock-keeping unit basis. The volume of sales is recorded for each package size of each brand on an average weekly basis. The weekly data are aggregated to the monthly level.

To establish comparable units of consumption for Rx and OTC products, we aggregate the data for each OTC brand across presentations and regional outlets so that the quantity measure reflects the total milligrams sold each month nationally. For instance, if 5,000 packages of Tagamet HB each with twenty-five tablets of 200 mg cimetidine are sold, we compute the to-

16. On this, see Rosenthal et al. (2002).
17. See Stata Corporation (1999).
18. For July 1995 onward (when the deflators first became available), we construct this deflator as the arithmetic average of the Producer Price Index for "Advertising agencies, ad creation, billed separately," and "Advertising agencies, media placement, including ad creation not billed." For months prior to July 1995, we employ the Producer Price Index for all finished goods.
19. See Information Resources Inc. (1997), Guadagni and Little (1983), and Bucklin and Gupta (1999). The IRI website is [http://www.infores.com].

tal number of mg of Tagamet HB sold that month as $5000 \times 25 \times 200 = 25$ million mg. Unlike the IMS Health data on Rx sales to drugstores, the IRI data record sales from drugstores, mass merchandisers, and food stores to consumers, so the IRI data include both wholesale and retail margins. Moreover, whereas the IMS data reflect inventory stocking behavior by, for example, chain drugstore warehouses, the IRI data only include actual transactions to final consumers.

To make the quantity units of the various OTC H_2 brands comparable with each other, we normalize the total number of milligrams per brand sold each month by the daily dosage recommended to treat active duodenal ulcers.[20] Although we describe our quantity measure as patient days of therapy, in fact this is not literally true. Both the Rx and OTC versions are used for the treatment of a number of related disorders, often at varying dosages, and by individuals having different body masses.[21] Rather, the quantity measures should be interpreted as the number of patient days of therapy that would be consumed were all the OTC H_2s used for the treatment of active duodenal ulcers at recommended Rx dosages. It is worth emphasizing that we do not wish to imply or suggest here that any or all patients actually (mis)use the OTC H_2s to treat active duodenal ulcers.[22] We make this transformation solely for the purpose of standardizing units of active ingredient.

Once quantity units are calculated, we divide total revenues by quantity, thereby obtaining a price per patient day of therapy. Both the revenue and price OTC data reflect the impacts of periodic "sales" and discounts as well as the effects of coupons redeemed by consumers at the time of the retail transaction.

Over-the-counter medications have been marketed intensively to consumers. For example, between 1990 and 1996 for the seven largest-selling antacid OTC products in 1994, the median real ratio of advertising to retail sales was approximately 34 percent.[23] To obtain measures of monthly advertising of the OTC H_2s, we employ data from Leading National Advertisers/Media Watch Multi-Media Service. Leading National Advertisers distinguishes consumer-oriented OTC brand advertising from that for Rx brands. Quarterly data on media advertising over the ten media mentioned earlier for the H_2 OTC brands are taken from Class D213, over-the-counter digestive aids and antacids. Currently these data are only available to us through 1998:4. The "ipolate" command in Stata is again employed to con-

20. This follows procedures utilized by Ling (1999) and Berndt et al. (1995, 1997).

21. Recommended dosages vary by indication. For example, whereas the recommended dosage of Zantac for treating active duodenal ulcers, active gastric ulcers, and GERD is 300 mg per day (either 300 mg once daily or 150 mg twice daily), the recommended dosage for duodenal ulcer maintenance therapy is only 150 mg per day.

22. For each of the four OTC H_2s, the transformation of OTC to Rx involves using twice the maximum daily recommended OTC dosages.

23. Ling (1999). The seven brands are Tums, Mylanta, Gaviscon, Maalox, Alka-Seltzer, Rolaids, and Pepto-Bismol.

vert expenditure data from quarterly to monthly. Monthly advertising expenditures in current dollars are then deflated by the BLS Producer Price Index for Advertising Agencies, as discussed above.

8.6   Observed Patterns Near the End of the Patented Product Life Cycle

"Nostalgia isn't what it used to be."
—Unknown

We now turn to a description and preliminary analysis of marketing and pricing developments as the Rx H_2 manufacturers anticipated and accommodated loss of patent protection of their own products or those of their competitors. We also examine the impacts of the preemptive launch of OTC H_2 variants and the effects of competition from generic Rx H_2 producers.

8.6.1   Marketing Intensity Near Patent Expiration

We begin by examining how branded pioneer firms changed their marketing behavior in anticipation of, and following, loss of patent protection. To assess the hypotheses advanced in section 8.3, we examine marketing efforts for the two H_2 antagonists losing patent expiration, Tagamet (May 1994) and Zantac (August 1997).[24] We compare average marketing efforts when the date of patent expiration is quite some time away (between 25 and 48 months ahead), as it becomes much closer (between 1 and 24 months ahead), and has passed (0 to 23 months after). For each time frame, we compute average monthly minutes of detailing and average journal pages, as well as the Dorfman-Steiner dollar ratio of average marketing expenditures to average sales revenues. Differences between the periods 1–24 and 25–48 months prior to patent expiration are called "near versus far away," and those between the periods 0–23 months after and 25–48 months before are called "after versus far away." The results of these calculations are given in table 8.1, the top panel in terms of marketing quantity levels, and the bottom in ratios of dollar marketing to sales.

For Tagamet, average monthly minutes of detailing fell by 30 percent as its patent expiration approached (May 1992–April 1994 vs. May 1990–April 1992) and by 87 percent following its patent expiration in May 1994 (May 1994–April 1996 vs. May 1990–April 1992). Journal page advertising fell even more sharply, by 55 percent and 97 percent, respectively. The ratio of total marketing (detailing plus medical journal advertising) expenditures to total sales revenue (bottom two rows of table 8.1) fell by 43 percent as Tagamet patent expiration approached, and then it subsequently fell by a smaller amount, 30, after patent expiration. The post-patent smaller decline

---

24. For Zantac, patent expiration actually occurred on Friday, 25 July 1997. Since this was near the end of July and began on a weekend, we approximate the beginning of patent expiration as August 1997.

Table 8.1   Changes in Marketing Efforts in Anticipation of and Following Patent Expiration, H₂-Antagonist Prescription Drugs (%)

	Tagamet Patent Loss	Zantac Patent Loss	Pepcid at Zantac Patent Loss	Axid at Zantac Patent Loss
Minutes of detailing				
Near vs. far away	−30.2	−59.3	−19.6	−36.0
After vs. far away	−86.6	−94.4	−28.3	−48.5
Pages of journal advertising				
Near vs. far away	−55.1	−99.3	257.7	−16.1
After vs. far away	−96.7	−100.0	−16.2	−94.7
Dollar Marketing to Dollar Sales Ratios				
Detailing dollars to sales ratio				
Near vs. far away	−37.8	−57.4	−39.1	−36.3
After vs. far away	−32.3	−71.2	−36.7	−35.1
Total detailing plus journal advertisingdollars to sales ratio				
Near vs. far away	−43.1	−59.8	−33.3	−36.0
After vs. far away	−30.1	−72.8	−35.3	−35.5

Notes: For Tagamet, "far away" is May 1990–April 1992, "near" is May 1992–April 1994, and "after" is May 1994–April 1996. For Zantac, Pepcid, and Axid, "far away" is August 1993–July 1995, "near" is August 1995–July 1997, and "after" is August 1997–July 1999.

in the ratio reflects in part the sharp decrease in the denominator—brand revenues—after patent expiration.

For Zantac, the decline in marketing efforts was even more dramatic. Average monthly minutes of detailing fell by 59 percent as Zantac patent expiration approached (August 1995–July 1997 vs. August 1993–July 1995), and by 94 percent following Zantac patent expiration in August 1997 (August 1997–July 1999 vs. August 1995–July 1997). As with Tagamet, journal page advertising fell even more sharply than detailing minutes, at 99 percent and 100 percent, respectively. The total marketing-sales ratio fell by almost 60 percent, and it fell by an additional 13 percent after patent expiration.

It is also of interest to examine how the competitors of Zantac, then the leading selling H₂, reacted when they observed Zantac cutting back on marketing in anticipation of and following Zantac's patent expiration. Because the entire H₂ prescription drug market was in decline during this time due to competition from the more potent PPIs and the introduction of OTC versions that potentially cannibalized H₂ Rx sales, would Pepcid and Axid Rx also cut back on marketing efforts? Or would they capitalize on a strategic opportunity to fill a void created by the dramatic cutbacks by Tagamet and Zantac, and instead increase their marketing efforts?[25] The marketing responses of Pepcid and Axid surrounding the time of Zantac's patent expiration are summarized in the last two columns of table 8.1.

25. Note that the patents of Axid and Pepcid did not expire until 2001.

Pepcid and Axid had rather different responses. For Axid, average minutes of detailing fell by about 36 percent as Zantac's patent expiration approached, and they fell another 13 percent following expiration. The journal advertising cutback was more varied: 16 percent as Zantac's patent expiration approached and 95 percent following it. For Pepcid, however, the decline in minutes of detailing was much more modest—only 20 percent in the time leading up to Zantac patent expiration, and an additional 8 percent following it. Journal page advertising for Pepcid actually increased by 258 percent (from rather low levels) as Zantac patent expiration approached, and after patent expiration it fell to 16 percent less than that 25–48 months before Zantac patent expiration occurred. Although the responses of Pepcid and Axid as Zantac cut back on its levels of marketing efforts differed, they were quite similar in terms of total marketing-sales ratios. Both reduced these ratios by about 33–36 percent as Zantac patent expiration approached and then maintained them at approximately those values after Zantac's patent expiration.

Finally, IMS data indicate zero recorded detailing efforts by generic manufacturers. However, for about twelve to eighteen months following patent expiration, generic manufacturers of cimetidine and ranitidine did a very modest amount of medical journal advertising.[26] Although the generic firms' medical journal advertisements announced the new availability of cimetidine or ranitidine, frequently these ads also noted the portfolio of other generic products offered by the manufacturer rather than focusing on their specific H_2 products.

8.6.2   Pricing of Rx Drugs in Anticipation of and Following Patent Expiration

Next we analyze pricing behavior prior to and following patent expiration. Figure 8.1 plots prices per day of therapy for Rx Tagamet and generic Rx cimetidine from January 1989 through December 1998, whereas figure 8.2 presents those for Rx Zantac and generic Rx ranitidine over the same period. Both figures include the average price per day of therapy over all Rx and OTC forms for each molecule ("Total Molecule") and the average price over branded Rx and generic Rx ("Total Rx"). All prices are in current (not deflated) dollars.

---

26. For cimetidine, medical journal pages with generic cimetidine advertisements in the eighteen months following Tagamet patent expiration were only about 14 percent of the corresponding Tagamet pages in the eighteen months prior to its patent expiration. For ranitidine, in the eighteen months prior to Zantac patent expiration, Zantac had no medical journal advertising, and thus no direct comparison with generic post-patent advertising is available. The number of pages of generic ranitidine advertising in the eighteen months following Zantac patent expiration was only about 17 percent of Tagamet's pages in the eighteen months prior to Tagamet's patent expiration. For both generic cimetidine and ranitidine, journal page advertising beyond eighteen months following the brand's patent expiration date is essentially zero.

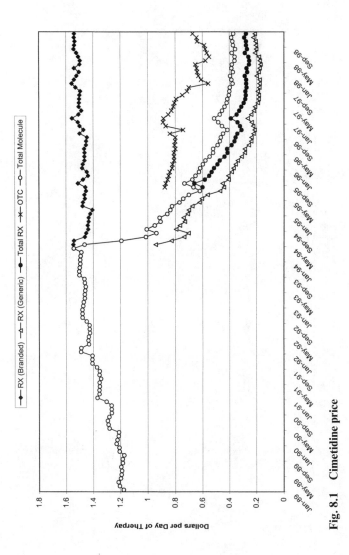

Fig. 8.1 Cimetidine price

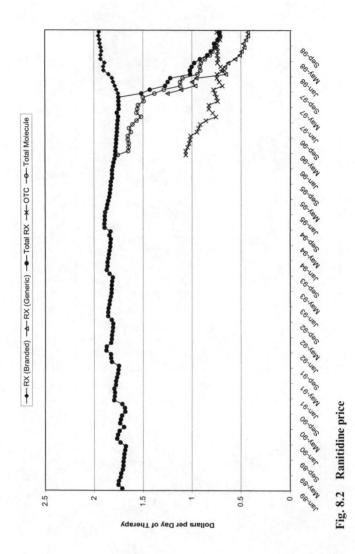

Fig. 8.2 Ranitidine price

As is seen in figure 8.1, Tagamet's Rx price continued to increase following patent expiration in May 1994, and by December 1998 it was about 5 percent greater than five years earlier when it lost patent protection. The price of generic cimetidine has fallen considerably since 1994 but has remained fairly constant since about mid-1997. By late 1998, the Tagamet Rx brand price was almost eight times that of generic Rx cimetidine. Instead of meeting price competition from the generics, Tagamet Rx maintained and even slightly increased its price.

Patent expiration provided considerable benefits for cimetidine consumers who switched to generic versions. In particular, the total Rx price of cimetidine (a sales-weighted average over Tagamet Rx and generic cimetidine Rx) has fallen to about 20 percent of its level at the time of patent expiration in May 1994. The total Rx price at late 1998 was about one-sixth that of the Tagamet Rx brand price.

Figure 8.2 presents the comparable price paths for Zantac Rx and generic Rx ranitidine. Following loss of market exclusivity in July 1997, the Zantac brand price increased steadily, and by late 1998 it was about 10 percent higher than at patent expiration. The rate of price decline for generic ranitidine immediately following patent expiration appears to be greater than that of cimetidine (compare figures 8.1 and 8.2). This difference could reflect greater entry incentives for ranitidine, because at the time of patent expiration the branded Zantac Rx was a larger dollar and unit sales market than was branded Tagamet Rx. In December 1998 the price of generic ranitidine was about one-quarter that of Zantac at the time of its patent expiration and one-fifth of the current Zantac price. Zantac pricing in the post–patent expiration era does not appear to differ in any dramatic way from the patent-protected time period, although its prices have increased more sharply than has Tagamet Rx since patent expiration.

Just as with cimetidine, consumers have realized far lower average prices for ranitidine following Zantac's patent expiration. By late 1998 the average ranitidine Rx price (a sales-weighted average over Zantac Rx and generic ranitidine Rx) was about 65 percent lower than it was at the time of Zantac patent expiration in July 1997.

In summary, neither Tagamet Rx nor Zantac Rx adopted a policy of competing with generics on price following patent expiration, and instead they increased prices. As a consequence, they lost a very substantial market share but retained sales to a small, relatively price-insensitive segment of brand-loyal customers.

8.6.3   Molecule Rx Volume Before and After Patent Expiration

Next we examine quantity (patient days of Rx therapy) data for cimetidine and ranitidine before and after patent expiration. For branded Tagamet, as is seen in figure 8.3, sales were relatively flat during the four years preceding patent expiration in May 1994 but plummeted afterward as

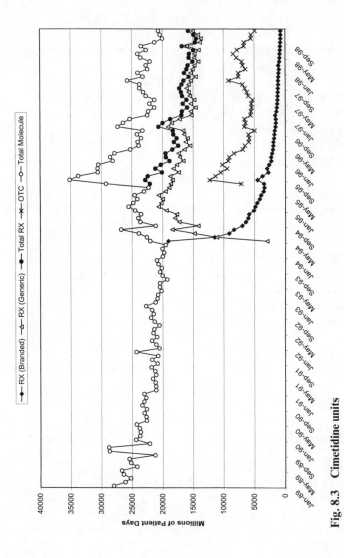

Fig. 8.3 Cimetidine units

generic entrants flourished. By late 1998, generic cimetidine had more than 95 percent market share of the prescription cimetidine market. Total quantity of brand plus generic Rx cimetidine sales (labeled "Total Rx" in figure 8.3) has shrunk by about one-third since Tagamet lost patent protection, even though the average price per day of therapy for the Rx cimetidine molecule (over its brand and generic Rx versions) declined precipitously (see figure 8.1). This cimetidine Rx sales decline reflects the combined impacts of new competition from generic ranitidine following Zantac Rx patent expiration, increased rivalry from the PPIs, cannibalization from the introduction of the OTC variant Tagamet HB, and sharply curtailed Rx marketing efforts.

For Rx ranitidine the picture is slightly different, as is seen in figure 8.4. In particular, branded Zantac Rx sales appear to have fallen steadily since early 1995 (around the time Pepcid AC, the first OTC H_2, came on the market), preceding its patent expiration by more than two years. Reflecting perhaps the effects of OTC cannibalization, branded Zantac Rx sales continued a steady decline until August 1997, when Rx patent expiration took place. Thereafter, as with branded Tagamet Rx, branded Zantac Rx quantity units fell dramatically, and by December 1998 Zantac Rx unit sales were about 10 percent of their 1994–95 peak levels. Total ranitidine Rx sales ("Total Rx" in figure 8.4) also experienced a continued decline following patent expiration. The post–patent expiration decline in total Rx sales for ranitidine is smaller than that for cimetidine (compare figures 8.3 and 8.4), but the fall in average Rx price for ranitidine from the time of patent expiration is also smaller for ranitidine Rx than with cimetidine Rx (compare figures 8.1 and 8.2).

8.6.4   L(a)unching with Cannibals: Effects of OTCs on Rx Sales

Next we turn to an exploratory empirical assessment of the impact of a brand's OTC introduction on its own Rx sales. In theory, this impact could be either positive or negative. If cannibalization is extensive, then patients taking Rx versions will switch to the OTC product, and the trend of overall OTC plus Rx sales for that brand will be largely unaffected. Alternatively, nonusers exposed to marketing for OTC products might seek advice from their physicians and be prescribed the stronger Rx version (whether as medically appropriate or as a consequence of insurance coverage), generating positive spillovers. If these spillovers are sufficiently large, overall OTC plus Rx sales for that brand could increase. Whether cannibalization or positive spillovers dominate is therefore an empirical issue.

We expect that because it was the largest-selling Rx product, Zantac faced the greatest threat of cannibalization of its Rx product by an OTC version. In contrast, with patent expiration already behind it, Tagamet had the most to gain from its OTC launch. We now assess the net effects on brand sales of OTC introductions by brand.

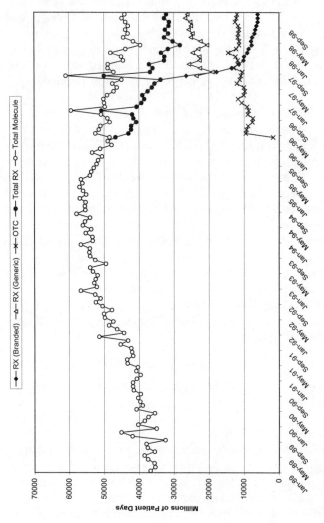

Fig. 8.4 Ranitidine units

First, we compare Rx and OTC prices. Recall that for comparability, the OTC price per day of therapy assumes twice the recommended daily OTC dosage, so that the Rx and OTC versions have the same amount of mg strength each day. By December 1998 the OTC Tagamet HB price per day of therapy is about 45 percent the Rx Tagamet price, but slightly more than three times the Rx generic cimetidine price, as shown in figure 8.1. Figure 8.2 shows that by late 1998, on a per-patient day of therapy basis, the price of OTC Zantac 75 is about one and one-half times that of Rx generic ranitidine, but only about 40 percent that of Zantac Rx. These estimates of the difference between the branded Rx and OTC versions are a lower bound of the true differential magnitude, since the Rx generic price does not include the retail margin, which is often larger than that for the branded Rx product, whereas the OTC price is gross of the retail margin. In spite of this OTC relative price overstatement, for consumers paying cash, purchasing a day of therapy is much less expensive with the OTC versions of Tagamet and Zantac than with their branded Rx variants. The OTC purchase also avoids the time and other costs of obtaining a physician's prescription.

Although to save on space we do not present comparable figures here for Pepcid and Axid, prices per day of therapy for Pepcid Rx and Axid Rx were about two and one-half times their comparable OTC price in late 1998.

The quantity of OTC Tagamet sold in late 1998 is about seven to eight times larger than Rx Tagamet. In 1995 OTC sales resuscitated overall brand sales following the 1994 loss of Tagamet patent protection. Tagamet's OTC introduction was a clear spillover winner: Because its brand Rx sales had fallen so sharply following patent expiration, there were few Rx sales left to cannibalize. By mid-1998, however, total Rx plus OTC Tagamet sales were again falling, and by late 1998 they reached levels about the same as just prior to patent expiration. Through its OTC launch, Tagamet averted and postponed the gradual brand franchise death, but only temporarily.

For Zantac, as seen in figure 8.4, the introduction of an OTC version in May 1996 appears to have revived the Zantac brand franchise, temporarily raising total Zantac Rx plus Zantac 75 OTC patient day sales. By fall 1997, immediately following Zantac Rx patent expiration, total Zantac unit sales were about the same as those in early 1996, just prior to the launch of Zantac 75. Zantac OTC unit sales have continued a slow but steady increase in recent years even as Zantac Rx sales have declined sharply, and by late 1998 patient days of Zantac OTC were twice those of Zantac Rx. Although (unlike Tagamet) in some ways the Zantac franchise benefited from an OTC introduction prior to its Rx patent expiration, it also appears that the Zantac franchise suffered cannibalization of Zantac Rx by Zantac 75. As the best-selling Rx therapy, Zantac was most susceptible to the various OTC introductions, including its own.

Tagamet OTC revenues (not shown) were about three times greater than those for Tagamet Rx in late 1998, whereas OTC Zantac 75 revenues were only slightly less than those from Zantac Rx. Summed over both OTC and Rx versions, however, Zantac revenues were about four to five times larger than those for Tagamet. Hence, although on a relative basis the OTC introductions appear to have benefited Tagamet more than Zantac, on an absolute revenue basis over both OTC and Rx forms, Zantac gained more.

8.7 Price Index Construction with Generic and Over-the-Counter "New Good" Entry

Constructing price and quantity measures on the basis of simple summed-up milligram units for a given molecule implicitly assumes that, for example, generic versions of cimetidine are perfectly substitutable with Tagamet (branded cimetidine). Similarly, aggregating milligrams of the OTC version of Zantac to milligrams of the Zantac Rx and generic Rx ranitidine, then obtaining price per milligram by dividing total revenue by these summed milligrams, also assumes perfect substitutability among OTC and Rx versions of ranitidine. Because perfect substitutability is clearly an unrealistic assumption (witness, for example, continued sales of Rx Zantac after much lower priced generic Rx ranitidine enters), it is useful to examine alternative methods for creating aggregate price indexes that allow for imperfect substitutability.

Recall from our earlier discussion in section 8.4 that in the context of medical care, we believe the traditional theory of consumer demand is best employed with great caution. In particular, principal-agent issues involving relationships between patients and their physicians, and the role of moral hazard and insurance in creating wedges between insurers' and consumers' marginal prices for covered Rx drugs, seriously compromise and constrain one's ability to draw any consumer welfare implications from observed aggregate price index trends.

We have implemented the methodologies of Feenstra and GC, as outlined in section 8.4. Specifically, to implement the Feenstra procedure using nonlinear estimation procedures, we have estimated parameters in the normalized quantity equation (6) derived from the CES brand-generic demand equations, using monthly data from both before and after patent expiration for Tagamet and Zantac; an analogous equation system based on the translog unit expenditure function was also estimated. In each case, the two-equation system (cimetidine and ranitidine) is estimated by maximum likelihood, allowing for contemporaneous correlation among residuals in the two equations.

To implement the GC methodology, single equation least squares procedures are employed in estimating the CES parameters in equation (5), using only post–patent expiration data for the cimetidine and ranitidine equations.

For both the Feenstra and GC procedures, aggregate CES price indexes for the cimetidine and ranitidine molecules are then constructed by inserting parameter estimates into equation (4). In the GC method, the assumed reservation price just prior to the time of initial generic entry is midway between the brand and generic price. Aggregate molecule price indexes incorporating the introduction of OTCs as new goods are calculated in an analogous manner. Notice that in the GC method these aggregate price indexes depend only on brand-generic substitutability within each molecule, and not on own-price elasticities for the molecule in aggregate.

Before proceeding with a discussion of results comparing the GC and Feenstra procedures, we emphasize that with both the GC and Feenstra procedures, our simplest demand specification is quite restrictive in that no account is taken of other, nonprice factors affecting demands, such as marketing efforts. In the GC specification that only employs post–patent expiration data, this restrictiveness may not be that undesirable, because only brand-generic substitutability within a given molecule is being modeled, and, as we observed earlier, in practice very few marketing efforts occur after patent expiration. On the other hand, in the Feenstra specification, because pre–patent expiration data are included, excluding nonprice factors as regressors in the total molecule demand equation (3), such as measures of relative brand marketing efforts, could well be expected to have a much larger impact. Moreover, although brand marketing variables could be introduced as additional regressors, since patent expiration could involve a regime shift, we would not be surprised if parameters on these price and marketing variables would differ in the pre– and post–patent expiration environments. It is possible that regime shifts are less evident in the Rx-to-OTC context than in the patent expiration and brand-generic entry environment.

8.7.1   Cimetidine and Ranitidine Price Indexes with Generic Entry

Despite a substantial amount of experimentation with alternative time periods, functional forms, and the incorporation of measures of marketing efforts, we were unable to obtain satisfactory estimates of the crucial within-molecule substitution elasticity estimates using the Feenstra procedure.

More specifically, with marketing effort measures excluded, and using data from the January 1989–June 1999 time frame, for both the CES and translog specifications we obtained reasonable estimates for the cimetidine and ranitidine aggregate molecule own-price elasticities of demand; these ranged from around –2.2 to –2.4 for the CES form for cimetidine and ranitidine, respectively, whereas the corresponding estimates based on the translog were about –2.6 and –2.3. However, estimates of the within-molecule brand-generic substitution elasticity were either of the wrong sign or of an unreasonable magnitude. For example, for cimetidine and ranitidine, based on the CES form, the estimates of σ were about –1.6 and 140, respectively;

assuming generic revenue shares of 67 percent, the comparable translog-based substitution elasticity estimates were about –0.6 and 70.

To check on the robustness of these unsatisfactory σ estimates, we systematically shortened the pre–patent expiration time period that ended first in May 1994 for Tagamet, sequentially dropping all observations in 1990, 1990–91, 1990–92, and then 1990–93; although estimates of both the own-price and cross-brand–generic substitution elasticity varied considerably with the choice of time period, in no case did satisfactory σ estimates result. We also experimented with a number of specifications that incorporated measures of marketing efforts; for each molecule, we cumulated physician-oriented detailing data over the previous twelve months and included in each of the molecule equations both own and others' cumulative marketing efforts. Although estimates of parameters on own-molecule cumulative marketing efforts were typically positive and significant, estimates on others' cumulative marketing efforts were negative and only occasionally significant. More importantly, however, inclusion of these additional Rx marketing effort measures did not entirely overcome our inability to obtain satisfactory estimates of the σ within-molecule elasticity of substitution between brand and generic. Unlike the situation with marketing efforts excluded, when marketing effort measures were included the molecule whose elasticity of substitution estimate was typically of the wrong sign was ranitidine (estimates ranged from –6.1 to –4,443), whereas elasticity of substitution estimates for cimitedine ranged from 1.02 (using January 1991–December 1998 data) to 3.26 (January 1994–December 1998).

If one instead implements the GC method using only post–patent expiration observations, own-price elasticity estimates for the aggregate molecule are not needed, and estimates of the brand-generic elasticities of substitution for the CES turn out to be plausible at 1.44 (standard error of 0.11) and 1.96 (0.18). For the translog, assuming generic revenue shares of 0.67, the GC parameter estimates imply elasticity of substitution estimates of 1.42 and 1.99 for cimetidine and ranitidine, respectively. Since only a very modest amount of medical journal advertising was conducted by generic entrants after patent expiration, and since generic physician detailing efforts were essentially zero, it is not surprising that incorporating brand-generic relative marketing efforts into the revenue share equations as an additional regressor did not change these results in any material manner.

8.7.2   Price Indexes for All Four Molecules Accounting for Over-the-Counter Entry

OTC entry occurred for Tagamet HB in August 1995, about fifteen months after Rx Tagamet lost patent expiration. In contrast, the OTC entry of Zantac 75 took place in April 1996, about eighteen months before the August 1997 loss of patent expiration for Rx Zantac. The Tagamet-Zantac OTC launch date experience is very different from that of both Pepcid AC

(June 1995) and Axid AR (July 1996), who launched their OTC version years before their patent expiration occurred (in 2001). We now examine aggregate price indexes for each of the four molecules, where the aggregate is over Rx brand, Rx generic (only in the case of cimetidine and ranitidine), and OTC brand versions.

We begin by constructing, for cimetidine and ranitidine, a price index over brand and generic Rx versions. Since, as discussed in the preceding subsection, our modeling efforts to construct price indexes over brand and generic versions were generally unable to yield satisfactory brand-generic substitution elasticity estimates, we use the nonparametric Divisia index procedure instead.

With the Feenstra method, we then model total generalized quantity for each molecule (Rx and OTC) using both pre– and post–OTC launch data, whereas with the GC method we employ only the post–OTC launch data. Measures of total marketing for each molecule include that for Rx marketing for each molecule (the sum of constant dollar expenditures for physician-oriented detailing, physician-oriented journal advertising, and DTC of the Rx brand), plus the OTC measure of Rx marketing for each molecule (only DTC marketing of the OTC brand). We then cumulated total marketing efforts for each molecule over the preceding twelve months. We also constructed a relative Rx-OTC marketing measure as the ratio of the Rx cumulative marketing efforts to OTC cumulative marketing efforts, where the cumulation encompasses the preceding twelve months. Because the DTC data available to us ended in December 1998, we utilize data over the ten-year time period January 1989–December 1998, yielding cumulative marketing effort measures for each molecule for the nine-year period January 1990–December 1998.

The Feenstra method involves maximum likelihood estimation of a four-equation system with cross-equation parameter restrictions and a balanced panel, whereas for the GC method single equation ordinary least squares (OLS) estimation is carried out using each molecule's post–OTC launch data only. In both the Feenstra and GC methods, for price index construction the crucial parameter is the Rx versus OTC substitution elasticity, which of course differs for each of the four molecules.

Using the Feenstra procedure and excluding marketing variables, we experienced considerable numerical convergence issues, with typically two or so of the within-molecule Rx-OTC elasticity estimates being very large in absolute value (sometimes positive, sometimes negative). Matters improved considerably, however, when we incorporated into each of the CES generalized quantity equations both that molecule's own total marketing efforts and the total marketing efforts summed over the other three molecules, where both marketing measures are logarithmically transformed. Specifically, estimates of the within-molecule Rx-OTC elasticity of substitution were 2.00 (standard error of 0.20) for famotidine (Pepcid), 1.42 (0.10) for ranitidine (Zantac), and 1.80 (0.25) for nizaditine (Axid). For cimetidine (Tagamet), however, the point estimate was an unreasonably large 9,069, with a standard error almost 100 times as large. Interestingly, for each of the four molecules the own (log) total marketing elasticity estimate was positive and significant (ranging from a low of 0.057 for famotidine to a high of 0.136 for ranitidine, with respective standard errors of 0.027 and 0.023), whereas those for the (log) of the sum of the other molecules' marketing efforts was negative, albeit only in the case of nizaditine was the −0.391 estimate significant (standard error of 0.106). Except for cimetidine, estimates of the own-price total molecule demand price elasticity were negative, significant, and plausible, whereas that for cimetidine was very imprecisely estimated.

Given the very large standard error estimates on the cimetidine own-price and within-molecule Rx-OTC elasticity of substitution estimates, we constrained the σ elasticity of substitution estimate for cimetidine to be 1.74, the mean of the corresponding σ estimates over famotidine, ranitidine, and nizaditine. We then substituted these σ estimates into equation (4) and computed exact price indexes for each of the four molecules, where these price indexes are an aggregate over Rx and OTC versions. These molecule-specific four aggregate price indexes are graphed in figure 8.5, where for each molecule the price index is 1.000 in January 1989. A number of points are worth noting.

First, for all four molecules, prices generally increase during the first five years from January 1989 to January 1994, and in the second half of the sample they take on different time paths.

The cimetidine price falls in early 1994 following patent expiration and generic entry and experiences another sharp fall in mid-1995 as OTC entry occurs. At the end of 1998, the cimetidine price index had fallen to a level of 0.548, about 42 percent of its April 1994 peak of 1.312.

For famotidine, the fall in price is also substantial, but because it had not lost patent protection by end 1998, its price decline reflects only the impact of OTC entry. As seen in figure 8.5, there is a sharp decline in the famotidine price in mid-1995 as Pepcid AC enters, and thereafter prices are roughly stable, ending at 0.793 in December 1998, about 29 percent less than its 1.112 value in May 1995 just prior to the OTC launch of Pepcid AC.

In contrast to both cimetidine and famotidine, for nizaditine the molecule price increases steadily from January 1989 through June 1996; it then drops about 15 percent to 1.04–1.06 in late 1996, and thereafter it experiences a steady increase, ending up at 1.147 in December 1998, down about 11 percent from the 1.289 level in June 1996 just prior to launch of the OTC Axid AR product. The Rx version of Axid did not lose patent protection until 2001, beyond the December 1998 last observation in this study.

For ranitidine, however, the combination of lost patent protection, very substantial low-priced generic entry, and substantial growth of the OTC

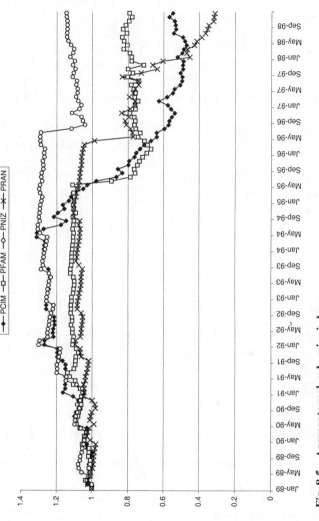

Fig. 8.5 Aggregate molecule price indexes

Zantac 75 product resulted in by far the largest price decline among the four molecules. As seen in figure 8.5, the ranitidine molecule experienced about a 25 percent price decline in May 1996 as OTC entry of Zantac 75 occurred, then another sharp price decline of about 25 percent between August and December 1997 as generic ranitidine initially entered the market, and continuing declines during 1998 with further generic ranitidine entry. In December 1998, the ranitidine molecule price index was 0.313, about 30 percent of its level just prior to the OTC launch of Zantac 75 and about 50 percent of its level just prior to entry of generic ranitidine.

These molecule price indexes are based on the Feenstra methodology that includes observations for each molecule both before and after OTC entry. Following GC, we have also estimated the Rx-OTC elasticity of substitution using equation (8) and, for each molecule, only the data following OTC launch. These results were somewhat disappointing. For all four molecules, GC-CES estimates of σ were less than 1.0, violating a necessary condition of the model that $\sigma > 1$. With relative Rx/OTC marketing variables excluded, the estimated σ (standard error follows in parentheses) was 0.802 (0.215) for cimetidine, 0.892 (0.164) for famotidine, -0.400 (0.581) for ranitidine, and -0.399 (0.186) for nizatidine. When a cumulative (log) relative Rx/OTC marketing variable was included as an additional regressor in equation (8), the relative marketing variable was typically significant and of the right sign, but all of the σ estimates remained below unity. These σ estimates were 0.848 (0.210) for cimetidine, 0.535 (0.134) for famotidine, $-$ 0.105 (0.312) for ranitidine, and -0.222 (0.273) for nizatidine. Since measures of consumer surplus are infinite when $\sigma < 1.0$, conditions for the validity of the CES exact price index are violated, and thus we do not report the corresponding price indexes.

8.8   Summary and Conclusions

In this paper we have reported results of our research examining the "sunset" H_2s up to and following their Rx patent expiration, as they encountered cannibalization from their own and competitors' OTC introductions, and as they faced forces of creative destruction from the next generation of more potent antiulcer and heartburn Rx drugs, the PPIs. Although the looming prospect of patent expiration had significant impacts on the behavior of the H_2 manufacturers in terms of their pricing and marketing behavior, it was more than the shadow of patent expiration that dimmed the H_2 prospects—undoubtedly, the forces of dynamic competition in the form of the newly dominant PPI products were equally foreboding.

Within this larger context, consumers appear to have benefited from generic entry and the introduction of OTC versions of previously prescription-only H_2s. One way to characterize these developments is to employ the exact aggregate price and quantity measures based on the CES function within the Feenstra framework (an aggregate over Rx and OTC versions for each molecule) and then construct aggregate Divisia price and quantity indexes encompassing all four molecules. These aggregate H_2 price and quantity measures, denoted PH2TOT and QH2TOT, are graphed in figure 8.6, with each indexed to 1.000 in January 1989. As is seen in figure 8.6, the aggregate H_2 price series increased steadily from January 1989 to about January 1992, was flat at about 1.15 for several years until early 1995, and then began to fall, with a particularly large decline in early 1996 (following OTC entry by several brands) and another substantial decline in late 1997 following Zantac loss of patent protection and Rx generic ranitidine entry. By the end of our sample in December 1998, the aggregate H_2 price index was 0.57, roughly 50 percent lower than in early 1995 just prior to the first OTC entry.

In terms of quantity of H_2s consumed, from January 1989 to early 1995 the quantity index increased from 1.00 to about 1.33, then grew more rapidly to about 1.86 by November 1996, and then began falling again, ending up at about 1.41 in December 1998.

It is worth emphasizing again, however, that how one interprets these price and quantity trends is somewhat ambiguous, given principal-agent relationships between physicians and patients, and the moral hazard arising from insurance coverage of Rx, but typically not OTC, versions of these products.

As expected, we find that the branded H_2 manufacturers have not competed on price with generic entrants following Rx patent expiration but instead have maintained or even slightly increased brand prices, losing market share and retaining sales to a small but relatively price-insensitive segment of brand-loyal customers.

We also find evidence strongly supporting the notion of protracted effects from marketing. In particular, we find very substantial declines in marketing efforts by branded firms as Rx patent expiration approaches, a phenomenon suggesting long-rather than short-lived anticipated sales impacts from marketing.

Even though generic entry results in average molecule prices (weighted over brand and generic) falling 65–80 percent of their pre–patent expiration levels, for both cimetidine and ranitidine the combined brand and generic quantity sales following patent expiration have also fallen considerably. This utilization decline could reflect the impacts of decreased marketing efforts, competition from the more potent PPIs, or cannibalization of Rx sales by the introduction and marketing of a same-brand OTC product. The relative importance of these various factors in explaining the post–patent expiration decline in sales is a topic worthy of further research.

On a per-patient-day basis, we find that in late 1998 brand OTC prices were 35–45 percent of their brand Rx prices, but brand OTC prices were still several times larger than same molecule generic Rx prices. These price

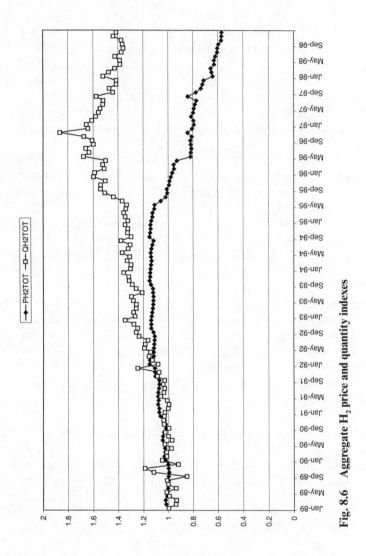

Fig. 8.6   Aggregate H$_2$ price and quantity indexes

ratios should be interpreted somewhat cautiously, however, since the Rx prices do not reflect retail margins, unlike the OTC prices based on scanner transaction data.

Since Zantac executed the OTC switch prior to its 1997 patent expiration, it suffered considerably from OTC cannibalization of Rx sales, but ultimately the substantial amount of OTC Zantac 75 sales has partially resuscitated the Zantac brand franchise. Because Tagamet lost patent protection prior to its OTC switch, it had the least to lose by going OTC, and in fact on a relative basis its OTC-Rx sales ratio has grown, although levels of both OTC Tagamet HB and Tagamet Rx are small.

Finally, we have compared two different approaches to incorporating the generic and OTC new goods into aggregate price indexes. The GC method yielded reasonably plausible elasticity of substitution estimates in the context of Rx generics' being the new good relative to Rx brands. However, in this brand-generic context, the Feenstra method did not fare as well, yielding estimates of the within-molecule elasticity of substitution that were either of the wrong sign or of an unreasonable magnitude. Matters did not improve much for the Feenstra method when demand equations were augmented by own and others' measures of cumulative marketing efforts. We note that in Feenstra (1997), the Feenstra method yielded plausible substitution elasticity estimates for cephalexin, but not for cephradine.

The Feenstra and GC methods reversed roles when the new good was instead defined to be an OTC version of the branded Rx drug. With the GC method, estimates of the elasticity of substitution were all less than unity, violating an integrability condition that requires $\sigma > 1$. In contrast, with the Feenstra method, in the Rx-to-OTC context three of the four estimates of σ were plausible and reasonably precisely estimated, whereas only one had an implausibly large value (and standard error). The addition of marketing variables to the molecule demand equation was particularly important in the Feenstra methodology, for there it greatly facilitated numerical convergence to plausible parameter estimates. Although detailed results were not presented in the paper, it is worth noting that the relative performance of the GC and Feenstra methods was unchanged when the CES functional form was replaced by a translog expenditure function.

Together, these results suggest that use of econometric methods in constructing price indexes that incorporate the effects of new goods requires considerably more experimentation, perhaps with other data sets and families of products, and with specifications that include nonprice factors affecting demand functions, such as measures of marketing efforts. Future research should focus on the conditions under which the Feenstra, the GC, or some other method is more likely to yield robust and plausible findings. Particular attention needs to be focused on the feasibility of integrating scanner price, quantity, and promotional data with more complete measures of marketing efforts from other publicly available data sources. Until more progress is made on these fronts, and reasonably robust findings are reported by a number of independent researchers, government statisticians may be understandably cautious in publishing price indexes based on econometrically estimated reservation prices or on econometric estimation of expenditure formulations that obviate the need for estimation of reservation prices. Apparently, the new goods problem is not simply solved by mechanical implementation of econometric estimation methods.

In terms of other future research, the impact of Rx-to-OTC switches on prices paid by consumers, after allowing for insurance coverage and patient copays, is a most interesting research topic, as is the more general issue of the effects of such switches on patient health and consumer welfare. The availability of scanner data helps make such research feasible. It would also be useful to exploit econometric procedures that allow for preference estimation even when the number of available products changes over time (see, e.g., Berry, Levinsohn, and Pakes 1995; Bresnahan, Stern, and Trajtenberg 1997). The existence of principal-agent and moral hazard issues, particularly important in the Rx market, however, makes such research very challenging.

Pepcid, Prozac, and Mevacor all lost patent protection and faced generic entry in 2001, and Prilosec could face generic entry in 2002, pending the outcome of patent litigation. Whether the long shadows of imminent patent protection for these drugs will display similar pricing, marketing, and Rx-OTC switching patterns to what we have observed in the H_2 market remains to be seen.

References

Berndt, Ernst R., Linda T. Bui, David H. Lucking-Reiley, and Glen L. Urban. 1995. Information, marketing, and pricing in the U.S. anti-ulcer drug market. *American Economic Review* 85 (2): 100–05.
———. 1997. The roles of marketing, product quality, and price competition in the growth and composition of the U.S. anti-ulcer drug industry. In *The economics of new products,* Studies in Income and Wealth, vol. 58, ed. Timothy F. Bresnahan and Robert J. Gordon, 277–322. Chicago: University of Chicago Press.
Berndt, Ernst R., Iain M. Cockburn, and Zvi Griliches. 1996. Pharmaceutical innovations and market dynamics: Tracking effects on price indexes for antidepressant drugs. *Brookings Papers on Economic Activity: Microeconomics,* issue no. 2:133–88. Washington, D.C.: Brookings Institution.
Berndt, Ernst R., Zvi Griliches, and Joshua G. Rosett. 1993. Auditing the producer price index: Micro evidence from prescription pharmaceutical preparations. *Journal of Business and Economic Statistics* 11 (3): 251–64.
Berry, Steven, James Levinsohn, and Ariel Pakes. 1995. Automobile prices in market equilibrium. *Econometrica* 63 (4): 841–90.
Bond, Ronald S., and David F. Lean. 1977. *Sales, promotion, and product differenti-*

ation in two prescription drug markets. Staff Report of the Bureau of Economics of the Federal Trade Commission. Washington, D.C.: February.

Bresnahan, Timothy F., Scott Stern, and Manuel Trajtenberg. 1997. Market segmentation and the sources of rents from innovation: Perosnal computers in the late 1980s. *RAND Journal of Economics* 28 (special issue): S17–S44.

Bucklin, Randolph E., and Sunil Gupta. 1999. Commercial use of UPC scanner data: Industry and academic perspectives. *Marketing Science* 18 (3): 247–73.

Caves, Richard E., Michael D. Whinston, and Mark A. Hurwitz. 1991. Patent expiration, entry, and competition in the U.S. pharmaceutical industry. *Brookings Papers on Economic Activity,* issue no. 1:1–48. Washington, D.C.: Brookings Institution.

Dell'Osso, Filippo. 1990. When leaders become followers: The market for anti-ulcer drugs. Case Series no. 12. London: London Business School, February.

Dorfman, Robert, and Peter O. Steiner. 1954. Optimal advertising and optimal quality. *American Economic Review* 44 (5): 826–36.

Electronic Orange Book. 2000. Approved drug products with therapeutic equivalence evaluations. Current through June 2000. Available at [http://www.fda/cder/default.htm]. Updated 28 July.

Eliasson, Gunnar, and Asa Eliasson. 1997. The pharmaceutical and biotechnological competence bloc and the development of losec. In *Technological systems: Cases, analyses, comparisons,* ed. Bo Carlsson, 217–43. Amsterdam: Kluwer Academic.

Ellison, Glenn, and Sara Fisher Ellison. 2000. Strategic entry deterrence and the behavior of pharmaceutical incumbents prior to patent expiration. Massachusetts Institute of Technology, Department of Economics. Manuscript, April.

Ellison, Sara Fisher, Iain Cockburn, Zvi Griliches, and Jerry Hausman. 1997. Characteristics of demand for pharmaceutical products: An examination of four cephalosporins. *RAND Journal of Economics* 28 (3): 426–46.

Feenstra, Robert C. 1994. New product varieties and the measurement of international prices. *American Economic Review* 84(1): 157–77.

———. 1997. Generics and new goods in pharmaceutical price indexes: Comment. *American Economic Review* 87 (4): 760–67.

Feenstra, Robert C., and Clinton R. Shiells. 1997. Bias in U.S. import prices and demand. In *The economics of new goods,* ed. Timothy F. Bresnahan and Robert J. Gordon, 249-273. Chicago: University of Chicago Press.

Frank, Richard G., and David S. Salkever. 1992. Pricing, patent loss, and the market for pharmaceuticals. *Southern Economic Journal* 59 (2): 165–79.

———. 1997. Generic entry and the pricing of pharmaceuticals. *Journal of Economics and Management Strategy* 6 (1): 75–90.

Grabowski, Henry, and John Vernon. 1992. Brand loyalty, entry, and price competition in pharmaceuticals after the 1984 Drug Act. *Journal of Law and Economics* 35 (2): 331–50.

Griliches, Zvi, and Iain M. Cockburn. 1994. Generics and new goods in pharmaceutical price indexes. *American Economic Review* 84 (5): 1213–32.

Guadagni, Peter M., and John D. C. Little. 1983. A logit model of brand choice calibrated on scanner data. *Marketing Science* 2 (3): 203–38.

Hurwitz, Mark A., and Richard E. Caves. 1988. Persuasion or information? Promotion and the shares of brand name and generic pharmaceuticals. *Journal of Law and Economics* 31 (October): 299–20.

IMS Health. 1998. *Information services manual 1998.* Plymouth Meeting, Penn.: IMS Health.

Information Resources Inc. 1997. *Store data measures.* Waltham, Mass.: Information Resources Inc.

King, Charles III. 2000. Marketing, product differentiation, and competition in the market for antiulcer drugs. Working Paper no. 01-014. Boston: Harvard Business School.

King, Charles III, Alvin J. Silk, Lisa R. Klein, and Ernst R. Berndt. 2000. Pepcid AC(A): Racing to the OTC market. Case N9-500-073. Boston, Mass.: Harvard Business School, February 4.

Leffler, Keith B. 1981. Promotion or information? The economics of prescription drug advertising. *Journal of Law and Economics* 24 (April): 45–74.

Leibowitz, Arleen. 1989. Substitution between prescribed and over-the-counter medications. *Medical Care* 27 (1): 85–94.

Leibowitz, Arleen, Willard G. Manning, and Joseph P. Newhouse. 1985. The demand for prescsription drugs as a function of cost-sharing. *Social Science in Medicine* 21 (10): 1063–68.

Ling, Davina. 1999. Advertising, competition, and prescription-to-nonprescription drug switches in the U.S. antacid market. Cambridge, Mass.: Massachusetts Institute of Technology, Department of Economics. Manuscript, April 9.

McCarthy, Robert. 1999. OTCs: The wild card in cost-effectiveness. *Business and Health* 17 (4): 33–35.

O'Brian, Bernie. 1989. The effect of patient charges on the utilization of prescription medicines. *Journal of Health Economics* 8 (1): 109–32.

Perloff, Jeffrey M., and Valerie Y. Suslow. 1994. Higher prices from entry: Pricing of brand-name drugs. Ann Arbor: University of Michigan, School of Business Administration. Unpublished manuscript.

Phelps, Charles, and Joseph P. Newhouse. 1974. Coinsurance, the price of time, and the demand for medical services. *Review of Economics and Statistics* 56 (3): 334–42.

Physicians' Desk Reference. 2000. Montvale, N.J.: Medical Economics Company.

Prevention Magazine. 1999. *National survey of consumer reactions to direct-to-consumer advertising.* Emmaus, Penn.: Prevention Magazine.

Robinson, William T., Gurumurthy Kalyanaram, and Glen L. Urban. 1994. First mover advantages for pioneering new products: A survey of empirical evidence. *Review of Industrial Organization* 9 (1): 1–23.

Rosenthal, Meredith B., Ernst R. Berndt, Julie M. Donohue, Richard G. Frank, and Arnold M. Epstein. 2002. Promotion of prescription drugs to consumers. *New England Journal of Medicine* 346 (7): 498–505.

Samuelson, William, and Richard Zeckhauser. 1988. Status quo bias in decision making. *Journal of Risk and Uncertainty* 1 (1): 349–65.

Scherer, F. Michael. 1993. Pricing, profits, and technological progress in the pharmaceutical industry. *Journal of Economic Perspectives* 7 (3): 97–115.

———. 2000. The pharmaceutical industry. In *Handbook of Health Economics,* Vol. 1B, ed. Anthony J. Culyer and Joseph P. Newhouse, 1297–336. Amsterdam: Elsevier Science.

Schmalensee, Richard L. 1972. *The economics of advertising.* Amsterdam: North-Holland.

———. 1982. Product differentiation advantages of pioneering brands. *American Economic Review* 72 (3): 349–65.

Stata Corporation. 1999. *Stata reference manual,* release 6. College Station, Tex.: Stata Press.

Stuart, Bruce, and James Grana. 1995. Are prescribed and over-the-counter medicines economic substitutes? *Medical Care* 33 (5): 487–501.

Temin, Peter. 1980. *Taking your medicine: Drug regulation in the United States.* Cambridge, Mass.: Harvard University Press.

———. 1983. Costs and benefits in switching drugs from Rx to OTC. *Journal of Health Economics* 2 (3): 187–205.
———. 1992. Realized benefits from switching drugs. *Journal of Law and Economics* 35 (2): 351–69.
Urban, Glen L., Theresa Carter, Steve Gaskin, and Zofia Mucha. 1986. Market share rewards to pioneering brands: An empirical analysis and strategic implications. *Management Science* 32 (6): 645–59.

Comment   Steve Morgan

In "The Long Shadow of Patent Expiration: Generic Entry and Rx-to-OTC Switches" Ernst R. Berndt, Margaret K. Kyle, and Davina C. Ling tackle two problems: one concerning producer theory, the other concerning price measurement based on consumer theory. In both regards, their focus is on the strategies used by manufactures of "sunset" branded pharmaceutical products—products for which patent expiry is imminent. They aptly illustrate how manufacturers can tailor marketing, pricing, and product lines to protect the profitability of their brands at this stage of the product life. Understanding the strategies of sunset brands is important because many leading pharmaceutical products are due to lose their patented status soon.

It is also of policy interest to assess the welfare impact of market dynamics associated with patent loss. This leads to the second problem addressed by Berndt, Kyle, and Ling: price measurement in the changing market environments of sunset branded drug products. In view of the theme of the conference, my comments focus on these measurement issues; they draw, however, on the practical realities of the pharmaceutical sector that make profitable the corporate strategies identified in the first half of their paper.

Berndt, Kyle, and Ling contrast two approaches to measuring the "new goods" effects of generic entry and the launch of over-the-counter versions of brand name products among a class of acid suppression drugs, histamine$_2$-receptor antagonists. They implement a reservation price estimation technique advocated by Griliches and Cockburn (1994, 1996) and a demand system estimation technique advocated by Feenstra (1997). Both methods have been use to address the generic drug problem elsewhere, but not the over-the-counter question.

The method advocated by Griliches and Cockburn is to use postentry market observations to estimate a reservation price for a generic entrant. Griliches and Cockburn simplify the task by assuming that consumers have a uniform distribution of reservation prices over the interval between the

Steve Morgan is a Canadian Institutes of Health Research postdoctoral fellow and a Canadian Associate of the Harkness International Health Care Policy Fellowship Program at the Centre for Health Services and Policy Research, University of British Columbia.

launch price of the generic and price of the brand at patent expiration. Berndt, Kyle, and Ling implement the approach using least squares procedures for estimating intraproduct class elasticity of substitution, upon which reservation price estimates are based.

The results gleaned from the Griliches and Cockburn method are intuitive for the prescription-only submarket. Indexes accounting for the price effect of generics fall upon their entry. Consumers, it would appear, are better off from increased competition among chemically equivalent prescription-only products. The econometric results pertaining to the over-the-counter availability of like-branded histamine$_2$-receptor antagonists, however, fail to meet necessary assumptions concerning the own-price elasticity when the Griliches and Cockburn method is employed. Postentry data generate unduly low elasticities.

The index method advocated by Feenstra is based on the estimation of the elasticity of substitution within and across products using both pre- and postentry data. It does not require the estimation of a reservation price and has been applied by Feenstra in other consumer product submarkets as well as on two classes of prescription drug products (Feenstra 1994). Others have advocated such a method as a generalized means of addressing substitution biases in product classes where the number of goods fluctuates over time (Balk 1999).

When Berndt, Kyle, and Ling implement this approach in the absence of marketing data, the parameter estimates are unstable and the implied indexes are counter-intuitive. As presented at the conference, their findings indicated that those price indexes went up after generic entry, implying that consumers are made worse off. Indexes that incorporate the impact of over-the-counter availability of like-branded products also produced inconsistent results in the absence of advertising data. When data on the marketing efforts are incorporated into the analysis, however, Feenstra-method findings related to the over-the-counter availability of like-molecule products were much improved. Three of four elasticity estimates converged at expected signs, and the implied price indexes showed substantial declines following the launch of over-the-counter versions of same-brand products.

Interpreting the index results—based on either Griliches and Cockburn's methods or Feenstra's method—that pertain to launch of over-the-counter products is particularly challenging due to a number of limitations in the data and the nature of the product class being analyzed.

The wholesale-level prescription data and the retail-level nonprescription data are not particularly comparable. This is because wholesale prices do not closely resemble the actual prices paid by large buyers of pharmaceuticals in the United States. Few but the uninsured pay list (wholesale plus markup) prices for pharmaceuticals. Instead, price-volume discounts and rebates are typically negotiated between manufacturers and pharmacy benefit providers (insurers, government agencies, or managed care corporations). The value of these negotiated discounts was substantial in the 1990s—sufficient to provoke the Health Care Financing Administration to revise its expenditure estimates to account for average discounts of approximately 24 percent (Genuardi and Stiller 1996). Moreover, discounts are achieved by pitting competing manufacturers' price offers against each other, which sets off a bidding war—the winner of which gets on, or receives preferential treatment within, the drug benefit provider's formulary. However important these pricing dynamics may be, they remain hidden.

Further challenges to the comparability of over-the-counter and prescription-only market segments come from the nature of the products being sold—including the nature of the information about those products contained in advertising. The prescription-only and over-the-counter products are marketed for quite different indications, even though they are comprised of the same active chemical ingredients.[1] As Berndt, Kyle, and Ling acknowledge, over-the-counter histamine$_2$-receptor antagonists are marketed and labeled for the prevention of minor heartburn, acid indigestion, and sour stomach. The packages of both Zantac 75 and Tagamet HB explain the dosing regimen for treating or avoiding heartburn due to acid indigestion or sour stomach, and warn patient not to use the drug for more than fourteen days unless directed to by a physician. Manufacturers cannot legally suggest that these nonprescription products be used for other purposes—neither in their packaging, nor in their advertising. However, to treat an ulcer with these over-the-counter drugs, patients must take twice the recommended dose for thirty to sixty days—two to four times the recommended duration of over-the-counter therapy. There is little doubt that some consumers do treat ulcers with the over-the-counter products—many, I suspect, do so on the advice of their physician. A vast majority of consumers in the over-the-counter market, however, are probably taking the drugs in small doses to ward off the annoyance of heartburn (e.g., as induced by eating spicy foods), not for the treatment of active ulcers. In light of these comparability issues, the index results concerning over-the-counter product launches are probably insufficient grounds to endorse one methodology over the other. With either the Feenstra or the Griliches and Cockburn method, it is unclear that one is comparing apples with apples.

On the other hand, the anomalous results found with Feenstra's preferred method of accounting for the impact of generic availability do provoke questions that may lead one to prefer the method of reservation-price estimation. In their presentation at the conference, Berndt, Kyle, and Ling

1. It is not uncommon for a single chemical to be marked for different indications. Two examples illustrate. Glaxo Wellcome markets *bupropion hydrochloride* as "Wellbutrin" for the treatment of depression and attention deficit disorder and as "Zyban" to help patients quit smoking. Merck markets *finasteride* as "Propecia" for male pattern baldness and as "Proscar" for the treatment of benign prostatic hyperplasia (non-cancerous enlargement of the prostate gland).

offer several possible reasons for the prescription-only price index discrepancies. One of these conjectured sources of inconsistency deserves elaboration, because it seems to point toward much-needed future research.

Feenstra's method requires the stability of parameters within the unit expenditure functions defined over equivalent brand and generic products (or over prescription and over-the-counter products) as well as the separability of these unit expenditure functions from the remainder of the consumer's utility function. Berndt, Kyle, and Ling remind us that their data span a period of more than ten years, raising a caution against the assumption of parameter stability (and possibly even separablility). In fact, the particular ten years for the particular products being analyzed may be less stable than might be the case in other commodity markets, including other classes of pharmaceuticals.

The nature of the demand for Histamine$_2$-receptor antagonists has been nothing if not unstable over the past two decades. These antiulcer drugs were the defining blockbuster drugs of the 1980s—their marketing hype and cash-box success earning them the Hollywood analogy. Soon after the stellar rise of this product class, the premise upon which much of its success was based came under scrutiny. Beginning in the early 1980s, clinical scientists began a protracted debate about the ulcer-causing role of bacteria known as Helicobacter-pylori. By 1994, evidence indicating that the presence of the bacteria was a causal factor in gastritis, duodenal ulcer, and some gastric ulcers had convinced even those who were outspoken critics of the Helicobacter-pylori theory (Therapeutics Initiative 1994). Combined with imminent patent expiration and serious prescription-only competition from the proton pump inhibitors, the widespread acceptance of the Helicobacter-pylori theory forced manufactures of Histamine$_2$-receptor antagonists to define and expand other uses of these acid suppressors.

One would hope that consumers' (or more specifically, physicians') appraisals of the prescription versions of Histamine$_2$-receptor antagonists changed over the 1990s. If so, the unit expenditure functions for antiulcer products would neither be stable nor separable from the remainder of consumers' utility functions. Consider, for example, the interaction between the marginal utility of Histamine$_2$-receptor antagonists and the antibiotic products used to eradicate the Helicobacter-pylori bacteria.

Notwithstanding changes unique to the antiulcer market, the availability of a generic alternative in a subclass can have several impacts on that class and others. The fact that branded products can "cream-skim" by raising prices following generic entry implies that the market is somehow segmented. It is quite possible that the most important segmentation is not with respect to tastes for branded versus generic products, but segmentation along financial incentives. Not only is there a distinction between the insured and uninsured, but many insured consumers now face forms of incentive pricing aimed at encouraging them to consider low-cost generics.

Knowing the financial incentives of the consumers in question is essential to understanding what is revealed by their consumption patterns.

Consider patients covered under the British Columbia Pharmacare Plan A. Plan A, which accounts for about 30 percent of drug spending in this Canadian province, is a tax-financed plan offering drug benefits for all residents in British Columbia who are sixty-five years of age and older. The plan covers ingredient costs of prescribed drugs; beneficiaries must pay associated pharmacists' dispensing fees. Before 1994, Plan A beneficiaries could obtain equivalent branded and generic drugs at the same cost: whatever the pharmacist charged for dispensing. Generic utilization under these incentives was understandably low (Grootendorst et al. 1996). Starting in April 1994, the government began an incentive pricing policy wherein the brand-name product was fully covered only for consumers who had medical reasons for obtaining the brand over generic alternatives. All other consumers who preferred the brand to the generic would have to pay the price difference—Pharmacare paying a share equal to the cost of the generic.

Figure 8C.1 illustrates how this simple change in financial incentives altered utilization patterns. The figure plots the average market share held by all (272) brand-name products that existed in 1988 and were subject to generic competition before 1998, grouped by the year of generic entry. The average price of brand-name drugs exceeded that of generics by approximately 40 percent in 1993. Although generics gradually penetrated markets before the incentive pricing policy was implemented, the process was slow and seldom complete. When the policy change took place in 1994:2, few brand-name firms matched generic prices, and the rate of generic drug utilization rose to the neighborhood of 80 to 90 percent.

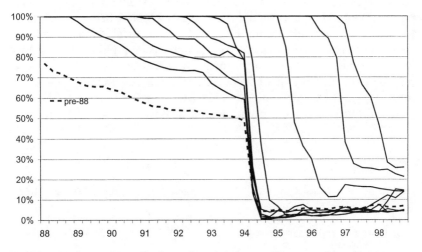

Fig. 8C.1   Average of brand's share of markets grouped by year subject to generic competition

A reservation price technique for capturing the impact of generics is probably better suited to deal with the discontinuity of financial incentives that occurs under an incentive pricing policy. For purchases made without such incentives (e.g., prior to the Pharmacare policy change), would the real revealed preferences be revealed under either the Feenstra or the Griliches and Cockburn method? Probably not.

An increasing number of insurance companies, pharmacy benefits managers, and health maintenance organizations in the United States are using incentive pricing policies to encourage generic drug utilization (Aventis 2000; Scott-Levin 2001). However, it is not clear if uninsured individuals are always aware of the generic option. In a recent survey of American consumers, 87 percent said they would choose a generic drug if it would save them money, yet fewer than half reported having been presented with the choice when purchasing drugs (Flemming 1999). Given the mix of financial incentives and product knowledge at the individual level, aggregate price and quantity observations are difficult—if not impossible—to interpret.

Berndt, Kyle, and Ling offer us an important, detailed description of firm behaviors when products are in their sunset phase, as well as a thought-provoking comparison of the indexes that economists might otherwise use to measure the impact of firm behaviors. Four times they caution readers about the difficulty of interpreting cost-of-living measures in the pharmaceutical sector due to the nonstandard financial incentives of consumers and potential imperfections in the physicians' agency role. Unfortunately, most readers, even trained economists, beg the welfare-theoretic question when they read price index results. Berndt, Kyle, and Ling rightfully (I believe) conclude that for measurement theorists and statistical agencies to address the welfare-theoretic question head-on, we do not necessarily need more sophisticated econometric techniques; we require better models of the principal agent relationships in the pharmaceutical sector and better sources of data. Even the detailed data sources employed by Berndt, Kyle, and Ling suffer from the fact that financial incentives are a dog's breakfast in the market as a whole. I believe the best future research in this area will probably come from drug-plan specific databases. With such databases, one can be (more) certain of consumers' financial incentives and tailor the price indexes accordingly.

References

Aventis. 2000. Hoechst Marion Roussel managed care series: 1999. Available at [http://www.managedcaredigiest.com/]. February.

Balk, B. M. 1999. On curing the CPI's substitution and new goods bias. Working paper. Voorburg, The Netherlands: Statistics Netherlands, Department of Statistical Methods.

Feenstra, R. C. 1994. New product varieties and the measurement of international prices. *American Economic Review* 84 (1): 157–77.

————. 1997. Generics and new goods in pharmaceutical price indexes: Comment. *American Economic Review* 87 (4): 760–67.

Flemming, H. 1999. Consumers don't mind generics. *Drug Topics* 143 (20): 91.

Genuardi, J. S., and J. M. Stiller. 1996. Changing prescription drug sector: New expenditure methodologies. *Health Care Financing Review* 17 (3): 191–205.

Griliches, Z., and I. M. Cockburn. 1994. Generics and new goods in pharmaceutical price indexes. *American Economic Review* 84 (5): 1213–32.

————. 1996. Generics and the producer price index for pharmaceuticals. In *Competitive Strategies in the Pharmaceutical Industry,* ed. R. B. Helms. Washington, D.C.: American Enterprise Institute.

Grootendorst, P., L. Goldsmith, J. Hurley, B. O'Brian, and L. Dolovich. 1996. *Financial incentives to dispense low cost drugs: A case study of British Columbia Pharmacare.* Report Submitted to the Health System and Policy Division, Health Canada. Hamilton, Ontario, Canada: McMaster University.

Scott-Levin. 2001. Managed care co-pays. Scott-Levin Press Release. 2 August. Available at [http://www.scottlevin.com/]. February.

Therapeutics Initiative. 1994. Definitive treatment of peptic ulcer disease by eradication of Helicobacter pylori. *British Columbia Therapeutics Letter,* issue no. 2 (November).

Measuring Change in Quality and Imputing Missing Observations

The Measurement of
Quality-Adjusted Price Changes

Mick Silver and Saeed Heravi

9.1 Introduction

A major source of bias in the measurement of inflation is held to be its inability to properly incorporate quality changes (Boskin 1996; Boskin et al. 1998; Diewert 1996; Cunningham 1996; Hoffmann 1998; Abraham, Greenless, and Moulton 1998). This is not to say statistical offices are unaware of the problem. Price collectors attempt to match the prices of "like with like" to minimize such bias. However, comparable items are often unavailable, and methods of implicit and explicit quality adjustment are not always considered satisfactory (Reinsdorf, Liegey, and Stewart 1995; Armknecht, Lane, and Stewart 1997; Moulton, LaFleur, and Moses 1998).

Alongside this is an extensive empirical literature concerned with the measurement of quality-adjusted price indexes at the product level. The

Mick Silver is professor of business statistics at Cardiff Business School, Cardiff University. Saeed Heravi is senior lecturer in quantitative methods at Cardiff Business School, Cardiff University.

This study is part of a wider project funded by the U.K. Office for National Statistics (ONS). The authors are grateful to the ONS for permission to reproduce some of this work in the form of this paper. The views expressed in the paper are those of the authors and not the ONS. Any errors and omissions are also the responsibility of the authors. Helpful advice during the working of this paper was received from David Fenwick (ONS), Adrian Ball (ONS), Dawn Camus (ONS), and Pat Barr (GfK Marketing), and valuable programming assistance was received from Bruce Webb (Cardiff University). The paper has also benefited from useful comments from Ernst Berndt (Massachusetts Institute of Technology), Erwin Diewert (University of British Columbia), Rob Feenstra (University of California, Davis), John Greenlees (Bureau of Labor Statistics), Christos Ioannidis (Brunel University), Matthew Shapiro (University of Michigan), and Ralph Turvey (London School of Economics). In particular, the authors had sight of a draft Organization for Economic Cooperation and Development manual by Jack Triplett (Brookings Institution), and this proved most useful for section 9.5, in which a variety of approaches are used. The usual disclaimers apply.

main approach is the use of hedonic regressions (but see Blow and Craw-ford 1999 for an exception) in which the price of a model, for example, of a personal computer is regressed on its characteristics. The data sources are often unbalanced, panel cross-sectional time series from catalogs or web pages. A hedonic regression is estimated that includes the characteristics of the variety and dummy variables on time, the coefficients on the time dum-mies being estimates of the changes in price having controlled for changes in characteristics. This is referred to as the *time dummy variable hedonic method.* The quality-adjusted price index is taken from the coefficients on the time dummies in the hedonic regression. There is usually little by way of data on quantities, and thus weights, in these estimates. Yet estimates from hedonic regressions have been used to benchmark the extent of bias due to quality changes in consumer price indexes (CPIs; Boskin 1996; Boskin et al. 1998; Hoffmann 1998).

In this first part of the paper (sections 9.2 to 9.4) we argue against the use of this widely adopted time dummy variable approach. It is set against the-oretical developments in the measurement of exact hedonic indexes by Fixler and Zieschang (1992), Feenstra (1995), and Diewert (chap. 10 in this volume) and superlative index number formulas by Diewert (1976, 1978). The exact hedonic approach also uses hedonic regressions, but it differs from the time dummy hedonic approach in two ways. First, the coefficients on the quality characteristics are not restricted to be the same over time, as is the case with the time dummy variable method. Use is made of repeated cross-section regressions in each period, rather than a single panel-data re-gression with dummy variables. Second, a formal sales weighting system is used in the exact approach, as opposed to implicit, equally weighted obser-vations. The exact approach also provides estimates of, and bounds for, cost-of-living indexes (COLI) based on economic theory. Cost-of-living in-dexes measure the ratio of the minimum expenditure required to maintain a given level of utility. The dummy variable approach is shown to be a re-stricted version of the exact hedonic approach. Concordant with the de-velopment of the theory for the exact hedonic approach has been devel-opments in data availability. Use is made of scanner data from electronic-point-of-sale bar code readings, which provide a sufficiently rich source to implement the exact hedonic approach and compare it with re-sults from the dummy variable method.

There are of course other variants of the time dummy variable method. A sales-weighted least squares estimator could be used, or estimates could be made on a chained basis with, for example, a comparison between January and February being based on hedonic regressions for these months only, with a time dummy for February, and similarly for February and March, March and April, and so on. The estimates of price changes over these bi-nary comparisons would be linked by successive multiplication to form a chained estimate over the whole period.

Against all of this Turvey (1999a,b) has proposed, on pragmatic grounds, a matched method akin to that adopted by statistical offices. The availability of scanner data with information on the relative expenditure of each product variety allows the compilation of matched indexes using exact and superlative formulas. The matched approach identifies the price of particular varieties and compares this with the prices of the same varieties in subsequent periods. It thus reduces the need to use regressions for the measurement of quality-adjusted price changes since "like" is being compared with "like." It is shown here how the exact hedonic approach based on Feenstra (1995) and the matched approach are related, having respective pros and cons for the measurement of quality-adjusted COLI. Also provided are estimates, using scanner data, of quality-adjusted price indexes for washing machines using all three of these approaches.

It is worth noting that scanner data are now available in Europe and North America for a wide range of consumer durables and fast-moving goods. The coverage of the data is often quite extensive, being supplemented by store audits for independent stores without bar code readers (see Hawkes and Smith 1999). Market research agencies including ACNielson and GfK Marketing Services collate and supply such data. Their use for validation and other purposes is now recommended for the compilation of consumer price indexes by Boskin (1996) and for direct use by Diewert (1993) and Silver (1995).

There have been a number of studies using matching on this rich data source in which prices of items with a particular specification are compared with their counterparts over time. These include Silver (1995), Saglio (1995), and Lowe (1999) for television sets and Reinsdorf (1996), Bradley et al. (1998), Haan and Opperdoes (1998), Dalen (1998), and Hawkes and Smith (1999) for selected food products. The matching used is often at a highly disaggregated level, matching individual item codes with their counterparts over time. There have been fewer studies that compare the results of alternative methodologies: these include Silver's (1999) study on TVs, which uses the dummy variable and exact hedonic approaches, and Moulton, LaFleur, and Moses' (1999) and Kokoski, Waehrer, and Rozaklis's (1999) studies on TVs and audio products, which use the dummy variable and hedonic quality-adjusted matching approaches. Studies, especially those using the dummy variable approach, invariably focus on a single methodology with little interest in the relationship between methods. An early and notable exception comparing the results from hedonic regressions and matching, although not based on scanner data, was Cole et al. (1986). In this study we show how all three approaches are related and contrast the results for the case of washing machines.

In section 9.2 we outline the three methods of measuring quality-adjusted price indexes and show how they are related. Section 9.3 provides a description of the data, the application in this study being to monthly data on washing machines in the United Kingdom in 1998. The implementation of the three methods and their results are also outlined in section 9.3. Conclusions on the appropriate method to measure quality-adjusted price changes using scanner data are in section 9.4.

The first part of the paper is concerned with how best to measure quality-adjusted price changes given scanner data. The second part is an initial attempt to replicate the practice of statistical offices with regard to quality adjustment. The same scanner data are used matching prices between product varieties in a base month, January, with their counterparts in February, and similarly for January with March, January with April, and so on. When a product variety is missing in the current month, different variants of implicit and (hedonic) explicit adjustments are undertaken, as would be used by a statistical office, and the results from these methods are compared. The methodology is explained and the results are presented and discussed in section 9.5.

9.2   Quality-Adjusted Price Indexes: Three Approaches Using Scanner Data

This section outlines three methods for measuring quality-adjusted price changes using scanner data: the time dummy variable hedonic method, an exact hedonic approach, and a matching technique, which can utilize exact and superlative formulas. It is reiterated that

- both the time dummy and exact hedonic methods use hedonic regressions, the former using a single panel-data regression, whereas the latter uses repeated cross-sectional ones;
- the time dummy hedonic method implicitly weights each observation equally in the regression, whereas the exact indexes have weighted formulations;
- the need for hedonic regressions is reduced when matching is effective.

9.2.1   Time Dummy Variable Hedonic Method

The hedonic approach involves the estimation of the implicit, shadow prices of the quality characteristics of a product. Products are often sold by a number of manufacturers, who brand them by their "make." Each make of product is usually available in more than one model, each having different characteristics. A set of $(z_k = 1, \ldots K)$ characteristics of a product is identified, and data over $i = 1, \ldots N$ product varieties (or models) over $t = 1, \ldots, T$ periods are collected. A hedonic regression of the price of model i in period t on its characteristics set z_{tki} is given by

$$(1) \qquad p_{ti} = \beta_0 + \sum_{t=2}^{T} \beta_t D_t + \sum_{k=1}^{K} \beta_k z_{tki} + \varepsilon_{ti}$$

where D_t is a dummy variable for the time periods, D_2 being 1 in period $t = 2$, zero otherwise; D_3 being 1 in period $t = 3$, zero otherwise, and so on.

The coefficients β_t are estimates of quality-adjusted price changes, that is, estimates of the change in the price between period 1 and period t, having controlled for the effects of variation in quality (via $\sum_{k=1}^{K}\beta_k z_{tki}$).

The theoretical basis for the method has been derived in Rosen (1974), in which a market in characteristic space is established (see also Triplett 1987; Arguea, Haseo, and Taylor 1994). There is a plethora of studies of the above form as considered by Griliches (1990), Triplett (1990), and Gordon (1990), but subsequently including Nelson, Tanguay, and Patterson (1994); Gandal (1994, 1995); Arguea, Haseo, and Taylor (1994); Lerner (1995); Berndt, Griliches, and Rappaport (1995); Moulton, LaFleur, and Moses (1999); Hoffmann (1998); and Murray and Sarantis (1999). An issue of specific concern is the choice of functional form to be used. There has been support for, and success in, the use of the linear form, including Arguea, Haseo, and Taylor (1994); Feenstra (1995); Stewart and Jones (1998); and Hoffmann (1998). The semilog formulation has also been successfully used in studies including Lerner (1995); Nelson, Tanguay, and Patterson (1994); and Moulton, LaFleur, and Moses (1999). Studies using, and testing for, more complex functional forms have been advocated by Diewert (chap. 10 in this volume) and generally applied to housing (Rasmussen and Zuehlke 1990; Mills and Simenauer 1996) with some success, such studies for consumer durable goods (using flexible functional forms and neural networks; Curry, Morgan, and Silver 2001) being more limited.

The data sources used may be scanner data but are often specialist magazines or mail-order catalogs. The approach as conventionally used is not without problems. First, it implicitly treats each model as being of equal importance, when some models will have quite substantial sales, whereas for others sales will be minimal. If data are available on sales values, a weighted least squares estimator may be employed (Ioannidis and Silver 1999). Second, the prices recorded are not the transaction price averaged over a representative sample of types of outlets, but often a single, unusual supplier.

A final problem arises with the manner in which the time dummy variable method takes account of changing marginal values (coefficients) over time. It is the usual practice that the coefficients are held constant and thus not allowed to reflect changes in the marginal worth of the characteristics. Dummy slope coefficients on each characteristic for each period would relax the constraint. Yet this would render the estimate of quality-adjusted price changes, the coefficient on the dummy (time) intercept, dependent on the values of the performance characteristics (Silver 1999; Kokoski, Waehrer, and Rozaklis 1999). We will see that the above problems are dealt with in the exact hedonic formulation, the dummy variable hedonic method being a restricted version of the exact hedonic approach.

9.2.2   Exact (and Superlative) Hedonic Indexes

Konüs (1939) and Diewert (1976) define a theoretical COLI, P_c, as the ratio of the minimum expenditure required to achieve a given level of utility, U, when the consumer faces period t prices compared with period $t - 1$ price, p_t, and p_{t-1}; that is,

$$(2) \qquad P_c(p_t, p_{t-1}, U) = \frac{E(p_t, U)}{E(p_{t-1}, U)}$$

The above does not recognize that changes may occur in the quality mix of the items compared. Fixler and Zieschang (1992) and Feenstra (1995) define an analogous hedonic COLI:

$$(3) \qquad P_c(p_t, p_{t-1}, z_t, z_{t-1}, U) = \frac{E(p_t, z_t, U)}{E(p_{t-1}, z_{t-1}, U)}$$

that is, the ratio of the minimum expenditure required to maintain a given level of utility when the consumer faces p_t and p_{t-1} prices and quality characteristics z_t and z_{t-1}.

The construction of such indexes requires the existence of a representative consumer whose expenditure functions are defined over the space of "characteristics," prices, and utility. When goods differ in their characteristics and consumers are heterogeneous in their preferences, only a specific class of functions describing the behavior of agents can be aggregated to some "representative" agent.

Theoretical frameworks are given by Feenstra (1995) and Diewert (chap. 10 in this volume). Feenstra uses aggregation results from McFadden (1983) to show that a representative agent formulation indeed arises from a discrete choice model, in which the individual consumers are deciding which of a discrete number of alternative varieties to choose. Feenstra proposes a reasonably broad class of utility functions for the individual consumers, which has two components: a subutility function over characteristics $z_i \in R_+^K$, which is the same across consumers; and an additive term obtained from each variety chosen, which differs across consumers. The latter additive terms are modeled as random across consumers, with a general "extreme value" distribution. Any pattern of correlation in the utility obtained from different models is allowed for, so this framework is much more general than the multinominal logit model, for example (in which the additive errors obtained from each variety are independent).

In this context, there exists an expenditure function for the representative consumer, $E(p_t, z_t, U_t)$, where $p_t = (p_{1t}, \ldots p_{Nt})$ is the vector of prices for the N varieties, and $z_t = (z_{1t}, \ldots z_{Nt})$ is the NK-dimensional vector of characteristics over all the product varieties. Social welfare, U_t, is interpreted as the sum of utilities over the individual consumers (i.e., utilitarian social welfare), and $E(p_t, z_t, U_t)$, measures the minimum expenditure summed over all consumers to obtain U_t. For each variety, we can also define the marginal value of characteristics to consumers, $\beta_i \in R_+^K$, which is the same across consumers. As characteristics change over time, bounds for the exact index can be constructed using these values. The current (Paasche) period and base (Laspeyres) weighted quality-adjusted bounds for a COLI, for an arithmetic aggregation using a linear hedonic equation, are given by Feenstra (1995) as

(4a)
$$\left(\frac{\sum_{i=1}^{N} x_{it} p_{it}}{\sum_{i=1}^{N} x_{it} \hat{p}_{it-1}} \right) \leq \frac{E(p_t, z_t, U)}{E(p_{t-1}, z_{t-1}, U)} \leq \left(\frac{\sum_{i=1}^{N} x_{it-1} \hat{p}_{it}}{\sum_{i=1}^{N} x_{it-1} p_{it-1}} \right)$$

where $E(\cdot)$ denotes the expenditure function, at periods t and $t-1$, evaluated at a fixed level of utility, and the arguments in the index are given by

(4b)
$$\hat{p}_{it} \equiv p_{it} - \sum \beta_{kt}(z_{ikt} - z_{ikt-1})$$
$$\hat{p}_{it-1} \equiv p_{it-1} + \sum \beta_{kt-1}(z_{ikt} - z_{ikt-1})$$

where Laspeyres and Paasche in equation (4a) are upper and lower bounds on their "true", economic theoretic COLIs: x is quantity sold, p is price, and z is a vector of characteristics with associated marginal values β_{kit} derived from a linear hedonic regressions over $i = 1 \ldots N$ product varieties (models) for each period t. Changes in the quality of models are picked up via changes in their characteristics $(z_{kt} - z_{kt-1})$, which are multiplied by estimates of their associated marginal values β_{kt}. With sales data available, the vector z can be the sales-weighted average usage or mix of each characteristic in each period. Note that $\hat{p}_{it}$ corrects the observed prices p_{it} for changes in the characteristics between the two periods, corresponding to the "explicit quality adjustment" described by Triplett (1990, 39).

Equation (4) has a simple intuition. In equation (4a) matched prices are being compared using current period quantities (weights) on the left-hand side and base period quantities on the right-hand side of the equation. However, the matching may not be perfect in that for each i, the quality may change over time. Consequently, predicted values are generated in equations (4b) to correct for such changes. For the left-hand side they adjust the base period prices for changes in the characteristics taking place between $t-1$ and t: maybe the goods are getting better over time. This change for each i is $\Delta z_{ik} = (z_{ikt} - z_{ikt-1})$, where z_{ikt} is the sales-weighted average of each k quality characteristic: say, the average spin speed or load capacity of washing machines has increased. However, some characteristics are more important, in a price-determining sense, than others, so each Δz is weighted by an estimate of its marginal value from a hedonic regression. For the left-hand side the hedonic regression is estimated using base period $t-1$ data to correct p_{t-1}, and for the right-hand side current period t data are used to correct p_t. It will be shown later how the i has to be defined in practice as product groups in which the quality mix changes but the intuition remains.

Economic theory provides further help with the choice between index number formulas. Cost-of-living index number formulas are defined in economic theory as exact for particular types of preferences if they equal the ratio of expenditure required to maintain constant utility for consumers with those types of preferences. Different index number formulas have been shown to have an exact correspondence to the functional form of the consumer's expenditure function. Laspeyres and Paasche price indexes (equation [4a]) correspond to fixed coefficient Leontief forms and act as upper and lower bounds on a true COLI. Base and current period weighted geometric means indexes could also be calculated, these being exact for (corresponding to) utility-maximizing consumers with constant elasticity of substitution (Feenstra 1995 and footnote 1). Diewert (1976, 1978) found that symmetric averages of these bounds provide index number formulas that correspond to flexible functional forms for the expenditure function, which are much less restrictive. He defined such index number formulas as being *superlative*. Fisher's index is the geometric mean of Laspeyres and Paasche and is superlative. The Törnqvist index[1] uses a symmetric mean of the weights of the bounds in equation (4a) and is superlative and exact for (corresponds to) a flexible translog utility function. Fisher's and Törnqvist indexes are thus quite special in that they are superlative, although Diewert (1995, 1997) has also shown the two formulas to be superior to many others from an axiomatic approach, with Fisher's in particular satisfying more "reasonable" tests than its competitors. The exposition here has been for arithmetic aggregation as opposed to a geometric one, although the results for geometric bounds and a Törnqvist index are noted in section 9.4 and are available from the authors.

The advantages of the exact hedonic approach are threefold. First, it utilizes the coefficients on the characteristics in an unconstrained manner to adjust observed prices for quality changes. Second, it incorporates a weighting system using data on the sales of each model and their characteristics, rather than treating each model as equally important. Finally, it has a direct correspondence to a constant utility index number formulation defined from theory.

9.2.3   Matching

We finally consider the process of matching. It compares the prices of matched identical varieties over time, so that the pure price changes are not tainted by quality changes. The aim is to compare only like with like. This is akin to the process used by price collectors for statistical offices in the

---

1. The geometric current and base-period bounds are given by $\Pi_{i=1}^{N}(p_{it}/\hat{p}_{it-1})^{s_{it}} \leq [E(p_t, z_t, U)]/[E(p_{t-1}, z_{t-1}, U)] \leq \Pi_{i=1}^{N}(\hat{p}_{it}/p_{it-1})^{s_{it-1}}$, where $\hat{p}_{it-1} \equiv p_{it-1} \exp[\Sigma\beta_{kt-1}(z_{ikt} - z_{ikt-1})]$ and $\hat{p}_{it} \equiv p_{it} \exp[-\Sigma\beta_{kt}(z_{ikt} - z_{ikt-1})]$, and the Törnqvist index is given by $\Pi(p_t/p_{t-1})^{[(w_t + w_{t-1})/2]} = [\Pi(p_t/p_{t-1})^{w_t} \times \Pi(p_t/p_{t-1})^{w_{t-1}}]^{1/2}$, where $w_t = (p_t x_t/\Sigma p_t x_t)$ and $w_{t-1} = (p_{t-1} x_{t-1}/\Sigma p_{t-1} x_{t-1})$.

Table 9.1   Illustration of Matching and Approaches to Quality Adjustment

Outlet type	Variety	Weight	January	February	March	April
Multiple	1	w_1	p_{11}	p_{12}	p_{13}	p_{14}
	2	w_2	p_{21}	p_{22}		
	3				p_{33}	p_{34}
	4			p_{42}	p_{43}	p_{44}
Mass merchandiser	5	w_5	p_{51}	p_{52}	p_{53}	p_{54}
	6	w_6	p_{61}	p_{62}		
	7				p_{73}	p_{74}

compilation of CPIs, but the matching is electronic using scanner data. Scanner data have a code to describe each model of a good. The code can be extended to include the type of outlet in which it is sold, in order that a particular model of a good in a particular type of outlet is matched against its counterpart in successive periods. Since individual retailers often have unique codes for the same model, the matching is in practice closer than by "model and outlet type." The problem with such matching is missing observations. For scanner data they arise when there is no transaction in that outlet (type) in a period, possibly because the item is no longer being sold or is on display but has not been bought.[2]

Turvey (1999a) proposed the use of chained matched indexes whereby the aggregate price change between, for example, January and February is spliced to that for February and March and so forth by successive multiplication. For example, the chained index between January and December, $CI_{J,D}$, is given by the product of the individual successive binary comparisons:

$$(5) \qquad CI_{J,D} = I_{J,F} \times I_{F,M} \times I_{M,A} \cdots I_{N,D}$$

Table 9.1 illustrates the matching procedure. There are seven varieties each with assumed equal weights (w_i), the distinction between outlet types being ignored for now.

The price index for January compared with February (J:F) involves price comparisons for varieties 1, 2, 5, and 6. For (F:M) it involves varieties 1, 4,

2. It is worth contrasting this with the way missing observations are recorded by price collectors. Price collectors may collect a display price even though the item is not sold in that particular month. Scanner data only pick up actual transactions. Alternatively, price collectors sampling from only some outlets may record a missing value if the model is not on display, even if the same model is being displayed and sold in other outlets. Scanner data match model numbers in types of outlets. Price collectors may not look at the number but use their own description of the main features of the item—for example, "a Bosch washing machine with 1400 spin speed"—which may be matched with a new or different model with similar, but not the same, characteristics. Price collectors match display prices of similar items from specific outlets; scanner data match unit values of all sales for identical items from types of outlets. Finally, the price collector has, within this context, an idea of replacement when a similar item is found to be almost taking the place of the old one. With scanner data this is something that can be explored, even automated, but it is not the subject of this study.

and 5, for (M:A) the same three varieties and, in addition, varieties 3 and 7. The sample composition changes for each comparison as varieties die and are born. The results for each comparison are chained to provide a single index for the whole period. Turvey advocates a chained geometric mean of matched observations.

> Where wholly new products reflecting rapid technical improvement are introduced into a market, overlap price ratios between old and new products usually change from month to month. Instead of proceeding as above, arbitrarily selecting just one month's overlap price ratio between a replacement product and the replaced product, this procedure takes into account the ratio during all overlap months so that the prices of both the old and new products enter into the index computation. When new products arrive on the market their prices should be brought into the index, the prices of old products only being removed from it when they disappear from the market. Thus a chained geometric index of matched observations will be used with a sample size which varies through time. (Turvey 1999a, 13)

The method involves some loss of information. No use, for example, is made of p_{42} for (J:F), and of p_{22}, p_{33}, p_{62}, and p_{73} for the (F:M) price comparisons, which is naturally to be regretted. This is to allow constant quality comparisons. However, it is on the birth and death of a product that price changes are unusual, and these are the very ones lost.[3] Some care, however, is needed in such statements. Table 9.1 illustrates how the loss of a matched observation takes place. For variety 2 in table 9.1, p_{22} is used for the January to February comparison, so it is not lost here. However, it is lost in the matching for the February to March comparison. It is tempting to argue that this loss is unimportant. It relates to a meaningless comparison because it does not exist in March and there is thus no basis for a price comparison. However, economic theory would assert otherwise. The economics of new goods is quite clear on the subject. If a new good is introduced, it is not sufficient to simply wait for two successive price quotations and then incorporate the good. This would ignore the welfare gain to consumers as they substitute from old technology to new technology. Such welfare gains are inseparably linked to the definition of a COLI defined as indexes, which measure the expenditure, required to maintain a constant level of utility (welfare). There exists in economic theory and practice the tools for the estimation of such effects (Hicks 1940; Diewert 1980, 498–503). This involves setting a "virtual" price in the period before introduction. This price is the one at which demand is set to zero. The virtual price is compared with the actual price in the period of introduction, and this is used to estimate the

---

3. A parallel issue arises for indexes of industrial production, especially in less developed countries, where new products are often new industries and ignoring their contribution to production when they are set up may seriously understate growth (Kmietowicz and Silver 1980).

welfare gain. Hausman (1997) provides some estimates for the introduction of a new brand of Apple-Cinnamon Cheerios. He concludes:

> The correct economic approach to the evaluation of new goods has been known for over fifty years since Hicks's pioneering contribution. However, it has not been implemented by government statistical agencies, perhaps because of its complications and data requirements. Data are now available. The impact of new goods on consumer welfare appears to be significant according to the demand estimates of this paper; the CPI for cereal may be too high by about 25 percent because it does not account for new cereal brands. An estimate this large seems worth worrying about.

Notwithstanding this, a curious feature of scanner data is that a missing transaction may arise simply because a model has not been purchased but is still on sale. A price collector would pick up the missing sales price not knowing it is above its reservation price, and there will thus be no need to estimate a virtual price.

9.2.4 Correspondence between the Methods

Matched versus Exact Hedonic Indexes

There is an interesting and useful correspondence here. Consider equation (4b). The $\hat{p}_t$ is the price (or unit value) of model i (in a given outlet) in period t, having been adjusted by changes in its quality characteristics between period $t - 1$ and t, the change in each characteristic being weighted by its associated marginal value in period t. If we are matching, no such adjustment is necessary. Matching does, however, have its failings in that information is lost. The exact hedonic formulation, as undertaken here in practice, aggregates not over each model, but over a subset of meaningful characteristics. For washing machines, for example, we might use makes and outlet types. The Laspeyres formulation on the right-hand side of equation (4) may be approximated by

(6a)
$$\frac{\sum_{j=1}^{J} x_{jt-1}\bar{\hat{p}}_{jt}}{\sum_{j=1}^{J} x_{jt-1}\bar{\hat{p}}_{jt-1}}$$

where we define a narrow set of G_j characteristics—say, dummy variables for makes and outlet types—that are present in most models of the product in each period, where $j = 1 \ldots J$ combinations of makes and outlet types. The $\bar{p}$ and x in equation (6a) are now the average prices and total quantities for each make in each outlet type, for example, for Zanussi washing machines sold in multiples, *within* a make and outlet type j for each period t. The adjusted average price for models i in each j in period t is given by

(6b)
$$\bar{\hat{p}}_{jt} = \bar{p}_{jt} - \left[\sum_{i \in G_j} \beta_{1t}\Delta\bar{z}_{j1t} + \sum_{i \in G_j} \beta_{2t}\Delta\bar{z}_{j2t} + \ldots \sum_{i \in G_j} \beta_{Kt}\Delta\bar{z}_{jKt} \right]$$

where $\bar{p}_{jt}$ is the sales-weighted average price for each j make in a particular outlet type, $\Delta\bar{z}_{jkt} = (\bar{z}_{jkt} - \bar{z}_{jkt-1})$, where $\bar{z}_{jkt}$ and $\bar{z}_{jkt-1}$ are sales-weighted averages (in each period) of the k characteristics other than makes and outlets (e.g., spin speed) and β_k is their estimated marginal value. In equation (6a) for, say, group $j = 1$, Zanussi washing machines in multiples, the average price in period t, $\bar{p}_{jt}$, is compared with that in period $t-1$, $\bar{p}_{jt-1}$. However, the quality of such machines may have changed over the period. This is adjusted for in equation (6b). For each j, say, $j = 1$, the quality-adjusted average price $\bar{\bar{p}}_{jt}$ in period t is the (sales-weighted) mean price of varieties in that group minus (adjusted for) the change in quality. For example, Δz_{1t} might be the change in the (sales-weighted) average spin speed of washing machines for that make or outlet type, multiplied by an estimate in period t, of the marginal value of a unit of spin speed from an hedonic regression. The summation is over the i varieties that are members of the $j = 1$ group. These adjustments continue for other quality characteristics $z_2 \ldots z_k$ in equation (6b). The $\bar{\bar{p}}_{jt}$ are thus quality-adjusted within each of the groups being aggregated in equation (6a). The more quality characteristics we aggregate over in the body of equation (6a), the fewer characteristics are used in determining $\bar{\bar{p}}$ in (6b). Equation (6a) should collapse down to the matched method, when aggregating over all characteristics. So why restrict the aggregation in (6a) to only makes and outlet types? The answer is that in doing so we use all the data. On matching in table 9.1 we lost p_{33} for the February to March comparison but regained it for March to April.

Note that there is a minimal loss of information in the exact hedonic formulation given by equation (6) because each model has a make and outlet type. There is an efficiency gain to the estimate akin to that from stratified sampling in which we correct for quality changes by matching for price changes between strata and use estimates within strata. If we aggregated over all characteristics in equation (6a), with no adjustments in (6b) we would have a matching process with some models having no price data for either period t or $t - 1$ in any two-way comparison. These would be excluded. However, when we allow the aggregation over a limited number of characteristics, which include models available in both periods, no information is lost. The adjustment for the variables not included in this weighted aggregation takes place in $\bar{\bar{p}}$. There is a trade-off. The more quality variables in the weighted aggregation, the more chance of losing information. We consider this in the empirical section.

Both the exact hedonic and matching approaches allow all forms of weighting systems, including Laspeyres, Paasche, and the superlative Fisher, to be used to gain insights into such things as substitution effects. The exact hedonic formulation uses statistical estimates of product "worth" to partial out quality changes for the characteristics excluded in the aggregation in equation (6a), rather than the more computational, and accurate, matching. The differences between the methods depend on the reliability of the $\bar{p}$ adjustment process, in terms of both the extent of changes in characteristics (Δz) and the values of β, and the relative loss of observations in bringing these characteristics into the aggregation process. Its extent is an empirical matter, and we will investigate this.

The equivalence of the two methods requires that the exact hedonic index take a chained formulation, as is the case for the matched approach. The chained approach has been justified as the natural discrete approximation to a theoretical Divisia index (Forsyth and Fowler 1981). Reinsdorf (1998) has formally determined the theoretical underpinnings of the index, concluding that in general chained indexes will be good approximations to the theoretical ideal—although they are prone to bias when prices changes "swerve and loop," as Szulc (1983) has demonstrated (see also Haan and Opperdoes 1998).

Direct versus Exact Hedonic

We include in the analysis results of the time dummy variable method, given its use in many studies and the taking of such estimates as indicators of potential errors due to lack of quality adjustment in CPIs (Boskin 1996; Hoffman 1998). However, as argued in Silver (1999), it is but a limited form of the exact hedonic approach, the limitations naturally arising from the limited catalog data upon which the estimates are often based and the absence of sales weights. Consider the time dummy variable method if we, first, used weighted average prices on the left-hand side of equation (1) and a sales-weighted least squares estimator and, second, introduced dummy slope variables for each characteristic against time to allow for changing marginal values. The improved specification would require estimates of the change in quality-adjusted price change to be conditioned on the change in characteristics. If we take the value-weighted mean usage of each characteristic as the average usage upon which the change in quality-adjusted prices is conditioned, we have a framework akin to the exact hedonic one. Each of the modifications outlined above is just a relaxation of a restrictive assumption of the time dummy variable approach. We nonetheless include in this study estimates from the time dummy variable approach in order to identify the extent of errors arising from its conventional use.

9.3   Data and Implementation

9.3.1   Data

Scope and Coverage

The study is for monthly price indexes for washing machines in 1998 using scanner data. Scanner data are compiled on a monthly basis from the scanner (bar code) readings of retailers. The electronic records of just about every transaction include the transaction price, time of transaction, place of sale, and a code for the item sold—for consumer durables we refer to this as the model number. Manufacturers provide information on the quality characteristics, including year of launch, of each model that can then be linked to the model number. Retailers are naturally interested in analyzing market share and pass on such data to market research agencies for analysis. By cumulating these records for all outlets (which are supplemented by visits to independent outlets without scanners) the agencies can provide comprehensive data on a monthly basis for each model for which there is a transaction, on the following: price (unit value), volume of sales, quality characteristics, make, and outlet type. Agencies are reluctant to provide separate data for a given model in a given outlet. This would not only allow competitors to identify how each outlet is pricing a particular model, and the resulting sales, but also allow manufacturers and governmental and other bodies to check on anticompetitive pricing. Data are, however, identifiable by broad types of outlets, and model codes often apply to specific outlets, although they are not identifiable.

It should be noted that the data, unlike those collected by price collectors, possess the following characteristics:

- They cover all time periods during the month.
- They capture the transaction price rather than the display price.
- They are not concerned with a limited number of "representative" items.
- They are not from a sample of outlets.
- They allow weighting systems to be used at an elementary level of aggregation.
- They include data on quality characteristics.
- They come in a readily usable electronic form with very slight potential for errors.

The data are not without problems, in that the treatment of multibuys and discounts varies between outlets and the coverage varies between product groups. For example, items such as cigarettes, which are sold in a variety of small kiosks, are problematic. Nonetheless, they provide a recognized alternative, first proposed by Diewert (1993) and used by Silver (1995) and Saglio (1995), but see also, for example, Lowe (1998) for Canada and Moulton, LaFleur, and Moses (1999) and Boskin (1996) for the United States. As Astin and Sellwood (1998, 297–98) note in the context of Harmonised Indices of Consumer Prices (HICP) for the European Union:

> Eurostat attaches considerable importance to the possible use of scanner data for improving the comparability and reliability of HICPs ([European Union] Harmonised Indices of Consumer Prices), and will be encouraging studies to this end. Such studies might consider the various ways in which scanner data might be used to investigate different issues in the compilation of HICPs for example . . . provide independent estimates as a control or for detection of bias in HICP sub indices; . . .

analyse the impact of new items on the index; [and] carry out research on procedures for quality control.

Our observations (observed values) are for a model of the product in a given month in one of four different outlet types: multiples, mass merchandisers, independents, and catalog. We stress that we differentiate models as being sold in different types of outlets. This is a very rich formulation since it allows us to estimate, for example, the marginal value of a characteristic in a particular month and a particular type of outlet and apply this to changes in the usage of such stores. Not all makes are sold in each type of outlet. In January 1998, for example, there were 266 models of washing machines with 500 observations; that is, each model was sold on average in 1.88 types of outlets.

The coverage of the data is impressive in terms of both transactions and features. For the United Kingdom, for example, in 1998, there were 1.517 million transactions involving 7,750 observations (models or outlet types) worth £550 million. The coverage of outlets is estimated (by GfK Marketing Services) to be "well over 90%" with scanner data being supplemented by data from price collectors in outlets that do not possess bar code readers.

The Variables

The variable set includes the following:

- *Price:* the unit value = value of sales or quantity sold of all transactions for a model in an outlet type in a month.
- *Volume:* the sum of the transactions during the period. Many of the models sold in any month have relatively low sales. Some only sell one of the model in a month or outlet type. Showrooms often have alongside the current models, with their relatively high sales, older models, which are being dumped, but need the space in the showroom to be seen. For example, 823 observations—models of washing machines in a month (on average) differentiated by outlet type—sold only one machine each in 1998. There were 1,684 observations (models in outlet types) selling between two and ten machines in a month, on average selling about 8,000 machines: so far, we have a total of 2,407 observations managing a sales volume of about 8,800. Yet the twelve models achieving a sales volume of 5,000 or more in any outlet or month accounted for 71,600 transactions.
- *Vintage:* the year in which the first transaction of the model took place. With durable goods, models are usually launched annually. The aim is to attract a price premium from consumers who are willing pay for the cachet of the new model, as well as to gain market share through any innovations that are part of the new model. New models can coexist with old models; 1.1787 million of the about 1.517 million washing machines sold in 1998 were first sold in 1997 or 1998—about 77.7 percent—leaving 22.3 percent of an earlier vintage coexisting in the market.

- *Makes:* the twenty-four different brands for which transactions occurred in 1998. The market was, however, relatively concentrated, with
  the three largest-selling (by volume) makes accounting for about 60
  percent of the market. Hotpoint had a substantial 40 percent of sales
  volume in 1998. This was achieved with 15 percent of models (observations). Zannusi, Hoover, and Bosch followed with not unsubstantial
  sales of around 10 percent each by volume.

The *characteristics* set includes the following:

- *Type of machine* (out of five types): top-loader; twin tub; washing machine (WM; about 90 percent of transactions); washer dryer (WD)
  with computer; WD without computer;
- *Condensors:* with or without (for WD; about 10 percent with);
- *Drying capacity* of WD: a mean 3.15 kg and standard deviation of 8.2
  kg for a standard cotton load;
- *Height* of machines in centimeters (cm)—(about 90 percent of observations being 85 cm tall);
- *Width and Depth* (94 percent being about 60cm wide; most observations taking depth values between 50 and 60 cm inclusive);
- *Spin speeds* of five main speeds: 800 rpm, 1,000 rpm, 1,100 rpm, 1,200
  rpm, and 1,400 rpm (which account for 10 percent, 32 percent, 11 percent, 24 percent, and 7 percent, respectively, of the volume of sales);
- *Water consumption,* which is advertised on the displays as "not a measure of efficiency since it will vary according to the programme, wash-
  load and how the machine is used." It is highly variable, with a mean
  of about 70 liters and standard deviation of 23liters;
- *Load capacity,* defined on the display as "a maximum load when loaded
  with cotton"—a mean about 50 kg with a standard deviation of
  about 13kg;
- *Energy consumption* (kWh per cycle), which is "based on a standard
  load for a 60 degree cotton cycle"—a mean of about 12 kWh with,
  again, a relatively large standard deviation of about 6 kWh.;
- *Free-standing*, built-under, and integrated; built-under, not integrated;
  built-in and integrated.
- *Outlet –type:* multiple, mass merchandiser, catalog, or independent.

9.3.2   Implementation of Each Method

The aim of this section is to compare the results of the three methods of
measuring quality-adjusted price changes using scanner data.

The Time Dummy Variable Approach

Both linear and semilog formulations were considered. Results for the linear model are considered here, although those from a semilogarithmic model
are referred to later and are available from the authors. The R^2 for the respec-

tive forms were relatively high, at 0.83 and 0.82. A Box-Cox transformation was used for testing functional form, the estimated λ being 1.003 with SE(λ) = 0.024 favoring the linear form.[4] A Bera-McAleer test based on artificial regressions was, however, inconclusive (the t-statistics for θ_1, θ_2 were 13.18 and 36.1, respectively).[5] The F-statistics for the null hypotheses of the results of coefficients all equal to zero were rejected for both functional forms at 314.6 and 297.2, respectively, for linear and semilog and p-values of 0.0000.

The results for the linear form are given in table 9.2. The coefficients were almost invariably statistically significant with appropriate signs and magnitudes. An additional spin speed of one rpm, for example, had a price premium of £0.30. Between December and January, other quality characteristics held constant and prices fell from the mean of £405.71 by £25.33, to £380.38—that is, a fall of 6.2 percent. There was some evidence of heteroskedasticity with the Breusch-Pagan test statistics of 27.7 and 9.0 for the linear and semilog forms respectively, both exceeding the critical value of Chisquared (3 degrees of freedom) = 7.815. However, the estimator remains unbiased, and the standard errors were adjusted to be heteroskedasticconsistent using a procedure by White (1980).

The regressions were estimated on a data set that excluded models with sales of thirty or less in any month and a minimal number of models with extreme prices arising from variables not included in the data, such as stainless steel washing machines. A failing of the dummy variable approach is that models with only one transaction are given the same importance in the regression as a model with, say, 10,000 transactions. The choice of thirty was based on some experimentation. The loss in the number of observations was quite severe for washing machines from 7,750 to 3,600, whereas the loss in terms of the *volume* of sales was minimal, from 1.517 million to 1.482 million. An alternative approach is to use a sales volume weighted least squares estimator, as considered later.

Exact (and Superlative) Hedonic Indexes

First, it is necessary to decide which quality-related variables are used in the aggregation in equation (6a) and which for the adjustment in equation

---

4. With this approach a variable Z is transformed to $(Z^\lambda - 1)/\lambda$. Since the limit of this as λ approaches zero is log Z, it is defined to be log Z when $\lambda = 0$. If all variables in a linear functional form are transformed in this way and then λ is estimated (in conjunction with the other parameters) via a maximum likelihood technique, significance tests can be performed on λ to check for special cases. If $\lambda = 0$, for example, the functional form becomes Cobb-Douglas in nature; if $\lambda = 1$ it is linear. A confidence interval on λ can be used to test whether or not it encompasses 0 or 1.

5. The Bera-McAleer test involves obtaining predicted values log $(\hat{z})$ and $(\tilde{z})$ from a semilogarithmic and a linear formulation, respectively. Artificial regressions are then computed using exp$\{$log $(\hat{z})\}$ and log$(\tilde{z})$ on the left-hand-side, and the residuals from each of these regressions, $\hat{v}_1$ and $\hat{v}_0$, are included in a further set of artificial regressions: log$(z) = \beta_0 + \beta_1 X_1 + \mu_0 \hat{v}_1 + \varepsilon_1; z = \beta_0 + \beta_1 X_1 + \mu_1 \hat{v}_0 + \varepsilon_2$. Using t-tests, if θ_0 is accepted we choose the log-linear model, and if θ_1 is accepted we choose the linear model, the test being inconclusive if both are rejected or both accepted.

Table 9.2   **Regression Results for Linear Hedonic Equation for 1998 (dependent variable: price)**

Variable	Estimated Coefficient	Standard Error
C	−981.290***	115.562
Months (benchmark: January)		
February	−0.214244	5.64587
March	6.71874	5.37602
April	0.220101	5.36765
May	−1.60710	5.37089
June	−5.02523	5.2291
July	−10.9314*	5.2195
August	−10.6569*	5.2936
September	−15.6103**	5.2193
October	−16.2413**	5.2970
November	−17.9056***	5.3397
December	−25.3343***	5.3068
Characteristics		
Height (cm)	−0.347469	0.291905
Depth (cm)	6.12143***	0.47413
Width (cm)	6.26849***	0.69974
Water consumption (liters)	−1.14070***	0.06825
Load capacity (kg)	−0.287457**	0.096536
Spin speed (rpm)	0.304251***	0.006965
Drying capacity—washer/dryer (kg)	−0.335703	0.368737
Condensor—washer/dryer	35.9352***	6.2530
Energy consumption (kWh per cycle)	0.331592**	0.104301
Vintage	4.24294***	0.90397
Type of machine (benchmark: front loader washing machine)		
Top loader	228.876***	12.125
Twin tub	−704.998***	20.251
Washer/dryer	64.6312***	9.1877
Washing machine with computer	127.455***	8.856
Washer/dryer with computer	129.682***	16.406
Installation (benchmark: free-standing)		
Built-under integrated	238.908***	10.1389
Built-under	−61.3298	42.8550
Built-in integrated	293.221***	27.349
Outlet type (benchmark: multiples)		
Mass merchandisers	23.1155***	2.9010
Independents	31.2458***	2.5882
Catalogs	71.8786***	3.3023
Makes (benchmark: Bosch)		
AEG	66.8428***	6.1338
Siemens	46.9125***	7.2096
Hoover	−68.0069***	3.65656
Miele	165.895***	10.316
Candy	−98.8340***	6.0759
English Electric	7.99810***	0.82048
Ariston	−21.9183*	8.5417
New Pol	−113.529	60.062

Table 9.2   (continued)

Variable	Estimated Coefficient	Standard Error
Beko	−134.695***	10.558
Zanussi	5.16116	4.12916
Electro	0.7362	11.8086
Indesit	−68.7762***	5.4285
Neff	109.284***	16.897
Philco	−108.286***	25.939
Ignis	−22.4469***	22.9162
Creda	−67.3200***	7.4762
Tricity/Bendi	−58.2687***	6.1059
Hotpoint	−32.5816***	3.9348
Servis	−76.1764***	5.7801
Asko	164.781**	60.226

N^a	3,600	
Mean of price	405.713	
Standard error of regression	59.8572	
Adjusted R^2	0.8299	
Breusch-Pagan	27.7	
F-statistic (zero slopes)	314.626	

[a]Volume of sales greater than thirty in a month or outlet type.
***Statistically significant at the 0.1 percent level for two-tailed t-tests.
**Statistically significant at the 1 percent level for two-tailed t-tests.
*Statistically significant at the 5 percent level for two-tailed t-tests.

(6b). The β_t estimates are then derived from *monthly* hedonic regressions and multiplied by changes in the sales-weighted change in the mix of quality characteristics to provide an adjustment to average prices ($\bar{p}$) for use in the main body of equation (6a).

The β coefficient is required for each K quality-related variable in equation (6b) *in each month*. The specification of the regression equations estimated for this purpose used all variables, to avoid omitted variable bias, with only the relevant β_t coefficient being used to generate $\bar{p}$. The specifications were therefore similar to the time dummy variable method except that separate regressions were estimated for each month.[6]

A weighted least squares estimator was used, the weights being the volume of sales. The mean $\bar{R}^2$ over the twelve monthly hedonic regressions was 0.842.[7] The coefficients were almost invariably statistically significant and

6. It is noted that observations with sales of 30 and less were not used for estimating the individual coefficients, but all the data were used for the average prices, quantities, values, and sales-weighted mix of qualities in formulas.

7. Test statistics here are illustrative, being based on semilog and linear models for the data as a whole, although they are indicative of the results for individual months (available from the authors). Estimates for log-log models were not feasible, given the large number of dummy variables on the right-hand side of the equation.

of reasonable magnitude with the appropriate sign.[8] As with the dummy variable method, the regressions were estimated using the linear and semilog forms. The coefficients from the linear form were used to derive quality-adjusted prices for use in an arithmetic framework—that is, for Laspeyres, Paasche, and (superlative) Fisher hedonic indexes (equation [4]). The coefficients from the semilog form were used to calculate base and current period weighted geometric means and (superlative) Törnqvist exact hedonic indexes given in footnote 1 and available from the authors. It is noted that the estimation of semilogarithmic functions as transformed linear regressions requires an adjustment to provide minimum variance unbiased estimates of parameters of the conditional mean. This involved the standard errors, which in any event were very small, although the adjustments were undertaken (Goldberger 1968).

As explained in section 9.2, the exact hedonic approach has the advantage over matching of minimal loss of data. However, the more variables included in the aggregation in equation (6a), the greater the information loss, as either $\bar{p}_{it-1}$ or $\bar{p}_{it}$ becomes unavailable in any period for comparison. In the limiting case of all variables being included, the method collapses to the matched approach. If we aggregate over makes, or even makes and outlet types, there is very little loss of data in terms of the number of observations and volume of sales. Aggregating only over the 21 makes leaves 99.67 percent of observations and 99.97 percent of sales volume. Extending the aggregation to the 21 makes and 4 outlets, 84 combinations still has little loss of data—99.08 percent of observations and 99.92 percent of sales volume. Any manufacturer operating in a particular outlet type continues to do so on a monthly basis. Extending the aggregation further to 24 spin speeds (i.e., over 2,016 combinations) reduces the coverage to 95.9 percent of observations and 99.6 percent of sales volume.

Matching

The matching procedure used incurred further loss of data: Only 83 percent of observations were used, although the missing ones were models in outlets that were being discarded with low sales, the volume of sales used in the matching being 97.8 percent.

The extent of the matching is illustrated for washing machines in 1998 in table 9.3. There were for example, 429 matched comparisons of a particular model in a specific outlet type in February 1998. These were selected from 500 and 488 observations available in February and January 1998, respectively. In total there were 6,020 matched comparisons for 1998, which compares with 7,750 available in 1998 or, more fairly, 7,750 – 500 = 7,256 to exclude the January figures because the matched comparisons are over eleven monthly comparisons as opposed to twelve months' data.

8. Results are available from the authors.

Table 9.3   Data on Matching for Washing Machines, 1998

Matched	Number of Observations		Volume of Sales (thousands)	
	Unmatched	Matched	Unmatched	Matched
January	500		126.2	
February	488	429	111.4	115.1
March	605	425	134.0	118.6
April	625	510	113.3	120.7
May	647	527	112.5	111.3
June	711	555	137.1	122.5
July	744	620	116.3	124.9
August	711	627	123.0	118.3
September	717	606	150.4	135.1
October	695	602	129.2	138.5
November	643	566	124.8	125.8
December	664	553	138.6	129.8

Note: Matched comparisons are between each month and the preceding one for chained indexes. There were, for example, 429 matched comparisons between February and January 1998 taken from 488 observations (model in a specific outlet type) in February and 500 in January 1998. Similarly, there were 425 matched comparisons between March and February 1998. Although the number of matched observations will not exceed those unmatched, the volume of sales may do so.

This difference of 1,236 observations is price data that exist in either period t or period $t + 1$ but do not have a counterpart to enable a comparison.[9] Since they are models just born or about to die, they should have low sales, and thus their omission should not unduly affect the index.[10] The total sales volume of matched comparisons was 1.3605 million, compared with 1.3906 million (unmatched but excluding January)—a difference of about 30,000 sales or about 2 percent of sales. From table 9.3 the monthly variation can be deduced. The worst loss of information was in the March to February comparisons: from $(111.4 + 134.0)/2 = 122.7$ thousand to 118.6 thousand—a loss of 3.3 percent. For the September to October and October to November comparisons the losses were less than 1 percent. A unit value index is given by

$$(7) \qquad \left[\frac{\sum p_t x_t}{\sum x_t} \right] \Bigg/ \left[\frac{\sum p_{t-1} x_{t-1}}{\sum x_{t-1}} \right],$$

which is a weighted measure of price changes *not* adjusted for changes in the quality mix. It is included in the analysis for comparison.

9. If, for example, the matched item had sales in period t of 100 and in period $t + 1$ of 50, and a new model was launched in period $t + 1$ with sales of 10, the matched volume would be $150/2 = 75$ and the unmatched 60 in period $t + 1$.

10. The data are transactions over the month, so recently born or dead models may only have been available for part of the month in question and have relatively low sales.

9.4   Results on the Three Methods for Scanner Data

Table 9.4 and figure 9.1 provide results using the matched approach for several different formulas.

First, the Laspeyres and Paasche provide outer upper and lower bounds, respectively, to the superlative Fisher index, the extent of the substitution being about 1.35 percent over the year, as consumers substituted away from machines with relatively high price increases. Note that because these indexes are chained on a monthly basis, they are different from those that arise from their fixed-base index counterparts. They allow the basket to be updated each month, the substitution in each month being compounded over the year. Second, figure 9.1 and table 9.4 show the unit value index, defined by index equation (7), to be unaffected by changes in the quality mix of models. Although the index shows only a slight overall fall in prices over

Table 9.4	Matched Quality-Adjusted Price Indexes by Formulas			
	Laspeyres	Paasche	Fisher	Unit Values
January	100	100	100	100
February	99.49	99.02	99.25	98.96
March	99.52	98.77	99.15	100.61
April	98.82	98.08	98.45	101.86
May	97.91	97.05	97.48	102.04
June	96.46	95.13	95.79	100.09
July	95.78	94.21	94.99	101.86
August	94.97	92.89	93.92	101.28
September	94.24	91.95	93.09	100.28
October	94.06	91.71	92.88	101.67
November	93.39	90.70	92.03	99.89
December	92.06	89.34	90.69	98.93

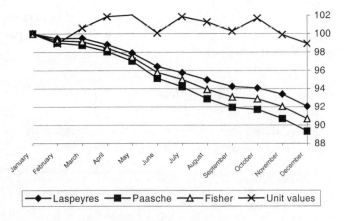

Fig. 9.1   Washing machines: Alternative formulas

the year of about 1 percent, and increases in other months compared with January 1998, quality-adjusted price changes have fallen by just under 10 percent over the year. The superlative matched index effectively adjusts for changes in the quality mix of purchases being based on computational matching as opposed to statistical models. Finally, not reported here but available from the authors, the results for the superlative Törnqvist index in footnote 1 are similar to those for the superlative Fisher, the Törnqvist in December being 90.711, compared to Fisher's 90.69. The geometric base and current-period weighted indexes can be seen in footnote 1 to be expected to be upper and lower inner bounds, respectively, on the superlative index because they incorporate some substitution effect (Shapiro and Wilcox 1997)—again, results are available from the authors. All of this is as predicted by economic theory. These indexes are the results of matched computations with different weighting systems. The matching, however, loses 2 percent of the data by sales volume. We consider below exact (and superlative) hedonic indexes, which lose only 0.4 percent of sales volume.

Figure 9.2 and table 9.5 provide results for different approaches to measuring quality-adjusted price indexes using an arithmetic formulation. The estimates from a linear model using the time dummy variable approach show a fall of only 6.0 percent, falling, in December, outside the Laspeyres and (what would be) Paasche bounds of the matched and exact approaches. In section 9.3 we found the hedonic regression to have a relatively high $\bar{R}^2$ with signs and values of the coefficients being as expected on a priori grounds. The linear formulation was supported by a Box-Cox test, although the results from a semilog formulation are very similar, the index falling to 93.85—by 6.15 percent. By conventional standards, these estimates are quite acceptable. The difference between the results from other approaches is more likely to be a result of the absence of a weighting system for the time dummy variable approach. If prices of more popular models are falling faster than those of unpopular ones, the weighted matched and exact approaches will take this into account, whereas the time dummy variable method will not. The concern here is with the time dummy variable approach as it is usually employed. However, a sales-weighted least squares estimator should in principle bring these estimates closer to the exact hedonic and matched results, although in practice the ordinary least squares and weighted least squares results were quite similar, a fall of 6.0 percent and 5.5 percent, respectively (and for semilog 6.0 percent and 5.7 percent, respectively). The results from the exact (and superlative) hedonic approach and matched estimates are not too dissimilar, a difference of about 2.0 and 1.7 percentage points for Laspeyres and Fisher over the year. In this case study, the loss of data for the matching, at about 2 percent by volume, was relatively low, giving confidence to the matched results.

Finally, figure 9.3 shows the results for the exact (superlative) hedonic approach at different levels of aggregation for Fisher indexes. As we expand

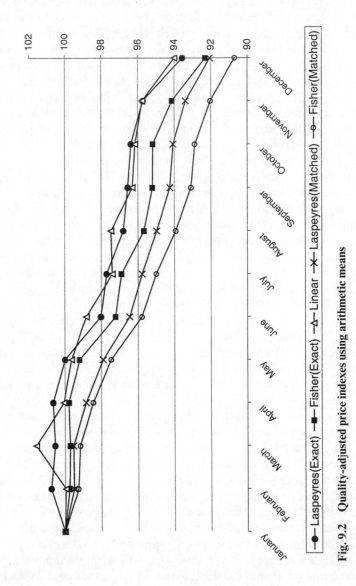

Fig. 9.2   Quality-adjusted price indexes using arithmetic means

— ● — Laspeyres(Exact)   — ■ — Fisher(Exact)   — △ — Linear   — ✳ — Laspeyres(Matched)   — ◯ — Fisher(Matched)

Table 9.5   **Quality-Adjusted Price Indexes Based on Arithmetic Means**

	Exact Hedonic by Make and Store Type		Time Dummy Variable:	Matched	
	Laspeyres	Fisher	Linear	Laspeyres	Fisher
January	100	100	100	100	100
February	101.04	99.93	99.95	99.50	99.25
March	101.26	100.23	101.59	99.52	99.15
April	100.99	99.86	100.05	98.82	98.45
May	100.25	99.11	99.62	97.91	97.48
June	98.41	97.27	98.81	96.46	95.79
July	98.19	97.02	97.41	95.78	94.99
August	97.10	95.61	97.47	94.97	93.92
September	96.96	95.24	96.30	94.24	93.09
October	97.05	95.23	96.15	94.06	92.88
November	96.14	94.18	95.76	93.39	92.03
December	94.12	92.42	93.99	92.06	90.69

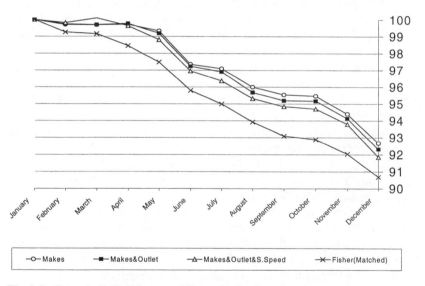

—○— Makes   —■— Makes&Outlet   —△— Makes&Outlet&S.Speed   —✕— Fisher(Matched)

Fig. 9.3   Exact hedonic indexes at different levels of aggregation

the weighted price changes in the body of the formula in equation (6a) from makes to makes within each outlet type, and then further by spin speed, the exact (superlative) hedonic index approaches the matched index.

In summary, this part of the paper uses scanner data to show how to measure quality-adjusted price changes using scanner data. It casts doubt on the use of the time dummy variable approach. It also argues for a matched approach as a special case of the theoretically based exact hedonic approach, the matched approach being based on computational matching and not being subject to the ideosyncrasies of the econometric estimation of hedonic indexes (Griliches 1990; Triplett 1990). Caution is, however, advised when the loss of data in matching is severe. In such a case an empirical investigation into the trade-off between including variables in the aggregation and the resulting loss of data is advised.

9.5   Quality Adjustment and Consumer Price Index Practice: An Experiment

9.5.1   Alternative Methods

The above account concerned the measurement of quality-adjusted price changes using scanner data. However, the problems of quality adjustment for the practical compilations of CPIs by statistical offices are quite different. In general, display prices are recorded by price collectors on a monthly basis for matched product varieties in a sample of individual stores. When a variety is missing in a month, the replacement may be of a different quality, and "like" may no longer be compared with "like." Its quality-adjusted price change has to be imputed by the statistical office. There is no problem of quality adjustment when varieties are matched. It is only when one is unavailable and its price change has to be imputed that there is a problem. The purpose of this experiment is to attempt to replicate the practices used by statistical offices in CPI compilation in order that the effects of different quality adjustment techniques can be simulated.

It should be noted that this is not a trivial matter. Moulton, LaFleur, and Moses (1999) examined the extent to which price collectors were faced with unavailable varieties of TVs in the U.S. CPI. Between 1993 and 1997, 10,553 prices on TVs were used, of which 1,614 (15 percent) were replacements, of which, in turn, 680 (42 percent) were judged to be not directly comparable. Canadian experience for TVs over an almost identical period found 750 of the 10,050 (7.5 percent) to be replacements, of which 572 (76 percent) were judged to be not directly comparable. For international price comparisons the problem is much more severe (Feenstra and Diewert 2000).

We should stress that sections 9.2–9.4 were concerned with how best to measure quality-adjusted price changes using scanner data. Here, the use of scanner data is to simulate CPI practices to help judge the veracity of alternative quality adjustment procedures that might be employed to supplement matched models procedures. A number of well-documented options are available and are outlined in Turvey (1989); Reinsdorf, Liegey, and Stewart (1995); Moulton and Moses (1997); Armknecht, Lane, and Stewart (1997); Armknecht and Maitland-Smith (1999); and Moulton, LaFleur, and Moses (1999), although the terminology differs; these options include

- *Imputation.* Where no information is available to allow reasonable estimates to be made of the effect on price of a quality change, the price change in the elementary aggregate group as a whole, to which the variety belongs, is assumed to be the same as that for the variety.
- *Direct comparison.* If another variety is directly comparable, that is, if it is so similar it can be assumed to have the same base price, its price replaces the missing price. Any difference in price level between the new and old is assumed to be due to price changes and not quality differences.
- *Direct quality adjustment.* Where there is a substantial difference in the quality of the missing and replacement varieties, estimates of the quality differences are made to enable quality-adjusted price comparisons to be made.

For illustration, consider a product variety with a price of £100 in January. In October, a replacement version with a widget attached is priced at £115. The direct comparison would use the price of an essentially identical variety. The direct quality adjustment method requires an estimate of the worth of the widget. For example, if it was found that the widget increased the product's flow of services by 5 percent, the £115 in October could be compared with an adjusted base-period price of £100 (1.05) = £105. The imputation approach would use the index for the relevant product group. If this was 110.0 in October (January = 100.0), the replacement item would have a revised base-period price of £115/1.10 = £104.55 to compare with the new price of £115; that is, 115/104.55 × 100 = 110.0, a 10 percent increase in price, the residual 5 percent being assumed to be due to quality differences.

Moulton, LaFleur, and Moses (1999) note that the direct or explicit quality adjustment approach can be used with data from manufacturers on the cost of quality changes or coefficients from hedonic regressions as explicit estimates of quality differences. Valuable insights into the validity of such methods can be gained by using a number of such methods on actual CPI data and comparing the results; seminal work in this area includes Lowe (1999) and Moulton, LaFleur, and Moses (1999). The alternative approach adopted here is to attempt to replicate such procedures using scanner data.

9.5.2   The Experiment

The purpose of this experiment is to replicate CPI data collection using scanner data to provide a means by which different CPI procedures can be emulated. The formulation here is relatively crude, being an initial attempt at the exercise. However, we hope it will be useful for illustrative purposes. The data are the same monthly data on washing machines in 1998 used in sections 9.3 and 9.4. We start by taking a January fixed basket of washing machines comprising all varieties for which there was a transaction in January. Our varieties are for a model in one of four outlet types: multiples, mass merchandisers, catalogs, and independents. Since many models are only sold in chains of particular outlets, the classification is in practice closer to a given model in a specific chain or even individual outlet, which is the price observed by a price collector. The unit value of each variety in January is treated as the average display price collected by the price collectors. Since the volume of transactions is known for each variety, the January sample is taken to be the universe of every transaction of each variety. This January universe is the base-period active sample. We can, of course, subsequently modify this by using different sampling procedures and identify their effects on the index.

If the variety in each outlet type continues to exist over the remaining months of the year, matched comparisons are undertaken between the January prices and their counterparts in successive months. Consider again for illustration table 9.1, the case of four varieties existing in January, each with relative expenditures of w_1, w_2, w_5, and w_6 and prices of p_{11}, p_{21}, p_{51}, and p_{61}. A Laspeyres price index for February compared with January $= 100.0$ is straightforward. In March the prices for varieties 2 and 6 are missing. Each of these was collected from different outlet types, multiples and mass merchandisers in this example. To enable Laspeyres price comparisons to be undertaken in such instances, a range of methods was utilized for the scanner data, including the following:

1. *Implicit imputation.* Price comparisons were only used when January prices could be matched with the month in question. In our example the January to March comparisons were based on varieties 1 and 5 only, the price changes of varieties 2 and 6 being assumed to be the same as these remaining varieties. The weights for varieties 1 and 5 would be $w_1/(w_1 + w_5)$ and $w_5/(w_1 + w_5)$, respectively.

2. *Targeted implicit imputation.* The price changes of missing varieties for a specific make within an outlet type were assumed to be the same as for the remaining active sample for that make within its outlet type. If we assumed varieties 1 and 2 and 5 and 6 are of the same make, then the weights for varieties 1 and 5 would be $(w_1 + w_2)/W$ and $(w_5 + w_6)/W$, respectively, where $W = (w_1 + w_2 + w_5 + w_6)$.

3. *Direct comparison.* Within each outlet type a search was made for the best match first, by matching brand, then in turn by type (see earlier section "The Variables"), width, and spin speed. If more than one variety was found, the selection was according to the highest value of transactions (expenditure). In our example, varieties 3 or 4 and 7 would, respectively, replace varieties 2 and 6 in March.

4. *Explicit hedonic: predicted versus actual.* A hedonic regression of the

(log of the) price of model i in period t on its characteristics set z_{tki} was estimated for each month, given by

$$(8) \qquad \ln p_{ti} = \beta_{0t} + \sum_{k=1}^{K} \beta_{kt} z_{kit} + \varepsilon_{it}.$$

Say the price of variety m goes missing in March, period $t + 2$. The price of variety m can be predicted for March if we insert the characteristics of variety m into the estimated regression equation for March and similarly for successive months. The predicted price for this "old" unavailable variety m in March and its price comparison with January (period t) are respectively given by

$$(9) \qquad \hat{p}_{m,t+2} = \exp\left[\hat{\beta}_{0,t+2} + \sum \hat{\beta}_{k,t+2} z_{k,m}\right] \quad \text{for} \quad \frac{\hat{p}_{m,t+2}}{p_{m,t}} - \text{old}$$

The "old" denotes that the comparison is based on a prediction of the price of the unavailable variety in the current period rather than the (new) replacement variety's price in the base period. In our example we would estimate $\hat{p}_{23}, \hat{p}_{24}$, and so on, and $\hat{p}_{63}, \hat{p}_{64}$, and so on, and compare them with p_{21} and p_{61}, respectively. We would effectively fill in the blanks for varieties 2 and 6.

An alternative procedure is to select for each missing m variety a replacement n variety using the routine described in step (3) above. In this case the price of n in period $t + 2$, for example, is known, and we require a predicted price for n in period t. The predicted price for the "new" variety and required price comparison are

$$(10) \qquad \hat{p}_{n,t} = \exp\left[\hat{\beta}_{0,t} + \sum \hat{\beta}_{k,t} z_{k,n}\right] \quad \text{for} \quad \frac{p_{n,t+2}}{\hat{p}_{n,t}} - \text{new},$$

that is, the characteristics of variety n are inserted into the right-hand side of an estimated regression for period t. The price comparisons of equation (9) would be weighted by $w_{m,t}$, as would those of its replaced price comparison in equation (10).

A final alternative is to take the geometric mean of the formulations in equations (9) and (10) on grounds akin to those discussed by Diewert (1997) for similar index number issues.

5. *Explicit hedonic: predicted versus predicted.* A further approach was the use of predicted values for, say, variety n in *both* periods, for example, $\hat{p}_{n,t+2}/\hat{p}_{n,t}$. Consider a misspecification problem in the hedonic equation. For example, there may be an interaction effect between a brand dummy and a characteristic—say, a Sony television set and Nicam stereo sound. Possession of both characteristics may be worth 5 percent more on price (from a semilogarithmic form) than their separate individual components (for evidence of interaction effects, see Curry, Morgan, and Silver 2001). The use of

$\hat{p}_{n,t+2}/\hat{p}_{n,t}$ would be misleading since the actual price in the numerator would incorporate the 5 percent premium, whereas the one predicted from a straightforward semilogarithmic form would not. A more realistic approach to this issue might be to use predicted values for *both* periods. We stress that in adopting this approach we are substituting for a recorded, actual price an imputation. This is not desirable, but neither would be the form of bias discussed above.

The comparisons using predicted values in both periods are given as

(11) $\dfrac{\hat{p}_{n,t+2}}{\hat{p}_{n,t}}$ for the "new" variety

$\dfrac{\hat{p}_{m,t+2}}{\hat{p}_{m,t}}$ for the disappearing or "old" variety, or

$$\left[\left(\frac{\hat{p}_{n,t+2}}{\hat{p}_{n,t}} \right) \left(\frac{\hat{p}_{m,t+2}}{\hat{p}_{m,t}} \right) \right]^{0.5}$$

as a (geometric) mean of the two.

6. *Explicit hedonic: adjustments using coefficients.* In this approach, a replacement variety was found using the routine in step (3) above and any differences between the characteristics of the replacement n in, for example, $t + 2$ and m in period t ascertained. A predicted price for n in period t, that is, $\hat{p}_{n,t}$, was determined and compared with the actual $p_{n,t+2}$. However, unlike the formulation in equation (10), $\hat{p}_{n,t}$ was estimated by applying the subset of the k characteristics that distinguished m from n to their respective marginal values in period t estimated from the hedonic regression and adjusting the price of $p_{m,t}$. For our illustration, if the nearest replacement for variety 2 was variety 3, then the characteristics that differentiate variety 3 from variety 2 were identified, and the price in the base period, p_{31} is estimated by adjusting p_{21} using the appropriate coefficients from the hedonic regression in that month. For example, if variety 2 had an 800 rpm spin speed and variety 3 a 1,100 rpm spin speed, other things being equal, the marginal value of the 300 rpm differential would be estimated from the hedonic regression, and p_{21} would be adjusted for comparison with p_{33}. Note that if the z variables in the characteristic set are orthogonal to each other the results from this approach will be identical to those from equation (10). A similar approach to equation (9) was also undertaken that only used the salient distinguishing characteristics and the geometric mean of the two calculated. These six methods provide in all twelve different measures of quality-adjusted price changes.

9.5.3   The Study

Table 9.6 provides a summary of the data used. In January 1998 there were 500 varieties (models in one of the four outlet types—multiples, mass merchandisers, catalogs, and independents) of washing machines accounting

Table 9.6   **Number of Observations and Expenditure Shares Used by Different Methods**

	Number of Observations, Models in Outlets	Number of Transactions, Thousands	Expenditure, £1000s	Imputation—No Replacements			Direct Comparisons—Replacements	
				% of January Observations Used	% of January Expenditure Used	% of Current Expenditure Used	% of January Observations Used	% of January Expenditure Used
January	500	126,171	45,727					
February	488	111,358	39,938	85.8	97.19	97.06	99.8	99.999
March	605	134,049	48,877	83.0	99.13	91.06	99.2	99.991
April	625	113,338	41,841	81.0	98.65	81.79	99.4	99.996
May	647	112,549	41,623	77.6	98.32	76.62	98.2	99.899
June	711	137,070	49,721	78.6	97.97	72.90	99.2	99.992
July	744	116,273	42,924	76.0	97.05	64.21	99.0	99.990
August	711	122,977	45,139	69.6	93.52	57.51	98.8	99.932
September	717	150,422	54,665	66.2	86.41	54.24	99.0	99.935
October	695	129,235	47,620	59.8	87.13	51.63	98.0	99.910
November	643	124,845	45,198	54.0	83.51	49.35	97.0	99.788
December	664	138,634	49,707	53.0	81.58	48.16	97.6	99.818

for 126,171 transactions. The distribution was highly skewed, with the top 5 percent and 10 percent of varieties (in an outlet type) accounting for 49 percent and 66 percent of transactions, respectively, in January. The indexes in this section are fixed-base January 1998 = 100.0 indexes compiled over the period January to December 1998. Unlike the chained indexes considered in previous sections, they take no account of varieties introduced after January unless they replace a variety that is "missing"—that is, it no longer has any transactions. The imputation approach does not replace missing varieties. Table 9.6 shows that by December, only 53 percent of the January basket of varieties were used for the December/January index, although these accounted for 81.6 percent of January expenditure. Varieties with lower sales values dropped out more quickly. However, the remaining 0.53 (500) = 265 varieties in December only accounted for 48.2 percent of the value of transactions *in December*. The active sample relating to the universe of transactions in December had deteriorated, and although they are not part of this current study, insights into the nature of the deterioration can be ascertained from the experiment. For example, this type of experiment could be used to consider the effects of renewing the item selection more frequently. The fall in the coverage of the active sample is mitigated by the introduction of replacements when using direct comparisons. The weights used remain, of course, those in January 1998. However, the sample of information used in successive months draws on the replacement varieties.

The search procedure outlined above for replacements for direct comparisons, and used in some of the hedonic methods, had a minimum condition—that the replacement must at least be of the same make in a given outlet type. This can be seen from table 9.6 to have been generally met, the fall-off being negligible. The hedonic approach benefited from use of information on the whole sample in each month for the estimation of the equations. The estimated regression equations were based on the whole sample in spite of the inclusion of varieties with limited transactions on the grounds that such varieties were more likely to be the ones going missing. The twelve regressions estimated in each month had a mean $\bar{R}^2$ of 0.80, and in each case the null hypothesis of the individual coefficients being jointly equal to zero was rejected by an F-test. The average monthly sample size was 558.

9.5.4   The Results

Table 9.7 provides the results. The extent of any bias arising from the imputation approach is dictated by the ratio of missing price comparisons to the total number of comparisons and by the difference between *quality-adjusted* price changes of the missing varieties, had they continued to exist, and those of other varieties (see the appendix). The bias from the class mean imputation approach should be smaller than the imputation approach, and these methods show the choice between the results matters—an approximately 2 percentage point difference over the year, for a roughly 10 percent fall.

Table 9.7 Laspeyres Indexes

	Imputation	Targeted Imputation	Direct Comparison	Predicted versus Actual			Adjustment via Coefficients			Predicted versus Predicted		
				Old	New	Geometric Mean	Old	New	Geometric Mean	Old	New	Geometric Mean
January	100.00	100.00	100.00	100.00	100.00	100.00	100.00	100.00	100.00	100.00	100.00	100.00
February	99.49	99.50	99.30	99.75	99.16	99.45	99.41	99.38	99.40	99.49	99.48	99.49
March	99.29	99.29	99.26	99.35	99.17	99.25	99.23	99.20	99.22	99.27	99.29	99.28
April	98.30	98.29	98.45	98.23	98.29	98.25	98.21	98.38	98.30	98.09	98.31	98.20
May	97.06	98.89	97.30	96.95	97.10	97.02	96.94	97.18	97.06	96.75	97.09	96.92
June	94.98	94.97	95.09	95.00	94.95	94.98	94.92	95.05	94.98	94.91	95.07	94.99
July	93.14	92.97	93.13	93.44	93.08	93.26	93.28	93.10	93.19	93.40	93.22	93.31
August	93.64	92.62	94.49	94.64	93.83	94.24	94.28	94.07	94.18	94.09	93.87	93.98
September	93.55	92.01	94.03	94.91	92.26	93.58	93.37	93.29	93.33	94.06	93.96	94.01
October	91.84	90.74	91.75	92.99	90.48	91.73	91.49	91.30	91.40	92.13	92.14	92.13
November	91.52	90.20	91.47	93.26	89.94	91.59	90.85	90.83	90.84	91.75	92.17	91.96
December	90.87	88.94	91.81	92.74	90.09	91.41	91.26	91.19	91.23	91.63	91.66	91.55

The price fall measured using direct comparisons was found to be smaller than the class mean result—a fall of 8.2 percent compared with 11.1 percent. A priori there is no expectation of the direction of bias from the targeted imputation approach (see the appendix), although for direct comparisons the replacements in varieties are more likely to be priced higher than the missing ones, the smaller fall in price thus being expected. However, given that the selection of replacement is not governed by the judicious selection of price collectors but by a computational procedure, the extent of the difference is smaller than expected.

The use of hedonic adjustment methods provides an explicit basis for the quality adjustments. The results for the predicted versus actual have a smaller fall for the "old" (equation [9]) than "new" (equation [10]) comparison (table 9.7). The actual old, disappearing varieties could be argued to be more likely to be below the hedonic surface as they price to clear the market, whereas the actual new varieties are more likely to be above the hedonic surface as they price-skim segments of consumers with higher price elasticities. However, the effect of both is to increase the price change. The geometric mean of an 8.6 percent fall is slightly higher than the other results, as expected.

The above estimates were also undertaken using a subset of the regression coefficients applied only to the characteristic differences that took place. If the variables for the characteristics are orthogonal to each other, the results will be the same as those for equations (9) and (10) discussed above. The adjustments are affected by multicollinearity as imprecise estimates of individual marginal values are utilized for the adjustment. Multicollinearity occurs when characteristics are bundled together, and it is not clear whether the differences between the results of the two formulations are some measure of this. Nonetheless, the results for the two geometric means are quite similar—a fall of 8.8 percent for the adjustment via coefficients.

The final set of estimates is the predicted versus predicted. The old and new estimates are very close, with a geometric mean and a fall of 8.4 percent. This compares with the geometric mean of the predicted versus actual of 8.6 percent, implying that the results, when averaged using the geometric mean, are not subject to serious misspecification error.

Thus, in summary, different hedonic adjustment techniques provide similar results, although the old and new predicted to actual appear to work best as a geometric mean. This similarity is encouraging, given the plethora of such approaches. These results are also similar to those from a computational, direct replacement method, but both imputation approaches lead to larger falls in prices, a result with no immediate explanation, given the analysis in the appendix.

9.5.5   Further Work

The results are exploratory in the sense that they arise from an experimental formulation that is subject to some limitations that cannot be easily remedied as well as some restrictions that can. A major limitation is that the observations are for a product variety in a specific outlet type, as opposed to in a specific outlet (in a geographical place). That some models are specific to some outlet chains helps, but we cannot distinguish here between the locations of the outlets, although in principle this is possible with scanner data. This in itself may not be problematic for price comparisons, since there is still some debate over the validity of using the aggregated unit values over outlets for price comparisons (Balk 1999; Diewert 1990; de Haan and Opperdoes 1998). However, the concept of "missing" prices used here is not appropriate since a price collector may, for example, find a price missing for a variety in an outlet in Cardiff while other price collectors may find price quotes for the same variety in different stores or locations. The experiment would only treat prices as missing if there were no transactions anywhere for the product variety. Scanner data provide a proxy variable on the extent to which each variety is sold in different outlets, and use of this is being considered to develop the experiment.

Further work might also include consideration of the effects of the following:

- different sampling schemes for the January selection as opposed to the use of the universe of transactions
- more frequent item selection (rebasing) on the need for quality adjustments
- more frequent item selection (rebasing) on the coverage of the universe of transactions
- variations in the specification and sample used for the hedonic regressions
- different selection criteria for replacements
- use of different formulas
- comparison with hedonic indexes
- different rules for deciding when a variety is "missing"
- more refined class imputation procedures
- missing market innovations
- extension to other products

Appendix

Triplett (2001) in a draft OECD manual has been responsible for a detailed analysis of the implicit bias from imputations, and although the formulation here is quite different, there is much that has been usefully applied from his analysis. For $i = 1 \ldots m$ varieties where $P_{m,t}$ is the price of variety m in period t, $P_{n,t+1}$ is the price of a replacement variety n in period $t + 1$, $A(h)$ is a quality adjustment to $P_{n,t+1}$ that equates its quality services to $P_{m,t+1}$ such that the quality-adjusted price $P^*_{m,t+1} = A(h)P_{n,t+1}$, and Q is the implicit adjustment that allows the method to work, the arithmetic formulation for one missing variety is given by

(A1)
$$\frac{1}{m}\left(\frac{P^*_{m,t+1}}{P_{m,t}} + \sum_{i=1}^{m-1} \frac{P_{i,t+1}}{P_{i,t}} \right) = \left[\frac{1}{(m-1)} \sum_{i=1}^{m-1} \frac{P_{i,t+1}}{P_{i,t}} \right] + Q$$

(A2)
$$Q = \frac{1}{m} \frac{P^*_{m,t+1}}{P_{m,t}} - \frac{1}{m(m-1)} \sum_{i=1}^{m-1} \frac{P_{i,t+1}}{P_{i,t}}$$

and for x missing varieties by

(A3)
$$Q = \frac{1}{m} \sum_{i=1}^{x} \frac{P^*_{m,t+1}}{P_{m,t}} - \frac{x}{m(m-x)} \sum_{i=1}^{m-x} \frac{P_{i,t+1}}{P_{i,t}}$$

The relationships are readily visualized if r_1 is defined as the respective geometric or arithmetic mean of price changes of varieties that continue to be recorded and r_2 that of quality-adjusted missing varieties, that is, for the arithmetic case where

(A4)
$$r_1 = \left[\sum_{i=1}^{m-x} \frac{P_{i,t+1}}{P_{i,t}} \right] \div (m - x)$$

$$r_2 = \left[\sum_{i=1}^{x} \frac{P^*_{i,t+1}}{P_{i,t}} \right] \div x$$

then the ratio of arithmetic mean biases from substituting equations (A4) in (A3) is

(A6)
$$Q_g = \frac{x}{m}(r_2 - r_1),$$

which equal zero when $r_1 = r_2$. The bias depends on the ratio of missing values and the difference between the mean of price changes for existing varieties and the mean of quality-adjusted replacement to missing price changes. Note that the bias is small if *either* (x/m) *or* the difference between r_1 and r_2 is small. Furthermore, note that the method is reliant on a comparison between price changes for existing varieties and *quality-adjusted* price changes for the replacement/missing comparison. This is more likely to be justified than a comparison without the quality adjustment. For example, suppose we had $m = 3$ varieties, each with a price of 100 in period t. Let the $t + 1$ prices be 120 for two varieties, but assume the third is missing—that is, $x = 1$—and is replaced by a variety with a price of 140, 20 of which is due to quality differences. Then the arithmetic bias as given in equation (A6), where $x = 1$, $m = 3$ and $r_2 = [(A(h) + P_{n,t+1})/P_{m,t}]$, is

$$\frac{1}{3}\left[\frac{140-20}{100} - \frac{240/2}{100}\right] = 0.$$

Had the bias depended on the *unadjusted price* of 140 compared with 100, the method would be prone to serious error. In this calculation the direction of the bias is given by $(r_2 - r_1)$ and does not depend on whether quality is improving or deteriorating, that is, whether $(A(h) > P_{n,t+1}$ or $A(h) < P_{n,t+1}$. If $A(h) > P_{n,t+1}$, a quality improvement, it is still possible that $r_2 < r_1$ and that the bias may be negative, a point stressed by Jack Triplett.

References

Abraham, K., J. Greenless, and B. Moulton. 1998. Working to improve the Consumer Price Index. *Journal of Economic Perspectives* 12 (1): 23–36.

Arguea, N. M., C. Haseo, and G. A. Taylor. 1994. Estimating consumer preferences using market data: An application to U.S. automobile demand. *Journal of Applied Econometrics* 9:1–18.

Armknecht, P. A., W. F. Lane, and K. J. Stewart. 1997. New products and the U.S. Consumer Price Index. In *The economic of new goods.* Studies in Income and Wealth, vol. 58, ed. T. F. Bresnaham and R. J. Gordon, 375–96. Chicago: University of Chicago Press.

Armknecht, P. A., and F. Maitland-Smith. 1999. Price imputation and other techniques for dealing with missing observations, seasonality, and quality changes in price indices. IMF Working Paper no. WP/99/78. Washington, D.C.: International Monetary Fund, Statistics Department.

Astin, J. A., and D. J. Sellwood. 1998. Harmonization in the European Union: A review of some technical issues. *Proceedings of the third meeting of the International Working Group on Price Indices*, ed. B. Balk, 291–308. Research Paper no. 9806. Voorburg, the Netherlands: Statistics Netherlands.

Balk, B. 1999. On the use of unit value indices as consumer price sub-indices. In *Proceedings of the fourth International Working Group on Price Indices,* ed. W. Lane, 112–20. Washington, D.C.: Bureau of Labor Statistics.

Berndt, E. R., Z. Grilches, and N. J. Rappaport. 1995. Econometric estimates of price indices for personal computers in the 1990s. *Journal of Econometrics* 68:243–68.

Blow, L., and I. Crawford. 1999. *Cost of living indices and revealed preference.* London: The Institute of Fiscal Studies.

Boskin, M. S., chairman. Advisory Commission to Study the Consumer Price Index. 1996. Towards a more accurate measure of the cost of living. Interim Report to the Senate Finance Committee. Washington, D.C.

Boskin, M. S., E. R. Delberger, R. J. Gordon, Z. Griliches, and D. W. Jorgenson. 1998. Consumer prices in the Consumer Price Index and the cost of living. *Journal of Economic Perspectives* 12 (1): 3–26.

Bradley, R., B. Cook, S. G. Leaver, and B. R. Moulton. 1998. An overview of research on potential uses of scanner data in the U.S. CPI. *Proceedings of the third meeting of the International Working Group on Price Indices*, ed. B. Balk, 169–182. Research Paper no. 9806. Statistics Netherlands.

Cameron, J., and A. Collins. 1997. Estimates of hedonic ageing for partner search. *Kyklos* 50 (3): 409–18.

Cole, R., Y. C. Chen, J. A. Barquin-Stolleman, E. Dulberger, N. Helvacian, and J. H. Hodge. 1986. Quality-adjusted price indexes for computer processors and selected peripheral equipment. *Survey of Current Business* 65 (1): 41–50.

Cunningham, A. 1996. Measurement bias in price indices: An application to the UK's RPI. Bank of England Working Paper Series, no. 47. London: Bank of England.

Curry, B., P. Morgan, and M. Silver. 2001. Hedonic regressions, misspecifications, and neural networks. *Applied Economics* 33:659–71.

Dalen, J. 1998. Experiments with Swedish scanner data. *Proceedings of the third meeting of the International Working Group on Price Indices*, ed. B. Balk, 163–68. Research Paper no. 9806. Voorburg, the Netherlands: Statistics Netherlands.

Diewert, W. E. 1976. Exact and superlative index numbers, *Journal of Econometrics* 4:115–45.

———. 1978. Superlative index numbers and consistency in aggregation. *Econometrica* 46:883–900.

———. 1980. Aggregation problems in the measurement of capital. In *The measurement of capital*, Studies in Income and Wealth, vol. 45, ed. Dan Usher, 433–528. Chicago: University of Chicago Press.

———. 1993. The early history of price index number research. In *Essays in index number theory*, vol. 1, ed. W. E. Diewert and A. O. Nakamura, 33–65. Amsterdam: North Holland.

———. 1995. Axiomatic and economic approaches to elementary price indices. Discussion Paper no. 95-01. Vancouver, Canada: University of British Columbia, Department of Economics.

———. 1996. Sources of bias in consumer price indices. Discussion Paper no. DP-96-04. University of New South Wales, School of Economics.

———. 1997. Alternative strategies for aggregating prices in the CPI: Comment. *Federal Reserve Bank of St Louis Review* 79 (3): 113–25.

Feenstra, R. C. 1995. Exact hedonic price indices. *Review of Economics and Statistics* 77:634–54.

Feenstra, R. C., and E. W. Diewert. 2000. Imputation and price indices: Theory and evidence from the International Price Program. BLS Working Paper no. 335. Washington, D.C.: Bureau of Labor Statistics, Office of Prices and Living Conditions.

Fixler, D., and K. Zieschang. 1992. Incorporating ancillary measures of processes and quality change into a superlative productivity index. *Journal of Productivity Analysis* 2:245–67.

Forsyth, F. G., and R. F. Fowler. 1981. The theory and practice of chain price index numbers. *Journal of the Royal Statistical Society*, series A, 144 (2): 224–47.

Gandal, N. 1994. Hedonic price indices for spreadsheets and empirical test for network externalities. *RAND Journal of Economics* 25 (1): 160–70.

———. 1995. Competing compatibility standards and network externalities in the PC market. *Review of Economics and Statistics* 77:599–608.

Goldberger, A. A. 1968. The interpretation and estimation of Cobb-Douglas functions. *Econometrica* 35 (3–4): 464–72.

Gordon, R. L. 1990. *The measurement of durable goods prices.* Chicago: University of Chicago Press.

Griliches, Z. 1990. Hedonic price indices and the measurement of capital and productivity: Some historical reflections. In *Fifty years of economic measurement: The Jubilee Conference of Research in Income and Wealth*, Studies in Income and

Wealth, vol. 54, ed. E. R. Berndt and J. E. Triplett, 185–206. Chicago: University of Chicago Press.

Haan, J. de, and E. Opperdoes. 1998. Estimation of the coffee price index using scanner data: The choice of the micro index. *Proceedings of the third meeting of the International Working Group on Price Indices*, ed. B. Balk, 191–202. Research Paper no. 9806. Voorburg, the Netherlands: Statistics Netherlands.

Hausman, J. R. 1997. Valuation of new goods under perfect and imperfect conditions. In *The economics of new goods*, Studies in Income and Wealth vol. 58, ed. T. Bresnahan and R. J. Gordon, 209–48. Chicago: University of Chicago Press.

Hawkes, W., and R. Smith. 1999. Improving consumer price measurements through the use of scanner data and market segmentation. In *Proceedings of the Measurement of Inflation Conference*, ed. M. Silver and D. Fenwick, 283–99. Cardiff, Wales: Cardiff Business School.

Hicks, J. R. 1940. The valuation of the social income. *Economica* 7:105–24.

Hoffmann, J. 1998. Problems of inflation measurement in Germany. Economic Research Group of Deutsche Bundesbank Discussion Paper no. 1/98. Frankfurt: Deutsche Bundesbank.

Ioannidis, C., and M. Silver. 1999. Estimating hedonic indices: An application to U.K. television sets. *Zeitschrift fur Nationalokonomie* (Journal of Economics) 69 (1): 71–94.

Kmietowicz, Z. W., and M. S. Silver. 1980. New products and the Index of Industrial Production. *Journal of Development Studies* 16 (4): 463–67.

Kokoski, M., K. Waehrer, and P. Rozaklis. 1999. Using hedonic methods for quality adjustment in the CPI: The consumer audio products component. BLS Working Paper. Washington, D.C.: Bureau of Labor Statistics, Division of Price and Index Number Research. Available at [http://www.bls.gov/cpi/cpiaudio.htm].

Konüs, A. A. 1939 (1924). The problem of the true index of the cost-of-living. *Econometrica* 7 (1): 10–29. First published in Russian.

Lerner, J. 1995. Pricing and financial resources: An analysis of the disk drive industry, 1980–88. *The Review of Economics and Statistics* 77:585–98.

Lowe, R. 1999. Televisions: Quality changes and scanner data. In *Proceedings of the fourth meeting of the International Working Group on Price Indices*, ed. W. Lane, 5–20. Washington, D. C.: Bureau of Labor Statistics.

McFadden, D. 1983. Econometric models of probabilistic choice. In *Structural analysis of discrete data with econometric applications*, ed. Charles F. Manski and Daniel McFadden, 198–272. Cambridge: MIT Press.

Mills, E. S., and R. Simenauer. 1996. New hedonic estimates of regional constant quality house prices. *Journal of Urban Economics* 39 (2): 209–15.

Moulton, B., T. J. LaFleur, and K. E. Moses. 1999. Research on improved quality adjustments in the CPI: The case of televisions. In *Proceedings of the fourth meeting of the International Working Group on Price Indices*, ed. W. Lane, 77–99. Washington, D.C.: Bureau of Labor Statistics.

Moulton, B., and K. E. Moses. 1997. Addressing the quality change issue in the Consumer Price Index. *Brookings Papers on Economic Activity*, issue no. 1:305–49.

Murray, J., and N. Sarantis. 1999. User cost, forward-looking behaviour, and the demand for cars in the U.K. *Journal of Economics and Business* 51 (3): 237–58.

Nelson, R. A., T. L. Tanguay, and C. D. Patterson. 1994. A quality-adjusted price index for personal computers. *Journal of Business and Economics Statistics* 12 (1): 23–31.

Rasmussen, D. W., and T. W. Zuehlke. 1990. On the choice of functional form for hedonic price functions. *Applied Economics* 22 (4): 431–38.

Reinsdorf, M. 1996. Constructing basic components for the U.S. CPI from scanner data: A test using data on coffee. Working Paper no. 277. Washington, D.C.: Bureau of Labor Statistics.

———. 1998. Divisia indices and the representative consumer problem. In *Proceedings of the fourth meeting of the International Working Group on Price Indices*, ed. W. Lane, 210–235. Washington, D.C.: Bureau of Labor Statistics.

Reinsdorf, M., P. Liegey, and K. Stewart. 1995. New ways of handling quality change in the U.S. Consumer Price Index. Working Paper no. 276. Washington, D.C.: Bureau of Labor Statistics.

Rosen, S. 1974. Hedonic prices and implicit markets: Product differentiation and pure competition. *Journal of Political Economy* 82:34–49.

Saglio, A. 1995. Comparative changes in average price and a price index: Two case studies. In *Proceedings of the first meeting of the International Working Group on Price Indices*, ed. L. M. Duchare. Ottawa: Statistics Canada. Available at [http://www4.statcan.ca/secure/english/ottawagroup/toc1.htm].

Shapiro, M. D., and D. W. Wilcox. 1997. Alternative strategies for aggregating prices in the CPI. *Federal Reserve Bank Review* 79 (3): 113–26.

Silver, M, 1995. Elementary aggregates, micro-indices, and scanner data: Some issues in the compilation of consumer prices. *Review of Income and Wealth* 41:427–38.

———. 1999. An evaluation of the use of hedonic regressions for basic components of consumer price indices. *Review of Income and Wealth* 45 (1): 41–56.

Stewart, K. G., and J. C. H. Jones. 1998. Hedonic and demand analysis: The implicit demand for player attributes. *Economic Inquiry* 36 (2): 192–202.

Szulc, B. J. 1983. Linking price index numbers. In *Price level measurement*, ed. W. E. Diewert and C. Montmarquette, 537–66. Ottawa: Statistics Canada.

Triplett, J. E. 1987. Hedonic functions and hedonic indices. In *The new Palgraves dictionary of economics*. 630–34. Bastingstoke, England: Palgrave Macmillan.

———. 1990. Hedonic methods in statistical agency environments: An intellectual biopsy. In *Fifty years of economic measurement: The Jubilee Conference on Research in Income and Wealth,* Studies in Income and Wealth, vol. 56, ed. E. R. Berndt and J. E Triplett, 207–38. Chicago: University of Chicago Press.

———. 2001. Draft of handbook on quality adjustment of price indexes for information and communication technology products. OECD Directorate for Science technology and Industry. Paris: Organization for Economic Cooperation and Development.

Turvey, R. 1989. *Consumer price indices.* Geneva: International Labour Organisation.

———. 1999a. Draft of elementary aggregate indices manual. Available at [http://www.turvey.demon.co.uk]. Revised April.

———. 1999b. Incorporating new models into a CPI: PCs as an example. In *Proceedings of the Measurement of Inflation Conference*, ed. M. Silver and D. Fenwick, 505–10. Cardiff, Wales: Cardiff Business School.

White, H. 1980. A heteroskedasticity-consistent covariance matrix and a direct test for heteroskedasticity. *Econometrica* 48:721–46.

Hedonic Regressions
A Consumer Theory Approach

Erwin Diewert

10.1 Introduction

This paper started out as a comment on Silver and Heravi (chap. 9 in this volume). This very useful and interesting paper follows in the tradition started by Silver (1995), who was the first to use scanner data in a systematic way in order to construct index numbers. In the present paper by Silver and Heravi, the authors collect an enormous data set on virtually all sales of washing machines in the United Kingdom for the twelve months in the year 1998. They use this detailed price and quantity information, along with information on the characteristics of each machine, in order to compute various aggregate monthly price indexes for washing machines, taking into account the problems associated with the changing quality of washing machines. In particular, the authors consider three broad types of approach to the estimation of quality-adjusted prices using scanner data:

- the usual time series dummy variable hedonic regression technique, which does not make use of quantity data on sales of models
- matched model techniques, in which unit values of matched models in each of the two periods being compared are used as the basic prices to go along with the quantities sold in each period (and then ordinary index number theory is used to aggregate up these basic prices and quantities)
- an exact hedonic approach based on the work of Feenstra (1995).

Erwin Diewert is professor of economics at the University of British Columbia and a research associate of the National Bureau of Economic Research.

The author is indebted to Paul Armknecht, Bert Balk, Ernst Berndt, Jeff Bernstein, Angus Deaton, Robert Feenstra, Dennis Fixler, Robert Gillingham, Alice Nakamura, Richard Schmalensee, Mick Silver, Yrjö Vartia, and Kam Yu for helpful comments and to the Social Sciences and Humanities Research Council of Canada for financial support.

The authors also used their scanner database on washing machines in order to replicate statistical agency sampling techniques.

What I found remarkable about the authors' results is that virtually all[1] of their calculated price indexes showed a very substantial drop in the quality-adjusted prices for washing machines, of about 6 percent to 10 percent over the year. Most of their indexes showed a drop in the aggregate price of washing machines in the 8–10 percent range. In the U.K. Retail Price Index (RPI), washing machines belong to the electrical appliances section, which includes a wide variety of appliances, including irons, toasters, refrigerators, and so on. From January 1998 to December 1998, the electrical appliances RPI component went from 98.6 to 98.0, a drop of 0.6 percentage points. Now it may be that the non-washing machine components of the electrical appliances index increased in price enough over this period to cancel out the large apparent drop in the price of washing machines, but I think that this is somewhat unlikely. Thus we have a bit of a puzzle: why do scanner data and hedonic regression studies of price change find, on average, much smaller increases in price compared to the corresponding official indexes that include the specific commodity being studied?[2] One explanation for this puzzle (if it is a puzzle) might run as follows. At some point in time, the statistical agency initiates a sample of models whose prices are to be collected until the next sample initiation period. Unless some of these models disappear, no other models will be added to the sample. Thus, what may be happening is that the market throws up new models over the period of time between sample initiations. These new models benefit from technical progress and tend to have lower prices (quality adjusted) than the models that the statistical agency is following. In theory, the producers of these outmoded models should drop their prices to match the new competition, but perhaps instead they simply stop producing these outmoded models, leaving their prices unchanged (or not dropping them enough). However, until every last model of these outmoded models is sold, the statistical agency continues to follow their price movements, which are no longer representative of the market.[3] If a model disappears, there is the possibility that the replacement model chosen by the statistical agency is not linked in at a low enough quality-adjusted price,[4] since the use of hedonic regressions is

1. The one exception was a unit value index that was the average price over all washing machines with no adjustments for the changing mix of machines. This quality-unadjusted index showed a drop of only 1 percent over the year. It is particularly interesting that Feenstra's (1995) exact hedonic approach gave much the same answers as the other approaches.

2. See Diewert (1998) for a review of the scanner data studies up to that point in time.

3. If this hypothesis is true, older models should have a tendency to have positive residuals in hedonic regressions. Berndt, Griliches, and Rappaport (1995, 264); Kokoski, Moulton, and Zieschang (1999, 155;); and Koskimäki and Vartia (2001, 4) find evidence to support this hypothesis for desktop computers, fresh vegetables, and computers, respectively.

4. Also when a model disappears, typically statistical agencies ask their price collectors to look for the model that is the closest substitute to the obsolete model, which means that the closest model is also approaching obsolescence.

not very widespread in statistical agencies. These two factors may help to explain why the hedonic regression approach tends to give lower rates of price increase in rapidly changing markets compared to the rates obtained by statistical agencies.

There is another factor that may help to explain why scanner data studies that use matched samples obtain lower rates of price increase (or higher rates of price decrease, as in the case of the washing machines) than those obtained by statistical agencies. Consider the list of models at the sample initiation period. Some of these models will turn out to be "winners" in the marketplace; that is, they offer the most quality-adjusted value.[5] Now, over time, consumers will buy increasing amounts of these winning models, but this in turn will allow the producers of these winning models to lower their prices, since their per unit output fixed costs will be lower as their markets expand. In a scanner data superlative index number computation of the aggregate market price over all models, these "winner" models that have rapid declines in price will get a higher quantity weighting over time, leading to a lower overall measure of price change than that obtained by the statistical agency, since the agency will be aggregating its sample prices using fixed weights.[6]

I do not have any substantial criticisms of the Silver and Heravi paper; I think that they have done a very fine job indeed.

Since I do not have any substantial criticisms of the paper, the question is: what should I do in the remainder of this comment? What I will do is discuss various methodological issues that the authors did not have the space to cover.[7]

Thus, in section 10.2 below, I revisit Sherwin Rosen's (1974) classic paper on hedonics in an attempt to get a much simpler model than the one that he derived. In particular, I make enough simplifying assumptions so that Rosen's very general model reduces down to the usual time series dummy variable hedonic regression model used by Silver and Heravi. The assumptions that are required to get this simple model are quite restrictive, but I hope that, in the future, other researchers will figure out ways of relaxing some of these assumptions. It should be mentioned that I take a traditional consumer demand approach to the problems involved in setting up an

5. These models should have negative residuals at the sample initiation period in a hedonic regression.

6. This point is made by Berndt and Rappaport (2001). However, it is interesting that both Silver and Heravi and Berndt, Griliches, and Rappaport (1995) find that this weighting bias was relatively low in their washing machine and computer studies in which they compared matched model superlative indexes with the results of unweighted hedonic regressions. Berndt, Griliches, and Rappaport found this weighting bias for computers to be around 0.7 percentage points per year.

7. I should mention that many of the methodology questions are discussed more fully in a companion paper that deals with television sets in the United Kingdom rather than washing machines; see Silver (1999b).

econometric framework for estimating hedonic preferences; that is, I do not attempt to model the producer supply side of the market.[8] Another major purpose of this section is to indicate why linear hedonic regression models (where the dependent variable is the model price and the time dummy enters in the regression in a linear fashion) are unlikely to be consistent with microeconomic theory.

In section 10.3, we look at the problems involved in choosing a functional form for the hedonic regression. Some of the issues considered in this section are

- a comparison between the three most commonly used functional forms for hedonic regressions;
- how hedonic regression techniques can be used in order to model the choice of package size;
- whether we should choose flexible functional forms when undertaking hedonic regressions; and
- whether we should use nonparametric functional forms.

Silver and Heravi noted that there is a connection between matched model techniques for making quality adjustments and hedonic regression techniques: essentially, the hedonic method allows information on nonmatching observations to be used, whereas information on models that suddenly appear or disappear in the marketplace must be discarded using the matched model methodology. Triplett (2001) has also considered the connection between the two approaches in an excellent survey of the hedonic regression literature. One of the most interesting results that Triplett derives is a set of conditions that will cause a hedonic regression model to give the same results as a matched model. In section 10.4, we generalize this result to cover a more general class of regression models than considered by Triplett, and we extend his results from the two-period case to the many-period case.

One of the features of the Silver and Heravi paper is their use of sales information on models as well as the usual model price and characteristics information that is used in traditional hedonic regression exercises. In section 10.5 below, we look at some of the issues involved in running hedonic regressions when sales information is available.

Section 10.6 provides some comments on Feenstra's (1995) exact hedonic price index approach, which is used by Silver and Heravi. Our tentative conclusion is that it is not really necessary to use Feenstra's approach if one is willing to make the simplifying assumptions that we make in section 10.2 below.

Section 10.7 generalizes our hedonic model presented in section 10.2 to a

---

8. Thus I am following Muellbauer's (1974, 977) example: he says that his "approach is unashamedly one-sided; only the demand side is treated. . . . Its subject matter is therefore rather different from that of the recent paper by Sherwin Rosen. The supply side and the simultaneity problems which may arise are ignored."

more general situation in which completely separate hedonic regressions are run in each period, as opposed to one big hedonic regression run over all periods in the sample.

Section 10.8 concludes.

10.2   The Theory of Hedonic Price Indexes Revisited

Hedonic regression models pragmatically regress the price of one unit of a commodity (a "model" or "box") on a function of the characteristics of the model and a time dummy variable. It is assumed that a sample of model prices can be collected for two or more time periods along with a vector of the associated model characteristics. An interesting theoretical question is whether we can provide a microeconomic interpretation for the function of characteristics on the right hand side of the regression.

Rosen (1974) in his classic paper on hedonics does this. However, his economic model turns out to be extremely complex. In this section, we will rework his model,[9] making two significant changes:

- We will assume that every consumer has the same *separable subutility function,* $f(z_1, \ldots, z_N)$, which gives the consumer the subutility $Z = f(\mathbf{z})$ from the purchase of one unit of the complex hedonic commodity that has the vector of characteristics $\mathbf{z} \equiv (z_1, \ldots, z_N)$.[10]
- The subutility that the consumer gets from consuming Z units of the hedonic commodity is combined with the consumption of X units of a composite "other" commodity to give the consumer an overall utility of $u = U^t(X, Z)$ in period t, where U^t is the period t "macro" utility function. Rosen (1974, 38) normalized the price of X to be unity. We will *not* do this; instead, we will have an explicit period t price , p^t, for one unit of the general consumption commodity X.

We start off by considering the set of X and Z combinations that can yield the consumer's period t utility level, u^t. This is the set $\{(X, Z): U^t(X, Z) = u^t\}$, which of course is the consumer's period t indifference curve over equivalent combinations of the general consumption commodity X and the hedonic commodity Z. Now solve the equation $U^t(X,Z) = u^t$ for X as a function of u^t and Z; that is, we have[11]

---

9. We used Rosen's notation, which was somewhat different from that used by Silver and Heravi.

10. We do not assume that all possible models exist in the marketplace. In fact, we will assume that only a finite set of models exists in each period. However, we do assume that the consumer has preferences over all possible models, where each model is indexed by its vector of characteristics, $\mathbf{z} = (z_1, \ldots, z_N)$. Thus each consumer will prefer a potential model with characteristics vector $\mathbf{z}^1 = (z_1^1, \ldots, z_N^1)$ over another potential model with the characteristics vector $\mathbf{z}^2 = (z_1^2, \ldots, z_N^2)$ if and only if $f(z^1) > f(\mathbf{z}^2)$.

11. If the period t indifference curve intersects both axes, then $g^t(u^t, Z)$ will only be defined for a range of nonnegative Z up to an upper bound.

(1) $$X = g^t(u^t, Z).$$

We will assume that this indifference curve slopes downward, and, in fact, we will make the stronger assumption that g^t is differentiable with respect to Z and

(2) $$\frac{\partial g^t(u^t, Z)}{\partial Z} < 0.$$

Let p^t and P^t be the prices for one unit of X and Z respectively in period t. The consumer's period t expenditure minimization problem may be defined as follows:

(3) $$\min_{X,Z} [p^t X + P^t Z : X = g^t(u^t,Z)] = \min_Z [p^t g^t(u^t,Z) + P^t Z].$$

The first-order necessary condition for Z to solve equation (3) is

(4) $$\frac{p^t \partial g^t(u^t,Z)}{\partial Z} + P^t = 0.$$

Equation (4) can now be rearranged to give the price of the hedonic aggregate P^t as a function of the period t utility level u^t and the price of general consumption p^t:

(5) $$P^t = -\frac{p^t \partial g^t(u^t, Z)}{\partial Z} > 0$$

where the inequality follows from the assumption in equation (2) above. We now interpret the right-hand side of equation (5) as the consumer's period t willingness-to-pay price function $w^t(Z, u^t, p^t)$:

(6) $$w^t(Z, u^t, p^t) \equiv -\frac{p^t \partial g^t(u^t, Z)}{\partial Z}.$$

Thus, as we travel down the consumer's period t indifference curve, for each point (indexed by Z) on this curve, equation (6) gives us the amount of money the consumer would be willing to pay *per unit of Z* in order to stay on the same indifference curve, which is indexed by the utility level u^t.

The period t willingness-to-pay value function v^t can now be defined as the product of the quantity of Z consumed times the corresponding per unit willingness-to-pay price, $w^t(Z, u^t, p^t)$:

(7) $$v^t(Z, u^t, p^t) \equiv Zw^t(Z, u^t, p^t) = -\frac{Zp^t \partial g^t(u^t, Z)}{\partial Z},$$

where the last equality follows using equation (6). The function v^t is the counterpart to Rosen's (1974, 38) value or bid function; it gives us the amount of money the consumer is willing to pay in order to consume Z units.

All of the above algebra has an interpretation that is independent of the hedonic model; it is simply an exposition of how to derive a willingness-to-pay price and value function using a consumer's preferences defined over two commodities. However, we now assume that the consumer has a separable subutility function, $f(z_1, \ldots, z_N)$, that gives the consumer the subutility $Z = f(z)$ from the purchase of one unit of the complex hedonic commodity[12] that has the vector of characteristics $z \equiv (z_1, \ldots, z_N)$. Note that we have assumed that the function f is time invariant.[13] We now assume that the consumer's period t utility function is $U^t(X, f(z))$. The above algebra on willingness to pay is still valid. In particular, our new period t willingness-to-pay price function, for a particular model with characteristics $z = (z_1, \ldots, z_n)$, is

$$(8) \qquad w^t(f(\mathbf{z}), u^t, p^t) \equiv -\frac{p^t \partial g^t(u^t, f(\mathbf{z}))}{\partial Z}.$$

Our new period t willingness-to-pay value function (which is the amount of money the consumer is willing to pay to have the services of a model with characteristics vector z) is

$$(9) \qquad v^t(f(\mathbf{z}), u^t, p^t) \equiv f(\mathbf{z}) w^t(f(\mathbf{z}), u^t, p^t) = -\frac{f(\mathbf{z}) p^t \partial g^t(u^t, f(\mathbf{z}))}{\partial Z}.$$

Now suppose that there are K^t models available to the consumer in period t, where model k sells at the per unit price of P_k^t and has the vector of characteristics $\mathbf{z_k^t} \equiv (z_{1k}^t, \ldots, z_{Nk}^t)$ for $k = 1, 2, \ldots, K^t$. If the consumer purchases a unit of model k in period t, then we can equate the model price P_k^t to the appropriate willingness-to-pay value defined by equation (9), where z is replaced by $\mathbf{z_k^t}$; that is, the following equations should hold:

$$(10) \qquad P_k^t = -\frac{f(\mathbf{z_k^t}) \, p^t \partial g^t(u^t, f(\mathbf{z_k^t}))}{\partial Z}; \quad t = 1, \ldots, T; \quad k = 1, \ldots, K^t.$$

What is the meaning of the separability assumption? Suppose the hedonic commodity is an automobile and suppose that there are only three char-

---

12. If a consumer purchases, say, two units of a model at price P that has characteristics $z_1, \ldots, z_N$, then we can model this situation by introducing an artificial model that sells at price $2P$ and has characteristics $2z_1, \ldots, 2z_N$. Thus the hedonic surface, $Z = f(z)$, consists of only the most efficient models including the artificial models.

13. We do not assume that $f(z)$ is a quasi-concave or concave function of z. In normal consumer demand theory, $f(z)$ can be assumed to be quasi-concave without loss of generality because linear budget constraints and the assumption of perfect divisibility will imply that "effective" indifference curves enclose convex sets. However, as Rosen (1974, 37–38) points out, in the case of hedonic commodities, the various characteristics cannot be untied. Moreover, perfect divisibility cannot be assumed, and not all possible combinations of characteristics will be available on the marketplace. Thus, the usual assumptions made in "normal" consumer demand theory are not satisfied in the hedonic context. Note also that although we placed a smoothness assumption on the macro functions $g^t(u, Z)$—the existence of the partial derivative $\partial g^t(u, Z)/\partial Z$—we do not place any smoothness restrictions on the hedonic subutility function $f(z)$.

acteristics: number of seats in the vehicle, fuel economy, and horsepower. The separability assumption means that the consumer can trade off these three characteristics and determine the utility of any auto with any mix of these three characteristics *independently of his or her other choices* of commodities. In particular, the utility ranking of automobile models is independent of the number of children the consumer might have or what the price of gasoline might be. Obviously, the separability assumption is not likely to be exactly satisfied in the real world, but in order to make our model tractable, we are forced to make this somewhat restrictive assumption.

Another aspect of our model needs some further explanation. We are explicitly assuming that consumers cannot purchase fractional units of each model; they can purchase only a nonnegative integer amount of each model; that is, we are explicitly assuming *indivisibilities* on the supply side of our model. Thus, in each period, there are only a finite number of models of the hedonic commodity available, so that while the consumer is assumed to have continuous preferences over all possible combinations of characteristics $(z_1, \ldots, z_N)$, in each period, only a finite number of isolated models are available on the market.

At this point, we further specialize our model. We assume that every consumer has the same hedonic subutility function[14] $f(\mathbf{z})$ and consumer i has the following linear indifference curve macro utility function in period t:

(11) $g_i^t(u_i^t, Z) \equiv -a^t Z + b_i^t u_i^t; \quad t = 1, \ldots, T; \quad i = 1, \ldots, I$

where a^t and b_i^t are positive constants. Thus for each period t and each consumer i, the period t indifference curve between combinations of X and Z is linear, with the constant slope $-a^t$ being the same for all consumers.[15] However, note that we are allowing this slope to change over time. Now differentiate equation (11) with respect to Z and substitute this partial derivative into equation (10). The resulting equations are[16]

---

14. The sameness assumption is very strong and needs some justification. This assumption is entirely analogous to the assumption that consumers have the same homothetic preferences over, say, food. Although this assumption is not justified for some purposes, for the purpose of constructing a price index for food, it suffices since we are mostly interested in capturing the substitution effects in the aggregate price of food as the relative prices of food components vary. In a similar fashion, we are interested in determining how the "average" consumer values a faster computer speed against more memory; that is, we are primarily interested in hedonic substitution effects.

15. We do not require a linear indifference curve globally but only locally over a certain range of purchases. Alternatively, we can view the linear indifference curve as providing a first-order approximation to a nonlinear indifference curve.

16. Comparing equation (12) with equation (10), it can be seen that the simplifying the assumptions in equation (11) enabled us to get rid of the terms $\partial g^t(u_i^t, f(z_k^t))/\partial Z$, which depend on individual consumer indifference curves between the hedonic commodity and other commodities. If we had individual household data on the consumption of hedonic and other commodities, then we could use normal consumer demand techniques in order to estimate the parameters that characterized these indifference curves.

(12) $\qquad P_k^t = p^t a^t f(\mathbf{z_k^t}); \quad t = 1, \ldots, T; \quad k = 1, \ldots, K^t.$

Now define the aggregate price of one unit of Z in period t as[17]

(13) $\qquad\qquad \rho_t \equiv p^t a^t; \quad t = 1, \ldots, T$

and substitute equation (13) into equation (12) in order to obtain our basic system of hedonic equations:[18]

(14) $\qquad P_k^t = \rho_t f(\mathbf{z_k^t}); \quad t = 1, \ldots, T; \quad k = 1, \ldots, K^t.$

Now all we need to do is postulate a functional form for the hedonic subutility function f and add a stochastic specification to equation (14) and we have our basic hedonic regression model. The unknown parameters in f along with the period t hedonic price parameters ρ_t can then be estimated.[19]

It is possible to generalize the above model but get the same model shown in equation (14) if we replace the composite "other" commodity X with $h(\mathbf{x})$, where $\mathbf{x}$ is a consumption vector and h is a linearly homogeneous, increasing, and concave aggregator function. Instead of equation (12), under these new assumptions, we end up with the following equations:

(15) $\qquad P_k^t = c(\mathbf{p^t})a^t f(\mathbf{z_k^t}); \quad t = 1, \ldots, T; \quad k = 1, \ldots, K^t,$

where $\mathbf{p^t}$ is now the vector of prices for the $\mathbf{x}$ commodities in period t, and c is the unit cost or expenditure function that is dual to h.[20] Now redefine ρ_t as $c(\mathbf{p^t})a^t$, and we still obtain the basic system of hedonic equation (14).

17. We have switched to subscripts from superscripts in keeping with the conventions for parameters in regression models; that is, the constants ρ_t will be regression parameters in what follows. Note also that ρ_t is the product of the price of the "other" commodity p^t times the period t slope parameter a^t. We need to allow this slope parameter to change over time in order to be able to model the demand for high-technology hedonic commodities, which have been falling in price relative to "other" commodities; that is, we think of a^t as decreasing over time for high-technology commodities.

18. Our basic model ends up being very similar to one of Muellbauer's (1974, 988–89) hedonic models; see in particular his equation (32).

19. It is possible to rework the above theory and give it a producer theory interpretation. The counterpart to the expenditure minimization problem in equation (3) is now the following profit maximization problem: $\max_{X, Z}[P^t Z - w^t X : X = g^t(k^t, Z)]$ where Z is hedonic output and P^t is a period t price for one unit of the hedonic output, w^t is the period t price of a variable input, and X is the quantity used of it, k^t is the period t quantity of a fixed factor (capital, say) and g^t is the firm's factor requirements function. Assuming that $Z = f(z)$, we end up with the following producer theory counterpart to equation (10): $P_k^t = f(z_k^t)\partial g^t(k^t, f(z_k^t))/\partial Z$. The counterpart to the assumption in equation (11) is for firm i, $g_k^i(k_i^t, Z) \equiv a^t Z - b_i^t k_i^t$, and the counterpart to equation (12) becomes $P_k^t = w^t a^t f(z_k^t)$. However, the producer theory model assumptions are not as plausible as the corresponding consumer theory model assumptions. In particular, it is not very likely that each producer will have the same period t aggregate price for a unit of variable input w^t, and it is not very likely that each firm producing in the hedonic market will have the same technology parameter a^t. However, the key assumption that will not generally be satisfied in the producer context is that each *producer is able to produce the entire array of hedonic models,* whereas, in the consumer context, it is quite plausible that each consumer has the possibility of purchasing and consuming each model.

20. Define c as $c(\mathbf{p^t}) \equiv \min_x\{\mathbf{p^t} \cdot \mathbf{x} : h(\mathbf{x}) = 1\}$ where $\mathbf{p^t} \cdot \mathbf{x}$ denotes the inner product between the vectors $\mathbf{p^t}$ and $\mathbf{x}$.

Equation (14) has one property that is likely to be present in more complex and realistic models of consumer choice. This property is that the model prices in period t are *homogeneous of degree one* in the general price level p^t. Thus, if p^t is replaced by λp^t for any $\lambda > 0$ (think of a sudden hyperinflation where λ is large), then equations (12) and (14) imply that the model prices should become λP_k^t. Note that this homogeneity property will *not* hold for the following additive hedonic model:

$$(16) \qquad P_k^t = \rho_t + f(z_k^t); \quad t = 1, \ldots, T; \quad k = 1, \ldots, K^t.$$

Thus, I would lean toward ruling out running hedonic regressions based on the linear model of equation (16) on a priori grounds. Note that hedonic models that take the logarithm of the model price P_k^t as the dependent variable will tend to be consistent with our basic hedonic equation (14), whereas linear models like equation (16) will not be consistent with the normal linear homogeneity properties implied by microeconomic theory.

We turn now to a discussion of some of the problems involved in choosing a functional form for the hedonic subutility function $f(\mathbf{z})$.[21]

10.3   Functional Form Issues

10.3.1   Frequently Used Functional Forms

The three most commonly used functional forms in the hedonic regression literature are the log-log, the semilog, and the linear.[22] We consider each in turn.

In the log-log model, the hedonic aggregator function f is defined in terms of its logarithm as

$$(17) \qquad \ln f(z_1, \ldots, z_N) \equiv \alpha_0 + \sum_{n=1}^{N} \alpha_n \ln z_n,$$

where the α_n is the unknown parameters to be estimated. If we take logarithms of both sides of equation (14), use equation (17), and add error term ε_k^t, we obtain the following hedonic regression model:

$$(18) \quad \ln P_k^t = \beta_t + \alpha_0 + \sum_{n=1}^{N} \alpha_n \ln z_{nk}^t + \varepsilon_k^t; \quad t = 1, \ldots, T; \quad k = 1, \ldots, K^t,$$

where $\beta_t \equiv \ln \rho_t$ for $t = 1, \ldots, T$. In order to identify all of the parameters, we require a normalization on the β_t and α_0. Typically, we set $\beta_1 = 0$, which is equivalent to $a^1 p^1 = 1$. If we want to impose linear homogeneity (or constant returns to scale) on the hedonic subutility function $f(z)$, we can do this by setting $\sum_{n=1}^{N} \alpha_n = 1$.

---

21. Our discussion draws heavily on Triplett (2001) and Berndt (1991, chap. 4).
22. See Berndt (1991, chap. 4) for historical references to the early use of these functional forms.

In the semilog model, the logarithm of the hedonic function $f(z)$ is defined as

$$(19) \qquad \ln f(z_1, \ldots, z_N) \equiv \alpha_0 + \sum_{n=1}^{N} \alpha_n z_n.$$

If we take logarithms of both sides of equation (14), use equation (18), and add error terms ε_k^t, we obtain the following hedonic regression model:

$$(20) \quad \ln P_k^t = \beta_t + \alpha_0 + \sum_{n=1}^{N} \alpha_n z_{nk}^t + \varepsilon_k^t; \quad t = 1, \ldots, T; \quad k = 1, \ldots, K^t,$$

where $\beta_t \equiv \ln \rho_t$ for $t = 1, \ldots, T$. Again, in order to identify all of the parameters, we require a normalization on the β_t and α_0, such as $\beta_1 = 0$, which is equivalent to $a^1 p^1 = 1$.

The semilog model has a disadvantage compared to the log-log model: it is not possible to impose constant returns to scale on the semilog hedonic function $f(z)$.[23] However, the semilog model has an advantage compared to the log-log model: the semilog model can deal with situations in which one or more characteristics z_{nk}^t are equal to zero, whereas the log-log model cannot. This is an important consideration if new characteristics come on to the market during the sample period.

In the linear model, the hedonic function $f(z)$ is a simple linear function of the characteristics

$$(21) \qquad f(z_1, \ldots, z_N) \equiv \alpha_0 + \sum_{n=1}^{N} \alpha_n z_n.$$

Substituting equation (21) into equation (14) and adding the error term ε_k^t, we obtain the following hedonic regression model:

$$(22) \quad P_k^t = \rho_t \left(\alpha_0 + \sum_{n=1}^{N} \alpha_n z_{nk}^t \right) + \varepsilon_k^t; \quad t = 1, \ldots, T; \quad k = 1, \ldots, K^t.$$

Again, in order to identify all of the parameters, we require a normalization on the ρ_t and α_n, such as $\rho_1 = 0$, which is equivalent to $a^1 p^1 = 1$. Unfortunately, equation (22) is a *nonlinear* regression model, whereas the earlier log-log and semilog models were *linear* regression models. Constant returns to scale on the linear hedonic function can be imposed by setting $\alpha_0 = 0$.

---

23. For some purposes, it is convenient to allow the hedonic utility function to be the type of utility function that is assumed in index number theory, where usually it is assumed that the utility function is homogeneous of degree one, increasing and concave. For example, if we want to use the hedonic framework to model *tied purchases* (i.e., two commodities are sold together at a single price), then the hedonic utility function becomes an ordinary utility function, $f(z_1, z_2)$, where z_1 and z_2 are the quantities of the two commodities that are in the tied package. In this situation, it may be reasonable to assume that f is homogeneous of degree one, in which case the price of a package consisting of z_1 and z_2 unit of the two commodities is $c(p_1, p_2) f(z_1, z_2)$, where $c(p_1, p_2) \equiv \min_{z, s} \{p_1 z_1 + p_2 z_2 : f(z_1, z_2) = 1\}$ is the unit cost function that is dual to the utility function f. There are many other applications in which it would be useful to allow f to be a linearly homogeneous function.

The model shown in equation (22) can also readily deal with the introduction into the marketplace of new characteristics.

It can be seen that none of the three models shown in equations (18), (20), and (22) totally dominates the other two models; each of the three models has at least one advantage over the other two.

Due to the nonlinear form of equation (22), this model has not been estimated very frequently, if at all. However, the following closely related model has been estimated countless times:

$$(23) \quad P_k^t = \rho_t + \alpha_0 + \sum_{n=1}^{N} \alpha_n z_{nk}^t + \varepsilon_k^t; \quad t = 1, \ldots, T; \quad k = 1, \ldots, K^t.$$

As was indicated in the previous section, the linear model shown in equation (23) is unlikely to be consistent with microeconomic theory, and so we cannot recommend its use.

10.3.2   Hedonic Regressions and the Problem of Package Size

For many commodities, the price declines as the volume purchased increases. How can this phenomenon be modeled using the hedonic regression framework?

Suppose that the vector of characteristics $z \equiv (z_1, \ldots, z_N)$ is a scalar, so that $N = 1$ and the single characteristic quantity z_1 is the *package size;* that is, it is the quantity of a homogeneous commodity that is contained in the package sold. In this case, it is natural to take the hedonic subutility function $f(z_1)$ to be a continuous monotonically nondecreasing function of one variable with $f(0) = 0$. We drop the subscript 1 in what follows.

A simple specification for $f(z)$ is to let it be a piecewise linear, continuous function or a *linear spline.* In the case of three linear segments, the system of estimating equation (14) would look like the following system after adding errors to equation (14): for $t = 1, \ldots, T$, we have:

$$(24) \quad P_k^t = \rho_t \alpha_1 z_k^t + \varepsilon_k^t \quad \text{if} \quad 0 \le z_k^t \le z_1^* = \rho_t [\alpha_1 z_1^* + \alpha_2 (z_k^t - z_1^*)] + \varepsilon_k^t$$

$$\text{if} \quad z_1^* \le z_k^t \le z_2^* = \rho_t [\alpha_1 z_1^* + \alpha_2 (z_2^* - z_1^*) + \alpha_3 (z_k^t - z_2^*)] + \varepsilon_k^t \quad \text{if} \quad z_2^* \le z_k^t.$$

The predetermined package sizes, z_1^* and z_2^*, where we switch from one linear segment to the next, are called break points. The unknown parameters to be estimated are $\rho_1, \ldots, \rho_T, \alpha_1, \alpha_2,$ and α_3. As usual, not all of these parameters can be identified, so it is necessary to impose a normalization such as $\rho_1 = 1$.

There are two difficulties with the system of estimating equations (24):

- The regression is nonlinear in the unknown parameters.
- The estimated coefficients $\alpha_1, \alpha_2,$ and α_3 should be nonnegative.[24] If an

---

24. Pakes (2001) argues that we should not expect our hedonic regression estimates to satisfy monotonicity restrictions based on the strategic behavior of firms as they introduce new

initial regression yields a negative α_i, then the regression can be rerun, replacing α_i with $(\alpha_i)^2$.

We turn now to a discussion of the flexibility properties of an assumed hedonic subutility function $f(\mathbf{z})$.

10.3.3 Flexibility Issues

In normal consumer demand theory, we usually ask that the functional form for the consumer's utility function (or any of its dual representations) be flexible; that is, we ask that our assumed functional form be able to approximate an arbitrary twice continuously differentiable utility function to the second order.[25] In the hedonic regression literature, this requirement that the functional form for the utility function be flexible has generally not been imposed.[26] For example, the functional forms considered in section 10.3.1 are only capable of providing a linear approximation rather than a quadratic one. The reason why flexible functional forms have not been used in the hedonic literature to a greater extent is probably due to the multicollinearity problem; that is, if we attempt to estimate a hedonic subutility function $f(z)$ that is capable of providing a second-order approximation, then it may have too many unknown parameters to be estimated accurately.[27] Nevertheless, it may be useful to consider the costs and benefits of using alternative flexible functional forms in the hedonic context.

For our first flexible functional form for $f(z)$, consider the following translog functional form (see Christensen, Jorgenson, and Lau 1975), which generalizes our earlier log-log hedonic aggregator function defined by equation (17) above:

$$(25) \qquad \ln f(z_1, \ldots, z_N) \equiv \alpha_0 + \sum_{n=1}^{N} \alpha_n \ln z_n + \frac{1}{2} \sum_{i=1}^{N} \sum_{j=1}^{N} \alpha_{ij} \ln z_i \ln z_j,$$

where the α_n and the α_{ij} are the unknown parameters to be estimated. If we take logarithms of both sides of equation (14), use equation (25), and add error term ε_k^t, we obtain the following translog hedonic regression model:

$$(26) \qquad \ln P_k^t = \beta_t + \alpha_0 + \sum_{n=1}^{N} \alpha_n \ln z_{nk}^t + \frac{1}{2} \sum_{i=1}^{N} \sum_{j=1}^{N} \alpha_{ij} \ln z_{ik}^t \ln z_{jk}^t + \varepsilon_k^t;$$

models. However, for credibility reasons, it is likely that statistical agencies will want to impose monotonicity restrictions.

25. See Diewert (1974, 127–33; 1993, 158–64) for examples of flexible functional forms.

26. An exception to this statement is the recent paper by Yu (2001). His discussion is similar to our discussion in many respects and is more general in some respects.

27. The situation in normal consumer demand theory can be more favorable to the accurate estimation of flexible functional forms because we will have an entire *system* of estimating equations in the normal context. Thus, if there are N commodities and price and quantity observations for T periods on H households, we will have $H(N-1)T$ degrees of freedom to work with in the usual systems approach to estimating consumer preferences. In the hedonic regression framework, we have $K^1 + K^2 + \ldots + K^T$ or roughly KT degrees of freedom, where K is the average number of models in each period.

$$\alpha_{ij} = \alpha_{ji}; \quad t = 1, \ldots, T; \quad k = 1, \ldots, K^t,$$

where $\beta_t \equiv \ln \rho_t$ for $t = 1, \ldots, T$. In order to identify all of the parameters, we require a normalization on the β_t and α_0. Typically, we set $\beta_1 = 0$, which is equivalent to $a^1 p^1 = 1$. If we want to impose linear homogeneity (or constant returns to scale) on the hedonic subutility function $f(z)$, we can do this by setting $\sum_{n=1}^{N} \alpha_n = 1$ and imposing the restrictions $\sum_{j=1}^{N} \alpha_{ij} = 0$ for $i = 1, \ldots,$ N. Obviously, the translog model shown in equation (26) contains the log-log model shown in equation (18) as a special case.[28]

The translog hedonic model shown in equation (26) has two nice properties:

- The right-hand side of equation (26) is linear in the unknown parameters so that linear regression techniques can be used in order to estimate the unknown parameters.
- Constant returns to scale can readily be imposed on the translog hedonic utility function $f(z)$ without destroying the flexibility of the functional form.

The main disadvantage of the translog hedonic model is that, like the log-log model, it cannot deal with the zero characteristics problem.

For our second flexible functional form, consider the following generalization of the semilog hedonic utility function in equation (19):

$$(27) \qquad \ln f(z_1, \ldots, z_N) \equiv \alpha_0 + \sum_{n=1}^{N} \alpha_n z_n + \frac{1}{2} \sum_{i=1}^{N} \sum_{j=1}^{N} \alpha_{ij} z_i z_j$$

where the α_n and the α_{ij} are the unknown parameters to be estimated. If we take logarithms of both sides of equation (14), use equation (27), and add error term ε_k^t, we obtain the following semilog quadratic hedonic regression model:

$$(28) \qquad \ln P_k^t = \beta_t + \alpha_0 + \sum_{n=1}^{N} \alpha_n z_{nk}^t + \frac{1}{2} \sum_{i=1}^{N} \sum_{j=1}^{N} \alpha_{ij} z_{ik}^t z_{jk}^t + \varepsilon_k^t;$$

$$t = 1, \ldots, T; \quad k = 1, \ldots, K^t$$

where $\beta_t \equiv \ln \rho_t$ for $t = 1, \ldots, T$. Again, in order to identify all of the parameters, we require a normalization on the β_t and α_0, such as $\beta_1 = 0$, which is equivalent to $a^1 p^1 = 1$.

The semilog quadratic model has a disadvantage compared to the translog model: it is not possible to impose constant returns to scale on the semilog quadratic hedonic function $f(z)$. Both models share the advantage of being linear in the unknown parameters. However, the semilog quadratic model has an advantage compared to the translog model: the semilog model

---

28. In view of our discussion in section 10.2, the translog $f(z)$ does not have to satisfy any curvature conditions.

can deal with situations in which one or more characteristics z_{nk}^t are equal to zero, whereas the translog model cannot. This is an important consideration if new characteristics come on to the market during the sample period.

For our third flexible functional form for the hedonic utility function $f(z)$, consider the following generalized linear functional form (see Diewert 1971).

$$(29) \qquad f(z_1, \ldots, z_N) \equiv \alpha_0 + \sum_{n=1}^{N} \alpha_n (z_n)^{1/2} + \frac{1}{2} \sum_{i=1}^{N} \sum_{j=1}^{N} \alpha_{ij} (z_i)^{1/2} (z_j)^{1/2}$$

where the α_n and the α_{ij} are the unknown parameters to be estimated. Note that equation (29) generalizes our earlier linear functional form shown in equation (21).[29] Substituting equation (29) into equation (14) and adding the error term ε_k^t, we obtain the following generalized linear hedonic regression model:

$$(30) \qquad P_k^t = \rho_t [\alpha_0 + \sum_{n=1}^{N} \alpha_n (z_{nk}^t)^{1/2} + \frac{1}{2} \sum_{i=1}^{N} \sum_{j=1}^{N} \alpha_{ij} (z_{ik}^t)^{1/2} (z_{jk}^t)^{1/2}] + \varepsilon_k^t;$$

$$t = 1, \ldots, T; \quad k = 1, \ldots, K^t.$$

As usual, in order to identify all of the parameters, we require a normalization on the ρ_t, α_n, and α_{ij} such as $\rho_1 = 0$, which is equivalent to $a^1 p^1 = 1$. Unfortunately, equation (30) is a nonlinear regression model, whereas the earlier translog and semilog quadratic models were linear regression models. Constant returns to scale on the generalized linear hedonic function can be imposed by setting $\alpha_n = 0$ for $n = 0, 1, \ldots, N$. The model in equation (22) can also readily deal with the introduction into the marketplace of new characteristics.

As was the case in section 10.3.1, none of the three flexible hedonic regression models presented in this section totally dominates the remaining two models. Equations (26) and (28) have the advantage of being linear regression models, whereas equation (30) is nonlinear. Equation (26) cannot deal very well with the introduction of new characteristics during the sample period, whereas equations (28) and (30) can. Constant returns to scale in characteristics can readily be imposed in equations (26) and (30), whereas this is not possible with equation (28). Thus each of the three models has two favorable characteristics and one unfavorable characteristic.

10.3.4 Nonparametric Functional Forms

It is possible to address the functional form problem in a nonparametric manner using generalized dummy variable techniques.[30]

---

29. Let the α_n and α_{ij} for $i \neq j$ all equal 0 in equation (29) and we obtain equation (21).

30. The material that we are going to present in this section is essentially equivalent to what statisticians call an analysis of variance model (a two-way layout with interaction terms); see chapter 4 in Scheffé (1959).

Suppose that there are only two characteristics that are important for the models on the market during periods $t = 1, \ldots, T$. Suppose further that there are only I configurations of the first characteristic and J configurations of the second characteristic during the sample period, where I and J are integers greater than 1.[31] Suppose further that in period t we have K_{ij}^t observations that have first characteristic in group i and second characteristic in group j. Denote the kth observation in period t in this i, j grouping as $z_{ijk}^t = (z_{1ijk}^t, z_{2ijk}^t)$. For this configuration of characteristics, we define the corresponding hedonic utility as follows:

$$(31) \quad f(z_{ijk}^t) \equiv \alpha_{ij}; \quad t = 1, \ldots, T; \ i = 1, \ldots, I; \ j = 1, \ldots, J; \ k = 1, \ldots, K_{ij}^t.$$

Let P_{ijk}^t denote the period t price for observation k that has model characteristics that put it in the i, j grouping of models. Substituting equation (31) into equation (14) and adding the error term ε_{ijk}^t leads to the following (nonlinear) generalized dummy variable hedonic regression model:

$$(32) \qquad\qquad P_{ijk}^t = \rho_t \alpha_{ij} + \varepsilon_{ijk}^t;$$

$$t = 1, \ldots, T; \quad i = 1, \ldots, I; \quad j = 1, \ldots, J; \quad k = 1, \ldots, K_{ij}^t.$$

As usual, not all of the parameters ρ_t for $t = 1, \ldots, T$ and α_{ij} for $i = 1, \ldots, I$ and $j = 1, \ldots, J$ can be identified and so it is necessary to impose a normalization on the parameters like $\rho_1 = 1$.

The hedonic regression model shown in equation (32) is nonlinear. However, in this case, we can reparameterize our theoretical model so that we end up with a linear regression model. Suppose that we take logarithms of both sides of equation (31). Then, defining $\ln \alpha_{ij}$ as γ_{ij}, we have

$$(33) \qquad\qquad \ln f(z_{ijk}^t) \equiv \gamma_{ij};$$

$$t = 1, \ldots, T; \quad i = 1, \ldots, I; \quad j = 1, \ldots, J; \quad k = 1, \ldots, K_{ij}^t.$$

Substituting equation (33) into equation (14) after taking logarithms of both sides of equation (14) and adding the error term ε_{ijk}^t leads to the following linear generalized dummy variable hedonic regression model:

$$(34) \qquad\qquad \ln P_{ijk}^t = \beta_t + \gamma_{ij} + \varepsilon_{ijk}^t;$$

$$t = 1, \ldots, T; \quad i = 1, \ldots, I; \quad j = 1, \ldots, J; \quad k = 1, \ldots, K_{ij}^t,$$

where $\beta_t \equiv \ln \rho_t$ for $t = 1, \ldots, T$. As usual, not all of the parameters β_t for $t = 1, \ldots, T$ and γ_{ij} for $i = 1, \ldots, I$ and $j = 1, \ldots, J$ can be identified, and

---

31. Alternatively, we *group* observations so that all models having a quantity z_1 of the first characteristic between 0 and z_1^* are in group 1, all models having a quantity z_1 of the first characteristic between z_1^* and z_2^* are in group 2, . . . , and all models having a quantity z_1 of the first characteristic between z_{I-1}^* and z_I^* are in group I. We do a similar grouping of the models for the second characteristic. Thus any model k in each period falls into one of IJ discrete groupings of models.

so it is necessary to impose a normalization on the parameters like $\beta_1 = 0$, which corresponds to $\rho_1 = 1$.

Which of the two generalized dummy variable hedonic regression model equations (32) or (34) is "better"? Obviously, they both have exactly the same economic content, but of course, the stochastic specifications for the two models differ. Hence, we would have to look at the statistical properties of the residuals in the two models to determine which is better.[32] However, without looking at residuals, the linear regression model equation (34) will be much easier to implement than the nonlinear model equation (32), especially for large data sets.

The linear generalized dummy variable hedonic regression model equations (32) and (34) have two major advantages over the traditional flexible functional form models listed in section 10.3.3:

- The dummy variable models shown in equations (32) and (34) are completely nonparametric and hence are much more flexible than traditional flexible functional forms.
- The dummy variable models can easily accommodate discrete characteristic spaces.

However, the dummy variable hedonic regressions also have some disadvantages:

- There can be an enormous number of parameters to estimate, particularly if there are a large number of distinct characteristics.
- If we attempt to reduce the number of parameters by having fewer class intervals for each characteristic, we will introduce more variance into our estimated coefficients.
- Different investigators will choose differing numbers of classification cells; that is, differing dummy variable hedonic specifications made by different hedonic operators will choose differing Is and Js, leading to a lack of reproducibility in the models.[33]
- If j is held constant, then the α_{ij} and γ_{ij} coefficients should increase (or at least not decrease) as i increases from 1 to I.[34] Similarly, if i is held constant, then the α_{ij} and γ_{ij} coefficients should increase (or at least not decrease) as j increases from 1 to J. The regression model equations

32. There is another consideration involved in choosing between equations (32) and (34). The parameters that we are most interested in are the ρ_i, not their logarithms, the β_i. However, as Berndt (1991, 127) noted, "explaining variations in the natural logarithm of price is not the same as explaining variations in price." Thus, Silver and Heravi and Triplett (2001) both note that the antilog of the least squares estimator for β_i will not be an unbiased estimator of ρ_i under the usual stochastic specification, and they cite Goldberger (1968) for a method of correcting this bias. Koskimäki and Vartia (2001, 15) also deal with this problem. These considerations would lead one to favor estimating equation (32) rather than equation (34).

33. The reproducibility issue is very important for statistical agencies.

34. We follow the usual convention that individual characteristics are defined in such a way that a larger quantity of any characteristic yields a larger utility to the consumer.

(32) and (34) ignore these restrictions, and it may be difficult to impose them.[35]

Nevertheless, I believe that these generalized dummy variable hedonic regression techniques look very promising. These models, along with other nonparametric models, deserve a serious look by applied researchers.

10.4   Hedonic Regressions and Traditional Methods for Quality Adjustment

Silver and Heravi demonstrated how traditional matched model techniques for making quality adjustments can be reinterpreted in the context of hedonic regression models. Triplett (2001) and Koskimäki and Vartia (2001, 9) also have some results along these lines. In this section, we review two of Triplett's results.

Suppose that the hedonic regression equation (14) holds in period t and we want to compare the quality of model 1 with that of model 2. Then it can be seen that the first two of equations (14) imply that the utility of variety 2 relative to variety 1 is

$$(35) \qquad \frac{f(\mathbf{z}_2^t)}{f(\mathbf{z}_1^t)} = \frac{(P_2^t/\rho_t)}{(P_1^t/\rho_t)} = \frac{P_2^t}{P_1^t};$$

that is, the utility or intrinsic value to the consumer of model 2 relative to the utility of model 1 is just the price ratio, P_2^t/P_1^t. Thus, in this case, a quality adjustment that falls out of a hedonic regression model is equivalent to a "traditional" statistical agency quality adjustment technique, which is to use the *observed price ratio* of the two commodities in the same period as an indicator of the relative quality of the two commodities.[36]

In a second example showing how traditional statistical agency quality adjustment techniques can be related to hedonic regressions, Triplett (2001) showed that under certain conditions, the usual matched model method for calculating an overall measure of price change going from one period to the next (using geometric means) was identical to the results obtained using a hedonic regression model.[37] We now look at Triplett's result in a somewhat more general framework.

Recall our standard hedonic regression model equation (14) above. Suppose further that the logarithm of $f(z)$ is a linear function in J unknown parameters, $\alpha_1, \ldots, \alpha_J$; that is, we have

$$(36) \quad \ln f(\mathbf{z}_k^t) \equiv \alpha_1 + \sum_{j=2}^{J} x_j(\mathbf{z}_k^t)\, \alpha_j; \quad t = 1, \ldots, T; \quad k = 1, \ldots, K^t$$

---

35. Note that there are comparable monotonicity restrictions that the continuous hedonic models listed in sections 10.3.1 and 10.3.3 should also satisfy, and it will be difficult to impose these conditions for these models as well.

36. We are ignoring the error terms in the hedonic regressions in making this argument.

37. Koskimäki and Vartia (2001, 9) state a similar more general result, which is very similar to the result that we obtain below.

where the functions $x_j(z_k^t)$ are known. Note that we have assumed that $x_1(\mathbf{z_k^t})$ $\equiv 1$; that is, we have assumed that the functional form for $\ln f(z)$ has a constant term in it. Now take logarithms of both sides of equation (14), substitute equation (36) into these logged equations, and add the stochastic term ε_k^t to obtain the following system of regression equations:

$$(37) \quad \ln P_k^t = \beta_t + \alpha_1 + \sum_{j=2}^{J} x_j(z_k^t)\alpha_j + \varepsilon_k^t; \quad t = 1, \ldots, T; \quad k = 1, \ldots, K^t$$

where, as usual, we have defined $\beta_t \equiv \ln \rho_t$ for $t = 1, \ldots, T$. A normalization is required in order to identify all of the parameters in equation (37). We choose the normalization $\rho_1 = 1$, which translates into the following normalization:

$$(38) \qquad\qquad\qquad \beta_1 = 0.$$

Using matrix notation, we can write the period t equations in equation (37) as

$$(39) \qquad\qquad \mathbf{y^t} = \mathbf{1^t}\,\beta_t + \mathbf{X^t}\,\alpha + \varepsilon^t; \quad t = 1, \ldots, T$$

where $\mathbf{y^t} \equiv [\ln P_1^t, \ldots, \ln P_{K^t}^t]'$ is a period t vector of logarithms of model prices (where $'$ denotes the transpose of the preceding vector), β_t is the scalar parameter $\ln \rho_t$, $\mathbf{1^t}$ is a column vector consisting of K^t ones, $\mathbf{X^t}$ is a K^t by J matrix of exogenous variables, $\alpha \equiv [\alpha_1, \ldots, \alpha_J]'$ is a column vector of parameters that determine the hedonic subutility function, and $\varepsilon^t \equiv [\varepsilon_1^t, \ldots, \varepsilon_{K^t}^t]'$ is a column vector of period t disturbances. Now rewrite the system of equations (39) in stacked form as

$$(40) \qquad\qquad\qquad \mathbf{y} = \mathbf{W}\gamma + \varepsilon$$

where $\mathbf{y}' \equiv [y^{1\prime}, \ldots, y^{T\prime}]$, $\varepsilon' \equiv [\varepsilon^{1\prime}, \ldots, \varepsilon^{T\prime}]$, $\gamma' \equiv [\beta_2, \beta_3, \ldots, \beta_T, \alpha_1, \ldots, \alpha_J]$, and the matrix $\mathbf{W}$ is a somewhat complicated matrix that is constructed using the column vectors $\mathbf{1^t}$ and the K^t by J matrices $\mathbf{X^t}$ for $t = 1, \ldots, T$.[38]

The vector of least squares estimators for the components of γ is

$$(41) \qquad\qquad\qquad \gamma^* \equiv (\mathbf{W'W})^{-1}\mathbf{W'y}.$$

Define the vector of least squares residuals $\mathbf{e}$ by

$$(42) \qquad\qquad \mathbf{e} \equiv \mathbf{y} - \mathbf{W}\gamma^* = \mathbf{y} - \mathbf{W}(\mathbf{W'W})^{-1}\mathbf{W'y}.$$

It is well known that the vector of least squares residuals $\mathbf{e}$ is orthogonal to the columns of $\mathbf{W}$; that is, we have

$$(43) \qquad \mathbf{W'e} = \mathbf{W'}[\mathbf{y} - \mathbf{W}(\mathbf{W'W})^{-1}\mathbf{W'y}] = \mathbf{W'y} - \mathbf{W'y} = \mathbf{0}_{T-1+J}'$$

where $\mathbf{0}_{T-1+J}$ is a vector of zeros of dimension $T - 1 + J$. Now premultiply both sides of $\mathbf{e} \equiv \mathbf{y} - \mathbf{W}\gamma^*$ by the transposes of the first $T - 1$ columns of $\mathbf{W}$. Using equation (43), we obtain the following equations:

38. Note that we used the normalization shown in equation (38) in order to eliminate the parameter β_1 from the parameter vector γ.

(44) $0 = \mathbf{1}^{t\prime}\mathbf{y}^t - \mathbf{1}^{t\prime}\mathbf{1}^t\boldsymbol{\beta}_t^* - \mathbf{1}^{t\prime}\mathbf{X}^t\boldsymbol{\alpha}^*;$ $t = 2, 3, \ldots, T$

where $\boldsymbol{\beta}_t^*$ is the least squares estimator for β_t and $\boldsymbol{\alpha}^* \equiv [\alpha_1^*, \ldots, \alpha_J^*]'$ is the vector of least squares estimators for $\boldsymbol{\alpha} \equiv [\alpha_1, \ldots, \alpha_J]'$. Now column T in $\mathbf{W}$ corresponds to the constant term α_1 and hence is a vector of ones. Premultiply both sides of equation (42) by this column, and by using equation (43), we obtain the following equation:

(45) $0 = \sum_{t=1}^{T}\mathbf{1}^{t\prime}\mathbf{y}^t - \sum_{t=2}^{T}\mathbf{1}^{t\prime}\mathbf{1}^t\boldsymbol{\beta}_t^* - \sum_{t=2}^{T}\mathbf{1}^{t\prime}\mathbf{X}^t\boldsymbol{\alpha}^*.$

Substitute equation (44) into equation (45) in order to obtain the following equation:

(46) $\mathbf{1}^{1\prime}\mathbf{y}^1 = \mathbf{1}^{1\prime}\mathbf{X}^1\boldsymbol{\alpha}^*.$

Noting that $\mathbf{1}^{t\prime}\mathbf{1}^t = K^t$ (the number of model prices collected in period t), we can rewrite equation (44) as follows:

(47) $\boldsymbol{\beta}_t^* = \dfrac{1}{K^t}\sum_{k=1}^{Kt}y_k^t - \dfrac{1}{K^t}\mathbf{1}^{t\prime}\mathbf{X}^t\boldsymbol{\alpha}^*;$ $t = 2, 3, \ldots, T.$

The $\boldsymbol{\beta}_t^*$ defined by the right-hand side of equation (47) can be given an interesting interpretation as an arithmetic average of the vector of quality-adjusted period t logarithmic prices $y^t - X^t\boldsymbol{\alpha}^*$. However, a very interesting result emerges from using equations (46) and (47) if we assume that the sample of model prices is *matched* for all T periods (so that in each period, exactly the same models are priced). If the sample is matched, then each $\mathbf{X}^t$ matrix is exactly the same (and all K^t equal a common sample size K). If the common $\mathbf{X}^t$ matrix is the K by $T - 1 + J$ matrix $\mathbf{X}$, then using equations (46) and (47) gives us the following formula for $\boldsymbol{\beta}_t^*$:

(48) $\boldsymbol{\beta}_t^* = \dfrac{1}{K}\sum_{k=1}^{K}y_k^t - \dfrac{1}{K}\sum_{k=1}^{K}y_k^1;$ $t = 2, 3, \ldots, T.$

Thus, in the matched sample case, taking the exponential of $\boldsymbol{\beta}_t^*$ as our estimator of ρ_t and recalling that $y_k^t \equiv \ln P_k^t$, we have

(49) $\rho_t^* \equiv \dfrac{\left(\prod_{k=1}^{K}P_k^t\right)^{1/K}}{\left(\prod_{k=1}^{K}P_k^1\right)^{1/K}} = \left[\prod_{k=1}^{K}\left(\dfrac{P_k^t}{P_k^1}\right)\right]^{1/K};$ $t = 2, 3, \ldots, T;$

that is, the hedonic regression approach in the matched model case gives exactly the same result for the overall measure of price change going from period 1 to t as what we would get by taking the geometric mean of the matched model price relatives for the two periods under consideration. Triplett indicated that this result was true for the case $T = 2$ and assuming that f was the log-log hedonic utility function described in section 10.3.1.

I think that the Silver and Heravi paper and the Triplett (2001) manual are both very useful in that they indicate very explicitly that traditional matched model techniques for quality adjustment can be quite closely related to the results of a hedonic regression approach. This correspondence between the two methods should help to demystify hedonic methods to some extent. Furthermore, as stressed by Silver and Heravi and Triplett, the statistical advantage in using the hedonic regression approach over the matched model approach increases as the lack of matching increases; that is, the hedonic technique uses all of the model information between the two periods under consideration, whereas the matched model approach can by definition use only the information on models that are present in the marketplace during both periods.

10.5   Hedonic Regressions and the Use of Quantity Weights

The hedonic regression study by Silver and Heravi is relatively unusual in that they not only had data on the prices and characteristics of washing machines sold in the United Kingdom in 1998, but they also had data on the sales of each model. The question that we want to address in this section is: how exactly should quantity data be used in a hedonic regression study?

We start out by considering a very simple model in which there is only one variety in the market during period t, but we have K price observations, P_k^t, on this model during period t, along with the corresponding quantity sold at each of these prices, q_k^t. Under these assumptions, our basic hedonic regression equation (14) for period t become

$$(50) \qquad P_k^t = \rho_t f(\mathbf{z_k^t}) = \rho_t; \quad k = 1, 2, \ldots, K$$

where we can set $f(\mathbf{z_k^t}) = 1$, since all K transactions are on exactly the same model.

From viewing equation (50), we see that ρ_t can be interpreted as some sort of average of the K period t observed transaction prices, P_k^t. The *relative frequency* at which the price P_k^t is observed in the marketplace during period t can be defined as

$$(51) \qquad \theta_k^t \equiv \frac{q_k^t}{\sum_{i=1}^{K} q_i^t}.$$

The expected value of the discrete distribution of period t prices is

$$(52) \qquad \rho_t^* \equiv \sum_{k=1}^{K} \theta_k^t P_k^t = \frac{\sum_{k=1}^{K} q_k^t P_k^t}{\sum_{i=1}^{K} q_k^t} \qquad \text{using equation (51).}$$

Note that the far right-hand side of equation (52) is a unit value. Thus quantity data on the sales of a model can be used to form a *representative average price* for the model in a period, and that representative price is an overall sales weighted average price for the model or a unit value.[39]

How can we derive the unit value estimator for the representative period t price ρ_t using a hedonic regression? There are at least two ways of doing this.

Look at equation k in the system of price equations (50). Since there are q_k^t sales at this price in period t, we could repeat the equation $P_k^t = \rho_t$ a number of times, q_k^t times to be exact. Let $\mathbf{1}_k$ be a vector of dimension q_k^t. Then, using vector notation, we could write rewrite the system of equations (50), repeating each price P_k^t the appropriate number of times that a transaction took place in period t at that price, as follows:

$$(53) \qquad \mathbf{1}_k P_k^t = \mathbf{1}_k \rho_t; \quad k = 1, 2, \ldots, K.$$

Now add error terms to each of equations (53) and calculate the least squares estimator for the resulting linear regression. This estimator turns out to be the unit value estimator ρ_t^* defined by equation (52).

The second way of deriving the unit value estimator for the representative period t price ρ_t using a hedonic regression is to multiply both sides of equation k in equations (50) by the square root of the quantity of model k sold in period t, $(q_k^t)^{1/2}$ and then add an error term, ε_k^t. We obtain the following system of equations:

$$(54) \qquad (q_k^t)^{1/2} P_k^t = (q_k^t)^{1/2} \rho_t + \varepsilon_k^t; \quad k = 1, 2, \ldots, K.$$

Note that the left-hand side variables in equation (54) are known. Now treat equation (54) as a linear regression with the unknown parameter ρ_t to be estimated. It can be verified that the least squares estimator for ρ_t is the unit value estimator ρ_t^* defined by equation (52).[40] Thus we can use a weighted least squares hedonic regression as a way of obtaining a more representative average model price for period t.

The above discussion may help to explain why Silver and Heravi used sales-weighted hedonic regressions in their regression models. The use of quantity-weighted regressions will diminish the influence of unrepresenta-

---

39. One could think of other ways of weighting the prices P_k^t. For example, we could use the expenditure share for all models sold at the price P_k^t during period t equal to $s_k^t \equiv P_k^t q_k^t / \sum_{i=1}^{K} P_i^t q_i^t$ for $k = 1, \ldots, K$ as a weighting factor for P_k^t. The representative period t average price using these weights becomes $\rho_t^{**} \equiv \sum_{k=1}^{K} s_k^t P_k^t$. Note that if we divide this price into the value of period t transactions, $\sum_{i=1}^{K} P_i^t q_i^t$, we obtain the corresponding quantity estimator, $(\sum_{i=1}^{K} P_i^t q_i^{t2} / \sum_{k=1}^{K} (P_k^t)^2 q_k^t$, which is not easy to interpret. On the other hand, if we divide the unit value estimator of aggregate period t price, ρ_t^* defined by equation (53), into the value of period t transactions, $\sum_{i=1}^{K} P_i^t q_i^t$, we obtain the simple sum of quantities transacted during period t, $\sum_{k=1}^{K} q_k^t$, as the corresponding quantity estimator. The use of unit values to aggregate over transactions pertaining to a homogeneous commodity within a period to obtain a single representative price and quantity for the period under consideration was advocated by Walsh (1901, 96; 1921, 88), Davies (1924, 187), and Diewert (1995, 20–24).

40. Berndt (1991, 127) presents a similar econometric argument justifying the weighted least squares model in equation (54) in terms of a model involving heteroskedastic variances for the untransformed model.

tive prices[41] and should lead to a better measure of central tendency for the distribution of quality-adjusted model prices; that is, the use of quantity weights should lead to more accurate estimates of the ρ_t parameters in equation (14).

10.6   Exact Hedonic Indexes

Silver and Heravi spend a considerable amount of effort in evaluating two of Feenstra's (1995) bounds to an exact hedonic index. In section 10.2, we made some rather strong simplifying assumptions on the structure of consumer preferences, assumptions that were rather different from those made by Feenstra. In this section, we look at the implications of our assumptions for constructing exact hedonic indexes.[42]

Recall our basic hedonic equation (14) again: $P_k^t = \rho_t f(\mathbf{z_k^t})$ for $t = 1, \ldots,$ T and $k = 1, \ldots, K^t$. We assume that the price P_k^t is the average price for all the models of type k sold in period t, and we let q_k^t be the number of units sold of model k in period t. Recall that the number of models in the marketplace during period t was K^t.

In this section, we will assume that there are K models in the marketplace over all T periods in our sample period. If a particular model k is not sold at all during period t, then we will assume that P_k^t and q_k^t are both zero. With these conventions in mind, the total value of consumer purchases during period t is equal to

$$(55) \qquad \sum_{k=1}^{K} P_k^t q_k^t = \sum_{k=1}^{K} \rho_t f(\mathbf{z_k}) q_k^t; \quad t = 1, \ldots, T.$$

The hedonic subutility function f has done all of the hard work in our model in converting the utility yielded by model k in period t into a "standard" utility $f(\mathbf{z_k})$ that is cardinally comparable across models. Then, for each model type k, we just multiply by the total number of units sold in period t, q_k^t, in order to obtain the total period t market quantity of the hedonic commodity, Q_t, say. Thus we have[43]

$$(56) \qquad Q_t \equiv \sum_{k=1}^{K} f(\mathbf{z_k}) q_k^t; \quad t = 1, \ldots, T.$$

The corresponding aggregate price for the hedonic commodity is ρ_t. Thus, in our highly simplified model, the aggregate exact period t price and

---

41. Griliches (1961; 1971, 5) made this observation many years ago.

42. Our assumptions are also quite different from those made by Fixler and Zieschang (1992), who took yet another approach to the construction of exact hedonic indexes.

43. This is a counterpart to the quantity index defined by Muellbauer (1974, 988) in one of his hedonic models; see his equation (30). Of course, treating ρ_t as a price for the hedonic commodity quantity aggregate defined by equation (57) can be justified by appealing to Hicks's (1946, 312–13) Aggregation Theorem, since the model prices $P_k^t = \rho_t f(z_k)$ all have the common factor of proportionality, ρ_t.

quantity for the hedonic commodity is ρ_t and Q_t defined by equation (56), which can readily be calculated, provided we have estimated the parameters in the hedonic regression equation (14) and provided that we have data on quantities sold during each period, the q_k^t.[44]

Once ρ_t and Q_t have been determined for $t = 1, \ldots, T$, then these aggregate price and quantity estimates for the hedonic commodity can be combined with the aggregate prices and quantities of nonhedonic commodities using normal index number theory.

We conclude this section by discussing one other aspect of the Silver and Heravi paper: namely, their use of matched model superlative indexes. A matched model price index for the hedonic commodity between periods t and $t + 1$ is constructed as follows. Let $I(t, t + 1)$ be the set of models k that are sold in both periods t and $t + 1$. Then the matched model Laspeyres and Paasche price indexes going from period t to period $t + 1$, P_L and P_P, respectively, are

$$(57) \qquad P_L^t \equiv \frac{\sum_{k \in I(t,t+1)} P_k^{t+1} q_k^t}{\sum_{k \in I(t,t+1)} P_t^k q_t^k} ;$$

$$(58) \qquad P_P^t \equiv \frac{\sum_{k \in I(t,t+1)} P_k^{t+1} q_k^{t+1}}{\sum_{k \in I(t,t+1)} P_k^t q_k^{t+1}}.$$

In the above matched model indexes, we compare only models that were sold in both periods under consideration. Thus we are throwing away some of our price information (on prices that were present in only one of the two periods). The matched model superlative Fisher Ideal price index going from period t to $t + 1$ is $P_F^t \equiv (P_L^t P_P^t)^{1/2}$; that is, it is the square root of the product of the matched model Laspeyres and Paasche indexes. Now it is possible to compare the matched model Fisher measure of price change going from period t to $t + 1$, P_F^t, to the corresponding measure of aggregate price change that we could get from our hedonic model, which is $\rho_t + 1/\rho_t$. We would hope that these measures of price change would be quite similar, particularly if the proportion of matched models is high for each period (as it is for the Silver and Heravi data). Silver and Heravi make this comparison for their hedonic models and find that the matched Fisher ends up about 2 percent lower for their U.K. washing machine data for 1998 compared to the hedonic models. It seems quite possible that this relatively large discrepancy could be due to the fact that the Silver and Heravi hedonic func-

---

44. If we have data for the q_k^t, then it is best to run sales-weighted regressions, as was discussed in the previous section. If we do not have complete market data on individual model sales but we do have total sales in each period, then we can run the hedonic regression model in equation (14) using a sample of model prices and then divide period t sales by our estimated ρ_t parameter in order to obtain an estimator for Q_t.

tional forms are only capable of providing a first-order approximation to arbitrary hedonic preferences, whereas the superlative indexes can provide a
second-order approximation, and thus substitution effects are bigger for the
superlative matched model price indexes.[45]

Thus an important implication of the Silver and Heravi paper emerges: it
is not necessary to undertake a hedonic study if the following conditions
hold:

- Detailed data on the price and quantity sold of each model are available.
- Between consecutive periods, the number of new and disappearing
  models is small, so that matching is relatively large.

We turn now to our final topic: a discussion of the additional problems
that occur if we relax the assumption that the hedonic subutility function
$f(z)$ is time invariant.

10.7   Changing Tastes and the Hedonic Utility Function

Several economists have suggested that there are good reasons why the
hedonic utility function $f(z)$ introduced in section 10.2 may depend on time
t.[46] In this section, we consider what changes need to be made to our basic
hedonic model outlined in section 10.2 if we replace our time invariant hedonic utility function $f(\mathbf{z})$ by one that depends on time, say $f^t(\mathbf{z})$.[47]

If we replace our old $f(\mathbf{z})$ in section 10.2 with $f^t(\mathbf{z})$ and make the same
other assumptions as we made there, we find that instead of our old equation (14), we now end up with the following equations.

$$(59) \qquad P_k^t = \rho_t f^t(\mathbf{z}_k^t); \quad t = 1, \ldots, T; k = 1, \ldots, K^t.$$

Up to this point, nothing much has changed from our previous 10.2
model that assumed a time-invariant hedonic subutility function $f(\mathbf{z})$, except that our new subutility function $f^t(\mathbf{z})$ will naturally have some time-

---

45. In favor of this interpretation is the fact that the matched model Laspeyres index was
roughly the same as the hedonic indexes computed by Silver and Heravi. However, there are
other factors at work, and this "explanation" may well be incomplete.

46. More precisely, Silver (1999a) and Pakes (2001) make very strong arguments (based on
industrial organization theory) that the hedonic regression coefficients that are estimated using period t data should depend on t. Griliches (1961) also argued that the hedonic regression
coefficients were unlikely to be constant over periods.

47. Before we proceed to our general discussion of time-dependent hedonic aggregator functions $f^t(\mathbf{z})$, we note a simple method originally due to Court (1939) and Griliches (1961) for allowing for time dependence that does not require any new methodology: simply use the previous time-independent methodology, but restrict the regression to two consecutive periods.
This will give us a measure of overall price change for the hedonic commodity going from period t to $t + 1$, say. Then run another hedonic regression using only the data for periods $t + 1$
and $t + 2$, which will give us a measure of price change going from period $t + 1$ to $t + 2$. And
so on.

dependent parameters in it. However, there is another major change that is associated with our new model, equation (59). Recall that in the time-invariant models discussed in section 10.3, we required only *one* normalization on the parameters, like $\rho_1 = 1$. In our new time-dependent framework, we require a normalization on the parameters in equation (59) for each period; that is, we now require T normalizations on the parameters instead of one in order to identify the ρ_t and the α parameters that characterize $f^t(\mathbf{z})$.

The simplest way to obtain the required normalizations is to make the hypothesis that the utility that *a reference model* with characteristics $\mathbf{z}^* \equiv (z_1^*, \ldots, z_N^*)$ gives the consumer the *same utility* across all periods in the sample. If we choose this reference utility level to be unity, then this hypothesis translates into the following restrictions on the parameters of $f^t(\mathbf{z})$:

$$(60) \qquad\qquad f^t(\mathbf{z}^*) = 1; \quad t = 1, \ldots, T.$$

Equations (59) and (60) now become our basic system of hedonic regression equations and replace our old system, equation (14) plus the normalization $\rho_1 = 1$.[48]

How should we choose the functional form for $f^t(\mathbf{z})$? Obviously, there are many possibilities. However, the simplest possibility (and it is the one chosen by Silver and Heravi) is to allow the α_n parameters that we defined for various functional forms in section 10.3 to depend on t; that is, the α_n defined in section 10.3 is replaced by α_n^t, and each period t parameter set is estimated by a hedonic regression that uses *only* the price and characteristics data for period t.[49] We leave to the reader the details involved in reworking our old algebra in section 10.3, changing the α_n into α_n^t and imposing the normalizations in equation (60) in place of our old normalization, $\rho_1 = 1$.

So far, so good. It seems that we have greatly generalized our old "static" hedonic model at virtually no cost. However, there is a hidden cost. Our new system of regression equations, (59) and (60), is in general *not invariant to the choice of the reference model with characteristics vector* $\mathbf{z}^*$. Thus if we choose a different reference model with characteristics vector $\mathbf{z}^{**} \neq \mathbf{z}^*$ and replace the normalizations in equation (60) with

---

48. If we define the imputed price of the reference model in period t as P^{t*}, it can be seen using equations (60) and (61) that $P^{t*} = \rho_t$ for $t = 1, \ldots, T$. Now in actual practice, when unrestricted period t hedonic regressions are run in isolation, researchers omit the time dummy and just regress, say, $\ln P_k^t$ on $\ln f^t(z_k^t)$, where the right-hand-side regression variables have a constant term. Then the researcher estimates the period t aggregate price of the hedonic commodity as $\rho^{t*} \equiv f^t(\mathbf{z}^*)$ where $\mathbf{z}^*$ is a conveniently chosen vector of reference characteristics. This procedure is equivalent to our time dummy procedure using the normalizations shown in equation (61).

49. If quantity sales data are available, then we recommend the weighted regression approach explained in section 10.5; recall equations (55). Also, in this case, if models are sold at more than one price in any given period, then we could weight each distinct price by its sales at that price or simply aggregate over sales of the specific model k in period t and let P_k^t be the unit value price over all of these sales. In what follows, we assume that the second alternative is chosen.

(61) $$f^t(\mathbf{z}^{**}) = 1; \quad t = 1, \ldots, T.$$

then in general, the new estimates for the aggregate hedonic commodity prices ρ_t will change. Thus the cost of assuming a time-dependent hedonic utility function is a lack of invariance in the relative prices of the aggregate hedonic commodity over time to our utility function normalization equations (60) or (61).

This lack of invariance in our estimated ρ_t need not be a problem for statistical agencies, provided that we can agree on a "reasonable" choice for the reference model that is characterized by the characteristics vector $\mathbf{z}^*$, since the important factor for the agency is to obtain "reasonable" and reproducible estimates for the aggregate hedonic commodity prices. Based on some discussion of this problem in Silver (1999b, 47), a preliminary suggestion is that we take $\mathbf{z}^*$ to be the sales-weighted average vector of characteristics of models that appeared during the sample period:

(62) $$\mathbf{z}^* \equiv \frac{\sum_{k=1}^{K} \sum_{t=1}^{T} q_k^t \mathbf{z_k}}{\sum_{k=1}^{K} \sum_{t=1}^{T} q_k^t},$$

where we have reverted to the notation used in section 10.6; that is, K is the total number of distinct models that we sold in the market over all T periods in our sample, and q_k^t is the number of models that have the vector of characteristics $\mathbf{z_k}$ that were sold in period t.[50]

Thus, once we pick functional forms for the $f^t(\mathbf{z})$ and add stochastic terms to equation (59), equations (60) and (61) and definition (62) completely specify our new hedonic regression framework. Of course, we still recommend that quantity weights (if available) be used in the econometric estimation for reasons explained in section 10.5; recall equation (54).

However, if the number of time periods in our sample T is large, then there is a danger that the overall characteristics vector $\mathbf{z}^*$ defined by equation (62) may not be very representative for any one or two consecutive periods. Thus we now suggest a different method of normalizing or making comparable the time dependent hedonic utility functions $f^t(\mathbf{z})$ that will deal with this lack of representativity problem. For each time period t, define $\mathbf{z}^{t*}$ to be the sales-weighted average vector of characteristics of models that appeared during period t:

(63) $$\mathbf{z}^{t*} \equiv \frac{\sum_{k=1}^{K} q_k^t \mathbf{z_k}}{\sum_{k=1}^{K} q_k^t}; \quad t = 1, \ldots, T.$$

Recall our basic hedonic regression equation (59), $P_k^t = \rho_t f^t(\mathbf{z_k^t})$. Now make the following normalizations:

---

50. If quantity information on sales of models, q_k^t, is not available, then define $\mathbf{z}^*$ as an unweighted arithmetic mean of the z_k.

(64) $$\rho_t = 1; \quad t = 1, \ldots, T.$$

Assuming that the parameters of the period t hedonic utility functions $f^t(\mathbf{z})$ have been estimated, we can now define the period t to $t + 1$ Laspeyres-, Paasche-,[51] and Fisher-type hedonic price indexes, respectively, as follows:

(65) $$P_L^{t,t+1} \equiv \frac{f^{t+1}(\mathbf{z}^{t*})}{f^t(\mathbf{z}^{t*})}; \quad t = 1, \ldots, T-1;$$

(66) $$P_P^{t,t+1} \equiv \frac{f^{t+1}(\mathbf{z}^{t+1*})}{f^t(\mathbf{z}^{t+1*})}; \quad t = 1, \ldots, T-1;$$

(67) $$P_F^{t,t+1} \equiv (P_L^{t,t+1} P_P^{t,t+1})^{1/2}; \quad t = 1, \ldots, T-1.$$

The Fisher-type hedonic price index is our preferred index. It can be seen that the Laspeyres and Paasche indexes defined by equations (65) and (66) can be quite closely related to Feenstra's upper and lower bounding indexes to his true index (and this superlative exact hedonic methodology is used by Silver and Heravi), depending on what functional form for f^t is chosen.

Once the parameters that characterize the time-dependent hedonic utility functions $f^t(\mathbf{z})$ have been estimated along with the associated aggregate period t hedonic commodity prices ρ_t,[52] then we can define period t aggregate demand for the hedonic commodity by[53]

(68) $$Q_t \equiv \sum_{k=1}^{K} f^t(\mathbf{z}_k) q_k^t; \quad t = 1, \ldots, T.$$

The above model is our suggested *direct method* for forming exact aggregate period t prices and quantities, ρ_t and Q_t, for the hedonic commodity.

It is possible to use the outputs of hedonic regressions in another, more indirect way, along with normal index number theory, in order to construct aggregate price and quantity indexes for the hedonic commodity.[54] Recall equations (57) and (58) in the previous section, which defined the matched model Laspeyres and Paasche price indexes over hedonic models going from period t to $t + 1$. The problem with these indexes is that they throw

---

51. Berndt, Griliches, and Rappaport (1995, 262–63) and Berndt and Rappaport (2001) define the Laspeyres- and Paasche-type hedonic indexes in this way. However, the basic idea dates back to Griliches (1971, 59) and Dhrymes (1971, 111–12). Note that equations (66) and (67) break down if the vector of characteristics in period t is totally different from the vector of characteristics in period $t + 1$. Similarly, problems can arise if some characteristics are zero in one period and nonzero in another period; recall the log of zero problem discussed in section 10.3 above.

52. In our second method, in which we set the ρ_t equal to unity, define $\rho_1 = 1$ and $\rho_t + 1 = \rho_t P_F^{t,t+1}$ or $t = 1, 2, \ldots, T-1$ where the Fisher-type hedonic chain index $P_F^{t,t+1}$ is defined by equation (68). In this second method, once the aggregate prices ρ_t have been determined, we obtain the aggregate quantities Q_t as the deflated values, $\sum_{k=1}^{K} P_k^t q_k^t / \rho_t$, rather than using equations (69).

53. If quantity weights are not available, then we cannot compute Q_t.

54. See Moulton (1996, 170) for an exposition of these methods.

away information on models that are sold in only one of the two periods under consideration. One way of using this discarded information is to use the hedonic regressions in order to *impute* the missing prices.[55]

Suppose that model k was either unavailable or not sold in period t (so that $q_k^t = 0$) but that it was sold during period $t + 1$ (so that P_k^{t+1} and q_k^{t+1} are positive). The problem is that we have no price P_k^t for this model in period t, when it was not sold. However, for period $t + 1$, our hedonic regression equation for this model is the following equation (neglecting the error term):

$$(69) \qquad P_k^{t+1} = \rho_{t+1} f^{t+1}(\mathbf{z_k}).$$

Now we can use the estimated period $t + 1$ hedonic utility function f^{t+1} and the estimated period t aggregate price for the hedonic commodity, ρ_t, in order to define an imputed price for model k in period t as follows:

$$(70) \qquad P_k^{t*} \equiv \rho_t f^{t+1}(\mathbf{z_k}) = \rho_t \left(\frac{P_k^{t+1}}{\rho_{t+1}} \right) \text{ using } (69) = \left(\frac{\rho_t}{\rho_{t+1}} \right) P_k^{t+1}.$$

Thus the imputed price for model k in period t, P_k^{t*}, is equal to the observed model k price in period $t + 1$, P_k^{t+1}, times the reciprocal of the estimated rate of overall change in the price of the hedonic commodity going from period t to $t + 1$, (ρ_t/ρ_t+1).

Now suppose that model k sold in period t (so that P_k^t and q_k^t are positive) but that model k either disappeared or was not sold in period $t + 1$ (so that P_k^{t+1} is 0). The problem is that we have no price P_k^{t+1} for this model in period $t + 1$, when it was not sold. However, for period t, our hedonic regression equation for model k is the following equation (neglecting the error term):

$$(71) \qquad P_k^t = \rho_t f^t(\mathbf{z_k}).$$

Now we can use the estimated period t hedonic utility function f^t and the estimated period $t + 1$ aggregate price for the hedonic commodity, ρ_{t+1}, in order to define an imputed price for model k in period $t + 1$ as follows:

$$(72) \qquad P_k^{t+1*} \equiv \rho_{t+1} f^t(\mathbf{z_k}) = \rho_{t+1} \left(\frac{P_k^t}{\rho_t} \right) \text{ using } (71) = \left(\frac{\rho_{t+1}}{\rho_t} \right) P_k^t.$$

Thus the imputed price for model k in period $t + 1$, P_k^{t+1*}, is equal to the observed model k price in period t, P_k^t, times the estimated rate of overall change in the price of the hedonic commodity going from period t to $t + 1$, (ρ_{t+1}/ρ_t).[56]

Now we can use the imputed prices defined by equations (70) and (72) in order to obtain price and quantity information on *all* models that were pres-

---

55. See Armknecht and Maitland-Smith (1999) for a nice review of imputation methods.

56. I believe that the approach outlined here is consistent with the approach used by Silver and Heravi to generate imputed prices for missing models. Triplett (2001) outlines other approaches.

ent in one or both of periods t and $t + 1$ and hence we can calculate the following completely matched Laspeyres and Paasche price indexes:

$$(73) \qquad P_L^t \equiv \frac{\sum_{k=1}^{K} P_k^{t+1} q_k^t}{\sum_{k=1}^{K} P_k^t q_k^t};$$

$$(74) \qquad P_P^t \equiv \frac{\sum_{k=1}^{K} P_k^{t+1} q_k^{t+1}}{\sum_{k=1}^{K} P_k^t q_k^{t+1}}$$

where we use the imputed price P_k^{t*} defined by equation (70) in place of the missing P_k^t if $q_k^t = 0$ but q_k^{t+1} is positive and we use the imputed price P_k^{t+1*} defined by equation (72) in place of the missing P_k^{t+1} if $q_k^{t+1} = 0$ but q_k^t is positive.[57] Comparing our new Laspeyres and Paasche price indexes defined by equation (73) and (74) to our old matched model Laspeyres and Paasche price indexes defined by equations (57) and (58), it can be seen that our new indexes do not throw away any relevant price and quantity information and hence can be expected to be more "accurate" in some sense.

10.8   Conclusion

A number of tentative conclusions can be drawn from the Silver and Heravi (2001) paper and this discussion of it:

- Traditional superlative index number techniques that aggregate up model data based on matched models can give more or less the same answer as a hedonic approach, provided that the amount of matching is relatively large.
- Linear hedonic regressions are difficult to justify on theoretical grounds (at least based on our highly simplified approach to hedonic regressions) and hence should be avoided if possible.
- If completely unconstrained hedonic regressions are run on the data of each period, then care should be taken in the choice of a reference model that allows us to compare the utility of the hedonic commodity across periods. In particular, the estimates of aggregate price change in the hedonic commodity will in general not be invariant to the choice of the reference model.
- The use of quantity weights in hedonic regression models is strongly recommended if possible.
- Under certain conditions, if models are matched in each period, then the hedonic regression approach will give exactly the same answer as a

---

57. Obviously, if both q_k^t and q_k^{t+1} are zero, then we do not require estimators for the missing prices P_k^t and P_k^{t+1} in order to compute the Laspeyres and Paasche indexes defined by equations (74) and (75).

traditional statistical agency approach to the calculation of an elementary index.

- We have not achieved a consensus on exactly what the "best practice" hedonic regression specification should be, but flexible functional form considerations should probably be a factor in the discussion of this problem.

References

Armknecht, P. A., and F. Maitland-Smith. 1999. Price imputation and other techniques for dealing with missing observations, seasonality, and quality change in price indices. In *Proceedings of the measurement of inflation conference,* ed. M. Silver and D. Fenwick, 25–49. London: Office for National Statistics.

Berndt, E. R. 1991. *The practice of econometrics: Classic and contemporary.* Reading, Mass.: Addison-Wesley.

Berndt, E. R., Z. Griliches, and N. J. Rappaport. 1995. Econometric estimates of price indexes for personal computers in the 1990's. *Journal of Econometrics* 68:243–68.

Berndt, E. R., and N. J. Rappaport. 2001. Price and quality of desktop and mobile personal computers: A quarter century historical overview. *The American Economic Review* 91 (2): 268–73.

Christensen, L. R., D. W. Jorgenson, and L. J. Lau. 1975. Transcendental logarithmic utility functions. *American Economic Review* 65:367–83.

Court, A. T. 1939. Hedonic price indexes with automotive examples. In *The dynamics of automobile demand,* 99–117. New York: General Motors Corporation.

Davies, G. R. 1924. The problem of a standard index number formula. *Journal of the American Statistical Association* 19:180–88.

Dhrymes, P. J. 1971. Price and quality changes in consumer capital goods: An empirical study. In *Price indexes and quality change,* ed. Z. Griliches, 88–149. Cambridge, Mass.: Harvard University Press.

Diewert, W. E. 1971. An application of the shephard duality theorem: A generalized Leontief production function. *Journal of Political Economy* 79:481–507.

———. 1974. Applications of duality theory. In *Frontiers of quantitative economics,* vol. 2, ed. M. D. Intriligator and D. A. Kendrick, 106–71. Amsterdam: North-Holland.

———. 1993. Duality approaches to microeconomic theory. In *Essays in index number theory,* vol. 1, ed W. E. Diewert and A. O. Nakamura, 105–75. Amsterdam: North-Holland.

———. 1995. Axiomatic and economic approaches to elementary price indexes. Discussion Paper 95-01. Vancouver, Canada: University of British Columbia, Department of Economics. Available at [http://web.arts.ubc.ca/econ/diewert/hmpgdie.htm].

———. 1998. Index number issues in the Consumer Price Index. *The Journal of Economic Perspectives* 12:47–58.

Feenstra, R. C. 1995. Exact hedonic price indices. *Review of Economics and Statistics* 77:634–54.

Fixler, D., and K. D. Zieschang. 1992. Incorporating ancillary measures of process and quality change into a superlative productivity index. *The Journal of Productivity Analysis* 2:245–67.

Goldberger, A. A. 1968. The interpretation and estimation of Cobb-Douglas functions. *Econometrica* 35:464–72.

Griliches, Z. 1961. Hedonic price indexes for automobiles: An econometric analysis of quality change. In *Price indexes and quality change,* ed. Z. Griliches, 55–87. Cambridge, Mass.: Harvard University Press.

———. 1971. Introduction: Hedonic price indexes revisited. In *Price indexes and quality change,* ed. Z. Griliches, 3–15. Cambridge, Mass.: Harvard University Press.

Hicks, J. R. 1946. *Value and capital.* 2d ed. Oxford, U.K.: Clarendon Press.

Kokoski, M. F., B. R. Moulton, and K. D. Zieschang. 1999. Interarea price comparisons for heterogeneous goods and several levels of commodity aggregation. In *International and interarea comparisons of income, output, and prices,* Studies in Income and Wealth, vol. 61, ed. A. Heston and R. E. Lipsey, 123–66. Chicago: University of Chicago Press.

Koskimäki, T., and Y. Vartia. 2001. Beyond matched pairs and Griliches-type hedonic methods for controlling quality changes in CPI sub-indices. Paper presented at the sixth Ottawa Group Meeting. 2–6 April, Canberra, Australia.

Muellbauer, J. 1974. Household production theory, quality, and the "hedonic technique." *The American Economic Review* 64 (6): 977–94.

Moulton, B. 1996. Bias in the Consumer Price Index: What is the evidence? *Journal of Economic Perspectives* 10 (4): 139–77.

Pakes, A. 2001. Some notes on hedonic price indices, with an application to PCs. Paper presented at the NBER Productivity Program Meeting. 16 March, Cambridge, Massachusetts.

Rosen, S. 1974. Hedonic prices and implicit markets: Product differentiation in pure competition. *Journal of Political Economy* 82 (1): 34–55.

Scheffé, H. 1959. *The analysis of variance.* New York: John Wiley and Sons.

Silver, M. 1995. Elementary aggregates, micro-indices, and scanner data: Some issues in the compilation of consumer prices. *Review of Income and Wealth* 41:427–38.

———. 1999a. Bias in the compilation of consumer price indices when different models of an item coexist. In *Proceedings of the fourth meeting of the International Working Group on Price Indices,* ed. W. Lane, 21–37. Washington, D.C.: Bureau of Labor Statistics.

———. 1999b. An evaluation of the use of hedonic regressions for basic components of consumer price indices. *The Review of Income and Wealth* 45 (1): 41–56.

Triplett, J. 2001. *Handbook on quality adjustment of price indexes for information and communication technology products.* Paris: Organization for Economic Cooperation and Development. Forthcoming.

Walsh, C. M. 1901. *The measurement of general exchange value.* New York: Macmillan and Company.

———. 1921. *The problem of estimation.* London: P. S. King and Son.

Yu, K. 2001. Trends in Internet access prices in Canada. Paper presented at the sixth Ottawa Group Meeting. 2–6 April, Canberra, Australia.

Price Index Estimation Using Price Imputation for Unsold Items

Ralph Bradley

11.1 Introduction

Although scanner price quotes and expenditures have great promise in improving the Consumer Price Index (CPI), their use has introduced new problems. One major problem confronting the Bureau of Labor Statistics (BLS) is the treatment of an item that experiences no purchases during a particular time period. Either a price can be explicitly imputed for this item or it can be implicitly imputed by ignoring it in the construction of the price index. This paper examines and compares different imputation methods. Indexes are then constructed using these various imputation methods using price and expenditure data from scanner sales of cereal in the New York area.

In scanner databases, when a particular item in a particular outlet does not sell in a certain time period, it is not possible to determine if this non-sale was the result of no inventories or of no consumer demand for the product, perhaps because the price was too high. Currently, under the BLS manual sampling system, if an item is still on the outlet shelf and experiences no purchase, the "list" price displayed on the shelf is sampled because the data collector can still observe the price on the shelf. In the scanner databases, when an item is not sold, it is not even possible to get a "list" price. Therefore, missing prices can be a result of at least one of two events in scanner data, but only one event in the current manual sampling system of the CPI.

Ralph Bradley is an economist at the Price and Index Number Research Division in the U.S. Bureau of Labor Statistics.

The author is grateful to Eva Sierminska for assistance and to David Richardson, Robert C. Feenstra, Eduardo Ley, and Matthew Shapiro for useful comments. The views expressed in this paper are solely those of the author and do not reflect either the policies or procedures of the U.S. Bureau of Labor Statistics.

Imputation of missing prices can be done implicitly or explicitly. Implicit imputation occurs when the missing item is ignored.[1] For example, similar items can be grouped together in such a way that the groups are large enough so that there is always at least one item sold in each group. One would calculate unit values of only the sold items in the groups and then compute a price index using the unit values. The reason that this is an implicit imputation method is that there is an *implied* imputation of the prices of the nonpurchased item with its group unit value. Explicit imputation involves the direct replacement of a missing price with an estimated price.

There is a rich literature on imputation of missing data. Little and Rubin (1987) provide a thorough method for imputing random variables that are "missing at random." Under these conditions, the probability that a random variable is missing is independent of the random variable itself, although one could use other exogenous variables to generate a replacement random variable whose distribution well approximates the distribution of the missing variable. Unfortunately, it is not possible to assume that the probability of a missing price is independent of its level. Therefore, an unbiased statistical imputation of prices needs to account for these selection effects.

Armknecht and Maitland-Smith (1999) and Feenstra and Diewert (2000) discuss alternative imputation methods for missing prices in the construction of price indexes. In their studies, missing prices are not necessarily the result of a nonsale. Seasonality, erratic reporting, and replacement with newer models are cited as possible causes. Feenstra and Diewert evaluate the alternatives in their study by their ability to both minimize the erratic movement in the price index and still incorporate all available information. This contrasts with the goal of Little and Rubin (1987), for whom the replacement variable should have a statistical distribution that closely approximates the distribution of the missing variable. The methods in this paper include the unit value approach, the carry forward approach, and the current BLS approach, as well as an economic approach that uses a combination of micro-theory and the methods of Little and Rubin. The reason that these methods are studied is that some are easy to implement but do not estimate the welfare effects of nonsales, whereas the economic approach is more difficult to implement and can be prone to specification and measurement error. Using the database that currently generates the BLS scanner cereal index for New York, I generate indexes for each of these methods and compare the results of the easier methods to the difficult ones. All of the methods except for the unit value approach produce indexes that are close in magnitude even though their pairwise differences are statistically significant.

---

1. Armknecht and Maitland-Smith (1999) discuss implicit and explicit imputation in great detail.

This study is organized as follows. Section 11.2 describes the various imputation methods that will be examined in this paper. Section 11.3 describes the cereal scanner data set, and finally section 11.4 describes the results of computing price indexes for cereal in New York using the alternative indexes imputation methods described in section 11.2.

11.2 Imputation Methods

11.2.1 Unit Values

Perhaps the easiest method from a computational standpoint is grouping items so that at least one item within each group is purchased and then calculating a unit value for each group. At a second-stage level, the "all-items" price index is computed from the group unit values. This grouping does not necessarily need to be across items within a time period, but can group across time periods. Hausman (1996) uses the unit value approach to get his elementary prices.

Suppose that there are G groups of goods. Then the unit value, UV_g, for the gth group with N_g items is

$$UV_g = \frac{\sum_{i=1}^{N_g} p_i q_i}{\sum_{i=1}^{N_g} q_i},$$

where p_i and q_i are, respectively, the price and quantity sold of item i. Since this is a quantity-weighted average, UV_g is not a sufficient statistic if q_i is also a function of p_i.

Although computationally simple, using unit values is still controversial. Diewert (1995) recommends using unit values, yet he does not show that the unit value index will "closely" approximate a true price index. In response to Diewert's article, Balk (1998) investigates the sufficient conditions for an index using unit values to be an appropriate price index. One of three independent criteria must be satisfied: (a) there is no variance in price within the group; (b) all the products within the group are perfect substitutes; (c) the group has a Leontieff cost function. However, when none of these conditions is satisfied, it is not clear how closely the unit value approximates the true price index, because these conditions are sufficient but not necessary.

Since unit values implicitly impute the missing prices, if items within a group are not perfect substitutes or complements but are differentiated, then the imputed price is based on quality characteristics that are not necessarily embodied in the product.

11.2.2 Bureau of Labor Statistics Method

Currently, when BLS collects its monthly sample of prices and an item in the sample is missing, the agency does a combined implicit and explicit imputation of the missing price. In the first month that an item is missing, the price of the missing item is ignored and the resulting price index is calculated by ignoring the item. If the item continues to be missing after the first month, then the BLS staff selects an item that is similar to the missing one and is available for sale and uses its price to impute a price for the missing item.

To describe this imputation adjustment fully, I give a simple example. Suppose in period s, item h and item i are available for sale, and both items have similar characteristics. If item h disappears in period $s + 1$, then the month-to-month index is computed by dropping the price of the missing item. This is an implicit imputation, in which the imputed price of the missing item is merely the previous price times the month-to-month index.

If the item is still missing in $s + 2$, the imputed prices, $\hat{p}_h^{s+1}$ and $\hat{p}_h^{s+2}$ for the index from period $s + 1$ to $s + 2$, are

$$\hat{p}_h^{s+1} = \hat{p}_h^{s+1} \frac{p_h^s}{p_i^s},$$

$$\hat{p}_h^{s+2} = \hat{p}_h^{s+2} \frac{p_h^s}{p_i^s}.$$

This is an explicit imputation. However, it is based on the implicit assumption that the consumer will buy this replacement item and that there is no welfare loss from the disappearance of the item.

As mentioned previously, if an item is available for sale in an outlet, its list price is still used in the index. However, one cannot observe the list price of unsold items in the scanner data set.

11.2.3   Carry-Forward Imputation

Missing prices can be explicitly imputed by "carrying forward" the last recorded price. Like the unit value, this is computationally simple, and it does not require the grouping of items as in the unit value approach. As Armknecht and Maitland-Smith (1999) point out, this method can produce abrupt changes in the index when the item reappears. Additionally, if the list or market price does not equal the imputed carry-forward price, then the index could be biased.

However, the carry-forward approach has certain advantages over the unit value approach. The explicit imputation is done with the price of the same item and therefore with the same quality characteristic. However, if the time period, itself, is an important characteristic, then this imputation approach suffers the same disadvantage of the unit value approach since the time characteristic embodied in the price differs from the true time characteristic.

It should be self-evident that if nonsold items were offered at a price greater than the carry-forward price, then using the carry-forward price could generate a bias in the price index. However, in these cases the carry-forward price could be greater than the price that makes the quantity demanded exactly equal to zero. For example, if there is a deeply discounted sale one week and consumers buy enough to supply themselves for over a week, in the second week there could be no sales at the deeply discounted price because consumers are saturated with a large inventory.[2]

11.2.4   An Economic Approach to Imputation

Unlike the methods of Little and Rubin (1987), the methods that are discussed above are not designed with the intent of generating a replacement random variable whose distribution closely approximates the distribution of the missing variable. The method in this section attempts to adapt the methods of Little and Rubin so that the imputed price method accounts not only for the expected value of the missing variable but also for the variance. If the imputed random variable has the same expectation as the missing random variable, but a different variance, then when these imputed values are used to compute regression parameters or are plugged into nonlinear functions, there can be resulting biases. Finally, when prices are missing one needs to account for the possibility that these prices are not missing at random but are missing because of their underlying value.

Fortunately, there is enough information in scanner databases to impute an estimate of the "reservation" or virtual price so that this imputed price estimate has a distribution that closely approximates the distribution of the true reservation price. This is the price that will make the quantity demanded equal to zero. To describe this method, I denote the $\mathbf{k}$ commodity vector as x with the associated price vector as $\mathbf{p}$. The consumer problem is typically

$$(1) \qquad \lim_{x} U(x)$$

$$s.t. \ \mathbf{p}x \leq y$$

$$x \geq 0$$

where $U(x)$ is the direct utility function with the standard regularity conditions. Let λ and γ be the Lagrangian multiplier for the first and second constraint, respectively. If the "desired" quantity for the ith good is negative, the first-order condition at the bound of $x_i = 0$ is then

$$(2) \qquad U_i(x)\big|_{x_i=0} - \lambda p_i + \gamma = 0,$$

where the subscript on U denotes the derivative of the ith item. The virtual price is then $U_i(x)\big|_{x_i} = 0/\lambda$. Although the "desired" $\{x_i^* = [x_i : U(x) - \lambda p_i = 0]\}$, is negative, we observe x_i is exactly zero. If the market price was $U_i(x)\big|_{x_i=0}/\lambda$ then the quantity demanded would be exactly zero. Letting π_i

---

2. Feenstra and Shapiro discuss this issue in chapter 5 in this volume.

denote the virtual or "reservation" price, the first-order conditions or tangency conditions are restated as

$$(3) \qquad\qquad U_i(x)\big|_{x_i=0} - \lambda\pi_i = 0.$$

The role of the virtual price can be displayed graphically using a $k = 2$ example. In figure 11.1, the market price line is MM and the "desired" quantities are x_1^* and x_2^*. However, this solution violates the nonnegativity constraint, since $x_1^* < 0$. Therefore, there is a corner solution at x_2, and there are no sales of good 1. The indifference curve U represents the equilibrium utility and is lower than U', which could be reached if there is no nonnegativity constraint. Therefore, the shadow price of this nonnegativity constraint is $U' - U$. The slope of the price line MM is the ratio $-p_1/p_2$. The price line RR is tangent to U at the equilibrium quantities of $(0, x_2)$. The slope of the price line RR is $-\pi_1/p_2$. If the market price for good 1 had been π_1, the consumer would have reached the same utility that she does under the constrained problem. It is necessary that $\pi_1 \leq p_1$.

If we knew the virtual prices in the scanner data sets, then we could correctly account for the effects of a missing price quote that was either the result of no inventory or of a market price that was "too high." In either case, the virtual price would satisfy condition (c), and if we knew the functional

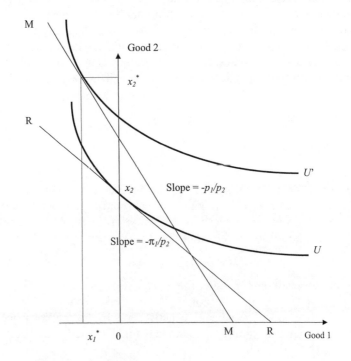

Fig. 11.1   A boundary condition

form of the consumer's utility function, we could use these virtual prices along with the prices of the purchased items to construct a true cost-of-living index. Additionally, we do not need to observe the "list" prices of the nonsold items because they would not be relevant in the construction of a cost of living index.

Unfortunately, one does not observe the virtual price. Instead, a demand system must be estimated, and, using the parameters of the estimated demand system and the prices of the purchased goods, one can impute an estimate of the virtual price. This method has been used in studies that attempt to determine the welfare effects in the introduction of new goods (see Hausman 1996 and Feenstra 1994, 1997). In this study, the indirect utility function is the "stochastic" translog:[3]

$$H(v; \alpha, \beta, \varepsilon) = -\sum_{i=1}^{k} \alpha_i v_i - \frac{1}{2}\sum_{i=1}^{k}\sum_{j=1}^{k} \beta_{ij} v_i v_j + \sum_{i=1}^{k} \varepsilon_i v_i$$

where $v_i = \ln(p_i/y)$ and ε_i is a mean zero random variable. The following homogeneity constraints are imposed: $\sum_{i=1}^{k}\alpha_i = 1$, $\sum_{j=1}^{k}\beta_{ij} = 0$, $\forall i$. Using these constraints and Roy's Identity, and not imposing the nonnegativity constraint for the quantities, we get the "desired" share equations for the ith share:

(4)
$$w_i^* = \alpha_i + \sum_{j=1}^{k} \beta_{ij} v_j + \varepsilon_i$$

However, suppose that for the first good $w_1^* < 0$. Then the observed shares $\{w_i\}_{i=1}^{k}$ will not equal the "desired" shares $\{w_i^*\}_{i=1}^{k}$, $w_1 = 0$, and $\sum_{i=1}^{k} w_i = 1$. Suppose further that $k = 3$, $w_2 > 0$, and $w_3 > 0$. Then the system of equations becomes

$$\pi_1 = -\frac{1}{\beta_{11}}(\alpha_1 + \beta_{12} v_2 + \beta_{13} v_3 + \varepsilon_1)$$

$$w_2 = \alpha_2 + \beta_{21}\pi_1 + \beta_{22} v_2 + \beta_{23} v_3 + \varepsilon_2$$

$$w_3 = \alpha_3 + \beta_{31}\pi_1 + \beta_{32} v_2 + \beta_{23} v_3 + \varepsilon_3$$

In order to impute π_1, we need to estimate the parameters of this demand system. Since v_1 is not observable, the resulting model is truncated rather than censored. In this example, the structural equation for the second good is

$$w_2 = \alpha_2 - \frac{\beta_{21}}{\beta_{11}}\alpha_1 + \left(\beta_{22} - \frac{\beta_{12}\beta_{21}}{\beta_{11}}\right)v_2 + \left(\beta_{23} - \frac{\beta_{13}\beta_{21}}{\beta_{11}}\right)v_3 + \tilde{\varepsilon}_2,$$

where

---

3. The superlative BLS price will have a Törnqvist functional form, and I posit the translog aggregator since this is the aggregator that makes the Törnqvist exact.

$$\tilde{\varepsilon}_2 = \varepsilon_2 - \frac{\beta_{21}}{\beta_{11}}\varepsilon_1$$

The parameter estimation in this example requires the accounting of "selection effects" because the following event has occurred:

(5) $\tilde{\varepsilon}_2 > -\left[\alpha_2 - \frac{\beta_{21}}{\beta_{11}}\alpha_1 + \left(\beta_{22} - \frac{\beta_{12}\beta_{21}}{\beta_{11}}\right)v_2 + \left(\beta_{23} - \frac{\beta_{13}\beta_{21}}{\beta_{11}}\right)v_3\right].$

This event is denoted as A_2, and A_3 is the event that the third good is purchased. Therefore, the following holds:

$$E(w_2 \mid A_2, A_3, v_2, v_3) = \alpha_2 + -\frac{\beta_{21}}{\beta_{11}}\alpha_1 + \left(\beta_{22} - \frac{\beta_{12}\beta_{21}}{\beta_{11}}\right)v_2$$

$$+ \left(\beta_{23} - \frac{\beta_{13}\beta_{21}}{\beta_{11}}\right)v_3 + E(\tilde{\varepsilon}_2 \mid A_2, A_3)$$

Since $E(\tilde{\varepsilon}_2 \mid A_2, A_3)$ is a function of the observed v_2, and v_3, and since the residuals across the equations are not independent (since each one will now contain ε_1), the regressors are now correlated with the residual. Therefore, the econometric estimation of the share equations cannot be solely done by nonlinear least squares estimation. It is these selection effects that make price imputation more difficult than the imputation in a "new goods" problem in which the time period of introduction is exogenous and therefore selection effects need not be incorporated. The appendix describes the estimation method used in this study in order to get the parameters of the demand system.

Once the parameters of the demand system have been estimated, it might be tempting to impute the virtual price $\hat{\pi}_1$ by

(6) $$\hat{\pi}_1 = -\frac{1}{\hat{\beta}_{11}}(\hat{\alpha}_1 + \hat{\beta}_{12}v_2 + \hat{\beta}_{13}v_3).$$

$\hat{\beta}_i$ denotes the parameter estimate of β_i. While $\mathrm{plim}(\hat{\pi}_1) = E(\pi_1)$, the variance of the imputed virtual price, $\hat{\pi}_1$, will be smaller than variance of the actual virtual price, π_1. One needs to account for the variance that comes from both the residual and the parameter estimates. The appendix describes this imputation method in greater detail.

11.3   The Cereal Scanner Data Set

The data set used in this study is the source data set that the BLS has used to construct its real time New York Cereal Index, which is described in the Richardson article of this publication. It contains the price and quantity sold for the supermarket outlets for New York City and its surrounding counties. Most large grocery chains, price clubs, and drugstores use scanner systems to monitor their inventory, to store prices, and to retrieve these stored prices when items pass through the checkout line. Each item has a twelve-digit bar code or Universal Product Code (UPC). It is the UPC that distinguishes the different items that are sold in an outlet. Different digits in the UPC are reserved to identify specific characteristics. For instance, there are five digits used to identify the manufacturer. These digits are assigned to the manufacturer by the Uniform Code Council. Another five digits are used by the manufacturer to identify each distinct product that is produced. Each new item or change in an existing item requires the issuing of a new UPC code.

When an item goes through the checkout line, the cash register scans the UPC code of the item, retrieves a price, and then records the sale on a computer tape or disk. From these records, one can find the weekly sales and prices for each bar-coded item in a grocery store. The outlet managers can use this information to monitor the turnover of the items on their shelves and make adjustments to improve their sales margins.

Even for a highly specified "item-area" such as cereal in New York, these data sets are extremely large. For instance, one month of data for New York cereal contains more observations than the entire data set that the BLS uses within a year. Because of this vast size, there is a need to establish a hierarchy. Figure 11.2 outlines the hierarchy for cereal. At the top level, the module identifies broad category type (ready-to-eat vs. hot cereal). At the next level is the brand name. Sometimes a brand name is the proprietary trademark of a firm (e.g., Cheerios) and other times it is not (e.g., Raisin Bran). At the lowest level is the UPC, each specific product having a unique UPC.

Table 11.1 lists the frequency of at least one unsold item for eight major brands over the 181-week period in the scanner data set. Except for Mini Wheats and Total, there is at least a 20 percent chance that for a given week that there will be at least one unsold UPC. It is evident that this probability increases with the number of UPCs within a brand. Although the probability of a nonsale is 20 percent for a particular brand, for every week in the data set used in this study, there are at least three nonsales.

In this study, when I compute indexes using the unit value approach, I group the UPCs by brand and then compute a unit value for each brand. I can do this since in this data set there is always at least one item within a brand that has strictly positive sales. I also investigate whether the items within a brand satisfy the Balk's criteria for a unit value index.

Even within brands and among outlets, there is evidence of product differentiation. The graphs in figure 11.3 plot the range of each week's prices for the top-selling UPCs in New York at different stores.[4] It is evident that the outlet differentiates the product, since consumers do not purchase only

4. These are prices per ounce.

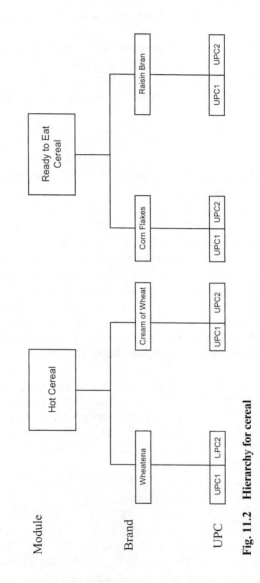

Fig. 11.2 Hierarchy for cereal

Table 11.1   **The Frequency of Unsold Items by Brand**

Brand	% of periods with Unsold Item	Number of Items (UPCs) within Brand
Cheerios	20.1	5
Corn Flakes	27.6	7
Raisin Bran	28.6	5
Rice Krispies	24.8	3
Honey Nut Cheerios	12.8	4
Frosted Flakes	33.1	7
Total	18.2	3
Mini Wheats	4.1	2

at the outlet offering the lowest price. Although Reinsdorf (1993) found evidence of outlet substitution bias, it seems clear that outlets are not perfect substitutes. Notice that the minimum price in general fluctuates more than the maximum price. The reason is that different stores put these items on sale at different times, and the percent reduction of the sale price varies across store. Most often the minimum price is a sale price.

When a brand has several UPCs assigned to it, it is usually the box size that distinguishes the two UPCs within the same brand. Conventional wisdom might conclude that box size is an "immaterial" characteristic. However, I find evidence to the contrary. I select three of the larger-selling brands and select two UPCs for each brand. The only characteristic that differentiates the two UPCs is box size. For each store, I subtract the price of the larger box from the price of the smaller box and then average these differences across stores. The results are listed in table 11.2, and the null hypothesis that the two prices are equal is always rejected. Therefore, we observe that outlets offer a choice of different box sizes for the same brand. These different box sizes have different per ounce prices. Both box sizes enjoy positive sales. Therefore, a 20-oz. box of Cheerios is not a perfect substitute for a 15-oz. box of Cheerios. Additionally, it is evident that a 20-oz. box of Cheerios in one store is not a perfect substitute for a 20-oz. box in another store. Therefore, both the outlet and the box size differentiate the product.

Based on this evidence, I conclude that the sufficient conditions for constructing a price index by taking unit values either across outlets or across items with a particular brand do not hold for the cereal market in New York. Obviously neither the items within a brand nor the outlets are complements. There is a variance of prices within a brand and among outlets. The items within a brand are not perfect substitutes. If they were perfect substitutes, then manufacturers and outlets would not be bearing the additional costs of offering different box sizes for the same item. However, it is still possible that a unit value approach might "closely" approximate a true price index.

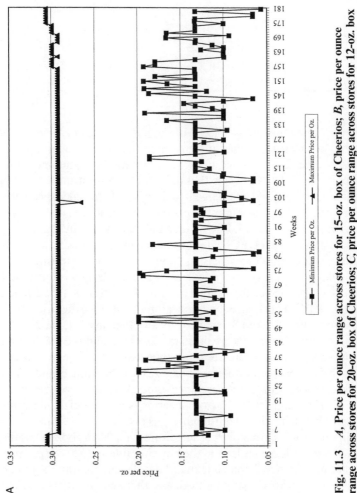

Fig. 11.3 *A*, Price per ounce range across stores for 15-oz. box of Cheerios; *B*, price per ounce range across stores for 20-oz. box of Cheerios; *C*, price per ounce range across stores for 12-oz. box of Kellogg's corn flakes; *D*, price per ounce range across stores for 24-oz. box of Kellogg's corn flakes; *E*, price per ounce range across stores for 11-oz. box of Kellogg's raisin bran; *F*, price per ounce range across stores for 20-oz. box of Kellogg's raisin bran

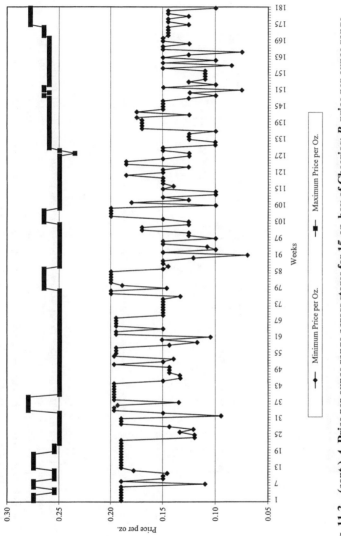

Fig. 11.3 (cont.) *A*, Price per ounce range across stores for 15-oz. box of Cheerios; *B*, price per ounce range across stores for 20-oz. box of Cheerios; *C*, price per ounce range across stores for 12-oz. box of Kellogg's corn flakes; *D*, price per ounce range across stores for 24-oz. box of Kellogg's corn flakes; *E*, price per ounce range across stores for 11-oz. box of Kellogg's raisin bran; *F*, price per ounce range across stores for 20-oz. box of Kellogg's raisin bran

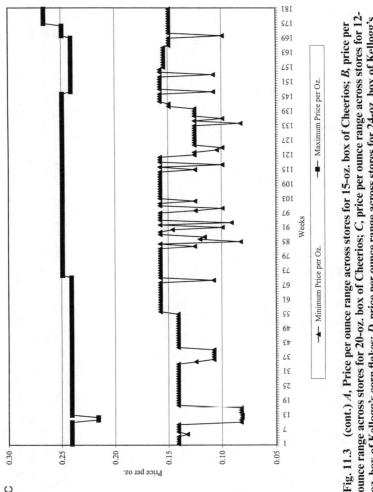

Fig. 11.3 (cont.) *A*, Price per ounce range across stores for 15-oz. box of Cheerios; *B*, price per ounce range across stores for 20-oz. box of Cheerios; *C*, price per ounce range across stores for 12-oz. box of Kellogg's corn flakes; *D*, price per ounce range across stores for 24-oz. box of Kellogg's corn flakes; *E*, price per ounce range across stores for 11-oz. box of Kellogg's raisin bran; *F*, price per ounce range across stores for 20-oz. box of Kellogg's raisin bran

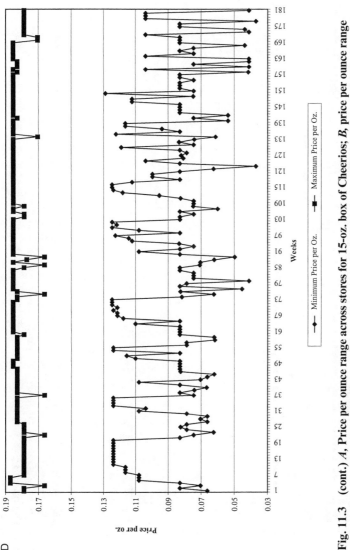

Fig. 11.3 (cont.) *A*, Price per ounce range across stores for 15-oz. box of Cheerios; *B*, price per ounce range across stores for 20-oz. box of Cheerios; *C*, price per ounce range across stores for 12-oz. box of Kellogg's corn flakes; *D*, price per ounce range across stores for 24-oz. box of Kellogg's corn flakes; *E*, price per ounce range across stores for 11-oz. box of Kellogg's raisin bran; *F*, price per ounce range across stores for 20-oz. box of Kellogg's raisin bran

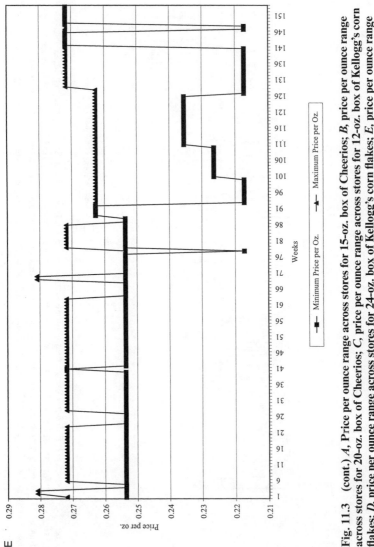

E

Fig. 11.3   (cont.) *A*, Price per ounce range across stores for **15-oz. box of Cheerios**; *B*, price per ounce range across stores for **20-oz. box of Cheerios**; *C*, price per ounce range across stores for **12-oz. box of Kellogg's corn flakes**; *D*, price per ounce range across stores for **24-oz. box of Kellogg's corn flakes**; *E*, price per ounce range across stores for **11-oz. box of Kellogg's raisin bran**; *F*, price per ounce range across stores for **20-oz. box of Kellogg's raisin bran**

F

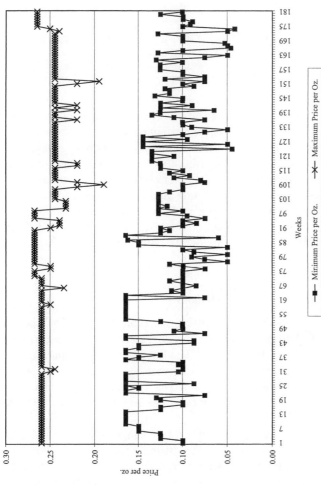

Minimum Price per Oz. ■ Maximum Price per Oz.

Weeks

Price per oz.

Fig. 11.3 (cont.) *A*, Price per ounce range across stores for 15-oz. box of Cheerios; *B*, price per ounce range across stores for 20-oz. box of Cheerios; *C*, price per ounce range across stores for 12-oz. box of Kellogg's corn flakes; *D*, price per ounce range across stores for 24-oz. box of Kellogg's corn flakes; *E*, price per ounce range across stores for 11-oz. box of Kellogg's raisin bran; *F*, price per ounce range across stores for 20-oz. box of Kellogg's raisin bran

Table 11.2   **Within-Store Differences in Price per Ounce**

Brand Name	Sizes	Average Difference in Price per Oz.	*t*-test Probability that Average Difference = 0	Maximum	Median	Minimum
General Mills Cheerios	15 oz, 20 oz	0.009024	0.0001	0.1665	0.017667	–0.16017
Kellogg's Corn Flakes	12 oz, 18 oz	0.043853	0.0001	0.1675	0.04125	–0.08375
Kellogg's Raisin Bran	11 oz, 22 oz	0.048706	0.0001	0.179136	0.045955	0.017773

To gain insight on the nonsale of items in this database, I define a sale as any price that is 95 percent or below the median price. Among the items that experience no sales, 28 percent of the nonsales follow its own sale *and* at the same time occur when at least one other item with its own brand experiences a sale. Twenty-one percent of the nonsales follow *only* its own sale, and 22 percent occur *only* during the sale of at least one other item within its own brand. The remaining 29 percent do not follow either its own sale or occur during the sale of at least one other sale in its own brand. These results should influence the results of the carry-forward imputation approach.

11.4   The Indexes Based on Five Methods

I estimate Törnqvist price indexes using one implicit imputation, the unit value, and four explicit methods. The first explicit method is the carry forward. The second is the BLS method. The last two are the imputations of the virtual price. I impute the virtual price two ways—first by using a simple direct approach using equation (6) and second by accounting for the selection effects and all the sources of variation. The imputation approach is described in the appendix.

My time series starts in August 1994 and ends in March 1998, and it has 181 weeks. The "cereal price war" occurs during this period as Kellogg's attempts to stop its falling market share. Price drops are most dramatic for those brands whose name is not proprietary, such as Raisin Bran and Corn Flakes.

I randomly select a store and start with the brands that have the highest expenditure share. I do this because the price indexes coming from these brands will be given a greater weight in the final index. It would almost be computationally impossible to do this for every brand, and therefore it is perhaps more important to correctly generate indexes for the brands that will get the most weight.

When I estimate the virtual prices, I first estimate the parameters of the model that is depicted in equation (4) by nonlinear least squares without adjusting for the selection effects of product exit and entry. I use the model parameters to impute a virtual price as described in equation (6). Then I estimate the model again and account for the selection effect as shown in equation (5) by using a simulated moment method, described in the appendix. When I impute a virtual price this time, I account for the additional sources of variation.

The UPCs that fall under each brand include both the national trademark brand and the private-label counterpart that is intended to serve as a substitute for the national brand. Therefore, for a brand such as Cheerios, I include all the different boxes of General Mills Cheerios and the store's private-label cereal that is intended to be a substitute for Cheerios. I include the private labels because they are specifically manufactured to be a substitute for a national brand even though the characteristics of the cereal are not exactly the same. In the case of the "Raisin Bran" brand, I combine both Kellogg's and Post Raisin Bran along with the private label that is intended to be a substitute for the Post Raisin Bran.

Finally, I construct Törnqvist indexes for the fourteen top-selling brands using five different imputation methods.[5] The first index uses unit values, and the second index uses the imputed virtual prices that come from the parameter estimates that are done without adjusting for the selection effects. The third index is calculated using the full imputation procedures described in the previous section. The fourth index uses the carry-forward imputation, and the fifth method is the BLS method.

Table 11.3 lists the parameter estimates for the nonlinear least squares estimation that does not incorporate the selection effects. (Table 11A.1 lists the results that do incorporate the selection effects.) Because of space limitations, I do not report the results for each brand. Instead, I give the results for the top-selling brands. The first results are for the Cheerios brand. There are five UPCs that fall within this brand. The UPCs are a private-label 7-oz. box, a 35-oz. box of Cheerios, a 20-oz. box of Cheerios, a 10-oz. box of Cheerios, and a 15-oz. box of Cheerios. Generally, the cross effects among the 20-oz., 10-oz., and 15-oz. boxes increase after the selection effects are incorporated. This should be expected. The absolute value of the own price coefficients increases for those UPCs with a relatively large share of the Cheerios brand.

The next set of results is for the Corn Flakes brand. The first five UPCs are, respectively, the 45-oz. box, the 7-oz. box, the 12-oz. box, the 18-oz. box, and the 24-oz. box for Kellogg's Corn Flakes. The last are respectively the 12-oz. and 18-oz. boxes of the private label. The highest cross effect is between the 18-oz. box of Kellogg's and the 24-oz. box. In the appendix, I

---

5. Again, I focus on the Törnqvist, since the chained Törnqvist will be the functional form of the newly published BLS superlative index.

Table 11.3 **Parameter Estimates of Lower-Level Demand Systems by Brand without Selection Effects**

	Item 1	Item 2	Item 3	Item 4	Item 5	Item 6	Item 7
	General Mills Cheerios ($R^2 = .808$)						
Own and Cross Effect							
Item 1	0.42						
	(.023)						
Item 2	0.04	−0.23					
	(.019)	(.031)					
Item 3	0.11	0.12	−0.86				
	(.040)	(.047)	(.084)				
Item 4	0.13	0.24	0.40	−0.93			
	(.029)	(.037)	(.058)	(.066)			
Item 5	0.13	−0.17	0.22	0.15	−0.32		
	(.044)	(.042)	(.061)	(.049)	(.084)		
Constant	0.31	0.49	0.66	1.10	−1.56		
	(.073)	(.066)	(.142)	(.101)	(.201)		
	Kellogg's Corn Flakes ($R^2 = .716$)						
Own and Cross Effect							
Item 1	−0.23						
	(.003)						
Item 2	0.00	−0.26					
	(.004)	(.060)					
Item 3	0.00	0.25	−0.51				
	(.012)	(.065)	(.104)				
Item 4	0.07	0.02	0.12	−0.87			
	(.020)	(.032)	(.061)	(.094)			
Item 5	−0.03	−0.06	0.07	0.51	−0.59		
	(.017)	(.032)	(.058)	(.065)	(.076)		
Item 6	0.01	0.03	0.05	0.10	0.06	−0.26	
	(.005)	(.019)	(.048)	(.048)	(.041)	(.023)	
Item 7	−0.31	0.01	0.01	0.05	0.05	0.00	−0.09
	(.007)	(.010)	(.030)	(.044)	(.037)	(.013)	(.022)
Constant	−0.16	0.57	1.05	0.26	−0.66	−0.09	0.04
	(.033)	(.053)	(.129)	(.209)	(.170)	(.068)	(.078)
	Kellogg's Raisin Bran ($R^2 = .663$)						
Own and Cross Effect							
Item 1	−0.06						
	(0.004)						
Item 2	0.07	−0.86					
	(0.038)	(0.097)					
Item 3	−0.05	0.47	−0.73				
	(0.032)	(0.088)	(0.135)				
Item 4	0.00	0.00	0.026	−0.27			
	(0.006)	(0.037)	(0.048)	(0.014)			
Item 5	0.03	0.32	0.05	0.00	−0.41		
	(0.027)	(0.078)	(0.099)	(0.039)	(0.116)		
Constant	0.21	0.98	−1.04	0.20	0.66		
	(.022)	(.169)	(.193)	(.042)	(.159)		

Table 11.3 (continued)

	Item 1	Item 2	Item 3	Item 4	Item 5	Item 6	Item 7
		Kellogg's Rice Krispies ($R^2 = .781$)					
Own and Cross Effect							
Item 1	−0.70						
	(.001)						
Item 2	0.21	−0.57					
	(.025)	(.046)					
Item 3	0.49	0.36	−0.85				
	(.032)	(.046)	(.055)				
Constant	−0.15	1.17	−0.02				
	(.141)	(.095)	(.123)				
		General Mills Honey Nut Cheerios ($R^2 = .835$)					
Own and Cross Effect							
Item 1	−0.32						
	(.034)						
Item 2	0.01	−0.12					
	(.019)	(.012)					
Item 3	0.18	0.01	−0.65				
	(.034)	(.026)	(.057)				
Item 4	0.14	0.10	0.47	−0.70			
	(.035)	(.025)	(.048)	(.054)			
Constant	−0.01	0.45	−0.58	1.13			
	(0.104)	(0.058)	(0.154)	(0.158)			

Brand/Item	Item Description
Cheerios	
Item 1	General Mills 7 oz.
Item 2	General Mills 35 oz.
Item 3	General Mills 20 oz
Item 4	General Mills 10 oz.
Corn Flakes	
Item 1	Kellogg's Corn Flakes 45 oz.
Item 2	Kellogg's Corn Flakes 7 oz.
Item 3	Kellogg's Corn Flakes 12 oz.
Item 4	Kellogg's Corn Flakes 18 oz.
Item 5	Kellogg's Corn Flakes 24 oz.
Item 6	Private Label 12 oz.
Item 7	Private Label 10 oz.
Raisin Bran	
Item 1	Kellogg's Raisin Bran 23.5 oz.
Item 2	Kellogg's Raisin Bran 20 oz.
Item 3	Post Raisin Bran 20 oz.
Item 4	Private Label 51 oz.
Item 5	Kellogg's 25.5 oz.
Rice Krispies	
Item 1	Kellogg's Rice Krispies 15 oz.
Item 2	Kellogg's Rice Krispies 10 oz.
Item 3	Kellogg's Rice Krispies 19 oz.
Honey Nut Cheerios	
Item 1	General Mills 27 oz.
Item 2	General Mills 48 oz.
Item 3	General Mills 14 oz.
Item 4	General Mills 20 oz.

Note: Standard errors in parentheses.

show that the cross effect is increased when the parameters are estimated with the selection effect. In both estimations, there are negative cross effects between the 45-oz. box and the private labels. This is a disturbing result.

When estimating these parameters, there is one factor that perhaps can create bias. Oftentimes, an outlet will place an item on sale and temporarily run out of the item during the sale period. In these situations, the desired quantity purchased does not equal the actual quantity purchase. Unfortunately, the event of an "item run-out" is not recorded on the scanner data sets. This measurement error problem should include a downward bias in the absolute value of both the own and cross effects since the magnitude of the quantity change coming from a price change is underreported. For the time being, this problem will persist, and it will also affect the values of any superlative index that is calculated from this data.

Additional results from the top-selling brands are also listed in table 11.2 but will not be discussed in this paper.

Table 11.4 gives summary statistics for the Törnqvist indexes generated in this study, and figures 11.4A and 11.4B plot the value of the indexes. I compute both a chained and a direct Törnqvist index for each method over the 181-week period. The column head "simple imputation" refers to the simple economic imputation that is done without incorporating the selection effects and that uses a price using the form in equation (6). Additionally, it does not account for all the sources of variation. The column head "full imputation" is the economic imputation that does account for selection effects and all source of variation. Besides giving summary statistics, this table also gives the last period value for each one of the methods.

Table 11.4   **Index Results Summary Statistics**

Method	Last Period Value	Average	Standard Deviation	Median	Minimum	Maximum
Unit value						
Direct	0.71174988	0.8690262	0.073431105	0.868337	0.575281	1.0302505
Chained	0.77702322	0.8805631	0.058646995	0.879293	0.66946	1.02783
Carry forward						
Direct	0.89017	0.9513015	0.031027043	0.95083	0.81719	1.00501
Chained	0.7946	0.9118548	0.051323889	0.89991	0.75456	1.00848
BLS method						
Direct	0.8584	0.9376107	0.034104332	0.93665	0.8141	1.00246
Chained	0.88219	0.9771714	0.035775544	0.97913	0.8512	1.05026
Simple imputation						
Direct	0.8312895	0.9277948	0.040486383	0.935425	0.751042	1.0178959
Chained	0.87883525	0.9484294	0.034320196	0.957048	0.841315	1.0136196
Full imputation						
Direct	0.833335324	0.9293684	0.039747923	0.936333	0.751782	1.0170632
Chained	0.88074915	0.9500644	0.0033277902	0.95858	0.845506	1.0123342

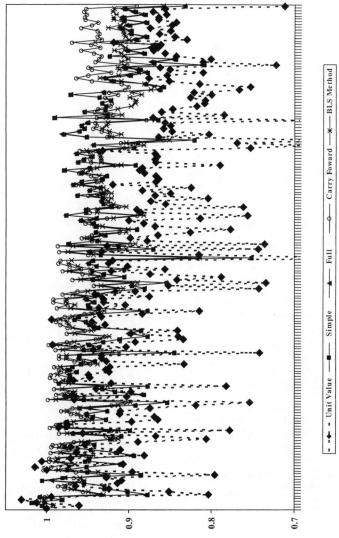

Fig. 11.4 *A*, A comparison of direct indexes; *B*, a comparison of chained indexes

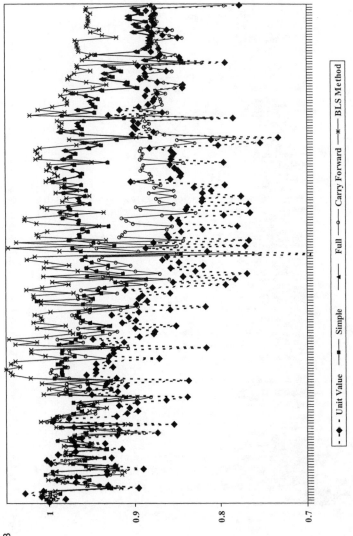

Fig. 11.4 (cont.) *A,* A comparison of direct indexes; *B,* a comparison of chained indexes

Figures 11.4A and 11.4B illustrate an important result. The lines that depict the indexes that are not based on unit values are indistinguishable. The line for the unit values is distinguishable and lies below the other indexes. While the other methods generate significantly different results when compared to each other, the magnitude of these differences is not as large as their difference with the indexes that use unit values. It is important to note that in the unit value method all the prices within each group are being replaced by their unit value. In the other methods, the prices of the sold items are always the same; therefore, the only difference is solely the result of the imputation method itself. For cereal in New York, the Balk criteria for using unit values do not hold, and the indexes using unit values produce dramatically different results.

What is surprising is that under the direct method there is the small magnitude of difference between the BLS method and the full and simple economic imputations. Clearly, the current BLS method is far simpler than the economic approach, and it seems that the BLS's current price replacement methods at least somewhat incorporate the welfare effects of a nonsale of an item.

Sections A and B of table 11.5 list the mean differences between indexes and give a standard errors for these differences. The index for each time period using the method listed in the row down the page is subtracted from the

Table 11.5   Difference across Methods in Estimates of Price Change

	Unit Value	Carry Forward	BLS Method	Simple Imputation	Full Imputation
		A. Direct			
Unit value	−0.082	−0.069	−0.059	−0.060	
		(0.003)	(0.003)	(0.004)	(0.004)
Carry forward	0.082		0.014	0.024	0.022
	(0.003)		(0.001)	(0.002)	(0.002)
BLS method	0.069	−0.014		0.010	0.008
	(00.003)	(0.001)		(0.002)	(0.002)
Simple imputation	0.059	−0.024	−0.010		−0.002
	(0.004)	(0.002)	(0.002)		(0.000)
Full imputation	0.060	−0.022	−0.008	0.002	
	(0.004	(0.002)	(0.002)	(0.000)	
		B. Chain			
Unit value		−0.0313	−0.0966	−0.0679	−0.0695
		(0.002)	(0.004)	(0.004)	(0.004)
Carry forward	0.0313		−0.0653	−0.0366	−0.0382
	(0.002)		(0.003)	(0.003)	(0.003)
BLS method	0.0966	0.0653		0.0287	0.0271
	(0.004)	(0.003)		(0.002)	(0.002)
Simple imputation	0.0679	0.0366	−0.0287		−0.0016
	(0.004)	(0.003)	(0.002)		(0.000)
Full imputation	0.0695	0.0382	−0.0271	0.0016	
	(0.004)	(0.003)	(0.002)	(0.000)	

Note: Standard errors in parentheses.

index method listed in the column and then averaged. All of the differences are significant at the 5 percent level. There is even a significant difference between the full and the simple economic imputation approach. Clearly, the regression results between the model that incorporated the selection effects and the one that did not were not large in magnitude, and thus the resulting differences in the price indexes are not large.

There is an interesting result for the chained index based on the carry-forward method. The chained index drifts below its direct value. Usually, the reverse happens. A major pitfall of the Törnqvist is that it is not reversible, so that if prices return to their base-period value, a chained Törnqvist will not necessarily equal one. It is very important to note from table 11.4 that the chained Törnqvist using the carry-forward method has a higher variance than the other explicit methods. This confirms the conclusions of Armknecht and Maitland-Smith (1999), and, as mentioned earlier, the carry-forward method carries forward a sales price for over 49 percent of the imputations, so that when the item is purchased again there is a "bounce" in the index. However, this "bounce" after reappearance does not completely offset the downward drift that occurs from deeply discounted sales. Perhaps these are important reasons that the carry-forward method might be avoided.

11.5   Conclusions

Among the alternative imputation methods that are reviewed in this study, it seems that the unit value methods generate the largest difference when applied to the scanner cereal database for New York. Clearly, the cereal market does not have the characteristics that are sufficient for a price index that uses unit values to be a true price index. However, there could easily be other product areas where at least one of Balk's criteria is met. For example, in the tuna market, Feenstra and Shapiro's study (chap. 5) in this volume indicates that the conditions for taking unit values across time might provide a true price index.

The economic approach in this study did not produce an index whose difference with the index using the BLS approach was large in magnitude even though the difference was statistically significant. At least in the cereal market, it seems that the BLS imputation method produces indexes with relatively smaller variances and whose results are close in magnitude to the indexes based on the economic approach.

Appendix

Here, I describe the full economic imputation method in detail. I posit the translog indirect utility function that generates the "desired" share equations depicted in equation (6).

Suppose in time period t goods that are indexed from 1 to m are unsold and the remaining $k - m$ goods experience positive sales. The system of equations for this time period is then

$$(7) \qquad w_{m+1}^t = \alpha_{m+1} + \sum_{j=1}^{m} \beta_{m+1,j} \overline{\pi}_j^t + \sum_{i=m+1}^{k} \beta_{m+1,j} v_j^t + \tilde{\varepsilon}_{m+1}^t$$

$$\cdots$$

$$w_k^t = \alpha_k + \sum_{i=1}^{m} \beta_{k,i} \overline{\pi}_i^t + \sum_{i=m+1}^{k} \beta_{k,i} v_i^t + \tilde{\varepsilon}_k^t,$$

where

$$(8) \qquad \begin{pmatrix} \overline{\pi}_1^t \\ \cdot \\ \overline{\pi}_m^t \end{pmatrix} = - \begin{pmatrix} \beta_{11} \cdots & \beta_{1m} \\ \cdots & \cdot \\ \beta_{m1} \cdots & \beta_{mm} \end{pmatrix}^{-1} \left[\begin{pmatrix} \alpha_1 \\ \cdot \\ \alpha_m \end{pmatrix} + \begin{pmatrix} \beta_{1,m+1} \cdots & \beta_{1,k} \\ \cdot & \cdot \\ \beta_{m,m+1} \cdots & \beta_{m,k} \end{pmatrix} \begin{pmatrix} v_{m+1}^t \\ \cdot \\ v_k^t \end{pmatrix} \right]$$

$$(9) \qquad \begin{pmatrix} \tilde{\varepsilon}_{m+1}^t \\ \cdot \\ \tilde{\varepsilon}_k^t \end{pmatrix} = - \begin{pmatrix} \beta_{m+1,1} \cdots & \beta_{m+1,m} \\ \cdots & \cdot \\ \beta_{k,1} \cdots & \beta_{k,m} \end{pmatrix} \begin{pmatrix} \beta_{11} \cdots & \beta_{1m} \\ \cdots & \cdot \\ \beta_{m1} \cdots & \beta_{mm} \end{pmatrix}^{-1} \begin{pmatrix} \varepsilon_1^t \\ \cdot \\ \varepsilon_m^t \end{pmatrix} + \begin{pmatrix} \varepsilon_{m+1}^t \\ \cdot \\ \varepsilon_k^t \end{pmatrix}$$

Note that $\overline{\pi}_i^t$ is that part of π_i^t that contains the effect of the prices and not the residuals. Likewise, the effect of the residuals in π_i are incorporated in $\tilde{\varepsilon}_{m+1}^t \ldots \tilde{\varepsilon}_k^t$. As mentioned in the study, the conditional expectation $E(\tilde{\varepsilon}_i^t \mid w_{m+1} > 0, \ldots, w_k > 0)$ for $i > m$ can be correlated with the right-hand-side regressors. To account for this residual correlation, I posit that $[\varepsilon_1, \ldots, \varepsilon_k]' \sim N(0_k, \Sigma)$, where 0_k is a k vector of zeros and Σ is a positive semidefinite $k \times k$ matrix. Then $[\tilde{\varepsilon}_{m+1}, \ldots, \tilde{\varepsilon}_k]' N(0, \Gamma)$ where

$$\Gamma = V \sum \Sigma V'$$

and

$$V = \left(\begin{pmatrix} \beta_{m+1,1} \cdots & \beta_{m+1,m} \\ \cdots & \cdot \\ \beta_{k,1} \cdots & \beta_{k,m} \end{pmatrix} \begin{pmatrix} \beta_{11} \cdots & \beta_{1m} \\ \cdots & \cdot \\ \beta_{m1} \cdots & \beta_{mm} \end{pmatrix}^{-1}, I_{k,k} \right)$$

The event $w_i > 0$ is the event

$$\tilde{\varepsilon}_i^t > -(\alpha_k + \sum_{j=1}^{m} \beta_{i,j} \overline{\pi}_j^t + \sum_{j=m+1}^{k} \beta_{i,j} v_j^t) = B_i$$

The pdf for the $k - m$ vector $\tilde{\varepsilon}^t = \{\tilde{\varepsilon}_{m+1}^t, \ldots, \tilde{\varepsilon}_k^t\}$ is denoted as $\phi[\tilde{\varepsilon}^t; 0_{m-k'}, \Gamma]$, which is a $k - m$ variate normal probability density function with mean $0_{k-k'}$ and variance covariance matrix equal to Γ. Denote the $k - m$ vector of $\{v_{m+1}^t, \ldots, v_k^t\}$ as v^t. Then, for $i > m$,

$$(10) \quad E\left(\tilde{\varepsilon}^t \,\middle|\, w^t_{m+1} > 0, \ldots, w^t_k > 0, v^t; \beta, \Sigma\right) = \frac{\int^\infty_{B_{m+1}} \cdots \int^\infty_{B_k} z \phi(z; 0_{m-k}, \Gamma) dz}{\int^\infty_{B_{m+1}} \cdots \int^\infty_{B_k} \phi(z; 0_{m-k}, \Gamma) dz}$$

The matrix of $\beta_{i,j}$ is β. The reason that β and v^t are conditioning values in equation (10) is that the integration limits B_i have these values in their domain. There is no analytical solution to equation (10). However, using a simulation technique that is essentially a variant of the Geweke-Hajivassiliou-Keane (GHK) simulator that is described in Gourieroux and Monfort (1996), I can generate a $k - m$ random vector whose expected mean is $E(\tilde{\varepsilon}^t \mid w_{m+1} > 0, \ldots, w_k > 0, v^t; \beta, \Sigma)$. In this study, I generate 200 simulations of this random variable and then average them. I denote this average as $h(v^t; \beta, \Sigma)$. Since this is an unbiased estimate of equation (10) of $O_p(1/\sqrt{200})$, the variance of $h(v^t; \beta, \Sigma)$ should be small. Letting

$$\hat{w}^t_i\left(v^t; \beta, \Sigma\right) = \alpha_i + \sum^m_{j=1} \beta_{i,j} \overline{\pi}^t_j + \sum^k_{j=m+1} \beta_{i,j} v^t_j + h\left(v^t; \beta, \Sigma\right)$$

and letting $\hat{w}^t(v^t; \beta, \Sigma)$ be the $k - m$ vector of $\hat{w}^t_i(v^t; \beta, \Sigma)$, I solve

$$\min_{\alpha, \beta, \Sigma} S^2 = \sum^T_{t=1}\left(w_t - \hat{w}_t\left(v^t; \beta, \Sigma\right)\right)' A_t\left(w_t - \hat{w}_t\left(v^t; \beta, \Sigma\right)\right)$$

A_t is a weighting matrix that accounts for the "within time period" variance covariance $E(\tilde{\varepsilon}^t - h(v^t; \beta, \Sigma))(\tilde{\varepsilon}^t - h(v^t; \beta, \Sigma))'$.[6] This model assumes independence across time for the residual.[7] The regression results of this estimation are listed in table 11A.1.

Once the parameters are estimated, I can impute the virtual prices. Here, I rely on the method of Little and Rubin (1987). The true virtual price vector is

$$(11) \quad \begin{pmatrix} \pi^t_1 \\ \cdot \\ \cdot \\ \pi^t_m \end{pmatrix} = -\begin{pmatrix} \beta_{11} \cdots & \beta_{1m} \\ \cdots & \\ \cdots & \\ \beta_{m1} \cdots & \beta_{mm} \end{pmatrix}^{-1}$$

$$\left[\begin{pmatrix} \alpha_1 \\ \cdot \\ \cdot \\ \alpha_m \end{pmatrix} + \begin{pmatrix} \beta_{1,m+1} \cdots & \beta_{1,k} \\ \cdots & \\ \cdots & \\ \beta_{m,m+1} \cdots & \beta_{m,k} \end{pmatrix}\begin{pmatrix} v^t_{m+1} \\ \cdot \\ \cdot \\ v^t_k \end{pmatrix} + \begin{pmatrix} \varepsilon^t_1 \\ \cdot \\ \cdot \\ \varepsilon^t_m \end{pmatrix}\right]$$

However, I only have parameter estimates in place of the true parameter, and I cannot observe the residuals. Therefore, to impute the virtual price I take

---

6. In this study, I estimate A_t by taking the 200 draws that are used to compute h and calculate a variance matrix around h.

7. Future study should focus on time dependence of the residual and on the possibility that historical prices influence demand.

Table 11A.1 **Parameter Estimates of Lower-Level Demand Systems by Brand with Selection Effects**

	Item 1	Item 2	Item 3	Item 4	Item 5	Item 6	Item 7
			General Mills Cheerios ($R^2 = .840$)				
Own and Cross Effect							
Item 1	−0.29						
	(0.019)						
Item 2	0.04	−0.28					
	(0.016)	(0.040)					
Item 3	0.10	0.14	−1.02				
	(0.037)	(0.051)	(0.100)				
Item 4	0.16	0.35	0.50	−1.25			
	(0.024)	(0.046)	(0.060)	(0.074)			
Item 5	−0.02	−0.24	0.28	0.24	−0.25		
	(0.036)	(0.045)	(0.069)	(0.040)	(0.089)		
Constant	0.25	0.83	0.91	1.66	−2.65		
	(0.080)	(0.095)	(0.168)	(0.114)	(0.232)		
			Kellogg's Corn Flakes ($R^2 = .723$)				
Own and Cross Effect							
Item 1	0.00						
	(0.001)						
Item 2	0.00	−0.25					
	(0.001)	(0.060)					
Item 3	0.00	0.27	−0.51				
	(0.004)	(0.065)	(0.106)				
Item 4	0.03	0.05	0.12	−0.91			
	(0.007)	(0.037)	(0.068)	(0.103)			
Item 5	−0.01	−0.11	0.05	0.57	−0.63		
	(0.006)	(0.037)	(0.058)	(0.071)	(0.081)		
Item 6	0.00	0.04	0.06	0.12	0.07	−0.31	
	(0.002)	(0.019)	(0.048)	(0.051)	(0.041)	(0.029)	
Item 7	−0.02	0.01	0.01	0.02	0.05	0.01	−0.09
	(0.003)	(0.010)	(0.030)	(0.050)	(0.045)	(0.011)	(0.023)
Constant	−0.08	0.71	1.05	0.35	−0.68	−0.03	−0.32
	(0.024)	(0.066)	(0.158)	(0.224)	(0.177)	(0.062)	(0.114)
			Kellogg's Raisin Bran ($R^2 = .667$)				
Own and Cross Effect							
Item 1	−0.07						
	(0.006)						
Item 2	0.07	−0.84					
	(0.033)	(0.108)					
Item 3	−0.06	0.48	−0.74				
	(0.039)	(0.093)	(0.138)				
Item 4	0.00	−0.01	0.030	−0.31			
	(0.007)	(0.037)	(0.052)	(0.019)			
Item 5	0.06	0.29	0.02	0.02	−0.39		
	(0.032)	(0.084)	(0.109)	(0.040)	(0.116)		
Constant	0.19	0.93	−1.10	0.33	0.65		
	(0.027)	(0.186)	(0.199)	(0.052)	(0.179)		

(*continued*)

Table 11A.1   (continued)

	Item 1	Item 2	Item 3	Item 4	Item 5	Item 6	Item 7

Kellogg's Rice Krispies ($R^2 =. 79$)

Own and Cross Effect

Item 1	−0.71						
	(0.038)						
Item 2	0.18	−0.53					
	(7.427)	(13.14)					
Item 3	0.52	0.35	−0.88				
	(0.033)	(0.042)	(0.054)				
Constant	−0.12	1.49	−0.36				
	(0.145)	(0.108)	(0.141)				

General Mills Honey Nut Cheerios ($R^2 = .836$)

Own and Cross Effect

Item 1	−0.37						
	(0.042)						
Item 2	0.00	−0.11					
	(0.019)	(0.012)					
Item 3	0.20	0.01	−0.68				
	(0.038)	(0.025)	(0.060)				
Item 4	0.16	0.10	0.48	−0.74			
	(0.036)	(0.026)	(0.056)	(0.065)			
Constant	0.03	0.42	−0.54	1.09			
	(0.124)	(0.128)	(0.156)	(0.199)			

Note: Standard errors in parentheses.

a random draw from the distribution of the parameter to account for the variance in the parameter estimates, and to account for the residual I take a random draw from $N(0_k, \hat{\Sigma})$ and then substitute these into equation (11).

References

Armknecht, P. A., and F. Maitland-Smith. 1999. Price imputation and other techniques for dealing with missing observations, seasonality, and quality change in price indices. IMF Working Paper no. WP/99/78. Washington, D.C.: International Monetary Fund.

Balk, B. M. 1998. On the use of the unit value indices as consumer price indices. In *Proceedings of the fourth meeting of the International Working Group on Price Indexes,* ed. Walter Lane, 112–20. Washington, D.C.: Bureau of Labor Statistics.

Diewert, W. E. 1995. Axiomatic and economic approaches to elementary price indexes. Discussion Paper no. 95-01. University of British Columbia, Department of Economics.

Feenstra, R. C. 1994. New product varieties and measurement of international prices. *American Economic Review* 84 (1): 157–77.

————. 1997. Generics and new goods in pharmaceutical price indexes: Comment. *American Economic Review* 87 (4): 760–67.

Feenstra, R. C., and E. W. Diewert. 2000. Imputation and price indexes: Theory and evidence from the international price program. Working Paper no. 00-12. University of California, Davis.

Gourieroux, C., and A. Monfort. 1996. *Simulation-based econometric methods.* London: Oxford University Press.

Hausman, J. 1996. Valuation of new goods under perfect and imperfect competition. In *The economics of new goods,* ed. T. Breshnahan and R. Gordon, 209–48. NBER Studies in Income and Wealth, vol. 58. Chicago: University of Chicago Press.

Little, R. J. A., and D. Rubin. 1987. *Statistical analysis with missing data.* New York: Wiley.

Reinsdorf, M. 1993. The effect of outlet price differentials in the U.S. Consumer Price Index. In *Price measurements and their uses,* ed. M. F. Foss, M. E. Manser, and A. H. Young, 227–54. NBER Studies in Income and Wealth, vol. 57. Chicago: University of Chicago Press.

Comment   Eduardo Ley

Congratulations to the author for a most interesting and informative paper. The paper deals with the issue of estimating price indexes when some price observations are missing because the quantity observed is zero—as is often the case with high-frequency highly disaggreggated data. The approach followed in the paper is to estimate demand systems that can then be used to attribute virtual (shadow) prices, π_is, to the zero-consumption goods (Lee and Pitt 1986). The paper develops an innovative two-stage estimation method for estimating the virtual prices. I will not comment on the econometric methodology but will, rather, focus on aggregation and data issues.

Aggregation Issues

Equation (1) in the paper displays what looks like a standard consumer-choice problem:

$$(1) \qquad \max_{\mathbf{x}} U(\mathbf{x})$$

$$s.t. \ \frac{\mathbf{px}}{y} = 1.$$

However, the problem treated in the paper is not a standard problem for two reasons (a) there is aggregation (separation) over goods—that is, y only represents the expenditure on cereal—and (b) there is aggregation over consumers—that is, y refers to the aggregated expenditure at a particular es-

Eduardo Ley is a senior economist at the International Monetary Fund Institute.

tablishment during one week. I would have liked to see these two aggregation issues addressed in the paper. (Furthermore, note that the relationship being estimated is not a proper consumer demand function but rather an "establishment sales function." Only after making further assumptions— for example, fixing the distribution of consumers across establishments—is it permissible to jump to demand functions.)

Although arguably the aggregation across goods could be easily handled—that is, through functional separability—the aggregation across consumers requires, in my opinion, further reflection. What is being assumed at the household level to give rise to this translog cost function at the retail-establishment level?

As an example, if we assumed translog preferences at the household level, the demand equation for good i by household h becomes

$$x_i^h = \left[\alpha_i^h + \sum_j \beta_{ij}^h \ln(p_i)\right] \frac{y^h}{p_i},$$

and—without making assumptions on the distribution of income—the aggregation condition requires linear Engel curves with identical slopes—that is, for all h: $\alpha^h = \alpha$ and $\beta_{ij}^h = \beta_{ij}$. The resulting household demands would generally result in positive shares for all cereal products—a highly unrealistic scenario. Because of the highly disaggregated data, I conjecture that most households only consume a small number of brands (typically one or two per household member), and the possibilities of substitution among brands are probably rather small, whereas the substitution among different-sized packages of the same product is large. I believe that aggregation over heterogeneous households would be a more realistic approach in this case.

In that vein, we could, for instance, get aggregate Cobb-Douglas consumption functions (a particular case of the translog) from individual Leontief-type preferences. In an extreme case, if households of type i buy 1 unit of x_i regardless of prices, the aggregate demands will be Cobb-Douglas:

$$\sum_h x_i^h = \left(\frac{H_i}{\sum_i H_i}\right) \frac{\sum_h y^h}{p_i},$$

where H_i is the number of type-i households. A better specification is probably given by linear preferences over x_is, which have the same or similar content but differ in package size and Leontief type over essentially different cereals. In any event, I would have liked to find in the paper some arguments providing some justification for what is ultimately done.

Generalized Axiom of Revealed Preference

There is, of course, a more basic question. Do the data satisfy the Generalized Axiom of Revealed Preference (GARP)? If the observed $(\mathbf{p}_t, \mathbf{x}_t)$ were generated by a utility-maximizing aggregate consumer, the data must satisfy GARP:

$$\mathbf{x}_t R \mathbf{x}_s \Rightarrow \mathbf{p}_s \mathbf{x}_s \leq \mathbf{p}_s \mathbf{x}_t,$$

where R is the transitive closure of the directly revealed preferred relation, R^D,

$$\mathbf{p}_t \mathbf{x}_t \geq \mathbf{p}_t \mathbf{x} \Leftrightarrow \mathbf{x}_t R^D \mathbf{x}.$$

If there are (large) violations to GARP it does not make much sense to worry about Slutsky symmetry implicit in the translog cost function— GARP is a necessary and sufficient condition for utility maximization. Thus, every maximizing consumer's behavior must satisfy GARP, and if the data satisfy GARP they can be interpreted as being generated by a utility-maximizing entity—see, for example, Samuelson (1948), and also Varian (1983) for tests on GARP. Jerison and Jerison (1999) relate violations of the Slutsky conditions to sizes of revealed preference conditions—the inconsistencies measured by the highest possible minimum rate of real income growth along revealed preference cycles in a particular region.

Therefore, the data should be checked for GARP before one attempts to estimate any demand functions. If the data violate the restrictions implied by the consumer optimization model, there is little justification in using that model to describe them.

Missing Data Are Observable

The motivation of the paper is that some weekly data pairs,

$$(x_{it}, p_{it})$$

are completely missing whenever $x_{it} = 0$; that is, p_{it} is not observed whenever $x_{it} = 0$. However, the reporting retail establishment does have available a much richer data set.

The establishment knows p_{it} regardless of the recorded sales whenever the stock of the product at the end-period, s_{it}, is not zero. When $s_{it} = 0$, provided that some sales were made during that week, the desired price data would also be available.

It follows that the problems raised in the paper can be easily circumvented if the reported data become

$$(x_{it}, p_{it}, s_{it})$$

whenever $s_{it} > 0$ or $x_{it} > 0$. Still, the problem of which price to use would arise when $s_{it} = x_{it} = 0$. Nevertheless, this case would be equally problematic for the method developed in the paper.

References

Jerison, David, and Michael Jerison. 1999. Measuring consumer inconsistency: Real income, revealed preference, and the Slutsky matrix. Discussion Paper no. 99-01. State University of New York at Albany, Department of Economics.

Lee, Lung-Fei, and Mark M. Pitt. 1986. Microeconometric demand systems with binding nonnegativity constraints: The dual approach. *Econometrica* 54 (5): 1237–42.

Samuelson, Paul. 1948. Consumption theory in terms of revealed preference. *Economica* 15:243–53.

Varian, Hal R. 1983. Non-parametric tests of consumer behaviour. *Review of Economic Studies* 50 (1): 99–110.

Contributors

Adrian Ball
U.K. Office for National Statistics
1 Drummond Gate
London SW1V 2QQ, England

Robert Barsky
Department of Economics
University of Michigan
Ann Arbor, MI 48109-1220

Mark Bergen
Marketing and Logistics Management
3-207 Carlson School of Management
321 19th Avenue South
Minneapolis, MN 55455

Ernst R. Bendt
Sloan School of Management, E52-452
Massachusetts Institute of Technology
50 Memorial Drive
Cambridge, MA 02142

Ralph Bradley
Bureau of Labor Statistics
2 Massachusetts Avenue, NE
Washington, DC 20212

Erwin Diewert
Department of Economics
University of British Columbia
#997-1873 East Mall
Vancouver, BC V6T 1Z1, Canada

Shantanu Dutta
The Marshall School of Business
    at USC
Marketing Department
Accounting Building 301E
Los Angeles, CA 90089-0443

Robert C. Feenstra
Department of Economics
University of California, Davis
Davis, CA 95616

David Fenwick
U.K. Office for National Statistics
1 Drummond Gate
London SW1V 2QQ, England

Dennis Fixler
Bureau of Economic Analysis
1441 L Street NW, BE-7
Washington, DC 20230

John S. Greenlees
Bureau of Labor Statistics
Room 3130
2 Massachusetts Avenue, NE
Washington, DC 20212

William J. Hawkes
814 East Lakeshore Drive
Barrington, IL 60010

Saeed Heravi
Office E30
Cardiff Business School
Cardiff University
Colum Drive
Cardiff, CF10 3EU
Wales, United Kingdom

Margaret K. Kyle
Department of Economics,
    E52-391G
Massachusetts Institute of
    Technology
50 Memorial Drive
Cambridge, MA 02142-1347

Daniel Levy
Department of Economics
Bar-Ilan University
Ramat-Gan 52900, Israel
and
Department of Economics
Emory University
Atlanta, GA 30322

Eduardo Ley
IMF Institute, Asian Division
International Monetary Fund
700 19th Street, NW
Washington, DC 20431

Davina C. Ling
Harvard University School of
    Public Health
University Place, Suite 410 South
124 Mount Auburn Street
Cambridge, MA 02138

Robin Lowe
Statistics Canada
Tunney's Pasture
Ottawa, Ontario K1A 0T6,
    Canada

Peter Morgan
Office B03
Cardiff Business School
Cardiff University
Colum Drive
Cardiff, CF10 3EU
Wales, United Kingdom

Steve Morgan
Centre for Health Services and
    Policy Research
University of British Columbia
109-2250 Wesbrook Mall
Vancouver, BC V6T 1W6, Canada

Frank Piotrowski
ACNielsen
177 Broad Street
Stamford, CT 06901

Marshall B. Reinsdorf
Bureau of Economic Analysis
Mail Stop BE-40
1441 L Street, NW
Washington, DC 20230

David H. Richardson
Bureau of Labor Statistics
Room 3615
2 Massachusetts Avenue, NE
Washington, DC 20212

Julio Rotemberg
Graduate School of Business
Harvard University, Morgan Hall
Soldiers Field
Boston, MA 02163

Candace Ruscher
Statistics Canada
Tunney's Pasture
Ottawa, Ontario K1A 0T6, Canada

Matthew D. Shapiro
Department of Economics
University of Michigan
Ann Arbor, MI 48109-1220

Mick Silver
Office C50
Cardiff Business School
Cardiff University
Colum Drive
Cardiff, CF10 3EU
Wales, United Kingdom

Jack E. Triplett
The Brookings Institution
1775 Massachusetts Avenue, NW
Washington, DC 20036

Author Index

Subject Index